MODERN
FIRST EDITIONS

MODERN FIRST EDITIONS

Their Value to Collectors

Joseph Connolly

Little, Brown and Company
BOSTON   TORONTO   LONDON

A LITTLE, BROWN BOOK

This Fourth Edition published in 1993 by Little, Brown and Company
First published as *Collecting Modern First Editions* by Studio Vista in 1977;
Second Edition published by Orbis Publishing Ltd in 1984; reprinted
twice (1985); Third Edition published by Macdonald & Co (Publishers)
Ltd in 1987

ISBN 0–316–90363–9
A CIP catalogue record for this book
is available from the British Library

Typeset by August Filmsetting, Haydock, St Helens
Printed and bound in Great Britain by
BPCC Hazell Books Ltd
Member of BPCC Ltd

Little, Brown and Company
165 Great Dover Street
London SE1 4YA

To the Memory of my Mother
and
For the future of my Children,
Victoria and Charles

Introduction

Welcome to the fourth edition of this garnering of all that is most desirable within the not-quite-so-po-faced-as-you-might-expect domain of the serious collector of modern first editions; to digress for a minute (although I am aware that this Introduction has not yet even begun to gather steam, and that at this stage of the game a digression might appear as an intrusion, not to say a misnomer) it is probably phrases just such as this ('serious collector of modern first editions') that serve to fill the uninitiated with dread: God, do I *really* want to be (or even *meet*) such a thing? Is it to do with speaking languages largely dead, having scant, white hair and peering donnishly over foolish spectacles? More alarming yet – does it require the sort of money that in these times may be viewed as no more than a perverse exercise in nostalgia, redolent with overtones of self-delusion? No no, not at all, not a bit of it: one is serious about *literature*, of course, and one is serious about devoting a reasonable amount of time, shelf-space and cash to forming a decent and lasting collection – but there the gravity ends: most bookish sorts are really quite jolly (some are mad, admittedly, but you learn to spot these early on): most can be quite the best company for not atrociously long periods. There is very little of the undertaker about professional booksellers or collectors, although intellectual snobbery is not unknown: it plays about the ankles of the unwary in the fashion of a seductive kitten which, if not reproved fairly energetically, will have its little claws in your knees before you can shriek 'clipped, bumped, frayed and torn but otherwise an excellent example!'

A good deal of the foregoing will strike the new collector as so much hallucinogenic rambling, the odd word now and again having been vaguely decipherable. Old hands will get the picture, while quite rightly nursing the reservation that all is not as rosy as it once so memorably was. One cannot pretend that the fabulous world of book collecting has been left untrammelled in the wake of the awful 'nineties (which began life as the 'caring' decade, few by now caring about much more than whether a roof over one's head may still be secured, in tandem with the odd meat meal). What the hardened campaigner and the unseasoned rookie both need to hear, however, is whether or not their collection of first editions (either actual or incipient) has gone the way of all other informed and canny purchases. Has the market collapsed? Have collectors' sensitive fingers been severely burnt? Is there a glut of unsaleable goodies? Has the bubble, in short, gone pop? The answers to these searching and frankly rather panic-inducing questions are, respectively, no, no, no and no. *Really*? Yes, really. The market is not *un*affected, of course (more about what this actually means later), and though one would not dream of suggesting that the cosy world of book collecting chugs along regardless, it does seem to have emerged not only relatively unscathed, but in a few key areas – dare one say it – more buoyant than ever.

Many booksellers – along with collectors who have been forced to cut back upon their acquisitions – by now might be struggling manfully to suppress the cultured equivalent of the big fat laugh (or, who knows, are letting it rip)

Introduction

and I can see that a little clarification is called for. Many bookshops and mail order dealers have folded during the last five years, while quite a lot of increasingly specialist booksellers have emerged to take their place. Sometimes, economic factors have contrived to strengthen a previously somewhat diffuse situation by the simple device of the merger. One of the most impressive modern first edition dealers in London at the moment in terms of stock, environment and professionalism is Ulysses, near the British Museum – a joint venture shared by at least four dealers: this trend will continue, I think, resulting in fewer costly outlets, but a stock level of the quality of the good old days. Further, almost without exception, the cream of one's collection has risen in value.

And what *of* prices? Well, in common with almost nothing else I can think of, with the exception perhaps of rock memorabilia, they have, as I say, risen – and sometimes dramatically. As ever, the rises are not constant: some books that I listed in 1987 as being worth up to £10 are still worth up to £10 (if you are lucky) while others have increased ten-fold and more. The hugest rises are accorded to the gilt-edged boys: Graham Greene and Evelyn Waugh, but of course – but also such as Dick Francis and P.D. James and, on the younger front (is he still classed as young? Is any of us?) Martin Amis. In the course of the Introduction to the third edition of this book, I sharply intook the breath while imparting the shock-horror truth that Amis's first novel *The Rachel Papers* would fetch '£100 + ', as opposed to a tenner or so a couple of years earlier; today I can see a specialist dealer demanding (and getting) £4–500 for an absolutely mint copy.

This whole business of prices and values (not always the same thing) continues to be the factor that most fascinates and divides people who have an interest in this sort of thing. In one sense, any form of valuation has an element of the arbitrary about it, and during times of extremes this becomes rather more marked. Moreover, if a book is legendarily rare, then even the very high valuation contained in this book just may turn out to be a fraction of what a determined and well-heeled collector would be willing to pay. If, freakishly, two copies of such a book appeared at auction during the same week, the price fetched for the second would almost certainly be a good deal less than for the first, this alone making any future valuation even more tricky (which price was 'right'?).

At the other end of the spectrum, there is the vast tidal wave of very run-of-the-mill first editions: you know the types – the ones you see in the W.H. Smith book sale, the most recent Richard Adams, almost anything by John Braine except *Room at the Top* or any old thing lacking the dustwrapper (more too about this now almost religious subject later). Such books have what I call a 'notional' value: up to £10 – or, on the A–Z price coding used throughout this book, grade B. The problem arises when people imagine that a whole shelf-full of nothing much at all is worth ten quid a time, and become peeved when a dealer offers them no more than 50p – or, more likely, refuses them altogether. The explanation is simple: firstly, the values given in this book are the prices *charged by booksellers for at least good-to-very-good copies* (a glossary of terms follows in a while) *in the dustwrapper*. So, if yours is a brilliant copy, and the dealer wants it, he will offer £3, £4 or *maybe* even £5 for it (which may or may not seem fair, but it *is* fair, and you maybe have to have been a bookseller to understand why – it's all boring stuff to do with economics and cash flow and appetite) but of course if it is damaged, written in, or wrapperless – or if the poor devil has been sitting on three copies for more years than he cares to contemplate – then the dealer will either offer a pittance or turn it down altogether. But this does not render a good copy of the book valueless, and hence the *notional* value: be warned.

So much for the rare and the commonplace; alas – wouldn't you know it – it is not as simple as that. What of a scarce little item in poor condition, or without its dustwrapper, or with a missing leaf? At this point it all becomes rather subjective, unless there are *reasons* for the imperfection. Early Orwell, for instance, is virtually never seen in glowing condition, and so therefore a so-so copy is not too worrying (whereas a sparkling copy, as I have explained, would for the same reason far outstrip its valuation in this book). Graham Greene, for instance, really *has* to be in fine state in dustwrapper if we are discussing anything much post-war, but the wrapper of, say, *Brighton Rock* is of legendary scarcity, so a crisp but denuded copy will do; early P.G. Wodehouse school stories often had rather boring black-and-white plates loosely tipped-in, and one or two are quite often missing: provided one is *aware* that photocopies have been substituted (and one is paying a commensurately lower price) such a copy can be acceptable. Of course, just how defective a copy a collector is willing to accept is entirely up to him or her – a temptingly low price often swinging it – but if there is a rule of thumb, it is this: *always* buy the very best copy you can afford, if only for peace of mind. You will never be hankering for anything better, and if in the future you consider the item expendable, you are pretty certain to find a ready market.

In terms of value, then, condition is crucial: truly excellent copies can double estimates, and nearly always find a buyer. I think it is less to do with the aspect of investment than the inherent sense of neatness and order evident in many book collectors: their houses may never feature in The World of Interiors and the attire of a good many can render a recently dipped Merino the very model of elegance and quiet good taste, but when it comes to the bookshelves, all must be perfect. This is either very healthy, or bordering on the insane, depending upon your outlook – but presumably if you have read thus far, you must sympathise to a degree.

So, bearing in mind the foregoing *caveats*, the English and American first editions of every title in this book are graded A–Z (see Scale of Values, following this Introduction) on the bookshop *selling* prices for decent, wrappered copies – although quite a few exceptions to this are specifically mentioned in the course of the listings. You will occasionally be fortunate enough to find a true bargain at the much touted jumble sale (it *can* still be done, but don't actively expect it) whereupon you can bore people into the ground with not so much your good stroke of luck as your connoisseurship in spotting such a prize. Similarly, you will attend auctions and book fairs and specialist shops where prices are higher or lower than those listed here; this doesn't necessarily mean that anyone is right or wrong – unless the disparity is positively chasmic – but can reflect anything from the location of the dealer to the price he himself paid for the book, as well as such other factors as the

Introduction

newsworthiness (which tends to mean death) of the author. Here, then, are the bones, and with time, experience and the not too frequent mistake, your own 'feel' will emerge. An experienced dealer or collector can 'feel' whether a book, a signature or a dustwrapper is right or not right: there is often no hard proof, but the 'feel' is something you contradict with care – unless your own 'feel' is so contrary as to engender fisticuffs.

We cannot conclude this chat on values without talking further about this blessed dustwrapper business. Outsiders who would be loth to buy a threadbare carpet or half a painting or a spoutless teapot call us mad for caring two hoots about the 'bit of paper around a book': let them. We are not mad (are we?) – we are simply *discerning:* the book should be in a condition as close as possible to that of first publication. There is also the aesthetic side: in general, wrappers are very much more attractive than the books they conceal.

That said, however, I feel we have to get a collective grip on ourselves: the supply of perfect copies has diminished greatly over the last decade, and although we may by all means insist upon the *presence* of a dustwrapper, we have to relax a little over its state: a bit of chipping, a closed tear (as opposed to a missing mouthful), a slightly faded spine and a price-clipped dustwrapper – all common and, I should have said, all acceptable: we do not wish our discernment to descend to a raving fetishism.

The other area that is not so cut-and dried is that of the 'special' edition: the 'special' edition can be a good thing, and it can be a white elephant. At the lowest scale, let us consider the book clubs: several of these offer newly published novels at a reduced retail price, but *nearly* all of them either add their colophon to the title page or else replace that of the original publisher – this, rightly or wrongly, rendering it negligible in the eyes of the collector: it's not *just* the snobbery factor but the knowledge that tens of thousands of the things have been printed, almost certainly later than the formally published trade edition. 'Special' in one way, then, but not so as to detain us here.

Some publishers regularly produce rather flashy editions simultaneously with the trade editions – these tend to be numbered (500 copies, generally – sometimes more) signed, divested of the dustwrapper we have just been crowing about, and stuck into a slipcase or – worse – a glassine cover. These are created for various 'First Edition Collectors' Clubs' that come and go, or for such prestigious stores as Harrods. Tread warily here: the last Len Deighton was given the treatment (cloth boards, cloth slipcase, signed and numbered) and appeared in quantity in the Harrods sale knocked down from £35 to just £3.50. Much more desirable would have been a signed copy of the straightforward Hutchinson edition.

Before we get into this area of author signatures and inscriptions, a word about the Private Presses. There is no doubt that there are fewer of them producing less glamorous work than ten years ago, though our more high-profile poets in particular continue to put out little bits and bobs tricked out like the Magna Carta and bound in the more yielding parts of ever more curious animals. You *may* buy these, if they appeal, you *may* come to love them, and they *may* rise in value (a good many have): more likely is that you will keep them in a drawer (many do not fit on shelves, the odd one that does resembling less a book than a fairly embarrassing celebratory box of chox). In my experience, collectors of Press books are interested in little else – it really is an alternative, though parallel, field of activity. Try not to be unduly put off nor perversely turned on by all this – nor, indeed, by anything else I or another might say: your book collection should reflect *your* taste in literature and visual appeal, so try to leave fashion and the pontifications of experts out of it or you will spend too much on things you never really cared for and fritter away the years wondering why.

Now then: author signatures, inscribed copies and all the other factors that render a book unique. The most lust-inducing items are fine copies of rare books, inscribed by the author (who, for preference, is known for signing very little) to someone who matters. These criteria came together beautifully in a Sotheby's sale in 1991, where Graham Greene's wife Vivienne decided to pop her heirlooms: the rare *The Man Within* (1929) was actually *dedicated* to Vivienne to boot, very smoochily inscribed, and estimated at £4–5000; it fetched £13,200. *Brighton Rock* (in the aforementioned rare dustwrapper) was inscribed 'For my love eternally, V.G.–G.G. June 1938' and fetched £6600 against an estimate of £1500–£2000. These – despite the dizzy prices – are sure-fire investments because each of them is unique, and Greene's future reputation is, of course, rock solid.

A step down from these heights might be a fine first with a particularly apposite inscription – a poem by a poet, a relevant drawing, a jokey allusion – as opposed to the merely baldest signature (although this is fine too if it's all you can get). If you meet a famous author, it's always rather pleasing if he writes in your name as well, but this must be seen as a purely personal pleasure unless you too are a celebrity; you could, I suppose, lie about your name in order to end up with something on the lines of 'To Elvis Presley, best wishes, Ted Hughes' – but on second thoughts, maybe not. Signing sessions are becoming increasingly popular in high street book chains (in common with anything else that might pull in more punters) and although their primary intention is to flog the author's latest offering, few writers object to signing one or two golden oldies – but *do* buy the current work, for courtesy's sake, and *do not* turn up with the man's entire output to date in a trunk. He *may* be flattered, but – if he is aware of market values – he is more likely to be suspicious. All this, of course, applies to *literary* authors; do by all means queue up for politicians, supermodels, TV cooks and comedians (all of which, these days, seem to be more or less interchangeable) but never assume that any of them has the remotest connection with book collecting *proper*: these are things you give to people you hardly know as presents, such people tending to briefly wonder why you did such a thing, while filing them for future use as presents for people they hardly know.

What *should* you collect? In practice, few collectors actually sit down and decide what to collect; they tend to start from a core of old favourites, upgrading to finer copies whenever possible, and being willing to be led by happenstance, browsing and bargains. Sometimes, thinning out will occur (but *please* make sure you really want to get rid of a book before you commit yourself – it's simply awful to see a grown collector cry). Some people have cut-off points – 1950, say. Some will start at the end of the War and come

Introduction

right up to date – and yet more will go for certain schools, cliques and genres, and even books that have translated into notable films. I once knew a collector who annually gathered up not only the Booker winner, but the whole of the shortlist; I can't really recommend this: by now – if he still pursues this faintly eccentric course – he must have an awful lot of dross. The Booker – still the biggest prize in terms of prestige if not cash – really has nothing to do with the collecting of modern first editions, I have decided. Since the first prize was awarded in 1969, very few winners have become scarce and desirable items, and nor have they become literary landmarks (with a few very considerable exceptions such as Golding's *Rites of Passage*, Rushdie's *Midnight Children* and Amis's *The Old Devils*). Some Booker prizewinning authors are not even listed in this book, for the very good reason that they are not collected: you rarely see queues forming for P.H. Newby, Bernice Rubens, J.M. Coatzee (or, let's face it, Keri Hulme) and at the moment I put both Michael Ondatje and Ben Okri into the same bracket; I have included 1992's joint winner, however – Barry Unsworth – and I rather wish I had done so before. But enough of the Booker: everyone collects what they *want* to collect, is what I'm driving at – and that is how it should be.

I am sometimes asked precisely where one should go to buy first editions – not so dumb a question as you might imagine, these days, as the specialist market has shrunk while it has strengthened. Salerooms – Sotheby's, Christie's, Phillips and all the lesser known and country auctions – continue to offer really quite startling items; sellers are happy to wait for their money, it appears, and even despite the sellers' premium, most seem happy with the prices realised. Specialist dealers can be expensive (many buy at auction, so work it out for yourself) but they tend to be dependable, honest and professional – and generally speaking, the stock quality is high. Provincial book fairs are always great fun (and always suffocatingly hot) and the prices usually reasonable, and sometimes low. General bookshops offer the best scope for bargains, of course, but one must be prepared to sift through an awful lot of sand in order to find the gold; mail order catalogues remove a good deal of the hard work and provide a valuable service, although the whole process can strike one as a bit bloodless and rather remote.

The next step is to be able to identify a first edition, and this is generally a fairly straightforward business, despite the fact that recent technological innovations have made it all a tad more complicated. And the *other* thing one needs to know, of course, is just what constitutes a literary first edition: *all* books were originally published in their 'first' edition – that is to say, the very first appearance of a book in print. This does *not* mean that every first edition of every book is desirable or valuable, just as I assume that no-one would believe every plate or saucer in the world with the word 'Wedgwood' on the back to be a museum piece. What one is searching for is a first edition of any author one chooses to collect; if the author is deemed 'collectable' (i.e. currently seen to be of lasting literary merit, or popular, or ultra-fashionable, or recently perceived to have been underrated, or a combination of any of these) then others too will be searching him out, few examples will be available, the dealers will be aware, and all this – couldn't you have guessed it? – will be reflected in the price.

Introduction

Usually, it is very easy to tell a first edition: on the verso (other side) of the title page is printed something to the effect of 'First published . . .' followed by the date. 'First printing' is an alternative, and many American publishers (rarely chaps to beat about the bush) come right out with it and state 'First edition'. What is absolutely vital, of course, is that this information is follow-ed by *nothing else whatever*: no 'second impression', no 'new edition', no 'this edition' – nor any other variation on the theme. With some very recent books, however – within the last five or so years – one has to be more vigilant: the verso might well state 'First published 1990', say, and beneath that no details of any subsequent printing – though there may well follow this riddle: 1 3 5 7 9 10 8 6 4 2. This, believe it or not, means that the book really is the first impression; were that first 1 missing, however, the book is a second impression (because the first has, as it were, gone) whereas if the 2 is also missing, the book in question is a third impression. Sneaky, huh? Why didn't they stick to the old method? Why indeed. And why didn't they simply print 1 to 10 in the *usual* way? Good question: it's progress, you see, and there's not an awful lot we can do about it.

There follows a guide on how to look after your firsts, once you have acquired them, and my old, ever-so-slightly-tongue-in-cheek Glossary of terms that you might encounter in book catalogues.

Understandably, if a collector has whacked out more than he anticipates earning during the coming quarter on a fine copy of some gorgeous rarity, he is fairly anxious to keep it that way. There is no special trick to this, and most of it is common sense, but here are a few tips anyway:

* If the dustwrapper is unlaminated, it can make good sense to cover it with *non-adhesive* transparent acetate. This improves the look (although it can make for irritating reflection) while proving resistant to the clamminess of collectors' (and – more to the point – others') fingers. It is also a good way of discouraging a slightly frayed or chipped dustwrapper from becoming more so. Do not Sellotape the front or rear of a dustwrapper. In time it becomes quite cancerously yellow, drops off in disgust, and leaves its tell-tale ochre stain.
* Do not pack books too tightly in shelves. This in itself does not damage them, but it risks disfigurement every time you want to pull one out. The correct method of pulling out a book, of course – and to know this will make you very popular in bookshops – is to first push back its neighbours, and then grasp the spine in the middle and not at its vulner-able top.
* Do not let books flop about, either. Pages sag, bindings warp, dust gets in – enough said.
* Avoid placing books directly opposite a sunny window – the spine colours will fade; particularly red and navy, for some reason or another.
* Glass-fronted bookcases are not a good idea. Books need air, or the pages go brown and smell stale. Open any glass-fronted case and you will see what I mean: they generally give off the odour of having recently played host to someone who died without leaving prior notice.
* Steer clear of radiators – they dry the air, suck the natural moisture out of

Introduction

the books, with twisted boards and foxing (that's the little brown spots like on granny's hands) as a result. If you are a serious collector, freeze.
* Damp is the arch-enemy. Damp will rapidly render your desirables not. Exposure to fire isn't a good idea, either – but that applies to most things.

The Glossary

All items in this catalogue are, unless otherwise stated, first English editions	means	All the choice items will be followed by the words 'second impression'
Limited edition, mint, un-opened in box, as issued	means	You will be as disinclined as the original owner to even so much as look at the thing
Mint	means	Fine
Fine	means	Fine also
Very Good	means	Good
Good	means	Not very good
Good +	means	Not very good also
Good −	means	No good at all
Fair	means	Filthy/Atrocious
Only fair	means	Filthy/Atrocious
Reading copy	means	Filthy/Atrocious
Working copy	means	Filthy/Atrocious
Some scoring	means	Illegible/Atrocious
Some marking	means	Dirty
Rubbed	means	Threadbare
Handled	means	You wouldn't care to touch it
Bumped	means	Distorted
Some loose pages	means	In its component parts
Neat inscription	means	Defaced endpaper
1st thus	means	Reprint
Rare	means	Uncommon, wildly expensive
Scarce	means	Not previously encountered by the bookseller

And a soupçon of Connolly's Law:
* The book that you have been searching for all your adult life was sold that morning to someone else. Cheap.
* The mint copy of *The Lord of the Flies* in your local Oxfam shop is, I assure you, a second impression.
* The book that you thought overpriced that the bookseller wouldn't reduce and twenty-four hours later does not seem so expensive because you can't live without it will be gone when you run all the way back for it.

* The bookseller who actually produces the book for which a customer has been searching all his adult life will watch said customer walking out of the door, thinking about it.
* Booksellers seldom have the books people *want*.
* People seldom want the books booksellers *have*.

And there, more or less, we have it. Next comes the listing of all the authors whom I believe to be of the most interest to collectors today: a few hitherto neglected oldies creep into this edition, a lot of new names and a sprinkling of dark horses – along with, of course, the strong, perennial backbone of avidly collected authors. The entries are updated to January 1993, and the A–Z Scale of Values follows the listings.

This book will not, alas, make you an expert, but it might just quicken the pulse: certainly it should provide most of the equipment you need. So, pursue the quarry, read the books, kiss them daily – and don't ever forget that it's meant to be fun!

Index of Authors

Index of Authors

Unsworth, Barry
Updike, John
Upward, Edward

Vidal, Gore
Vonnegut, Kurt

Wallace, Edgar
Waterhouse, Keith

Waugh, Evelyn
Wesker, Arnold
Wesley, Mary
Wheatley, Dennis
White, Patrick
White, T.H.
Williams, Nigel
Williams, Tennessee

Wilson, A.N.
Wilson, Angus
Wilson, Colin
Winterson, Jeanette
Wodehouse, P.G.
Wolfe, Tom
Woolf, Leonard
Woolf, Virginia
Wyndham, John

Ackroyd, Peter   Born in London, 1949.

Still a huge seller, and still very popular with collectors – some of whom rather wish he would slow down a bit (his output is phenomenal) while others would prefer he stuck to fiction. It is always a problem when a novelist one admires produces a biography of some worthy in whom one has not the slightest interest – do you buy it for the sake of completion or not? In Ackroyd's case, though, the subjects (Eliot, Dickens) cannot fail to interest. There is a school of thought that believes Ackroyd is beginning to become a bit too clever-clever with his extraordinary pastiches and devices (and in the case of *English Music* one sees the point) but he is still very much a man to watch and to gather.

1 **Ouch** (poetry)
Ackroyd tells me that this was a few sheets Xeroxed in an edition of 'around 500 copies'. — Curiously Strong Press 1971 — **K**

2 **London Lickpenny** (poetry) — Ferry Press 1973 — **I**

3 **Notes for a New Culture** (criticism) — Vision Press 1976 — **G**

4 **Country Life** (poetry) — Ferry Press 1978 — **I**

5 **Dressing Up** (social history) — Thames & Hudson 1979 — **E**
Simon & Schuster 1979 — **D**

6 **Ezra Pound and His World** (biography) — Thames & Hudson 1980 — **D**

7 **The Great Fire of London** (novel) — Hamilton 1982 — **F**

8 **The Last Testament of Oscar Wilde** (novel) — Hamilton 1983 — **E**
Harper & Row 1983 — **C**

9 **T.S. Eliot** (biography) — Hamilton 1984 — **C**
Simon & Schuster 1984 — **C**

10 **Hawksmoor** (novel) — Hamilton 1985 — **D**
Harper & Row 1985 — **C**

11 **The Diversions of Purley and other poems** — Hamish Hamilton 1987 — **C**

12 **Chatterton** (novel) — Hamish Hamilton 1987 — **C**
Grove Press 1988 — **B**

13 **First Light** (novel) — Hamish Hamilton 1989 — **C**
Grove Weidenfeld 1989 — **B**

14 **Dickens** (biography) — Sinclair-Stevenson 1990 — **C**
HarperCollins 1990 — **C**

15 **English Music** (novel) — Hamish Hamilton 1992 — **B**
Ballantine 1992 — **B**

Adams, Richard   Born in Berkshire, 1920.

It has been coming for years – Adams simply isn't interesting collectors (or reviewers) very much at all, these days. Of course, he remains the author of a twentieth-century classic – and I duly list it below.

1	**Watership Down**	Rex Collings 1972	**O**
		Macmillan (NY) 1974	**G**

Albee, Edward   Born in Washington D.C, 1928.

Albee continues not to produce – and writers (particularly playwrights) tend to get forgotten when this happens. When they *die*, of course, they can be joyously rediscovered, but until that time...

1	**The Zoo Story, The Death of Bessie Smith, The Sandbox: Three Plays**	Coward McCann (NY) 1960	**H**
2	**The Zoo Story**	*Evergreen Review* March–April 1960	**D**
3	**Fam and Yam**	Dramatists Play Service (NY) 1961	**C**
4	**The American Dream**	Coward McCann (NY) 1961	**D**
5	**Who's Afraid of Virginia Woolf?**	Atheneum 1962	**H**
		Cape 1964	**F**
6	**The Zoo Story** and **Other Plays** (same as 1)	Cape 1962	**D**
7	**The Ballad of the Sad Café**	Atheneum 1963	**D**
		Cape 1965	**C**
8	**Tiny Alice**	Atheneum 1965	**C**
		Cape 1966	**B**
9	**Malcolm**	Atheneum 1966	**C**
		Cape 1967	**B**
10	**A Delicate Balance**	Atheneum 1966	**C**
		Cape 1968	**B**
11	**Box** and **Quotations from Chairman Mao Tse-Tung**	Atheneum 1969	**C**
		Cape 1970	**B**
12	**All Over**	Atheneum 1971	**C**
		Cape 1972	**B**
13	**Seascape**	Atheneum 1975	**C**
		Cape 1976	**B**
14	**Counting the Ways** and **Listening: Two Plays**	Atheneum 1977	**C**
15	**The Lady from Dubuque**	Atheneum 1980	**C**

Aldiss, Brian   Born in Norfolk, England, 1925.

I wonder if there is such a thing as a complete Aldiss collection in private hands? Or even in *public* hands? Could be – people who like Aldiss *really* like Aldiss, but he still is not in the mainstream of the collecting world; probably the most famous 'cult' writer of them all, though.

1	**The Brightfount Diaries** (novel)	Faber 1955	H
2	**Space, Time and Nathaniel** (stories)	Faber 1957	G
3	**Non-Stop** (novel)	Faber 1958	G
4	**Starship** (same as 3)	Criterion (NY) 1959	E
5	**Vanguard from Alpha** (novel)	Ace (NY) 1959	G
6	**No Time Like Tomorrow** (stories)	NAL (NY) 1959	F
7	**The Canopy of Time** (stories)	Faber 1959	F
8	**Bow Down to Nul** (novel)	Ace 1960	F
9	**Galaxies Like Grains of Sand** (novel)	NAL 1960	G
10	**Equator** (novel)	Digit 1961	F
11	**The Interpreter** (novel)	Digit 1961	F
12	**The Male Response** (novel)	Beacon Press, Boston 1961	G
		Dobson 1963	E
13	**The Primal Urge** (novel)	Ballantine (NY) 1961	F
		Sphere 1967	C
14	**Hothouse** (novel)	Faber 1962	F
15	**The Long Aftermath of Earth** (same as 14)	NAL 1962	D
16	**The Airs of Earth** (stories)	Faber 1963	E
17	**Starswarm** (stories)	NAL 1964	D
18	**The Dark Light Years** (novel)	Faber 1964	E
		NAL 1964	D
19	**Greybeard** (novel)	Faber 1964	E
		Harcourt Brace 1964	D
20	**Best SF Stories of Brian Aldiss** (rev. ed. 1971)	Faber 1965	C
21	**Earthworks** (novel)	Faber 1965	D
		Doubleday 1966	C
22	**Who Can Replace a Man?** (same as 20)	Harcourt Brace 1966	C
23	**The Saliva Tree and Other Strange Growths** (stories)	Faber 1966	C
24	**Cities and Stones: A Traveller's Jugoslavia** (non-fiction)	Faber 1966	C
25	**An Age** (novel)	Faber 1967	C
26	**Cryptozoic** (same as 25)	Doubleday 1968	C
27	**Report on Probability A** (novel)	Faber 1968	C
		Doubleday 1968	C

28 **A Brian Aldiss Omnibus** (stories)	Sidgwick & Jackson 1969	C
29 **Intangibles Inc. and Other Stories**	Faber 1969	C
30 **Barefoot in the Head** (novel)	Faber 1969	C
	Doubleday 1970	B
31 **Neanderthal Planet** (stories)	Avon (NY) 1970	C
32 **The Shape of Further Things** (non-fiction)	Faber 1970	C
	Doubleday 1971	C
33 **The Hand-Reared Boy** (novel)	Weidenfeld 1970	D
	McCann 1970	C
34 **A Soldier Erect** (novel)	Weidenfeld 1971	C
	McCann 1971	C
35 **The Moment of Eclipse** (stories)	Faber 1971	B
	Doubleday 1971	B
36 **Brian Aldiss Omnibus 2**	Sidgwick & Jackson 1971	B
37 **The Comic Inferno** (stories)	Daw Books 1972	C
38 **The Book of Brian Aldiss** (same as 37)	NEL 1973	C
39 **Frankenstein Unbound** (novel)	Cape 1973	C
	Random House 1974	C
40 **Billion Year Spree: The History of Science Fiction**	Weidenfeld 1973	C
	Doubleday 1973	C
41 **The Eighty Minute Hour** (novel)	Cape 1974	C
	Doubleday 1974	C
42 **The Malacia Tapestry** (novel)	Cape 1976	C
	Harper 1977	C
43 **Brothers of the Head** (novel)	Pierrot 1977 (UK & US)	C
44 **Last Orders and Other Stories**	Cape 1977	C
45 **Enemies of the System: A Tale of Homo Uniformis** (novel)	Cape 1978	C
	Harper & Row 1978	C
46 **A Rude Awakening** (novel)	Weidenfeld 1978	C
With 33 and 34, this completes the trilogy of Horatio Stubbs novels.	Random House 1979	C
47 **New Arrivals, Old Encounters** (essays)	Cape 1979	C
	Harper 1979	C
48 **This World and Nearer Ones: Essays Exploring the Familiar**	Weidenfeld 1979	C
	Kent State 1981	C
49 **Pile** (illustrated)	Cape 1979	C
50 **Life in the West** (novel)	Weidenfeld 1980	C
51 **Moreau's Other Island** (novel)	Cape 1980	C
52 **An Island Called Moreau** (same as 51)	Simon & Schuster 1981	C
53 **Helliconia Spring** (novel)	Cape 1982	C
	Atheneum 1982	C
54 **Helliconia Summer** (novel)	Cape 1983	C
	Atheneum 1983	C

55	**Seasons in Flight** (novel)	Cape 1984	**C**
		Atheneum 1986	**C**
56	**Helliconia Winter** (novel)	Cape 1985	**C**
		Atheneum 1985	**C**
57	**Trillion Year Spree:**	Gollancz 1986	**C**
	The History of Science Fiction	Atheneum 1986	**C**
	With David Wingrove		
58	**The Year Before Yesterday** (novel)	Watts (US) 1987	**B**
59	**Cracken at Critical** (same as 58)	Kerosina (UK) 1987	**B**
60	**Ruins** (novel)	Hutchinson 1987	**B**
61	**Best Science Fiction Stories**	Gollancz 1988	**B**
	of Brian W. Aldiss		
62	**Man in His Time** (same as 61)	Atheneum 1989	**B**
63	**Forgotten Life** (novel)	Gollancz 1988	**B**
		Atheneum 1989	**B**
64	**A Romance of the Equator:**	Gollancz 1989	**B**
	Best Fantasy Stories	Atheneum 1990	**B**
65	**Bury My Heart at W.H. Smith's:**	Hodder & Stoughton	**B**
	A Writing Life	1990	
66	**Dracula Unbound** (novel)	Grafton 1991	**B**
		HarperCollins 1991	**B**
67	**Remembrance Day** (novel)	HarperCollins 1992	**B**

Amis, Kingsley   Born in London, 1922.

Amis vaults from strength to strength – he is surely now our greatest living novelist, if such a mantle isn't too wince-making. That is the wonder of writers – as they get older, they get *better* (well – not all of them. Not many of them, actually – but it's certainly true in Kingsley's case). Of course, he now tends to dwell upon characters at various stages of decrepitude instead of the sallow youths of yore, but the zest, the Amis bite has strengthened. If you doubt it, read the Memoirs. That he is not beyond experimentation is demonstrated by the risky but eventually masterful *The Russian Girl*, and the word is that there are many more good things to come. Collectors have now thoroughly woken up to how rich a vein there is to be mined here, and prices have perked up accordingly: no matter – Sir Kingsley is well worth it.

1	**Bright November** (verse)	Fortune Press 1947	**M**
2	**A Frame of Mind** (verse)	Reading School of Art	**L**
		1953	
3	**Lucky Jim** (novel)	Gollancz 1953	**O**
		Doubleday 1954	**I**
4	**Fantasy Poets No. 22** (verse)	Fantasy Press 1954	**I**
5	**That Uncertain Feeling** (novel)	Gollancz 1955	**G**
		Harcourt Brace 1956	**D**
6	**A Case of Samples:**	Gollancz 1956	**I**
	Poems 1946–1956	Harcourt Brace 1957	**E**

7	**Socialism and the Intellectuals**	Fabian Society 1957	E
8	**I Like It Here** (novel)	Gollancz 1958	F
		Harcourt Brace 1958	C
9	**Take a Girl Like You** (novel)	Gollancz 1960	E
		Harcourt Brace 1961	C
10	**New Maps of Hell: A Survey**	Harcourt Brace 1960	H
	of Science Fiction	Gollancz 1961	F
11	**My Enemy's Enemy** (stories)	Gollancz 1962	E
		Harcourt Brace 1963	C
12	**The Evans Country** (verse)	Fantasy Press 1962	J
13	**One Fat Englishman** (novel)	Gollancz 1963	D
		Harcourt Brace 1964	C
14	**The Egyptologists** (novel)	Cape 1965	D
	With Robert Conquest.	Random House 1966	C
15	**The James Bond Dossier**	Cape 1965	E
	(non-fiction)	NAL 1965	D
16	**The Anti-Death League** (novel)	Gollancz 1966	D
		Harcourt Brace 1966	C
17	**A Look Round the Estate:**	Cape 1967	E
	Poems 1957–1967	Harcourt Brace 1968	C
18	**Colonel Sun: A James Bond**	Cape 1968	D
	Adventure (pseud. Robert Markham)	Harper 1968	C
19	**Lucky Jim's Politics**	Conservative Centre	E
		1968	
20	**I Want It Now** (novel)	Cape 1968	D
		Harcourt Brace 1969	C
21	**The Green Man** (novel)	Cape 1969	D
		Harcourt Brace 1970	C
22	**What Became of Jane Austen?**	Cape 1970	C
	and Other Questions (essays)	Harcourt Brace 1971	B
23	**Girl, 20** (novel)	Cape 1971	D
		Harcourt Brace 1972	C
24	**On Drink** (non-fiction)	Cape 1972	C
		Harcourt Brace 1973	B
25	**Dear Illusion** (story)	Covent Garden Press	D
	(limited to 600 copies, 100 numbered and signed) (**G**)	1972	
26	**The Riverside Villas Murder** (novel)	Cape 1973	D
		Harcourt Brace 1973	C
27	**Ending Up** (novel)	Cape 1974	D
		Harcourt Brace 1974	C
28	**Rudyard Kipling and His World**	Thames & Hudson 1975	C
	(biography)	Scribner 1975	C
29	**The Alteration** (novel)	Cape 1976	C
		Viking Press 1977	B
30	**Harold's Years** (edited by)	Quartet 1977	B
31	**The New Oxford Book of Light Verse** (edited by)	OUP 1978	C

32	**The Darkwater Hall Mystery** (story) Sherlock Holmes spoof, limited to 165 copies.	Tragara Press 1978	**K**
33	**Jake's Thing** (novel)	Hutchinson 1978	**E**
		Viking 1979	**C**
34	**The Faber Popular Reciter** (verse, edited by)	Faber 1978	**B**
35	**Collected Poems 1944–1979**	Hutchinson 1979	**C**
		Viking 1980	**B**
36	**An Arts Policy?** (lecture)	Centre for Policy Studies 1979	**C**
37	**Russian Hide-and-Seek** (novel)	Hutchinson 1980	**C**
38	**Collected Short Stories**	Hutchinson 1980	**C**
39	**The Golden Age of Science Fiction** (selected by)	Hutchinson 1981	**C**
40	**Every Day Drinking** (articles)	Hutchinson 1983	**B**
41	**How's Your Glass? A Quizzical Look at Drinks and Drinking**	Weidenfeld 1984	**B**
42	**Stanley and the Women** (novel)	Hutchinson 1984	**C**
		Summit 1985	**B**
43	**The Old Devils** (novel)	Hutchinson 1986	**D**
		Summit 1986	**C**
44	**The Great British Songbook** (edited by, with John Cochrane)	Pavilion 1986	**C**
45	**The Crime of the Century** (novel)	Dent 1987	**C**
		Mysterious Press 1989	**C**
46	**Difficulties With Girls** (novel)	Hutchinson 1988	**C**
		Summit 1989	**B**
47	**The Amis Anthology: A Personal Choice of English Verse**	Hutchinson 1988	**B**
48	**The Folks That Live on the Hill** (novel)	Hutchinson 1990	**B**
		Summit 1990	**B**
49	**The Pleasure of Poetry** (edited by)	Cassell 1990	**B**
50	**Memoirs**	Hutchinson 1991	**C**
		Summit 1991	**C**
51	**The Kingsley Amis Omnibus** (novels)	Hutchinson 1992	**B**
52	**The Russian Girl** (novel)	Hutchinson 1992	**B**
53	**The Amis Story Anthology** (edited by) (stories by other hands)	Hutchinson 1992	**B**

In addition to the above, Amis has edited two books on one of his heroes: **G.K. Chesterton: Selected Stories** (Faber 1972) and **G.K. Chesterton: A Century Appraisal** (Elek 1974) and one on yet another: **Tennyson** (Penguin 1973). Also notable are five anthologies of science fiction stories (**Spectrum I–V**, Gollancz 1961–65) edited with Robert Conquest. (**I : D,** rest **C**)

Amis, Martin   Born in Oxford, 1949.

Many of those who argue against Kingsley Amis being our best novelist will put forward his son instead: between them they certainly seem to have things sewn up. Martin Amis writes beautifully and powerfully and often quite shockingly (in the literal sense, of course) – and although it is true that he has not *quite* recaptured the full glory of *Money*, he has lost none of his hold upon readers and collectors. It is already extremely difficult (and surprisingly expensive) to form a complete collection, but if any of the young(ish) bloods are worth it, he is.

1	**The Rachel Papers** (novel)	Cape 1973	**N**
		Knopf 1974	**K**
2	**Dead Babies** (novel)	Cape 1975	**L**
		Knopf 1976	**I**
3	**Dark Secrets** (same as 2)	Triad 1977	**G**
4	**Success** (novel)	Cape 1978	**G**
		Harmony 1987	**C**
5	**Mixed Doubles** (screenplay)	Saturn 3 1980	**D**
6	**Other People: A Mystery Story** (novel)	Cape 1981	**F**
		Viking Press 1981	**D**
7	**Invasion of the Space Invaders** (non-fiction)	Hutchinson 1982	**G**
8	**Money** (novel)	Cape 1984	**F**
		Viking 1985	**D**
9	**The Moronic Inferno and Other Visits to America** (journalism)	Cape 1986	**D**
		Viking 1987	**C**
10	**Einstein's Monsters** (stories)	Cape 1987	**D**
		Harmony 1987	**C**
11	**London Fields** (novel)	Cape 1989	**C**
		Harmony 1990	**C**
12	**Time's Arrow** (novel)	Cape 1991	**C**
		Harmony 1991	**C**

Asimov, Isaac   Born in Russia, 1920. Naturalized American, 1928. Died 1992.

Asmov continues to pour forth. A glance at the *American Books in Print* or even at the Export issue of *The Bookseller* is more than enough to induce groan after groan in the hapless bibliographer: anthologies, reprints, new editions, essays, non-fiction – and novels. As previously, we limit ourselves to the fiction; otherwise I should have to retitle this book *Collecting Isaac Asimov*, and everyone else would have to go.

1 **Pebble in the Sky** (novel)	Doubleday 1950	**G**
	Sidgwick & Jackson 1968	**C**
2 **I, Robot** (stories)	Gnome Press 1950	**F**
	Grayson 1952	**D**
3 **The Stars, Like Dust** (novel)	Doubleday 1951	**F**
4 **Foundation** (novel)	Gnome Press 1951	**F**
	Weidenfeld 1953	**D**
5 **Foundation and Empire** (novel)	Gnome Press 1952	**E**
6 **The Currents of Space** (novel)	Doubleday 1952	**E**
	Boardman 1955	**C**
7 **Second Foundation** (novel)	Gnome Press 1953	**E**
8 **The Caves of Steel** (novel)	Doubleday 1954	**E**
	Boardman 1954	**C**
9 **The End of Eternity** (novel)	Doubleday 1955	**E**
10 **The Martian Way and Other Stories**	Doubleday 1955	**E**
	Dobson 1964	**C**
11 **The Naked Sun** (novel)	Doubleday 1957	**D**
	Joseph 1958	**C**
12 **Earth Is Room Enough** (stories)	Doubleday 1957	**D**
13 **Nine Tomorrows: Tales of the Near Future**	Doubleday 1959	**D**
	Dobson 1963	**C**
14 **The Rest of the Robots** (stories plus 8 and 11)	Doubleday 1964	**C**
	Dobson 1967	**C**
15 **Fantastic Voyage** (novel)	Houghton Mifflin 1966	**C**
	Dobson 1966	**C**
16 **Through a Glass, Clearly** (stories)	New English Library 1967	**C**
17 **A Whiff of Death** (novel)	Walker 1968	**C**
	Gollancz 1968	**C**
18 **Asimov's Mysteries** (stories)	Doubleday 1968	**C**
	Rapp & Whiting 1968	**C**
19 **Nightfall and Other Stories**	Doubleday 1969	**C**
	Rapp & Whiting 1969	**C**
20 **The Gods Themselves** (novel)	Doubleday 1972	**C**
	Gollancz 1972	**C**
21 **The Early Asimov** (stories)	Doubleday 1972	**C**
22 **The Best of Isaac Asimov** (stories)	Sidgwick & Jackson 1973	**C**
	Doubleday 1974	**C**
23 **Tales of the Black Widowers** (stories)	Doubleday 1974	**C**
	Gollancz 1975	**B**
24 **Buy Jupiter and Other Stories**	Doubleday 1975	**C**
	Gollancz 1976	**B**
25 **Authorised Murder** (novel)	Doubleday 1976	**C**
	Gollancz 1976	**B**
26 **The Bicentennial Man and Other Stories**	Doubleday 1976	**C**
	Gollancz 1977	**B**

27	**More Tales of the Black Widowers** (stories)	Doubleday 1976 Gollancz 1977	C B
28	**Murder at the Aba** (novel)	Doubleday 1976	C
29	**The Key Word and Other Mysteries**	Walker (US) 1977	C
30	**The Casebook of the Black Widowers** (stories)	Doubleday 1980 Gollancz 1980	C B
31	**Foundation's Edge** (novel) A signed limited edition was published simultaneously by Whispers at $51.	Doubleday 1982 Granada 1982	C B
32	**Robots of Dawn** (novel)	Doubleday 1983 Granada 1984	C B
33	**Nine Tomorrows** (stories)	Doubleday 1984 Granada 1985	C B
34	**Banquets of the Black Widowers** (stories)	Doubleday 1985 Granada 1985	B B
35	**Foundation and Earth** (novel)	Doubleday 1986 Grafton 1986	B B
36	**Alternative Asimovs** (stories)	Doubleday 1986	B
37	**Robot Dreams** (stories)	Berkley 1986 Gollancz 1987	B B
38	**The Best Science Fiction of Isaac Asimov**	Doubleday 1986 Grafton 1987	B B
39	**The Best Mysteries of Isaac Asimov**	Doubleday 1986 Grafton 1987	B B
40	**Fantastic Voyage II: Destination Britain** (novel)	Doubleday 1987 Grafton 1987	B B
41	**Prelude to Foundation** (novel)	Doubleday 1988 Grafton 1988	B B
42	**Azazel** (novel)	Doubleday 1988 Doubleday UK 1989	B B
43	**Nemesis** (novel)	Doubleday 1989 Doubleday UK 1989	B B
44	**The Asimov Chronicles: Fifty Years of Isaac Asimov**	Dark Harvest NY 1989 Century 1991	B B
45	**Robot Visions** (stories & essays)	NAL 1990 Gollancz 1990	B B
46	**Puzzles of the Black Widowers** (stories)	Doubleday 1990 Doubleday UK 1990	B B
47	**The Complete Stories I**	Doubleday 1990	B
48	**Nightfall** (novel) With Robert Silverberg.	Doubleday 1990 Gollancz 1990	B B
49	**The Complete Stories**	HarperCollins UK 1992	B
50	**The Positronic Man** (novel) With Robert Silverberg.	Gollancz 1992	B

Asimov has also published six juveniles under the pseudonym of Paul French:

David Starr: Space Ranger	Doubleday 1952	**F**
Lucky Starr and the Pirates of the Asteroids	Doubleday 1954	**E**
Lucky Starr and the Oceans of Venus	Doubleday 1954	**E**
Lucky Starr and the Big Sun of Mercury	Doubleday 1956	**D**
Lucky Starr and the Moons of Jupiter	Doubleday 1957	**D**
Lucky Starr and the Rings of Saturn	Doubleday 1958	**D**

These were published in England –
under Asimov's real name – by NEL in
1972–73.

Atwood, Margaret   Born in Ottawa, 1939.

A Canadian novelist of increasing reputation who has, rather surprisingly,
published more poetry than anything – not something she is really known for
here, but I think Atwood is on the verge of becoming highly collectable, and
so I list the lot. The novels will always be the most sought after, however –
particularly *The Handmaid's Tale* and very probably the extraordinarily
complex *Cat's Eye*.

1 **Double Persephone** (verse)	Hawkshead Press 1961	**H**
2 **The Circle Game** (poem)	Cranbrook Academy 1964	**E**
3 **Talismans for Children** (verse)	Cranbrook Academy 1965	**D**
4 **Kaleidoscopes: Baroque** (verse)	Cranbrook Academy 1965	**D**
5 **Speeches for Doctor Frankenstein** (verse)	Cranbrook Academy 1966	**D**
6 **The Circle Game** (verse)	Contact Press 1966	**D**
7 **Expeditions** (verse)	Cranbrook Academy 1966	**D**
8 **The Animals in that Country** (verse)	OUP Toronto 1968	**F**
	Little, Brown US 1969	**E**
9 **Who Was in the Garden**	Unicorn US 1969	**E**
10 **The Edible Woman** (novel)	McClelland & Stewart (Canada) 1969	**G**
	Deutsch 1969	**F**
	Little, Brown US 1970	**D**
11 **The Journals of Susanna Moodie** (verse)	OUP Toronto 1970	**D**
12 **Oratorio for Sasquatch, Man and Two Androids: Poems for Voices**	CBC 1970	**C**

Atwood

32	**Bluebeard's Egg and Other Stories**	McClelland & Stewart (Canada) 1983	**D**
		Houghton Mifflin 1986	**C**
		Cape 1987	**C**
33	**Unearthing Suite** (story)	Grand Union Press 1983	**D**
34	**Interlunar** (verse)	OUP Toronto 1984	**C**
		Cape 1986	**C**
35	**The Handmaid's Tale** (novel)	McClelland & Stewart (Canada) 1985	**F**
		Houghton Mifflin 1986	**E**
		Cape 1986	**D**
36	**Hurricane Hazel and Other Stories**	Eurographica, Helsinki 1986	**C**
37	**Selected Poems 2**	OUP Toronto 1986	**C**
		Houghton Mifflin 1987	**C**
38	**Cat's Eye** (novel)	McClelland & Stewart (Canada) 1988	**D**
		Doubleday 1989	**C**
		Bloomsbury 1989	**C**
39	**Selected Poems 1966–1984**	OUP Toronto 1990	**C**
40	**Margaret Atwood: Conversations**	Ontario Review Press 1990	**B**
		Virago 1992	**B**
41	**For the Birds** (juvenile)	Douglas & McIntyre (Canada) 1990	**C**
42	**Poems 1965–1975**	Virago 1991	**B**
43	**Wilderness Tips** (novel)	McClelland & Stewart (Canada) 1991	**C**
		Doubleday 1991	**B**
		Bloomsbury 1991	**B**
44	**Good Bones** (stories)	Doubleday 1992	**B**
		Bloomsbury 1992	**B**

In addition to the above, Margaret Atwood has edited **The New Oxford Book of Canadian Verse in English** (OUP 1982) and **The Oxford Book of Canadian Short Stories in English** (OUP 1986).

Auden, W.H.   Born in York, England, 1907. Died 1973.

Auden remains steady. There will never be a time when he is not collected – indeed, each successive generation of right-minded people guarantees that – but something of a huge revival of attention is required to hurl Auden back to the pinnacle of collectors' attention that he enjoyed ten or twelve years ago: a previously unpublished (major) manuscript, say – or a biography on the lines of Peter Ackroyd's *T.S. Eliot*. But Auden's greatness and position are secure despite the vagaries of book collectors, as is the memory of his extraordinary face. My daughter once had a way of remembering who was whom in the literary world: Shakespeare, for instance, was 'the bald one with a beard who we've got a bust of' while Auden was merely 'the wrinkly'.

It has been necessary to limit the list that follows to books and pamphlets written by Auden and published by commercial English and American publishers, and those he edited and translated that seemed to be most pertinent to his *œuvre*. However, an excellent bibliography of Auden exists: *W.H. Auden: A Bibliography 1924–1969* (University Press of Virginia, 2nd ed. 1972). This contains everything – including contributions to periodicals – within 420 pages. The first edition of this work, incidentally, is desirable in that Auden wrote the intro., though as it was published in 1964, it is not of such practical use as the current edition.

1	**Poems**	SHS 1928	**Z+**

Spender hand-printed this little volume in Frognal, Hampstead, in an edition of less than thirty. No collector has any hope of finding one, unless one of the known owners decides to sell, but the price could easily be £12,000 or more. It is one of the legendary 1sts of the century. Three facsimiles of the book have been published, however, and one of these might be an acceptable substitute:
University Microfilms Xerox 1960
University of Cincinnatti Library 1964 (limited to 500 copies)
Ilkley Literature Festival 1973
The Cincinnatti facsimile is cloth-bound, with an introduction by Spender, but the Ilkley copy is faithful to the orange wrpps, reproduces the erratum slip for the first time, and has a separate foreword by B.C. Bloomfield, Auden's bibliographer.

2	**Poems**	Faber 1930	**N**
3	**The Orators: An English Study**	Faber 1932	**K**
4	**The Dance of Death** (verse)	Faber 1933	**J**
5	**Poems** (contains nos. 3 & 4)	Random House US 1934	**G**
6	**The Dog Beneath the Skin** (play)	Faber 1935	**I**
	With Christopher Isherwood.	Random House 1935	**G**
7	**The Ascent of F6** (play)	Faber 1936	**H**
	With Christopher Isherwood.	Random House 1937	**F**
8	**Look, Stranger!** (verse)	Faber 1936	**J**
9	**On This Island** (same as 8)	Random House 1937	**H**
10	**Spain** (poem)	Faber 1937	**H**
11	**Letters from Iceland** (prose)	Faber 1937	**I**

	With Louis MacNeice.	Random House 1937	G
12	**Selected Poems**	Faber 1938	D
13	**On the Frontier** (play)	Faber 1938	F
	With Christopher Isherwood.	Random House 1939	D
14	**Education Today and Tomorrow** (essay, with T.C. Worsley)	Hogarth Press 1939	G
15	**Journey to a War** (prose)	Faber 1939	H
	With Christopher Isherwood.	Random House	G
16	**Another Time** (verse)	Random House 1940	F
		Faber 1940	F
17	**Some Poems**	Faber 1940	D
18	**The Double Man** (verse)	Random House 1941	J
19	**New Year Letter** (same as 18)	Faber 1941	F
20	**For the Time Being** (verse)	Random House 1944	F
		Faber 1945	F
21	**The Collected Poetry**	Random House 1945	E
22	**The Age of Anxiety** (verse)	Random House 1947	E
		Faber 1948	E
23	**Collected Shorter Poems 1930–1944**	Faber 1950	E
24	**The Enchafed Flood** (criticism)	Random House 1950	G
		Faber 1951	G
25	**Nones** (verse)	Random House 1951	G
		Faber 1952	G
26	**Mountains** (Ariel Poem)	Faber 1954	C
27	**The Shield of Achilles** (verse)	Random House 1955	F
		Faber 1955	E
28	**The Magic Flute** (libretto translation)	Random House 1956	E
	With Chester Kallman.	Faber 1957	E
29	**Making, Knowing and Judging** (lecture)	OUP 1956	F
30	**W.H. Auden: A Selection by the Author**	Penguin 1958	B
31	**Selected Poetry of W.H. Auden** (same as 30)	Modern Library US 1959	C
32	**Homage to Clio** (verse)	Random House 1960	E
		Faber 1960	E
33	**The Dyer's Hand** (essays)	Random House 1962	E
		Faber 1963	E
34	**Selected Essays**	Faber 1964	C
35	**About the House** (verse)	Random House 1965	D
		Faber 1966	D
36	**Collected Shorter Poems 1927–1957**	Faber 1966	D
		Random House 1967	D
37	**Selected Poems**	Faber 1968	C
38	**Collected Longer Poems**	Faber 1968	D
		Random House 1969	D
39	**Secondary Worlds** (lecture)	Faber 1969	D
		Random House 1969	D

40 **City Without Walls** (verse)	Faber 1969	**D**
	Random House 1970	**D**
41 **A Certain World** (commonplace book)	Viking 1970	**D**
	Faber 1971	**D**
42 **Academic Graffiti** (clerihews)	Faber 1971	**C**
	Random House 1972	**B**
43 **Epistle to a Godson** (verse)	Faber 1972	**D**
	Random House 1972	**C**
44 **Forewords and Afterwords** (essays)	Viking 1973	**C**
	Faber 1973	**C**
45 **Auden/Moore: Poems and Lithographs**	British Museum 1974	**C**
46 **Thank You, Fog** (verse)	Faber 1974	**C**
	Random House 1974	**C**
47 **Collected Poems**	Faber 1976	**C**
	Random House 1976	**C**
48 **The English Auden: Poems, Essays, & Dramatic Writings 1927–1939**	Faber 1977	**C**
	Random House 1978	**C**

Auden was also the editor of many works. A selection appears below.

The Poet's Tongue (2 vols) With John Garrett.	Bell 1935	**H**
The Oxford Book of Light Verse	OUP 1938	**E**
Poets of the English Language (5 vols)	Viking Press 1950	**I**
	Eyre & Spottiswoode 1952	**I**
An Elizabethan Song Book	Doubleday 1955	**G**
	Faber 1957	**G**
The Faber Book of Modern American Verse	Faber 1956	**D**
Selected Writings of Sydney Smith	Farrar Straus 1956	**E**
	Faber 1957	**E**
Van Gogh: A Self-Portrait	New York Graphic Society 1961	**F**
	Thames & Hudson 1961	**F**
The Viking Book of Aphorisms	Viking 1962	**D**
The Faber Book of Aphorisms	Faber 1965	**D**
A Choice of de la Mare's Verse	Faber 1963	**C**
Selected Poems, by Louis MacNeice	Faber 1964	**C**
Nineteenth Century British Minor Poets	Delacorte 1966	**D**
	Faber 1967	**D**
G.K. Chesterton: A Selection from his Non-Fiction Prose	Faber 1970	**C**
A Choice of Dryden's Verse	Faber 1973	**B**
George Herbert	Penguin 1973	**B**

Auster, Paul   Born in New Jersey, 1947.

This American author has not really come to the attention of collectors yet, but this could change if only on the strength of his *New York Trilogy* – quite a classic already. Auster writes very entertainingly in a rather intellectual sort of way – but don't let that put you off.

1	**Unearth: Poems 1970–1972**	Living Hand US 1974	F
2	**Wall Writing: Poems 1971–1975**	Figures US 1976	D
3	**Fragments from Cold** (verse)	Parenthese US 1977	D
4	**Facing the Music** (verse)	Station Hill US 1980	C
5	**White Spaces** (prose)	Station Hill US 1980	C
6	**The Art of Hunger and Other Essays**	Menard Press UK 1982	C
7	**The Random House Book of Twentieth Century French Poetry** (editor)	Random House UK 1982	C
		Vintage 1984	C
8	**The Invention of Solitude** (prose)	Sun US 1982	C
		Faber 1988	C
9	**City of Glass** (novel)	Sun and Moon Press US 1985	F
10	**Ghosts** (novel)	Sun and Moon Press US 1986	E
11	**The Locked Room** (novel)	Sun and Moon Press US 1987	E
12	**The New York Trilogy** (contains 9, 10 & 11)	Faber 1987	D
		Penguin US 1990	B
13	**In the Country of Last Things** (novel)	Viking US 1987	C
		Faber 1988	C
14	**Disappearances** (verse)	Overlook Press US 1988	C
15	**Moon Palace** (novel)	Viking US 1989	C
		Faber 1990	C
16	**The Music of Chance** (novel)	Viking US 1990	C
		Faber 1991	C
17	**Ground Work: Selected Poems and Essays 1970–1979**	Faber 1990	B
18	**Leviathan** (novel)	Viking US 1992	B
		Faber 1992	B

Ayckbourn, Alan   Born in Hampstead, London, 1939.

Possibly because his output is so enormous, or possibly because he writes only comedy (the British adore comedy, but rarely see fit to promote its creator to the ranks of the artists who make them cry) Ayckbourn has not been seen to be the highly talented and important playwright that he is. Quite apart from the fact that his plays are intensely funny, and allow for such good acting from his favourite stable of performers, his understanding and wielding of stagecraft can sometimes be nothing short of phenomenal, as seen in the *Norman Conquest* trilogy, where we the audience can be in three places at once, as it were, and the deviousness, vanity, hypocrisy and sheer lunacy of these prime examples of the British middle class is magnified and enhanced that we might relish it all the more. And being British, and middle class, we adore it.

1	**Relatively Speaking**	Evans 1968	**F**
		French (US) 1968	**C**
2	**Ernie's Incredible Illucinations**	Hutchinson	
	Included in *Playbill One*, edited by Alan Durband. There were three volumes in this series of non-net paperbacks intended for schools.	Educational 1969	**B**
3	**Countdown**	Methuen 1970	**B**
	Included in an anthology of plays entitled *We Who Are About To . . .*		
4	**How the Other Half Loves**	French (US) 1972	**C**
		Evans (UK) 1972	**C**
5	**Time and Time Again**	French (UK & US) 1973	**C**
6	**Absurd Person Singular**	French (UK & US) 1974	**C**
7	**The Norman Conquests**	French (UK & US) 1975	**D**
	A hardcover edition – Ayckbourn's first – was published in the same year by Chatto & Windus (**D**).		
8	**Absent Friends**	French (UK & US) 1975	**C**
9	**Bedroom Farce**	French (UK & US) 1977	**C**
10	**Three Plays**	Chatto & Windus 1977	**D**
	Includes 6, 8 and 9.	Grove Press 1979	**C**
11	**Just Between Ourselves**	French (UK & US) 1978	**B**
12	**Ten Times Table**	French (UK & US) 1978	**B**
13	**Joking Apart**	French (UK & US) 1979	**B**
14	**Confusions**	French (UK & US) 1979	**B**
	Includes *Mother Figure, Drinking Companion, Between Mouthfuls, Gosforth's Fete*, and *A Talk in the Park*.		
15	**Joking Apart**	Chatto & Windus	**D**

Includes 13, 11 and 12.

		1979	
16	**Sisterly Feelings**	French (UK & US) 1981	B
17	**Taking Steps**	French (UK & US) 1981	B
	16 and 17 were published together in hardcover by Chatto and Windus in the same year (**C**).		
18	**Suburban Strains**	French (UK & US) 1982	B
19	**Season's Greetings**	French (UK & US) 1982	B
20	**Way Upstream**	French (UK & US) 1983	B
21	**Intimate Exchanges** (2 vols.)	French (UK & US) 1985	C
22	**Chorus of Disapproval**	French (UK & US) 1985	B
23	**Woman in Mind**	Faber 1986	B
24	**Henceforward**	Faber 1988	B
25	**Mr A's Amazing Maze Plays**	Faber 1989	B
26	**A Man of the Moment**	Faber 1990	B
27	**Invisible Friends**	Faber 1991	B
28	**Callisto 5**	French 1992	B
29	**My Very Own Story**	French 1992	B

Bailey, Paul   Born in London, 1937.

Bailey publishes quietly and not terribly often, sells moderately and gathers respectful reviews. Hardly surprising, then, that many had not even heard of him when his latest novel was nominated for the 1986 Booker Prize – this guaranteeing him rather more attention in the future. Bailey is what we call a 'fine' writer (professional and non-prolific) but be warned – there aren't many laughs in his novels, dwelling as they do on isolation, loss, bereavement, suicide, death and associated horrors. Something of an acquired taste, to my way of thinking. His one work of non-fiction concerns a brothel, which may or may not mean something; I haven't the slightest idea.

1	**At the Jerusalem** (novel)	Cape 1967	E
		Atheneum 1967	B
2	**Trespasses** (novel)	Cape 1970	D
		Harper 1971	B
3	**A Distant Likeness** (novel)	Cape 1973	C
4	**Peter Smart's Confessions** (novel)	Cape 1977	C
5	**Old Soldiers** (novel)	Cape 1980	C
6	**An English Madam: The Life and Work of Cynthia Payne** (non-fiction)	Cape 1982	B

7 **Gabriel's Lament** (novel)	Cape 1986	**B**
8 **An Immaculate Mistake: Scenes from Childhood and Beyond** (autobiography)	Bloomsbury 1990	**B**

Bainbridge, Beryl   Born in Liverpool, 1934.

I am pleased to be able to report that since the last edition of this book dear Beryl has made a welcome return to fiction – not only this, but she has lost none of her touch. Elegant, moving and stylish – these slim novels are very memorable indeed. The early stuff is even more difficult to find than ever, but surprisingly low in price.

1	**A Weekend with Claude** (novel)	Hutchinson 1967	**H**
2	**Another Part of the Wood** (novel)	Hutchinson 1968	**F**
3	**Harriet Said ...** (novel)	Duckworth 1972	**E**
		Braziller 1972	**C**
4	**The Dressmaker** (novel)	Duckworth 1973	**D**
5	**The Secret Glass** (same as 4)	Braziller 1974	**C**
6	**The Bottle Factory Outing** (novel)	Duckworth 1974	**D**
		Braziller 1974	**C**
7	**Sweet William** (novel)	Duckworth 1975	**C**
		Braziller 1975	**B**
8	**A Quiet Life** (novel)	Duckworth 1976	**C**
		Braziller 1977	**B**
9	**Injury Time** (novel)	Duckworth 1977	**C**
		Braziller 1977	**B**
10	**Young Adolf** (novel)	Duckworth 1978	**C**
		Braziller 1979	**B**
11	**Winter Garden** (novel)	Duckworth 1980	**C**
		Braziller 1981	**B**
12	**Watson's Apology** (novel)	Duckworth 1984	**C**
		McGraw Hill 1985	**B**
13	**English Journey; or, the Road to Milton Keynes** (non-fiction)	Duckworth 1984	**C**
		Braziller 1984	**B**
14	**Mum and Mr. Armitage: Selected Short Stories**	Duckworth 1985	**C**
		McGraw Hill 1987	**B**
15	**Filthy Lucre** (novel)	Duckworth 1986	**B**
16	**Forever England: North and South** (non-fiction)	Duckworth 1987	**B**
17	**An Awfully Big Adventure** (novel)	Duckworth 1989	**B**
		HarperCollins 1991	**B**
18	**A Bainbridge Omnibus** (contains 3, 4 & 6)	Duckworth 1989	**B**
19	**Birthday Boys** (novel)	Duckworth 1991	**B**

Baker, Nicholson   Born in New York, 1957.

A subtle, funny and rather rude writer who is still something of a secret outside the Granta-reading elite, despite receiving ever more prominent reviews. One to watch.

1	**The Mezzanine** (novel)	Weidenfeld & Nicolson US 1988	**F**
		Granta Books 1989	**D**
2	**Room Temperature** (novel)	Grove Weidenfeld 1990	**D**
		Granta Books 1990	**C**
3	**U and I** (prose)	Grove Weidenfeld 1991	**C**
		Granta Books 1991	**C**
4	**Vox** (novel)	Random House 1992	**C**
		Granta Books 1992	**C**

Ballard, J.G.   Born in Shanghai, China, 1930.

If *Crash* remains Ballard's culty classic, *Empire of the Sun* surely represents some other kind of landmark – the acclaim it received on publication seems to have encouraged Ballard to break out of the SF mould and produce some really startling work. Still *reasonably* easy to collect, but as his reputation continues to rise, this situation seems certain to change.

1	**The Wind from Nowhere** (novel)	Berkley (NY) 1962	**L**
2	**The Voices of Time and Other Stories**	Berkley 1962	**I**
3	**Billenium and Other Stories**	Berkley 1962	**H**
4	**The Drowned World** (novel)	Berkley 1962	**H**
		Gollancz 1963	**F**
5	**The Four-Dimensional Nightmare** (stories)	Gollancz 1963	**F**
6	**Passport to Eternity and Other Stories**	Berkley 1963	**F**
7	**The Terminal Beach** (stories)	Gollancz 1964	**E**
8	**The Drought** (novel)	Cape 1965	**E**
9	**The Crystal World** (novel)	Cape 1966	**E**
		Farrar Straus 1966	**D**
10	**The Disaster Area** (stories)	Cape 1967	**D**
11	**The Day of Forever** (stories)	Panther 1968	**C**
12	**The Overloaded Man** (stories)	Panther 1968	**C**
13	**The Atrocity Exhibition** (novel)	Cape 1970	**D**
14	**Vermilion Sands** (stories)	Berkley 1971	**D**
		Cape 1973	**E**
15	**Crash!** (novel)	Cape 1973	**E**
		Farrar Straus 1973	**D**

16 **Concrete Island** (novel)	Cape 1974	**C**
	Farrar Straus 1974	**C**
17 **High Rise** (novel)	Cape 1975	**D**
18 **Low-Flying Aircraft** (stories)	Cape 1976	**C**
19 **The Best of J.G. Ballard**	Sidgwick & Jackson 1977	**B**
20 **The Unlimited Dream Company** (novel)	Cape 1979	**C**
	Holt Rinehart 1979	**C**
21 **The Venus Hunters** (stories)	Granada 1980	**C**
22 **Hello America** (novel)	Cape 1981	**C**
23 **Myths of the Near Future** (stories)	Cape 1982	**C**
24 **Empire of the Sun** (novel)	Gollancz 1984	**C**
	Simon & Schuster 1985	**C**
25 **The Day of Creation** (novel)	Gollancz 1987	**B**
	Farrar Straus 1988	**B**
26 **Running Wild** (novella)	Hutchinson 1988	**B**
	Farrar Straus 1989	**B**
27 **Memories of the Space Age** (stories)	Arkham House US 1988	**B**
28 **War Fever** (stories)	Collins 1990	**B**
	Farrar Straus 1991	**B**
29 **The Kindness of Women** (novel)	HarperCollins 1991	**B**
	Farrar Straus 1991	**B**

Banks, Iain   Born in Fife, Scotland, 1954.

Although Banks's new books are always expansively reviewed, he seems to have if anything a rather lower profile than when he burst on the scene nearly ten years ago with his repellent (but really rather good) *The Wasp Factory*. But he retains a hard core of devotees; it remains to be seen whether he will once and for all become a mainstream collectable, or whether he will wither into the backwaters of cultdom.

1 **The Wasp Factory** (novel)	Macmillan 1984	**G**
	Houghton Mifflin 1984	**C**
2 **Walking on Glass** (novel)	Macmillan 1985	**D**
	Houghton Mifflin 1986	**B**
3 **The Bridge** (novel)	Macmillan 1986	**C**
	St Martin's 1989	**B**
4 **Consider Phlebas** (novel)	Macmillan 1987	**C**
	St Martin's 1988	**B**
5 **Espedair Street** (novel)	Macmillan 1987	**B**
6 **The Player of Games** (novel)	Macmillan 1988	**B**
	St Martin's 1989	**B**
7 **Canal Dreams** (novel)	Macmillan 1989	**B**
	Doubleday 1991	**B**
8 **Use of Weapons** (novel)	Orbit 1990	**B**
	Bantam 1992	**B**

9 **The State of the Art** (novel)	Orbit 1991	**B**
10 **The Crow Road** (novel)	Scribners 1992	**B**

Banks, Lynne Reid   Born in London, 1929.

Although still producing, the author is more of a 'get it out of the library or wait for the paperback' type of animal. I am not aware of any collector seeking out any of her books except *The L-Shaped Room,* and possibly the pair of sequels that make up the trilogy, and I list these here. What would estate agents have done without that title to actually *glorify* two small, rather awkward rooms that have been knocked into one?

1 **The L-Shaped Room** (novel)	Chatto & Windus 1960	**E**
	Simon & Schuster 1962	**B**
2 **The Backward Shadow** (novel)	Chatto & Windus 1970	**B**
	Simon & Schuster 1970	**B**
3 **Two Is Lonely** (novel)	Chatto & Windus 1974	**B**
These three form a trilogy: 1 is in itself a	Simon & Schuster 1974	**B**
milestone, and a desirable work.		

Banville, John   Born in Wexford, Ireland, 1945.

A very stylish and literary writer who is either a big noise or else a complete unknown, depending upon the circles in which one moves, and the journals one takes. The point of all this from the collector's point of view is that to many booksellers, Banville might yet be undiscovered: seize the opportunity.

1 **Long Lankin** (stories)	Secker & Warburg 1970	**F**
2 **Nightspawn** (novel)	Secker & Warburg 1971	**J**
	Norton 1971	**F**
3 **Birchwood** (novel)	Secker & Warburg 1973	**E**
	Norton 1973	**C**
4 **Doctor Copernicus** (novel)	Secker & Warburg 1976	**D**
	Norton 1976	**C**
5 **Kepler** (novel)	Secker & Warburg 1981	**D**
	Godine 1983	**C**
6 **The Newton Letter: an Interlude** (novel)	Secker & Warburg 1982	**C**
	Godine 1987	**C**
7 **Mefisto** (novel)	Secker & Warburg 1986	**C**
	Godine 1989	**B**
8 **The Book of Evidence** (novel)	Secker & Warburg 1989	**C**
	Scribner 1990	**B**

Barnes, Julian Born in Leicester, 1946.

In the last edition of this book I suggested that there might still be booksellers who were unaware of Barnes; well, you can forget that now. Julian Barnes now has a very high reputation (well deserved) and is that rare breed of novelist – like Ackroyd – where you never quite know what on earth he is going to come up with next. Which is why, maybe, *Talking it Over* was received less rapturously than, say, the quite brilliant *History of the World* – it was merely a good novel, without all the tricks. I believe that this was a sound direction to take, however, because as soon as writers feel they have to top the special effects of the last effort, they become conjurors, and increasingly desperate. Barnes is a man to watch – but already difficult to gather, I'm afraid.

1	**Duffy** (novel)	Cape 1980	G
	(pseud. Dan Kavanagh)	Pantheon 1986	B
2	**Metroland** (novel)	Cape 1980	H
		St Martin's Press 1980	C
3	**Fiddle City** (novel)	Cape 1981	D
	(pseud. Dan Kavanagh)	Pantheon 1986	B
4	**Before She Met Me** (novel)	Cape 1982	E
5	**Flaubert's Parrot** (novel)	Cape 1984	E
		Knopf 1985	C
6	**Putting the Boot In** (novel)	Cape 1985	C
	(pseud. Dan Kavanagh)		
7	**Staring at the Sun** (novel)	Cape 1986	C
		Knopf 1987	B
8	**Going to the Dogs** (novel)	Viking UK 1987	C
	(pseud. Dan Kavanagh)	Pantheon 1987	C
9	**A History of the World in 10½ Chapters** (novel)	Cape 1989	D
		Knopf 1989	C
10	**Talking it Over** (novel)	Cape 1991	C
		Knopf 1991	B
11	**The Porcupine** (novella)	Cape 1992	B

Barstow, Stan Born in Yorkshire, 1928.

Barstow is still producing, but I cannot in all conscience continue listing him in his entirety – I have never, in truth, met a Barstow collector. Nonetheless, *A Kind of Loving* remains a key work in any collection of post-war literature, and so I list it – together with the two follow-ups that form the Vic Brown Trilogy.

1	**A Kind of Loving** (novel)	Joseph 1960	F
		Doubleday 1961	C
2	**The Watchers on the Shore** (novel)	Joseph 1966	B

		Doubleday 1967	**B**
3	**The Right Tube End** (novel)	Joseph 1976	**B**

Beckett, Samuel   Born near Dublin, 1906. Died 1989.

One somehow thought Beckett would never die – although it was equally difficult to imagine him ever having been born. I expected a great surge in Beckett-collecting following his demise, however, but it never came and it still hasn't. There certainly was a degree of impatience with his last, very slight works – and completists became increasingly resentful at having to fork out between ten and twenty pounds for new books when they contained roughly as many pages – and I do not even mention the limited stuff at up to £1000 a time. Still, the later stuff is still something of a bargain, while the 1950s and 1960s Faber items continue to get scarcer. I suppose there will be little books of parings for years to come.

In the list that follows, I have recorded the first editions in the English language, but as the French-language edition precedes many of these, the following bibliography should be consulted for the fullest information:

Raymond Federman and John Fletcher *Samuel Beckett, His Works And His Critics: An Essay in Bibliography* University of California Press, Berkeley 1970.

1	**Our Exagmination Round His Factification for Incamination of Work in Progress**	Shakespeare & Co. (Paris) 1929	**O**
		Faber 1936	**L**
	Cont. Dante... Bruno... Vico... Joyce. By S.B.	New Directions 1939	**J**
2	**Whoroscope** (verse)	Hours Press (Paris) 1930	**Q,S**
	Beckett's first separately published work. Limited to 300 copies, 100 signed. Wrpps.		
3	**Proust**	Chatto & Windus 1931	**M**
		Grove Press 1957	**F**
4	**More Pricks than Kicks** (texts)	Chatto & Windus 1934	**Q**
		Grove Press 1970	**D**
5	**Echo's Bones** (verse)	Europa Press (Paris) 1935	**P**
6	**Murphy** (novel)	Routledge 1938	**Q**
	Scarce.	Grove Press 1957	**E**
7	**Molloy** (novel)	Olympia Press (Paris) 1955	**K**
	(French-language ed. 1951 **M**)		
		Grove Press 1955	**I**
		Calder 1959	**G**
8	**Waiting for Godot** (play)	Grove Press 1954	**K**
	(French-language ed. 1952 **N**)	Faber 1956	**H**
9	**Malone Dies** (novel)	Grove Press 1956	**I**
	(French-language ed. 1951 **J**)	Calder 1958	**H**

43

10	**All That Fall** (play)	Grove Press 1958	**G**
		Faber 1958	**G**
11	**Endgame** (play)	Grove Press 1958	**F**
	(French-language ed. 1957 **H**)	Faber 1958	**F**
12	**The Unnamable**	Calder 1959	**F**
	(French-language ed. 1953 **H**)		
13	**From an Abandoned Work**	Faber 1958	**G**
	Wrpps.		
14	**Krapp's Last Tape** and **Embers**	Faber 1959	**H**
	(plays)	Grove Press 1960	**D**
	Wrpps.		
15	**Watt** (novel)	Olympia Press (Paris) 1953	**K**
		Grove Press 1959	**F**
		Calder 1963	**F**
16	**Poems in English**	Calder 1961	**D**
		Grove Press 1963	**C**
17	**Happy Days** (play)	Grove Press 1961	**E**
		Faber 1962	**E**
18	**Play and Two Short Pieces for Radio** (incl. *Words & Music* and *Cascando*)	Faber 1964	**E**
19	**How It Is** (novel)	Grove Press 1964	**D**
	(French-language ed. 1961 **F**)	Calder 1964	**D**
20	**Imagination Dead Imagine** (text)	Calder 1965	**C**
	(French-language ed. 1965 **E**)		
21	**Proust and Three Dialogues with Georges Duthuit**	Calder 1965	**C**
22	**Come and Go: Dramaticule**	Calder 1967	**C**
23	**Eh Joe and Other Writings** (play)	Faber 1967	**D**
	Incl. *Act Without Words* II and *Film*.		
24	**No's Knife: Selected Shorter Prose 1945–1966**	Calder 1967	**C**
	Incl. *Stories and Texts for Nothing, From an Abandoned Work, Imagination Dead Imagine, Enough* and *Ping*.		
25	**Film** (screenplay)	Grove Press 1969	**C**
		Faber 1972	**C**
26	**Breath and Other Shorts**	Faber 1971	**D**
	Incl. *Come and Go, Act Without Words* I and II, *From an Abandoned Work*.		
27	**Lessness** (story)	Calder 1971	**C**
	(French-language ed. 1969 **D**)		
28	**First Love** (story)	Calder 1973	**C**
	(French-language ed. 1970 **D**)	Grove Press 1974	**C**
29	**The Lost Ones** (story)	Calder 1972	**C**
	(French-language ed. 1971 **D**)		
30	**Not I** (play)	Faber 1973	**C**

31 **The North** — Enitharmon Press 1973 — **N**
Limited to 137 numbered and signed
copies.

32 **Mercier and Camier** (novel) — Calder 1974 — **C**
(French-language ed. 1970 **C**) — Grove Press 1975 — **C**

33 **Footfalls** (play) — Faber 1976 — **C**

34 **That Time** (play) — Faber 1976 — **C**

35 **For to End Yet Again, and Other** — Calder 1977 — **C**
Fizzles
Published as **Fizzles** by Grove Press in
1977 (**C**)

36 **Collected Poems in English and** — Calder 1977 — **C**
French

37 **Four Novellas** — Calder 1977 — **C**

38 **Ends and Odds** (plays) — Grover Press 1977 — **C**
Incl. 30, 33, 34. — Faber 1977 — **C**

39 **Six Residua** (reprinted pieces) — Calder 1978 — **C**

40 **All Strange Away** (prose) — Calder 1979 — **C**
First published in a limited edition
ilustrated by Edward Gorey in 1976 by
the Gotham Book Mart (**I**).

41 **Company** (prose) — Grove Press 1980 — **C**
Translated by S.B. from his *Compagnie*, — Calder 1980 — **C**
Editions de Minuit, 1979.

42 **Rockaby and Other Short Pieces** — Grove Press 1981 — **C**
Contains *Rockaby, Ohio Impromptu, All
Strange Away* and *A Piece of Monologue*.

43 **Ill Seen Ill Said** (prose) — Grove Press 1981 — **C**
— Calder 1982 — **C**

44 **Three Occasional Pieces** (plays) — Faber 1982 — **C**

45 **Worstward Ho** (prose) — Calder 1983 — **C**

46 **Collected Shorter Plays** — Faber 1984 — **C**

47 **Disjecta: Miscellaneous Writings** — Calder 1984 — **C**
and Dramatic Fragments

48 **Collected Shorter Prose 1945–1980** — Calder 1984 — **C**

49 **Collected Poems 1930–1978** — Calder 1984 — **C**

50 **Complete Dramatic Works** — Faber 1986 — **C**
— Grove Press 1986 — **C**

51 **Happy Days: The Production** — Faber 1986 — **F**
Notebook — Grove Press 1986 — **F**

52 **Nohow On** — Calder 1988 — **C**
(contains *Company, Ill Been Ill Said,
Worstword Ho*)

53 **Stirrings Still** (texts) — Calder 1988 — **Q**
(a signed, de luxe edition published at £750)

54 **As the Story was Told** — Calder 1990 — **C**
(trade edition of 53)

55 **Beckett's Theatrical Notebooks:** — Faber 1992 — **F**
Krapp's Last Tape

56 **Dream of Fair to Middling Women** (Beckett's first, long-suppressed novel)	Black Cat Press 1992	C
57 **Collected Poems 1930–89**	Calder 1992	C
58 **The Theatrical Notebooks of Samuel Beckett: Endgame**	Faber 1992	F

Becket translated the following:

Anthology of Mexican Poetry	Indiana University, Bloomington 1958	E
	Thames & Hudson 1959 Ed. by Octavio Paz.	E

Robert Pinget **The Old Tune** inc:

Robert Pinget **Three Plays**	Hill & Wang (NY) 1966	C
Robert Pinget **Plays**	Calder 1966	C
Guillaume Apollinaire **Zone**	Calder 1972	C
	Dolmen Press 1972	C

Samuel Beckett: An Exhibition (Turret Books 1971) is also a useful book to the collector.

Behan, Brendan   Born in Dublin, 1923. Died 1964.

His books fetch *decent* prices, when they come up – and they sell, but never for very much. No one seems actively to go after them, which is a shame, for the best are really excellent. We may reflect upon the fact that if Behan were pursued by as many people as those who claim to have gone drinking with him, he would be the most avidly collected author in the world.

1 **The Quare Fellow** (play)	Methuen 1956	F
2 **The Hostage** (play)	Methuen 1958	E
These two plays pub. in America in one vol.	Grove Press 1964	B
3 **Borstal Boy**	Knopf 1957	F
	Hutchinson 1958	F
4 **Brendan Behan's Island** (non-fiction)	Hutchinson 1962	C
	Geis 1962	C
5 **Hold Your Hour and Have Another**	Hutchinson 1963	C
	Little, Brown 1964	C
6 **Brendan Behan's New York**	Hutchinson 1964	C
	Geis 1964	C
7 **The Scarperer** (novel)	Doubleday 1964	C
	Hutchinson 1966	C
8 **Confessions of an Irish Rebel**	Hutchinson 1965	C
	Geis 1966	C
9 **Borstal Boy** (play)	Random House (NY) 1971	B

10 **Richard's Cork Leg** (play)	Methuen 1973	**B**
	Grove Press 1974	**B**
11 **After the Wake: Uncollected Prose**	O'Brien Press 1983	**B**
First published in Ireland, and then by Allison & Busby in UK, and by Devin in US.		

Bellow, Saul   Born in Canada, 1915. American.

Although Bellow's first two (and most sought-after) novels would never fetch in Britain what they would in America, the prices have risen, and Bellow's reputation continues to grow despite (because of?) his very slim output. Another factor that might contribute to the growing popularity of Bellow is the fresh attention that has been drawn to him by a new and younger generation of USA-watchers, notably Martin Amis – with whom he has been compared.

1 **Dangling Man** (novel)	Vanguard Press 1944	**P**
	Lehmann 1946	**K**
2 **The Victim** (novel)	Vanguard Press 1945	**M**
	Lehmann 1948	**I**
3 **The Adventures of Augie March** (novel)	Viking 1953	**G**
	Weidenfeld 1954	**F**
4 **Seize the Day, with Three Short Stories and a One Act Play**	Viking 1956	**E**
	Weidenfeld 1957	**E**
5 **Henderson the Rain King** (novel)	Viking Press 1959	**E**
	Weidenfeld 1959	**D**
6 **Herzog** (novel)	Viking 1964	**D**
	Weidenfeld 1965	**C**
7 **The Last Analysis** (play)	Viking 1965	**C**
	Weidenfeld 1966	**C**
8 **Mosby's Memoirs and Other Stories**	Viking 1968	**C**
	Weidenfeld 1969	**C**
9 **Mr Sammler's Planet** (novel)	Viking 1970	**C**
	Weidenfeld 1970	**C**
10 **Humboldt's Gift** (novel	Viking 1975	**C**
	Alison Press/	
	Secker & Warburg 1975	**C**
11 **To Jerusalem and Back** (non-fiction)	Viking 1976	**C**
	Secker & Warburg 1976	**B**
12 **The Nobel Lecture**	US Information Service, Stockholm 1977	**H**
13 **The Dean's December** (novel)	Harper 1982	**C**
	Secker & Warburg 1982	**B**
14 **Him with His Foot in His Mouth and Other Stories**	Harper 1984	**C**
	Secker & Warburg 1984	**B**

47

15 **More Die of Heartbreak** (novel)	Morrow 1987	C
	Alison Press 1987	B
16 **A Theft** (story)	Penguin 1989	B
17 **The Bellarosa Connection** (stories)	Penguin 1989	B
18 **Something to Remember Me By**	Secker & Warburg 1992	B
(story – also contains nos. 16 and 17)		

Bennett, Alan   Born in Yorkshire, 1934.

Bennett was always a hugely popular playwright in this country – but since the success of his TV playlets *Talking Heads*, critics have practically deified him: certainly Bennett never fails to entertain, but he is also a very thought-provoking writer – one laughs at the jokes at the time, but all the darker stuff lingers on. If Bennett were a novelist, he would be far more collected than he is (such is the way) but although the books that follow will never be terribly expensive, they will – for the most part – prove to be damnably elusive.

1 **Beyond the Fringe** (play)	Souvenir Press 1962	H
	Random House 1963	D
2 **Forty Years On** (play)	Faber 1969	G
3 **Getting On** (play)	Faber 1972	C
4 **Habeas Corpus** (play)	Faber 1973	C
5 **The Old Country** (play)	Faber 1978	C
6 **Enjoy** (play)	Faber 1980	C
7 **Office Suite**	Faber 1981	C
Includes *Green Forms* and *A Visit From Miss Prothero*.		
8 **Objects of Affection** (play)	BBC 1983	C
9 **A Private Function** (screenplay)	Faber 1985	C
10 **The Writer in Disguise** (plays)	Faber 1985	C
Includes *Me, I'm Afraid of Virginia Woolf*, *All Day on the Sands*, *One Fine Day*, *The Old Crowd* and *Afternoon Off*.		
11 **Two Kafka Plays**	Faber 1987	B
(includes *Kafka's Dick* and *The Insurance Man*)		
12 **Talking Heads**	BBC 1987	C
13 **Prick Up Your Ears**	Faber 1987	B
(screenplay)		

Bentley, E.C.   Born 1875. Died 1956.

As well as having written one excellent detective novel, Bentley is famous for having created a rather daft four-line poem format, which he called the

Clerihew (his middle name). A previously unpublished cache of the things was recently discovered in Bentley's old school (St Paul's) and so now, in addition to the established canon, we may thrill to such stuff as:

Which was more tall?
Chapman or Hall?
The mystery thickens
When you learn that they published Dickens!

Yes, well, anyway. Here are the highlights.

1	**Trent's Last Case** (novel)	Nelson 1913	**H**
2	**The Complete Clerihews**	OUP 1981	**B**
3	**The First Clerihews**	OUP 1982	**B**
	With collaborators.		

Berger, John Born in London, 1926.

A somewhat elitist taste, but Berger retains his royal band of followers. The early fiction would be the most looked for, but his art criticism might yet be underrated, and is certainly worth a glance.

1	**A Painter of Our Time** (novel)	Secker & Warburg 1958	**F**
		Simon & Schuster 1959	**D**
2	**Permanent Red: Essays in Seeing**	Methuen 1960	**D**
3	**The Foot of Clive** (novel)	Methuen 1962	**D**
4	**Corker's Freedom** (novel)	Methuen 1964	**D**
5	**The Success and Failure of Picasso**	Penguin 1965	**C**
6	**A Fortunate Man: The Story of a Country Doctor** (photo-documentary)	Lane 1967	**B**
		Holt Rinehart 1967	**B**
7	**Art in Revolution** (non-fiction)	Weidenfeld 1969	**B**
		Pantheon 1969	**B**
8	**The Moment of Cubism and Other Essays**	Weidenfeld 1969	**C**
		Pantheon 1969	**C**
9	**The Look of Things: Selected Essays and Articles**	Penguin 1971	**B**
		Viking 1974	**B**
10	**Ways of Seeing** (art)	Penguin 1972	**B**
		Viking 1973	**B**
11	**G** (novel)	Weidenfeld 1972	**D**
		Viking 1972	**C**
12	**A Seventh Man** (photo-documentary)	Penguin 1975	**B**
13	**Pig Earth** (novel)	Writers & Readers 1979	**B**
		Pantheon 1980	**B**
14	**About Looking** (art)	Writers & Readers 1980	**B**
		Pantheon 1980	**B**
15	**Another Way of Telling** (prose, with Jean Mohr)	Writers & Readers 1982	**B**
		Pantheon 1982	**B**

49

16 **And Our Faces, My Heart,**	Writers & Readers 1984	**B**
Brief as Photos (prose)	Pantheon 1984	**B**
17 **The White Bird** (prose)	Chatto & Windus 1985	**C**
18 **The Sense of Sight** (same as 17)	Pantheon 1986	**B**
19 **Once in Europa** (stories)	Pantheon 1987	**B**
	Granta 1989	**B**
20 **A Question of Geography** (play)	Faber 1987	**B**
With Nella Bielski.		
21 **Goya's Last Portrait: The**	Faber 1989	**B**
Painter Played Today (play)		
With Nella Bielski.		
22 **Lilac and Flag: An Old Wives'**	Pantheon 1990	**B**
Tale of a City (novel)	Granta 1991	**B**

Berryman, John Born in Oklahoma, 1914. Died 1972.

It really is rather difficult to judge whether or not Berryman is actively sought in Britain, as so few of the titles seem to come up – even in the Faber editions. Certainly, he is not as *fashionable* as he was in the sixties and seventies, but that is no bad thing. At least when firsts *do* come up they will go to people who genuinely appreciate the verse, and not to the trend-conscious bandwagoneers.

1 **Five American Poets**	New Directions (NY)	**K**
With others.	1940	
2 **Poems**	New Directions 1942	**I**
3 **The Dispossessed** (verse)	Sloane (NY) 1948	**H**
4 **Stephen Crane** (criticism)	Sloane 1950	**G**
	Methuen 1951	**E**
5 **Homage to Mistress Bradstreet**	Farrar Straus (NY) 1956	**J**
(verse)		
The Amer. ed. is just the title poem,	Faber 1959	**H**
whereas the Faber ed. includes a		
selection from 3 and 6.		
6 **His Thoughts Made Pockets & The**	Frederick (NY) 1958	**I**
Plane Buckt		
7 **77 Dream Songs** (verse)	Farrar Straus 1964	**G**
	Faber 1964	**F**
8 **Berryman's Sonnets** (verse)	Farrar Straus 1967	**E**
	Faber 1968	**D**
9 **Short Poems**	Farrar Straus 1967	**C**
The same as the Eng. ed. of 5, without		
the title poem, but with one new poem.		
10 **His Toy, His Dream, His Rest**	Farrar Straus 1968	**G**
(verse)	Faber 1969	**F**
11 **Love and Fame** (verse)	Farrar Straus 1970	**D**
	Faber 1971	**C**

12 **Delusions, etc.** (verse)	Farrar Straus 1972	C
	Faber 1972	C
13 **Selected Poems 1938–1968**	Faber 1972	C
14 **Recovery** (novel)	Farrar Straus 1973	C
	Faber 1973	C
15 **The Freedom of the Poet**	Farrar Straus 1977	C
(essays)	Faber 1977	C
16 **Henry's Fate** (verse)	Farrar Straus 1977	C
	Faber 1978	C

Betjeman, John Born in Highgate, London, 1906. Died 1984.

Dear Sir John – still one of the most loved English poets, partly because he makes you smile, and partly because you do not have to rack your brains in order to divine what the blazes he is banging on about – as is so often the way with some of our, um, more *ambitious* poets. He must have published as and when he produced, as no posthumous collection has emerged, alas. But there are plenty of riches for the collector here, as may be seen. The trouble is, the rare is getting rarer, and the not so rare is getting pricier – a story, I daresay, you have heard before. But Betj is truly an all-time classic – no flash in the pan, he – and so the effort, I think, simply must be made.

1 **Mount Zion** (verse)	James Press 1931	P
2 **Ghastly Good Taste** (architecture)	Chapman & Hall 1933	J
(with a rear gatefold)		
3 **Devon** (architecture)	Architectural Press 1936	I
4 **Continual Dew: A Little Book of Bourgeois Verse**	Murray 1937	J
5 **An Oxford University Chest**	Miles 1938	J
6 **A Handbook on Paint**	Silicate Paint Co.	J
(an oddity – one essay by J.B., one by Hugh Casson)	J.B. Orr & Co. Ltd 1939	
7 **Antiquarian Prejudice** (essay)	Hogarth Press 1939	E
8 **Old Light for New Chancels** (verse)	Murray 1940	F
9 **Vintage London** (architecture)	Collins 1942	E
10 **English Cities and Small Towns** (architecture)	Collins 1943	C
11 **John Piper** (art)	Penguin 1944	C
12 **New Bats in Old Belfries** (verse)	Murray 1945	E
13 **Slick, But Not Streamlined: Poems and Short Pieces** (1,750 copies, edited by W.H. Auden)	Doubleday US 1947	I
14 **Murray's Buckinghamshire Architectural Guide** With John Piper.	Murray 1948	D

15	**Selected Poems** Edited by John Sparrow.	Murray 1948	C
16	**Murray's Berkshire Architectural** **Guide**	Murray 1949	D
17	**Murray's Shropshire Architectural** **Guide**	Murray 1951	E
18	**First and Last Loves** (essays)	Murray 1952	E
19	**A Few Late Chrysanthemums** (verse)	Murray 1954	E
20	**Poems in the Porch**	SPCK 1954	C
21	**The English Town in the Last** **Hundred Years** (architecture)	CUP 1956	D
22	**Collins Guide to English Parish** **Churches**	Collins 1958 Obolensky 1959	D C
23	**Collected Poems** Edited by Earl of Birkenhead.	Murray 1958	C
24	**Summoned by Bells** (verse autobiography)	Murray 1960 Houghton Mifflin 1963	D C
25	**A Ring of Bells** Edited by Irene Slade, for children. Extracts from 24.	Murray 1963 Houghton Mifflin 1963	C C
26	**English Churches** (architecture) With Basil Clarke.	Studio Vista 1964	C
27	**Cornwall** (architecture)	Faber 1965	D
28	**High and Low** (verse)	Murray 1966 Houghton Mifflin 1967	D C
29	**London's Historic Railway** **Stations** (architecture)	Murray 1972	C
30	**A Pictorial History of English** **Architecture**	Murray 1972 Macmillan US 1972	C C
31	**A Nip in the Air** (verse)	Murray 1974	C
32	**Archie and the Strict Baptists** (juvenile)	Murray 1977 Lippincott 1978	C B
33	**The Best of Betjeman** Edited by John Guest.	Murray 1978	B
34	**Church Poems**	Murray 1981	B
35	**Uncollected Poems**	Murray 1982	C

Bowen, Elizabeth   Born in Dublin, 1899. Died 1973.

As the keen interest in women writers continues to grow – fuelled in part by the olive-green tidal wave of Virago paperback reprints that threatens to engulf us – so the Bowen camp gets bigger. Extremely difficult to assemble a complete collection – and you will be up against dedicated pros. Female, in all probability. If *you* are female, ignore this. If you are not, be warned.

1 **Encounters: Stories**	Sidgwick & Jackson 1923	**K**
	Boni & Liveright 1926	**G**
2 **Ann Lee's and Other Stories**	Sidgwick & Jackson 1926	**J**
	Boni & Liveright 1926	**G**
3 **The Hotel** (novel)	Constable 1927	**I**
	Dial Press 1928	**F**
4 **The Last September** (novel)	Constable 1929	**H**
	Dial Press 1929	**F**
5 **Joining Charles and Other Stories**	Constable 1929	**H**
	Dial Press 1929	**F**
6 **Friends and Relations** (novel)	Constable 1931	**G**
	Dial Press 1931	**E**
7 **To the North** (novel)	Gollancz 1932	**G**
	Knopf 1933	**E**
8 **The Cat Jumps and Other Stories**	Gollancz 1934	**G**
9 **The House in Paris** (novel)	Gollancz 1935	**G**
	Knopf 1936	**E**
10 **The Death of the Heart** (novel)	Gollancz 1938	**E**
	Knopf 1939	**D**
11 **Look at All Those Roses** (stories)	Gollancz 1941	**D**
	Knopf 1941	**C**
12 **Bowen's Court** (non-fiction)	Longman 1942	**C**
	Knopf 1942	**C**
13 **English Novelists** (non-fiction)	Collins 1942	**C**
	Hastings House 1942	**C**
14 **Seven Winters** (non-fiction)	Cuala Press, Dublin 1942	**G**
	Longman 1943	**C**
	Knopf 1943	**C**
15 **The Demon Lover and Other Stories**	Cape 1945	**D**
16 **Ivy Gripped the Steps and Other Stories** (same as 15)	Knopf 1946	**C**
17 **Selected Stories**	Fridberg, Dublin 1946	**D**
18 **Anthony Trollope: A New Judgement**	OUP (UK & US) 1946	**D**
19 **Why Do I Write?: An Exchange of Views Between Elizabeth Bowen, Graham Greene, and V.S. Pritchett**	Marshall 1948	**C**
20 **The Heat of the Day** (novel)	Cape 1949	**C**
	Knopf 1949	**C**
21 **Collected Impressions**	Longman 1950	**C**
	Knopf 1950	**C**
22 **The Shelbourne** (non-fiction)	Harrap 1951	**E**
23 **The Shelbourne Hotel** (same as 22)	Knopf 1951	**D**

Boyd

24 **A World of Love** (novel)	Cape 1955	C
	Knopf 1955	C
25 **Stories**	Knopf 1959	C
26 **A Time in Rome** (non-fiction)	Longman 1960	C
	Knopf 1960	C
27 **Afterthought: Pieces About Writing**	Longman 1962	C
	Knopf 1962	C
28 **The Little Girls** (novel)	Cape 1964	C
	Knopf 1964	B
29 **A Day in the Dark and Other Stories**	Cape 1965	C
30 **The Good Tiger** (juvenile)	Knopf 1965	C
	Cape 1970	C
31 **Eva Trout** (novel)	Knopf 1968	C
	Cape 1969	C
32 **Pictures and Conversations**	Knopf 1975	C
33 **The Collected Stories**	Cape 1981	C
	Random House 1982	C

Elizabeth Bowen also edited the
following two important works:

The Faber Book of Modern Stories	Faber 1937	
Stories (by Katherine Mansfield)	Knopf 1956	
34 **Short Stories** (same as above)	Collins 1957	

Boyd, William   Born in Ghana, 1952. British.

Maybe not quite such a big noise as a few years ago, though still command-
ing a good deal of respect: in Oxford, of course, he is still a god. Not at all as
prolific as some of our younger writers (a good thing) although he does write
a lot of screenplays and the occasional television adaptation (one of which –
unpublished – was of Evelyn Waugh's *Scoop*: not terribly well reviewed, but I
enjoyed it immensely). *A Good Man in Africa* still fetches a dizzy price, but the
rest – as you can see – are not too heart-stopping.

1 **A Good Man in Africa** (novel)	Hamilton 1981	L
	Morrow 1982	G
2 **On the Yankee Station** (stories)	Hamilton 1981	J
3 **An Ice-cream War** (novel)	Hamilton 1983	E
	Morrow 1983	C
4 **Stars and Bars** (novel)	Hamilton 1984	C
	Morrow 1985	B
5 **School Ties** (plays)	Hamilton 1985	C
Includes *Good and Bad at Games*,	Morrow 1986	B
Dutch Schulz, and an essay on public		
schools.		
6 **The New Confessions** (novel)	Hamilton 1987	C
	Morrow 1988	B

7 **Brazzaville Beach** (novel)	Sinclair-Stevenson 1990	**B**
	Morrow 1991	**B**

Bradbury, Malcolm Born in Yorkshire, 1932.

The balance between Bradbury's twin careers of bestselling novelist and academic seems to have tipped in favour of the latter, lately – which is, frankly, a crashing disappointment. Not that his non-fiction works are without interest or merit – quite the reverse; but the novels are what one is really waiting for – and this is certainly true of collectors. *The History Man* remains the classic.

1 **Eating People is Wrong** (novel)	Secker & Warburg 1959	**H**
	Knopf 1960	**D**
2 **How to Have Class in a Classless Society**	Parrish 1960	**F**
3 **All Dressed Up and Nowhere to Go**	Parrish 1962	**E**
4 **Evelyn Waugh** (Writers & Critics Series)	Oliver & Boyd 1964	**D**
5 **Stepping Westward** (novel)	Secker & Warburg 1965	**D**
	Houghton Mifflin 1966	**B**
6 **What is a Novel?**	Arnold 1969	**C**
7 **The Social Context of Modern English Literature**	Blackwell 1971	**C**
	Schocken 1971	**C**
8 **Possibilities: Essays on the State of the Novel**	OUP 1973	**C**
9 **The History Man** (novel)	Secker & Warburg 1975	**G**
	Houghton Mifflin 1976	**D**
10 **Who Do You Think You Are** (stories)	Secker & Warburg 1976	**C**
11 **Saul Bellow** (criticism)	Methuen 1982	**C**
In the Contemporary Writers Series.		
12 **The Modern American Novel** (prose)	OUP 1983	**C**
13 **Rates of Exchange** (novel)	Secker & Warburg 1983	**C**
	Knopf 1983	**B**
14 **Why Come to Slaka?** (prose)	Secker & Warburg 1986	**B**
	Penguin US 1988	**B**
15 **Cuts** (novella)	Hutchinson 1987	**B**
	Harper 1987	**B**
16 **My Strange Quest for Mensonge: Structuralism's Hidden Hero** (prose)	Deutsch 1987	**B**
	Penguin US 1988	**B**
17 **No, Not Bloomsbury** (essays)	Deutsch 1987	**B**
	Columbia U.P. 1988	**B**
18 **The Modern World: Ten Great Writers**	Secker & Warburg 1988	**C**
	Viking 1989	**C**

Bradbury, Ray

19 **Unsent Letters: Irreverent Notes** **From a Literary Life** (prose)	Secker & Warburg 1988 Viking 1988	B B
20 **From Puritanism to Post-** **modernism: The Story of** **American Literature** With Richard Ruland.	Routledge 1991	B
21 **Doctor Criminale** (novel)	Secker & Warburg 1992	B

Bradbury, Ray   Born in Illinois, 1920. American.

An increasingly cultish author – although there is still enormous interest in anything from the 1950s and early 1960s – especially *Dark Carnival, The Illustrated Man* and – the classic – *Fahrenheit 451*.

Bradbury has published a huge array of rather arcane material, but here I confine myself to the complete novels and stories.

1 **Dark Carnival** (stories)	Arkham House 1947 Hamish Hamilton 1948	K I
2 **The Martian Chronicles** (stories)	Doubleday 1950	H
3 **The Silver Locusts** (same as 2)	Hart Davis 1951	F
4 **The Illustrated Man** (stories)	Doubleday 1951 Hart Davis 1952	H G
5 **The Golden Apples of the Sun** (stories)	Doubleday 1953 Hart Davis 1953	G F
6 **Fahrenheit 451** (novel)	Ballantine 1953 Hart Davis 1954	L I
7 **The October Country** (stories)	Ballantine 1955 Hart Davis 1956	E D
8 **Dandelion Wine** (novel)	Doubleday 1957 Hart Davis 1957	F E
9 **A Medicine for Melancholy** (stories)	Doubleday 1959	E
10 **The Day it Rained Forever** (same as 9)	Hart Davis 1959	E
11 **Something Wicked This Way Comes** (novel)	Simon & Schuster 1962 Hart Davis 1963	H G
12 **The Machineries of Joy** (stories)	Simon & Schuster 1964 Hart Davis 1964	D C
13 **The Vintage Bradbury** (stories)	Random House 1965	C
14 **The Autumn People** (stories)	Ballantine 1965	D
15 **Tomorrow Midnight** (stories)	Ballantine 1966	D
16 **Twice Twenty Two** (stories)	Doubleday 1966	D
17 **I Sing the Body Electric!** (stories)	Knopf 1969 Hart Davis 1970	C C
18 **Bloch and Bradbury** (stories) With Robert Bloch.	Tower US 1969	E
19 **Fever Dreams and Other Fantasies** (same as 18)	Sphere 1970	D

20 **Long After Midnight** (stories)	Knopf 1976	**C**
	Hart Davis MacGibbon 1977	**C**
21 **The Best of Bradbury**	Bantam 1976	**C**
22 **To Sing Strange Songs** (stories)	Wheaton UK 1979	**C**
23 **The Stories of Ray Bradbury**	Knopf 1980	**C**
	Granada 1980	**C**
24 **The Last Circus** and **The Electrocution** (stories)	Lord John Press 1980	**E**
25 **Dinosaur Tales** (stories)	Bantam 1983	**C**
26 **A Memory of Murder** (stories)	Dell 1984	**B**
27 **Death is a Lonely Business** (novel)	Knopf 1985	**B**
	Grafton 1986	**B**
28 **The Toynbee Convector** (stories)	Knopf 1988	**B**
	Grafton 1989	**B**
29 **A Graveyard for Lunatics: Another Tale of Two Cities** (novel)	Knopf 1990	**B**
	Grafton 1990	**B**

Braine, John   Born in Yorkshire, 1922. Died 1986.

It's no good pretending any more that people collect John Braine – his critical reputation has taken a real knocking, lately, and practically all of his books may be picked up for a song. It is a shame that he lost that superb cutting edge so brilliantly displayed in his first, great book – and, to a lesser extent, in its sequel. I list the pair here: Joe Lampton lives.

1 **Room at the Top** (novel)	Eyre & Spottiswoode 1957	**I**
	Houghton Mifflin 1957	**D**
2 **Life at the Top** (novel)	Eyre & Spottiswoode 1962	**C**
	Houghton Mifflin 1962	**B**

Braithwaite, E.R.   Born in British Guiana (Guyana), 1922.

Not a collected author, but I stubbornly continue to include him just for this one desirable novel, its theme of black-white relations being (alas) no less relevant today.

To Sir, With Love	Bodley Head 1959	**E**

Brooke, Rupert Born in Rugby, 1887. Died 1915.

As with all the war poets, killed so young, a great deal of the *œuvre* is posthumous, collected, and recollected. The very early publications – brought out when Brooke was still a schoolboy – are of legendary rarity, and therefore would command a massive price. As will be seen from the ensuing checklist, Brooke is not an author one has any hope of assembling in full, but a fair idea of availability and price should be achieved.

1	**The Pyramids**	Rugby Press 1904	U
2	**The Bastille**	Rugby Press 1905	T
3	**Prize Compositions**	Rugby Press 1905	S
4	**Poems 1911**	Sidgwick & Jackson 1911	M
5	**1914 and Other Poems** An American edition seems to have been printed by Doubleday in 1915 for copyright reasons only, and never published.	Sidgwick & Jackson 1914	L
6	**1914: Five Sonnets**	Sidgwick & Jackson 1915	I
7	**The Collected Poems of Rupert Brooke**	Lane (NY) 1915	I
		Sidgwick & Jackson 1918	H
8	**Lithuania** (drama)	Chicago Little Theatre 1915	K
		Sidgwick & Jackson 1935	G
9	**Letters from America**	Scribner 1916	H
		Sidgwick & Jackson 1916	I
10	**John Webster** (drama)	Lane 1916	F
		Sidgwick & Jackson 1916	E
11	**Selected Poems**	Sidgwick & Jackson 1917	E
12	**The Complete Poems of Rupert Brooke**	Sidgwick & Jackson 1932	E
13	**Twenty Poems**	Sidgwick & Jackson 1935	D
14	**The Poetical Works of Rupert Brooke**	Faber 1946	D
15	**Democracy and the Arts**	Hart-Davis 1946	C
16	**The Prose of Rupert Brooke**	Sidgwick & Jackson 1956	C
17	**The Letters of Rupert Brooke**	Faber 1968	C

For fullest information on Brooke, see
the following:

Christopher Hassall **Rupert Brooke: A Biography**	Faber 1964
Geoffrey Keynes **Rupert Brooke: A Bibliography**	Soho Bibliographies, Hart-Davis 1959

Brookner, Anita   Born in London, 1928.

Although they are by far the best things she has done, I am omitting Dr. Brookner's art monographs on such as Watteau, Greuze and David, because I feel sure that collectors – female to a man, as it were – will not be interested. Apart from anything else, their sheer bulk would mess up the ordered line of slim little novels.

1	**A Start in Life** (novel)	Cape 1981	E
2	**The Debut** (same as 1)	Linden Press US 1981	C
3	**Providence** (novel)	Cape 1982	D
		Pantheon 1984	B
4	**Look at Me** (novel)	Cape 1983	D
		Pantheon 1983	B
5	**Hotel Du Lac** (novel)	Cape 1984	E
		Pantheon 1985	C
6	**Family and Friends** (novel)	Cape 1985	C
		Pantheon 1985	B
7	**A Misalliance** (novel)	Cape 1986	C
	(US edition: *The Misalliance*)	Pantheon 1987	B
8	**A Friend From England** (novel)	Cape 1987	C
		Pantheon 1988	B
9	**Latecomers** (novel)	Cape 1988	C
		Pantheon 1989	B
10	**Lewis Percy** (novel)	Cape 1989	B
		Pantheon 1990	B
11	**Brief Lives** (novel)	Cape 1990	B
		Random House 1991	B
12	**A Closed Eye** (novel)	Cape 1991	B
		Random House 1992	B
13	**Fraud** (novel)	Cape 1992	B

Buckeridge, Anthony   Born in London, 1912.

One of the very few children's authors in this book, but a classic. Buckeridge – at the age of eighty – produced a new Jennings book recently, and although it must be said that it was but a poor shade of things that were, it was nonetheless good to see good old Jen and Darbi in a book cover again. You should have collected these years ago, of course, when you were first told: if you haven't, you've made a bish – but there's still time! And do make sure you are buying the originals, and not the later, Bowdlerized versions which are, frankly, ozard.

All, except where stated, are published by Collins.

1	**Jennings Goes to School**	1950	H
2	**Jennings Follows a Clue**	1951	E
3	**Jennings' Little Hut**	1951	E
4	**Jennings and Darbishire**	1952	D
5	**Jennings' Diary**	1953	D
6	**According to Jennings**	1954	D
7	**Our Friend Jennings**	1955	D
8	**Thanks to Jennings**	1957	D
9	**Take Jennings, for Instance**	1958	D
10	**Jennings, as Usual**	1959	D
11	**The Trouble with Jennings**	1960	C
12	**Just Like Jennings**	1961	C
13	**Leave It to Jennings**	1963	C
14	**Jennings, of Course!**	1964	C
15	**Especially Jennings!**	1965	C
16	**Jennings Abounding**	1967	C
17	**Jennings in Particular**	1968	C
18	**Trust Jennings!**	1969	C
19	**The Jennings Report**	1970	C
20	**Typically Jennings!**	1971	C
21	**Speaking of Jennings**	1973	C
22	**Jennings at Large**	1977	B

This was a paperback 'Armada' original.

23	**Jennings Again!**	Macmillan 1991	B

Buckeridge has also published the following, all from the Lutterworth Press:

A Funny Thing Happened!	1953	C
Rex Milligan's Busy Term	1953	C
Rex Milligan Raises the Roof	1955	C
Rex Milligan Holds Forth	1955	C
Rex Milligan Reporting	1961	C

Burgess, Anthony Born in Manchester, 1917.

Difficult to find anything new to say about this chap. He continues to be prolific (although he seems to have got some sort of a grip on himself these days, and tends to set the limit at one paltry book a year) and yet the quality seems to go up all the time. Still very much collected – always will be. The scarce titles are fetching really quite extraordinary prices now, as will be seen below. A bit too late to start on Burgess, then – unless you are rich and lucky, in which case you are presumably doing other things.

1 **Time for a Tiger** (novel)	Heinemann 1956	N
2 **English Literature: A Survey for Students**	Longman 1958	H
(pseud. John Burgess Wilson)		
3 **The Enemy in the Blanket** (novel)	Heinemann 1958	J
4 **Beds in the East** (novel)	Heinemann 1959	J
This, together with 1 and 3, forms the Malayan Trilogy.		
5 **The Right to an Answer** (novel)	Heinemann 1960	I
	Norton 1961	F
6 **The Doctor is Sick** (novel)	Heinemann 1960	H
	Norton 1966	F
7 **The Worm and the Ring** (novel)	Heinemann 1961	M
Suppressed book.		
8 **Devil of a State** (novel)	Heinemann 1961	D
	Norton 1962	C
9 **One Hand Clapping** (novel)	Davies 1961	M
(pseud. Joseph Kell)	Knopf 1971	C
10 **A Clockwork Orange** (novel)	Heinemann 1962	L
	Norton 1963	F
11 **The Wanting Seed** (novel)	Heinemann 1962	G
	Norton 1963	D
12 **Honey for the Bears** (novel)	Heinemann 1963	F
	Norton 1964	D
13 **Inside Mr Enderby** (novel)	Heinemann 1963	L
(pseud. Joseph Kell)		
14 **The Novel Today** (non-fiction)	Longman 1963	D
15 **Nothing Like the Sun: A Story of Shakespeare's Love-Life**	Heinemann 1964	D
	Norton 1964	C
16 **The Eve of Saint Venus** (novel)	Sidgwick & Jackson 1964	D
	Norton 1967	C
17 **Languages Made Plain** (non-fiction)	English Universities Press 1964	C
	Crowell 1965	C
18 **The Long Day Wanes** (inc. 1, 3 and 4)	Norton 1965	C
19 **A Vision of Battlements** (novel)	Sidgwick & Jackson 1965	D
	Norton 1966	C
20 **Here Comes Everybody: An Introduction to James Joyce for the Ordinary Reader**	Faber 1965	F

21 **Re Joyce** (same as 20)	Norton 1965	**D**
22 **Tremor of Intent** (novel)	Heinemann 1966	**E**
	Norton 1966	**C**
23 **The Novel Now** (non-fiction)	Faber 1967	**D**
	Norton 1967	**C**
24 **Enderby Outside** (novel)	Heinemann 1968	**E**
25 **Enderby** (inc. 13 and 24)	Norton 1968	**C**
26 **Urgent Copy: Literary Studies**	Cape 1968	**C**
	Norton 1969	**C**
27 **Shakespeare** (non-fiction)	Cape 1970	**C**
	Knopf 1971	**C**
28 **MF** (novel)	Cape 1971	**C**
	Knopf 1971	**C**
29 **Joysprick: An Introduction to the Language of James Joyce**	Deutsch 1972	**D**
30 **Napoleon Symphony** (novel)	Cape 1974	**C**
	Knopf 1974	**B**
31 **The Clockwork Testament: or, Enderby's End** (novel)	Hart-Davis MacGibbon 1974	**C**
	Knopf 1974	**B**
32 **Moses: A Narrative** (prose)	Dempsey & Squires 1976	**C**
33 **A Long Trip to Teatime** (prose)	Dempsey & Squires 1976	**B**
34 **Beard's Roman Women** (novel)	McGraw Hill 1976	**B**
	Hutchinson 1977	**B**
35 **Abba Abba** (novel)	Faber 1977	**B**
	Little, Brown 1977	**B**
36 **Ernest Hemingway and His World** (biography)	Thames & Hudson 1978	**C**
	Scribner 1978	**B**
37 **1985** (novel)	Hutchinson 1978	**C**
	Little, Brown 1978	**B**
38 **The Land Where Ice-cream Grows** (juvenile)	Benn 1979	**D**
	Doubleday 1979	**C**
39 **Man of Nazareth** (adaptation)	McGraw Hill 1979	**B**
	Magnum 1980	**B**
40 **Earthly Powers** (novel)	Hutchinson 1980	**C**
	Simon & Schuster 1980	**B**
41 **On Going to Bed** (anthology) Edited and introduced by A.B.	Deutsch 1982	**B**
42 **The End of the World News** (novel)	Hutchinson 1982	**B**
	McGraw Hill 1983	**B**
43 **This Man and His Music** (non-fiction)	Hutchinson 1982	**B**
	McGraw Hill 1983	**B**
44 **Ninety-nine Novels: The Best in English Since 1939**	Allison & Busby 1984	**B**
	Simon & Schuster 1984	**B**
45 **Enderby's Dark Lady** (novel)	Hutchinson 1984	**B**
	McGraw Hill 1984	**B**

46 **The Kingdom of the Wicked** (novel)	Hutchinson 1985	B
	Arbor House 1985	B
47 **Homage to QWERTYUIOP** (journalism)	Hutchinson 1985	B
	McGraw Hill 1986	B
48 **Oberon Old and New** (opera)	Hutchinson 1985	B
49 **The Pianoplayers** (novel)	Hutchinson 1986	B
50 **Carmen** (opera)	Hutchinson 1986	B
51 **Little Wilson and Big God, Being The First Part of the Confessions of Anthony Burgess**	Weidenfeld & Nicholson US 1986	B
	Heinemann 1987	B
52 **A Clockwork Orange** (play)	Hutchinson 1987	B
53 **They Wrote in English** (prose)	Hutchinson 1988	B
54 **The Devil's Mode and Other Stories**	Hutchinson 1989	B
	Random House 1989	B
55 **Any Old Iron** (novel)	Hutchinsom 1989	B
	Random House 1989	B
56 **You've Had Your Time, Being The Second Part of the Confessions of Anthony Burgess**	Heinemann 1990	B
	Grove Weidenfeld 1991	B
57 **Mozart and the Wolf Gang** (prose)	Hutchinson 1991	B
	Ticknor & Fields 1991	B
58 **A Mouthful of Air** (non-fiction)	Hutchinson 1992	B

Burgess has also edited and translated a number of works. For complete details, see:

Paul W. Boytinck **Anthony Burgess: A Bibliography**	West 1978

Burroughs, Edgar Rice   Born in America, 1875. Died 1950.

Decent of Burroughs to give Tarzan a Jane. Poor old Robinson Crusoe, remember, got stuck with Man Friday. Hard to see, speaking from a vantage point of snappy sophistication, quite what Jane saw in the man; mind you, she had little choice.

There were very many Tarzan books. I list here the first of them, which is very scarce and expensive. Subsequent titles, though, should be in the £10–£50 class.

Tarzan of the Apes	McClurg (Chicago) 1914	R

Burroughs, William S. Born in Missouri, 1914.
American.

Still rather popular with a younger set who wish they were old enough to not remember a single thing about the sixties, and I doubt whether even the recent film version of *The Naked Lunch* is sufficient to dim their enthusiasm. I list below all the fiction.

1. **Junkie: Confessions of an Unredeemed Drug Addict** (novel) (pseud. William Lee). A complete edition was published by Penguin in 1977, entitled *Junky*.	Ace US 1953 Digit UK 1957	**L** **H**
2 **The Naked Lunch** (novel) (US ed. lacks the *The*)	Olympia Press, Paris 1959 Grove Press US 1962 Calder 1964	**I** **H** **E**
3 **The Soft Machine** (novel)	Olympia Press, Paris 1961 Grove Press US 1966 Calder & Boyars 1968	**F** **D** **C**
4 **The Ticket That Exploded** (novel)	Olympia Press, Paris 1962 Grove Press US 1967 Calder & Boyars 1968	**F** **D** **C**
5 **Dead Fingers Talk** (novel)	Calder 1963	**D**
6 **Nova Express** (novel)	Grove Press 1964 Cape 1966	**E** **D**
7 **The Wild Boys: A Book of the Dead** (novel)	Grove Press 1971 Calder & Boyars 1972	**C** **C**
8 **Exterminator!** (stories)	Viking Press 1973 Calder & Boyars 1974	**C** **C**
9 **Short Novels**	Calder 1978	**C**
10 **Blade Runner: A Movie** (novel)	Blue Wind Press US 1979	**C**
11 **Port of Saints** (novel)	Blue Wind Press US 1980 Calder 1983	**C** **C**
12 **Cities of the Red Night: A Boy's Book** (novel)	Calder 1981 Holt Rinehart 1981	**C** **C**
13 **Early Routines** (stories)	Cadmus US 1981	**C**
14 **The Streets of Chance** (stories)	Red Ozier Press US 1981	**D**
15 **The Place of Dead Roads** (novel)	Holt Rinehart 1983 Calder 1984	**C** **C**
16 **Queer** (novel)	Viking US 1987 Picador 1988	**C** **C**

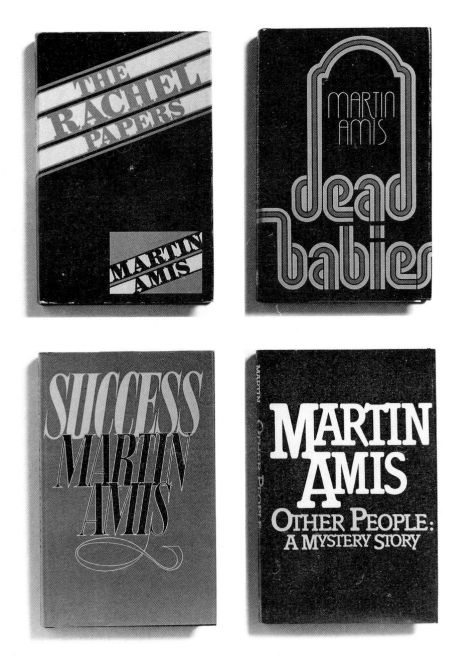

The first four novels of Martin Amis

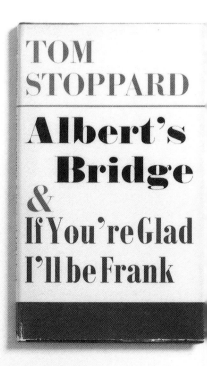

A selection of Stoppards from his most eloquently irresistible period

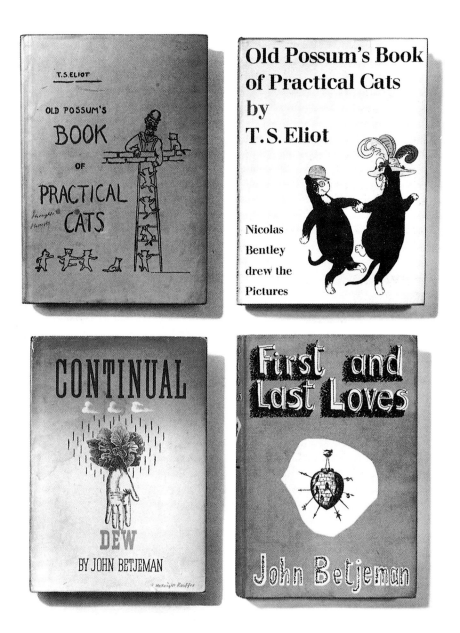

The first and the first illustrated editions of Old Possum, and a brace from the late, lamented Laureate

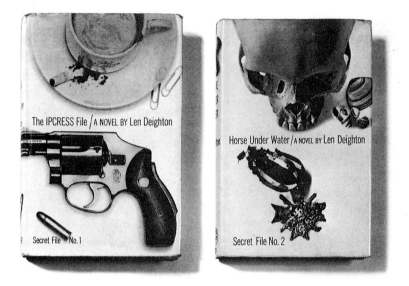

Deighton's first three novels, comprising the 'Secret Files' – all with dust-wrappers
by Raymond Hawkey

Poetry, prose and poser in the theatre

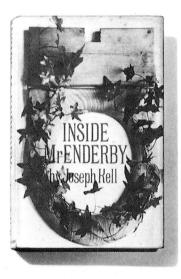

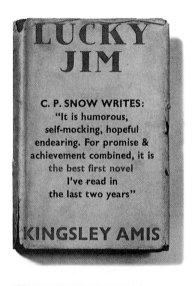

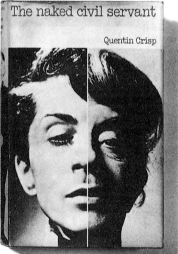

A scarce pseudonymous Anthony Burgess, Amis's first and famous novel, the first English edition of Donleavy's first novel, and the autobiography of Britain's noisiest Crisp

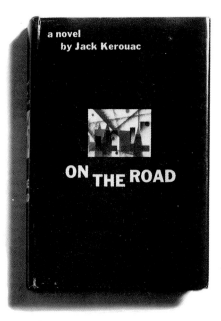

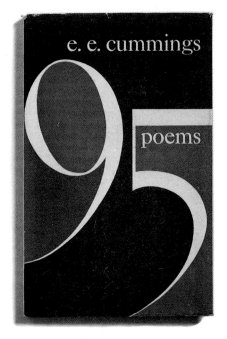

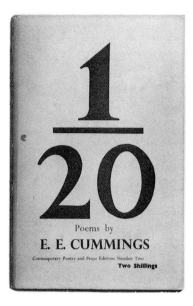

The seminal Kerouac, Bellow's first book, and a couple of
representative works by cummings

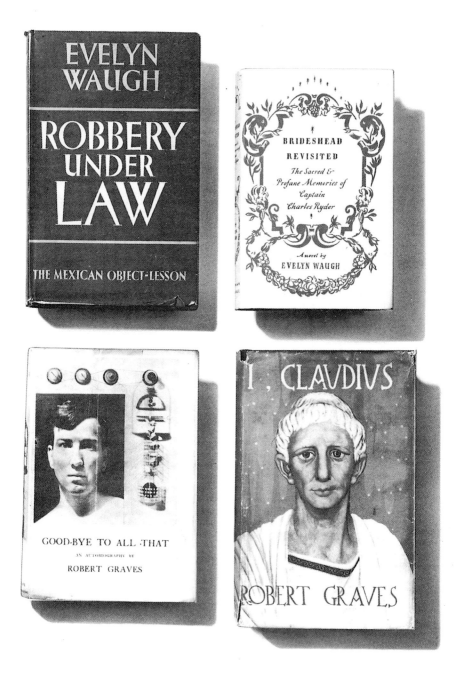

A very scarce Waugh, with his celebrated novel, and the two best-known titles by
Robert Graves

17 **The Western Lands** (novel)	Viking US 1987	C
	Picador 1988	C

Byatt, A.S.   Born in Yorkshire, 1936.

Not so much an invigorating novelist as a thought provoker. The books are not to everyone's taste, it is true – *Possession*, despite its Booker-winning acclaim (Byatt said she would spend the prize money on a swimming pool) is pretty heavy going – but Antonia Susan's profile in the book collecting world slowly edges forward.

1 **Shadow of a Sun** (novel)	Chatto & Windus 1964	F
	Harcourt Brace 1964	D
2 **Degrees of Freedom: The Novels**	Chatto & Windus 1965	C
of Iris Murdoch (non-fiction)	Barnes & Noble 1965	C
3 **The Game** (novel)	Chatto & Windus 1967	C
	Scribner 1968	C
4 **Wordsworth and Coleridge**	Nelson 1970	C
in their Time (non-fiction)	Crane-Russak 1973	C
5 **Iris Murdoch** (non-fiction)	Longman 1976	C
6 **The Virgin in the Garden** (novel)	Chatto & Windus 1978	C
	Knopf 1978	B
7 **Ford Madox Ford and the Prose**	Chatto & Windus 1982	B
Tradition (non-fiction)	Knopf 1982	B
8 **Still Life** (novel)	Chatto & Windus 1985	B
	Scribner 1985	B
9 **Sugar and Other Stories**	Chatto & Windus 1987	B
	Scribner 1987	B
10 **Possession** (novel)	Chatto & Windus 1990	B
	Random House 1990	B
11 **Passions of the Mind** (essays)	Chatto & Windus 1991	B
12 **Angels and Insects** (novellas)	Chatto & Windus 1992	B

Camus, Albert   Born in Algeria, 1913. Died 1960. French.

Camus – although still very much read – is not strongly collected in Britain, as is often true with modern work appearing in translation, for all the true firsts are, of course, French. For this reason, I am listing only his first and most interesting work, and although this too is just the first *English* edition, it has points that make it very desirable in its own right, as will be seen below.

The Outsider	Hamilton 1946	E
Though first published as *L'Etranger* in		
France in 1942, this English edition is of		
great interest to collectors, as it is		
translated by Stuart Gilbert, introduced		

Canetti

by Cyril Connolly, and has a d/w by
Edward Bawden. It is also, of course, the
first appearance of Camus in English.
Very undervalued, however. It must
soon be worth much more. The Knopf
edition is entitled *The Stranger*.

Canetti, Elias Born in Bulgaria, 1905.

Always very much more appreciated in Europe than in Britain, Canetti's
winning of the Nobel Prize in 1981 brought him to a wider audience as Cape
rushed back into print his best known work, hailing it (rightly) as a masterpiece, many cynically wondering why such a masterpiece had been allowed
to go out of print in the first place.

Although Canetti has written quite a few books of importance (such as
Crowds and Power) I record here his highlight which was also, incidentally, his
first book and his only novel. It was originally published in German in 1935
(firsts of this edition have fetched up to £300) and was put out in this country
after the war, in a translation by C.V. Wedgwood 'under the personal super-
vision of the author' as the title page records.

Auto da Fe (novel)   Cape 1946   **J**
The book went into several impressions
in its first year, and it is scarce.

Capote, Truman Born in New Orleans, 1924. Died 1984.

Although his persona, his outspokenness and his, well – *presence* were somewhat more jaw-sagging than his prose, Capote remains a much-read and
admired writer to the end, his highlights as diverse as the slight but very
attractive short story *Breakfast at Tiffany's* and one of the earliest examples of
'faction', *In Cold Blood*. As is almost always the way, much more popular and
collected in America than in Britain.

1	**Other Voices, Other Rooms** (novel)	Random House (NY) 1948	**G**
		Heinemann 1948	**D**
2	**A Tree of Night and Other Stories**	Random House 1949	**F**
3	**Local Color** (non-fiction)	Random House 1950	**D**
4	**The Grass Harp** (novel)	Random House 1951	**D**
		Heinemann 1952	**D**
5	**The Grass Harp** (play)	Random House 1952	**C**
6	**The Muses Are Heard: An Account**	Random House 1956	**C**
7	**Breakfast at Tiffany's** (stories)	Random House 1958	**H**
		Heinemann 1959	**G**

8 **Observations**	Simon & Schuster 1959	F
With Richard Avedon.	Weidenfeld 1959	E
9 **Selected Writings**	Modern Library (NY) 1963	C
	Hamilton 1963	C
10 **A Christmas Memory** (story)	Random House 1966	C
11 **In Cold Blood: A True Account of a Multiple Murder and Its Consequences**	Random House 1966	E
	Hamilton 1966	C
12 **House of Flowers** (play)	Random House 1968	C
13 **The Thanksgiving Visitor** (play)	Random House 1968	C
	Hamilton 1969	C
14 **The Dogs Bark: Public People and Private Places**	Random House 1973	C
	Weidenfeld 1974	C
15 **Then It All Came Down: Criminal Justice Today Discussed by Police, Criminals and Correcting Officers With Comments by Truman Capote**	Random House 1976	C
16 **Music for Chameleons** (essays)	Random House 1980	B
	Hamilton 1981	B
17 **One Christmas** (novel)	Random House 1982	B
	Hamilton 1983	B
18 **Answered Prayers** (unfinished novel)	Random House 1986	B
	Hamilton 1986	B
Also of note: **Conversations with Capote** Lawrence Grobel	Hutchinson 1985	B

Carey, Peter   Born in Victoria, Australia, 1943.

Young Carey's novels are about Australia – but don't go away, it's all right, they're really amusing in a funny-sad sort of a way. Very elegant too, despite being something of an acquired taste. *Illywhacker* (Australian for a conman) is a good read – but most will have come to Carey through his Booker-winning *Oscar and Lucinda*. At the moment, not too troublesome or expensive to gather up.

1 **The Fat Man in History** (stories)	University of Queensland Press 1974	F
	Faber 1980	C
	Random House 1980	C
2 **War Crimes** (stories)	University of Queensland Press 1979	E
3 **Bliss** (novel)	University of Queensland Press 1981	F
	Faber 1981	E
	Harper 1981	D

Carter

4 **Illywhacker** (novel)	Faber 1985	C
	Harper 1985	C
5 **Bliss: The Screenplay**	University of Queensland Press 1986	C
6 **Bliss: The Film** (same as 5)	Faber 1986	C
7 **Oscar and Lucinda** (novel)	Faber 1988	C
	Harper 1988	C
8 **The Tax Inspector** (novel)	Faber 1991	B
	Knopf 1991	B

Carter, Angela Born in Sussex, 1940. Died 1992.

Since her untimely death, we have heard a greal deal of praise for Angela Carter – certainly her last two novels were very fine pieces of work. Always a *wise* writer, and very popular for a long time, her position in the collecting world has yet to be defined, but a rise in interest is inevitable.

1 **Shadow Dance** (novel)	Heinemann 1966	J
2 **Honeybuzzard** (same as 1)	Simon & Schuster 1966	F
3 **The Magic Toyshop** (novel)	Heinemann 1967	H
	Simon & Schuster 1968	D
4 **Several Perceptions** (novel)	Heinemann 1968	F
	Simon & Schuster 1968	C
5 **Heroes and Villains** (novel)	Heinemann 1969	F
	Simon & Schuster 1960	C
6 **Miss Z, The Dark Young Lady** (juvenile)	Heinemann 1970	E
	Simon & Schuster 1970	C
7 **Love** (novel)	Hart-Davis 1970	E
8 **The Donkey Prince** (juvenile)	Simon & Schuster 1970	E
9 **The Infernal Desire Machines of Doctor Hoffman** (novel)	Hart-Davis 1972	D
10 **The War of Dreams** (same as 9)	Harcourt Brace 1974	C
11 **Fireworks** (stories)	Quartet 1974	C
	Harper & Row 1981	C
12 **The Passion of New Eve** (novel)	Gollancz 1977	D
	Harcourt Brace 1977	C
13 **Comic and Curious Cats** Illus. Martin Leman.	Gollancz 1979	D
	Crown 1979	C
14 **The Sadeian Women** (non-fiction)	Virago 1979	C
	Pantheon 1979	C
15 **The Bloody Chamber** (novel)	Gollancz 1979	C
	Harper 1980	C
16 **Sleeping Beauty and Other Favourite Fairy Tales**	Gollancz 1983	C

17 **Come Unto These Yellow Sands** (four radio plays)	Bloodaxe Books 1984	C
18 **Nights at the Circus** (novel)	Chatto & Windus 1984	D
	Viking 1986	C
19 **Black Venus** (stories)	Chatto & Windus 1985	C
20 **Saints and Strangers** (same as 19)	Viking US 1986	C
21 **Wise Children** (novel)	Chatto & Windus 1991	C
	Farrar Straus 1992	C
22 **Expletives Deleted** (miscellany)	Chatto & Windus 1992	B

Chandler, Raymond   Born in Chicago, 1888. Died 1959.

Chandler was both very good *and* unique. That combination usually ensures collectability, for the very good reason that collectors are no fools (I trust you all agree) and they tend to steer clear of perishable goods. Chandler is here to stay. So are the high prices – OK, sister?

1 **The Big Sleep** (novel)	Knopf 1939	T
	Hamilton 1939	R
2 **Farewell, My Lovely** (novel)	Knopf 1940	S
	Hamilton 1940	R
3 **The High Window** (novel)	Knopf 1942	P
	Hamilton 1943	N
4 **The Lady in the Lake** (novel)	Knopf 1943	O
	Hamilton 1944	L
5 **Five Murderers** (stories) This, along with 6 and 7, was published in wrappers.	Avon (NY) 1944	J
6 **Five Sinister Characters** (stories)	Avon 1945	J
7 **The Finger Man** (stories)	Avon 1946	J
8 **The Little Sister** (novel)	Knopf 1949	M
	Hamilton 1949	K
9 **Trouble is My Business** (stories)	Penguin 1950	F
	Houghton Mifflin 1951	F
10 **The Simple Art of Murder** (miscellany)	Houghton Mifflin 1950	I
	Hamilton 1950	H
11 **The Long Goodbye** (novel)	Hamilton 1953	I
	Houghton Mifflin 1953	H
12 **Playback** (novel)	Houghton Mifflin 1958	H
	Hamilton 1958	G
13 **Raymond Chandler Speaking** (non-fiction)	Houghton Mifflin 1962	G
	Hamilton 1962	F
14 **Killer in the Rain** (stories)	Houghton Mifflin 1964	H
	Hamilton 1964	H
15 **The Smell of Fear** (stories)	Hamilton 1965	F

16 **The Blue Dahlia** (screenplay)	S. Illinois	
	University Press 1976	**E**
	Elm Tree 1976	**D**
17 **The Notebooks of Raymond**	Ecco Press 1976	**F**
Chandler	Weidenfeld 1977	**C**
18 **The Selected Letters of Raymond**	Cape 1981	**C**
Chandler		

Charteris, Leslie Born in Singapore, 1907. Pseudonym for Leslie Charles Bowyer Yin

I attended some book award lunch in 1991 – *Sunday Express*, if I remember – and who should I find myself sitting next to but the creator of the Saint. Charteris was very tall, tanned and lean, and he stared straight ahead a good deal of the time through pale blue, milky eyes. Could have even *been* the Saint! He liked Roger Moore's portrayal, apparently, but he thought George Sanders rather better. I, for my part, could think of nothing intelligent to say at all.

I list here only Charteris's first book, the first Saint book, and the first to carry the word in the title.

1 **X Esquire** (novel)	Ward Lock 1927	**L**
2 **Meet the Tiger** (novel)	Ward Lock 1928	**I**
3 **Enter the Saint** (3 novelettes)	Hodder & Stoughton	**K**
	1930	

Cheever, John Born in Massachusetts, 1912. Died 1983.

A sleeper for very many years in this country, and then a cult; the cult grew during the immediate aftermath of his death, but now already shows signs of waning. Still sought-after, though with demonstrably less trendy and wide-eyed fervour. The stories remain his best work.

1 **The Way Some People Live: A Book**	Random House 1943	**I**
of Stories		
2 **The Enormous Radio and Other**	Funk & Wagnall 1953	**G**
Stories		
3 **Stories** (with others)	Farrar Straus 1956	**E**
4 **A Book of Stories** (same as 3)	Gollancz 1957	**D**
5 **The Wapshot Chronicle** (novel)	Harper Row 1957	**H**
	Gollancz 1957	**F**
6 **The Housebreaker of Shady Hill**	Harper Row 1958	**F**
and Other Stories	Gollancz 1959	**D**
7 **Some People, Places and Things**	Harper Row 1961	**E**
That Will Not Appear in My Next	Gollancz 1961	**D**
Novel (stories)		

8 **The Wapshot Scandal** (novel)	Harper Row 1964	**E**
	Gollancz 1964	**D**
9 **The Brigadier and the Golf Widow**	Harper Row 1964	**D**
(stories)	Gollancz 1965	**C**
10 **Bullet Park** (novel)	Knopf 1969	**F**
	Cape 1969	**E**
11 **The World of Apples** (stories)	Knopf 1973	**D**
	Cape 1974	**C**
12 **Falconer** (novel)	Knopf 1977	**C**
	Cape 1977	**C**
13 **The Stories of John Cheever**	Knopf 1978	**C**
	Cape 1979	**C**
14 **Oh What a Paradise It Seems**	Knopf 1982	**C**
(novel)	Cape 1982	**C**
15 **The Journals of John Cheever**	Knopf 1991	**C**
	Cape 1991	**C**

Also of note:
Home Before Dark (Weidenfeld 1985) – a memoir by Susan Cheever, his daughter

Chesterton, G.K. Born in London, 1874. Died 1936.

Chesterton was extremely prolific, and a very entertaining author. It must be admitted, though, that an awful lot of his books would nowadays be wanted *only* by the collector for the sake of completeness, for he did put out a lot of very topical, religious and rhetorical literature that admirers of his poetry, say, or of the Father Brown stories would hardly warm to. This tends to be reflected in prices, of course. It is perfectly possible to build up a fairly large collection of first editions by Chesterton, or Wells or Shaw, none of which anyone particularly wants, none of which will you read, and all of which the bookseller will be pleased to be shot of. With the gems, though, the story is rather different. There follows, therefore, a list of his best-known works, and those which are probably the most desirable as first editions.

Fuller information might very well be required, however – particularly for his very many non-fiction works – and for this I refer you to: John Sullivan *G.K. Chesterton: A Bibliography* University of London 1958

1 **Napoleon of Notting Hill**	Bodley Head 1904	**N**
2 **The Man Who was Thursday**	Arrowsmith 1908	**M**
3 **The Innocence of Father Brown**	Cassell 1911	**O**
4 **Manalive**	Nelson 1912	**I**
5 **The Flying Inn**	Methuen 1914	**I**
6 **The Wisdom of Father Brown**	Cassell 1914	**N**
7 **The Man Who Knew Too Much**	Cassell 1922	**M**
8 **The Incredulity of Father Brown**	Cassell 1926	**N**

9 **The Collected Poems of G.K. Chesterton**	Palmer 1927	E
10 **The Secret of Father Brown**	Cassell 1927	I
11 **The Scandal of Father Brown**	Cassell 1935	G
12 **Autobiography**	Hutchinson 1936	D

Christie, Agatha Born in Devon, 1890. Died 1976.

Even people who don't collect detective fiction or crime want Agatha Christie – if not all, then at least a representation. Trouble is, they don't want just *any* old representation, oh no: they would settle for a mint *The Mysterious Affair at Styles*, or *Murder on the Orient Express* or *Ten Little Niggers* or *The Murder of Roger Ackroyd* – well, you get the idea. It's the old story, I'm afraid – the scarce becomes rare, the rare unheard-of. I agree that some of the prices listed below are scarcely believable – but hey! I'm just the messenger.

1 **The Mysterious Affair at Styles** (novel)	Lane (US) 1920	T
	Lane (UK) 1921	S
2 **The Secret Adversary** (novel)	Lane 1922	S
	Dodd Mead 1922	R
3 **Murder on the Links** (novel)	Lane 1923	R
	Dodd Mead 1923	P
4 **The Man in the Brown Suit** (novel)	Lane 1924	R
	Dodd Mead 1924	P
5 **Poirot Investigates** (stories)	Lane 1924	R
	Dodd Mead 1925	P
6 **The Secret of Chimneys** (novel)	Lane 1925	P
	Dodd Mead 1925	N
7 **The Road of Dreams** (verse)	Bles 1925	L
8 **The Murder of Roger Ackroyd** (novel)	Collins 1926	S
	Dodd Mead 1926	Q
9 **The Big Four** (novel)	Collins 1927	N
	Dodd Mead 1927	L
10 **The Mystery of the Blue Train** (novel)	Collins 1928	O
	Dodd Mead 1928	M
11 **The Seven Dials Mystery** (novel)	Collins 1929	N
	Dodd Mead 1929	L
12 **Partners in Crime** (stories)	Collins 1929	L
	Dodd Mead 1929	K
13 **The Underdog** (story) With *Blackman's Wood* by E. Phillips Oppenheim.	Reader's Library 1929	K
14 **The Murder at the Vicarage** (novel)	Collins 1930	M
	Dodd Mead 1930	K
15 **The Mysterious Mr Quin** (stories)	Collins 1930	L
	Dodd Mead 1930	J

16	**Giant's Bread** (novel)	Collins 1930	K
	As Mary Westmacott.	Doubleday 1930	I
17	**The Sittaford Mystery** (novel)	Collins 1931	K
18	**The Murder at Hazelmoor** (same as 17)	Dodd Mead 1931	K
19	**Peril at End House** (novel)	Collins 1932	K
		Dodd Mead 1932	I
20	**The Thirteen Problems** (stories)	Collins 1932	J
21	**The Tuesday Club Murders** (same as 20)	Dodd Mead 1933	J
22	**Lord Edgware Dies** (novel)	Collins 1933	L
23	**Thirteen at Dinner** (same as 22)	Dodd Mead 1933	K
24	**The Hound of Death and Other Stories**	Odhams 1933	F
25	**Parker Pyne Investigates** (stories)	Collins 1934	K
26	**Mr Parker Pyne, Detective** (same as 25)	Dodd Mead 1934	I
27	**The Listerdale Mystery and Other Stories**	Collins 1934	K
28	**Black Coffee** (play)	Ashley 1934	H
29	**Why Didn't They Ask Evans?** (novel)	Collins 1934	O
30	**Murder on the Orient Express** (novel)	Collins 1934	R
31	**Murder on the Calais Coach** (same as 30)	Dodd Mead 1934	O
32	**Murder in Three Acts** (novel)	Dodd Mead 1934	O
33	**Unfinished Portrait** (novel)	Collins 1934	I
	As Mary Westmacott.	Doubleday 1934	G
34	**Boomerang Clue** (same as 29)	Dodd Mead 1935	H
35	**Three Act Tragedy** (same as 32)	Collins 1935	K
36	**Death in the Clouds** (novel)	Collins 1935	L
37	**Death in the Air** (same as 36)	Dodd Mead 1935	I
38	**The A.B.C. Murders: A New Poirot Mystery**	Collins 1936	N
		Dodd Mead 1936	K
39	**Cards on the Table** (novel)	Collins 1936	M
		Dodd Mead 1936	L
40	**Murder in Mesopotamia** (novel)	Collins 1936	M
		Dodd Mead 1936	L
41	**Murder in the Mews and Other Stories**	Collins 1937	L
42	**Dead Man's Mirror and Other Stories** (same as 41)	Dodd Mead 1937	I
43	**Death on the Nile** (novel)	Collins 1937	N
		Dodd Mead 1938	I
44	**Dumb Witness** (novel)	Collins 1937	L
45	**Poirot Loses a Client** (same as 44)	Dodd Mead 1937	L
46	**Appointment With Death: A**	Collins 1938	L

Christie

	Poirot Mystery	Dodd Mead 1938	J
47	**The Regatta Mystery and Other Stories**	Dodd Mead 1939	L
48	**Hercule Poirot's Christmas** (novel)	Collins 1939	O
49	**Murder for Christmas: A Poirot Story** (same as 48)	Dodd Mead 1939	M
50	**Murder Is Easy** (novel)	Collins 1939	L
51	**Easy to Kill** (same as 50)	Dodd Mead 1939	J
52	**Ten Little Niggers** (novel)	Collins 1939	R
53	**And Then There were None** (same as 52)	Dodd Mead 1940	O
54	**One, Two, Buckle My Shoe** (novel)	Collins 1940	K
55	**Sad Cypress** (novel)	Collins 1940	K
		Dodd Mead 1940	H
56	**The Patriotic Murders** (same as 54)	Dodd Mead 1941	H
57	**Evil Under the Sun** (novel)	Collins 1941	L
		Dodd Mead 1941	I
58	**N or M?** (novel)	Collins 1941	M
		Dodd Mead 1941	J
59	**The Body in the Library** (novel)	Collins 1942	K
		Dodd Mead 1942	H
60	**The Moving Finger** (novel)	Dodd Mead 1942	J
		Collins 1943	J
61	**Five Little Pigs** (novel)	Collins 1942	I
62	**Murder in Retrospect** (same as 61)	Dodd Mead 1942	G
63	**Death Comes as the End** (novel)	Dodd Mead 1942	I
		Collins 1945	I
64	**Towards Zero** (novel)	Collins 1944	I
		Dodd Mead 1944	G
65	**Absent in the Spring** (novel) As Mary Westmacott.	Collins 1944	G
		Farrar & Rinehart (NY) 1944	E
66	**Ten Little Niggers** (play)	French 1944	H
67	**Sparkling Cyanide** (novel)	Collins 1945	J
68	**Remembered Death** (same as 67)	Dodd Mead 1945	G
69	**Appointment with Death** (play)	French 1945	E
70	**The Hollow** (novel)	Collins 1946	H
		Dodd Mead 1946	F
71	**Come Tell Me How You Live** (travel)	Collins 1946	F
		Dodd Mead 1946	D
72	**Ten Little Indians** (play) (same as 66)	French (NY) 1946	D
73	**Murder on the Nile** (play)	French 1946	D
		French (NY) 1946	D
74	**The Labours of Hercules: Short Stories**	Collins 1947	H

75 **Labors of Hercules** (same as 74)	Dodd Mead 1947	**F**
76 **Taken at the Flood** (novel)	Collins 1948	**G**
77 **There Is a Tide . . .** (same as 76)	Dodd Mead 1948	**E**
78 **The Rose and the Yew Tree** (novel)	Heinemann 1948	**E**
As Mary Westmacott.	Rinehart 1948	**D**
79 **Witness for the Prosecution** (stories)	Dodd Mead 1948	**G**
80 **Crooked House** (novel)	Collins 1949	**G**
	Dodd Mead 1949	**F**
81 **A Murder is Announced** (novel)	Collins 1950	**G**
	Dodd Mead 1950	**F**
82 **Three Blind Mice and Other Stories**	Dodd Mead 1950	**G**
83 **Under Dog and Other Stories**	Dodd Mead 1951	**E**
84 **They Came to Baghdad** (novel)	Collins 1951	**F**
	Dodd Mead 1951	**D**
85 **The Hollow** (play)	French 1952	**C**
	French (NY) 1952	**C**
86 **They Do It with Mirrors** (novel)	Collins 1952	**F**
87 **Murder with Mirrors** (same as 86)	Dodd Mead 1952	**D**
88 **Mrs McGinty's Dead** (novel)	Collins 1952	**F**
	Dodd Mead 1952	**D**
89 **A Daughter's a Daughter** (novel) As Mary Westmacott.	Heinemann 1952	**C**
90 **After the Funeral** (novel)	Collins 1953	**F**
91 **Funerals are Fatal** (same as 90)	Dodd Mead 1953	**D**
92 **A Pocket Full of Rye** (novel)	Collins 1953	**E**
	Dodd Mead 1954	**C**
93 **Witness for the Prosecution** (play)	French 1954	**C**
	French (NY) 1954	**C**
94 **Destination Unknown** (novel)	Collins 1954	**E**
95 **So Many Steps to Death** (same as 94)	Dodd Mead 1955	**C**
96 **Hickory, Dickory, Dock** (novel)	Collins 1955	**E**
97 **Hickory, Dickory, Death** (same as 96)	Dodd Mead 1955	**C**
98 **The Mousetrap** (play)	French 1956	**N**
	French (NY) 1956	**K**
99 **Dead Man's Folly** (novel)	Collins 1956	**E**
	Dodd Mead 1956	**C**
100 **The Burden** (novel) As Mary Westmatcott.	Heinemann 1956	**C**
101 **The Spider's Web** (play)	French 1957	**C**
	French (NY) 1957	**C**
102 **Towards Zero** (play)	French 1957	**C**
	Dramatists Play Service 1957	**C**

103	**4.50 from Paddington** (novel)	Collins 1957	**E**
104	**What Mrs McGillicuddy Saw!** (same as 103)	Dodd Mead 1957	**E**
105	**Verdict** (play)	French 1958	**C**
106	**The Unexpected Guest** (play)	French 1958	**C**
107	**Ordeal by Innocence** (novel)	Collins 1958	**D**
		Dodd Mead 1958	**C**
108	**Cat Among the Pigeons** (novel)	Collins 1959	**D**
		Dodd Mead 1959	**C**
109	**The Adventure of the Christmas Pudding** (stories)	Collins 1960	**D**
110	**Go Back for Murder** (play) Adaptation of 61.	French 1960	**C**
111	**Double Sin and Other Stories**	Dodd Mead 1961	**C**
112	**13 for Luck** (stories)	Dodd Mead 1961	**C**
		Collins 1966	**C**
113	**The Pale Horse** (novel)	Collins 1961	**D**
		Dodd Mead 1962	**C**
114	**The Mirror Crack'd from Side to Side** (novel)	Collins 1962	**D**
115	**The Mirror Crack'd** (same as 114)	Dodd Mead 1963	**C**
116	**Rule of Three** (plays) Cont. *Afternoon at the Seaside, The Patient* and *The Rats*.	French 1963	**C**
117	**The Clocks** (novel)	Collins 1963	**C**
		Dodd Mead 1964	**B**
118	**A Caribbean Mystery** (novel)	Collins 1964	**C**
		Dodd Mead 1965	**B**
119	**Star over Bethlehem and Other Stories** As A.C. Mallowan.	Collins 1965	**C**
		Dodd Mead 1965	**C**
120	**Surprise! Surprise!** (stories)	Dodd Mead 1965	**C**
121	**13 Clues for Miss Marple** (stories)	Dodd Mead 1965	**C**
122	**At Bertram's Hotel** (novel)	Collins 1965	**C**
		Dodd Mead 1965	**C**
123	**Third Girl** (novel)	Collins 1966	**C**
		Dodd Mead 1967	**C**
124	**Endless Night** (novel)	Collins 1967	**C**
		Dodd Mead 1968	**C**
125	**By the Pricking of My Thumbs** (novel)	Collins 1968	**C**
		Dodd Mead 1968	**C**
126	**Passenger to Frankfurt** (novel)	Collins 1970	**C**
		Dodd Mead 1970	**C**
127	**Nemesis** (novel)	Collins 1971	**C**
		Dodd Mead 1971	**B**
128	**The Golden Ball and Other Stories**	Dodd Mead 1971	**B**

129 **Elephants Can Remember** (novel)	Collins 1972	**B**
	Dodd Mead 1972	**B**
130 **Postern of Fate** (novel)	Collins 1973	**C**
	Dodd Mead 1973	**B**
131 **Akhmaton** (play)	Collins 1973	**C**
	Dodd Mead 1973	**C**
132 **Poems**	Collins 1973	**C**
	Dodd Mead 1973	**C**
133 **Hercule Poirot's Early Cases** (stories)	Collins 1974	**C**
	Dodd Mead 1974	**B**
134 **Murder on Board: Three Complete Mystery Novels** Cont. **The Mystery of the Blue Train, Death in the Air, What Mrs McGillicuddy Saw!**	Dodd Mead 1974	**C**
135 **Curtain: Hercule Poirot's Last Case**	Collins 1975	**C**
	Dodd Mead 1975	**B**
136 **Sleeping Murder** (novel)	Collins 1976	**C**
	Dodd Mead 1976	**B**
137 **Miss Marple's Final Cases and Others** (stories)	Collins 1979	**C**
	Dodd Mead 1979	**B**
138 **Autobiography**	Collins 1979	**C**
139 **Remembrance** (story)	Souvenir Press 1988	**B**
140 **My Flower Garden**	Souvenir Press 1989	**B**

Clarke, Arthur C. Born in Somerset, 1917.

Clarke continues to be very prolific, which provides plenty of scope, of course – but he can still be collected without too much trouble or expense, with the exceptions of his very earliest work, and classics such as *2001*. Although Clarke has now published nearly forty non-fiction works, I continue to limit the listing to the stuff in which most collectors are interested – the novels and the short stories.

1 **Prelude to Space** (novel)	New World (NY) 1951	**I**
	Sidgwick & Jackson 1953	**G**
2 **The Sands of Mars** (novel)	Sidgwick & Jackson 1951	**F**
	Gnome Press 1952	**D**
3 **Islands in the Sky** (novel)	Winston, Philadelphia 1952	**F**
	Sidgwick & Jackson 1952	**D**
4 **Against the Fall of Night** (novel)	Gnome Press 1953	**E**
5 **Childhood's End** (novel)	Ballantine 1953	**E**

		Sidgwick & Jackson 1954	D
6	**Expedition to Earth** (stories)	Ballantine 1953	E
		Sidgwick & Jackson 1954	D
7	**Earthlight** (novel)	Balantine 1955	E
		Muller 1955	D
8	**The City and the Stars** (novel)	Harcourt Brace 1956	E
		Muller 1956	D
9	**Reach for Tomorrow** (stories)	Ballantine 1956	E
		Gollancz 1962	D
10	**Tales from the White Hart** (stories)	Ballantine 1957	D
		Sidgwick & Jackson 1972	B
11	**The Deep Range** (novel)	Harcourt Brace 1957	D
		Muller 1957	C
12	**The Other Side of the Sky** (stories)	Harcourt Brace 1958	D
		Gollancz 1961	C
13	**Across the Sea of Stars** (incl. 5, 7 and stories)	Harcourt Brace 1959	C
14	**A Fall of Moondust** (novel)	Harcourt Brace 1961	D
		Gollancz 1961	C
15	**From the Oceans, From the Stars** (incl. 11, 8 and stories)	Harcourt Brace 1962	D
16	**Tales of Ten Worlds** (stories)	Harcourt Brace 1962	C
		Gollancz 1963	C
17	**Dolphin Island** (novel)	Holt Rinehart 1963	D
		Gollancz 1963	C
18	**Glide Path** (novel)	Harcourt Brace 1963	D
		Sidgwick & Jackson 1969	C
19	**Prelude to Mars** (incl. 1, 2 and stories)	Harcourt Brace 1965	C
20	**An Arthur C. Clarke Omnibus** (incl. 1, 5 and 6)	Sidgwick & Jackson 1965	C
21	**The Nine Billion Names of God** (stories)	Harcourt Brace 1967	C
22	**2001: A Space Odyssey** (novel)	NAL 1968	H
		Hutchinson 1968	G
23	**An Arthur C. Clarke Second Omnibus** (incl. 2, 7, and 14)	Sidgwick & Jackson 1968	C
24	**The Lion of Comarre** (novel)	Harcourt Brace 1968	C
		Gollancz 1970	C
25	**A Meeting with Medusa** (stories)	Harcourt Brace 1972	C
26	**The Wind from the Sun** (stories)	Harcourt Brace 1972	C
27	**Of Time and Stars** (stories)	Gollancz 1972	C
28	**The Lost Worlds of 2001** (miscellany)	NAL 1972	C
		Sidgwick & Jackson 1972	C

29 **Report on Planet Three and Other Speculations** (stories)	Gollancz 1972	C
	NAL 1973	C
30 **The Best of Arthur C. Clarke (1937–1971)**	Sidgwick & Jackson 1973	C
31 **Rendezvous with Rama** (novel)	Harcourt Brace 1973	B
	Gollancz 1973	B
32 **Imperial Earth** (novel)	Gollancz 1975	B
	Harcourt Brace 1976	B
33 **The Fountains of Paradise** (novel)	Gollancz 1979	B
	Harcourt Brace 1979	B
34 **2010: Odyssey Two** (novel)	Granada 1982	C
	Ballantine 1982	C
35 **The Sentinel** (stories)	Berkley US 1983	B
	Panther 1985	B
36 **The Songs of Distant Earth** (novel)	Grafton 1986	B
	Ballantine 1986	B
37 **2061: Odyssey Three** (novel)	Ballantine 1988	C
	Grafton 1988	C
38 **Cradle** (novel) With Gentry Lee.	Gollancz 1988	B
	Warner 1988	B
39 **Rama II** (novel) With Gentry Lee.	Gollancz 1989	B
	Bantam 1989	B
40 **Tales from Planet Earth** (stories)	Century 1989	B
	Bantam 1990	B
41 **Beyond the Fall of Night** (novel) With Gregory Benford.	Putnam 1990	B
42 **Against the Fall of Night** (same as 41)	Gollancz 1991	B
43 **The Ghost from the Grand Banks** (novel)	Bantam 1990	B
	Gollancz 1990	B
44 **The Garden of Rama** (novel) With Gentry Lee.	Gollancz 1991	B
	Bantam 1991	B

Cleese, John   Born in England, 1939.

Listed under 'recreations' in his *Who's Who* entry are 'gluttony and sloth'. It will be seen that Cleese is a ceaseless producer of inimitably wonderful things and bears the physique of a Brobdingnagian stick insect, and so we may take these self-penned put-downs with a cellar of salt. The *really* interesting thing about his entry, however, is his appending his book *Families, and How to Survive Them* under publications (this is an intermittently amusing and reve-latory collaboration with his analyst) but omits all mention of the supreme *Fawlty Towers*. Finally, the twelve episodes have been published, though in a rather quirky manner, as will be seen below.

1 **Fawlty Towers** (teleplays) With Connie Booth.	Contact Futura 1977	D

79

Contains *The Builders, The Hotel Inspectors* and *Gourmet Night.*

2 **Fawlty Towers Book 2** (teleplays)   Contact Futura 1979   **C**
With Connie Booth.
Contains *The Wedding, A Touch of Class* and *The Germans.*

3 **The Complete Fawlty Towers**   Methuen 1988   **C**
Contains the six listed above, as well as – for the first time – *Communication Problems, The Psychiatrist, Waldorf Salad, The Kipper and the Corpse, The Anniversary, Basil the Rat.*

Connolly, Cyril   Born in Coventry, 1903. Died 1974.

At Eton with George Orwell, Anthony Powell, Henry Green and John Lehmann, and then later on to Balliol under Maurice Bowra, who dubbed Connolly 'the cleverest boy of his generation'. This is quite something to live up to, and there still seems to be a feeling abroad that Connolly did not. I believe this to be as unjust as it is illogical, for he failed to do only what others decided he should have done. In his own endeavours he was invariably successful – as Palinurus, as the founder and editor of *Horizon*, as novelist and critic – although it is true that in later life he observed that his position as star reviewer at *The Sunday Times* brought in far more money than would the writing of books, and therefore he no longer wrote books. This may be said to be a disappointing attitude for an artist, though it should be remembered that by then Connolly was no longer the coming young man of promise, but an established man of letters. First editions are becoming increasingly scarce, and for some reason or another are very rarely in truly fine condition (*Enemies of Promise* being particularly prone to shabbiness) and this would have gratified Connolly (he is still being *read*) and it also would have given him pause, for he was himself a passionate and devoted collector of modern firsts in fine state, most with a personal inscription from the author. There is a (probably apocryphal) story concerning Connolly hearing with great sadness that Huxley lay on his death bed, and rushing round in a taxi clutching a *Brave New World* for inscription before Huxley could quite quit this one.

His final 'Comment' in the last issue of *Horizon* (nos. 120–121) is now in the Oxford Dictionary of Quotations, and is worth repeating here: 'It is closing time in the gardens of the West and from now on an artist will be judged only by the resonance of his solitude or the quality of his despair.'

1 **The Rock Pool** (novel)   Obelisk Press, Paris,   **O**
    1936
    Scribner 1936   **L**
    Hamilton 1947   **F**

2 **Enemies of Promise**   Routledge 1938   **H**
    Little, Brown 1939   **E**

3 **The Unquiet Grave**   Horizon 1944   **K**
(published under the pseudonym
Palinurus, limited to 1000 copies. A
revised edition was published in 1945
by Hamish Hamilton and by Harper in
US – **E**).
4 **The Condemned Playground** (essays) Routledge 1945   **F**
                                          Macmillan 1946   **D**
5 **The Missing Diplomats** (prose)   Queen Anne Press 1952   **F**
6 **Ideas and Places** (essays)   Weidenfeld 1953   **E**
                                          Harper 1953   **D**
7 **Les Pavillons** (architecture)   Macmillan US 1962   **F**
   (with Jerome Zerbe)   Hamilton 1962   **F**
8 **Bond Strikes Camp** (satire)   London Magazine 1963   **C**
   (this forms a good part of the
   April issue)
9 **Previous Convictions** (essays)   Hamilton 1963   **E**
                                          Harper 1964   **C**
10 **The Modern Movement: 100 Key**   Deutsch/Hamilton 1965   **F**
   Books from England, France and   Atheneum 1966   **C**
   America 1880–1950
11 **The Evening Colonnade** (essays)   Bruce & Watson 1973   **D**
                                          Harcourt Brace 1975   **C**
12 **A Romantic Friendship: The Letters** Constable 1975   **C**
   of Cyril Connolly to Noel Blakiston
13 **Journal and Memoir**   Collins 1983   **C**
                                          Ticknor & Fields 1984   **C**

Another item of note is:
Cyril Connolly: A Memoir by
Stephen Spender (Tragara Press 1978,
limited to 165 numbered copies). The
memoir first appeared in the *Times
Literary Supplement* (**G**)

Connolly edited the following:
Horizon Stories   Faber 1943   **C**
                                          Vanguard Press 1946   **C**
Great English Short Novels   Dial Press (NY) 1953   **C**
The Golden Horizon   Weidenfeld 1953   **C**
                                          University Books 1956   **C**

Connolly translated the following:
Vercors **Put Out the Light**   Macmillan 1944
This translation of *Le Silence de la Mer*
was published in America by
Macmillan in the same year under the
more reasonable title *Silence of the Sea*.

Cope, Wendy   Born in Kent, 1945.

I listed young Wendy in the last edition, when she had just published *Cocoa* –
she had that certain *je ne sais*. Anyway – although she has published only two
real collections to date, Cope is now the best selling British poet, including
Betjeman, Larkin, Heaney – you name it. Parts of *Serious Concerns* are maybe
a little *too* light and glib, but great fun nonetheless. I list here her complete –
and already quite extensive – oeuvre including a couple of things I have just
discovered which predate *Cocoa*.

1	**Across the City** (poem)	Priapus Press 1980	E
2	**Hope and the 42** (poem)	Other Branch 1984	C
3	**Making Cocoa for Kingsley Amis** (verse)	Faber 1986	E
4	**Poem from a Colour Chart of Houseplants**	Priapus Press 1986	C
5	**Men and Their Boring Arguments** (poem)	Wykeham Press 1988	C
6	**Does She Like Word Games**	Anvil Press 1988	B
7	**Twiddling Your Thumbs** (juvenile)	Faber 1988	C
8	**Is That the New Moon?** (edited by)	Collins 1989	B
9	**The River Girl** (children's verse)	Faber 1991	B
10	**Serious Concerns** (verse)	Faber 1992	B

Crisp, Quentin   Born in Sutton, 1908.

By his own description, one of the 'stately homos of England' is now resident
in America, living in a rather sad and dingy room which he apparently loves,
and which is fast assuming the characteristic loveliness of his old room in
Chelsea which he had not cleaned in thirty years, telling us that after the first
three years, it had got no worse. Whatever you think of Crisp, he is difficult to
ignore.His calm and truthful philosophies make him beguiling reading, and
most of his little books (*Love Made Easy, How to have a Lifestyle, The Wit and
Wisdom of Quentin Crisp*, etc.) may be picked up, dare I say it, very cheaply.
But the classic is elusive – as it should be, dear boy.

The Naked Civil Servant (autobiography)	Cape 1968	H

Crispin, Edmund   Born in Buckinghamshire, 1921. Died 1978.

He started life as Robert Bruce Montgomery, Oxford scholar, music teacher, and composer. He then became Edmund Crispin, highly successful author of detective fiction – the J.I.M. Stewart variety (literary and Varsity), not that of Mickey Spillane (blood, broads and booze).

The reason for the very long gap in the ensuing checklist (1953 until 1977) is that during this period Crispin chose to edit a series of short stories and to review other books, instead of writing his own, although he did return to fiction in 1977, the year before he died.

1	**The Case of the Gilded Fly** (novel)	Gollancz 1944	**L**
2	**Obsequies at Oxford** (same as 1)	Lippincott 1945	**H**
3	**Holy Disorders** (novel)	Gollancz 1946	**J**
		Lippincott 1946	**G**
4	**The Moving Toyshop** (novel)	Gollancz 1946	**I**
		Lippincott 1946	**G**
5	**Swan Song** (novel)	Gollancz 1947	**H**
6	**Dead as Dumb** (same as 5)	Lippincott 1947	**G**
7	**Love Lies Bleeding** (novel)	Gollancz 1948	**H**
		Lippincott 1948	**G**
8	**Buried for Pleasure** (novel)	Gollancz 1948	**G**
		Lippincott 1948	**E**
9	**Frequent Hearses** (novel)	Gollancz 1950	**G**
10	**Sudden Vengeance** (same as 9)	Dodd Mead 1950	**E**
11	**The Long Divorce** (novel)	Gollancz 1951	**F**
	This was reissued in 1952 by Spivak under the title *A Noose for Her*.	Dodd Mead 1951	**D**
12	**Beware of the Trains: 16 Stories**	Gollancz 1953	**F**
		Walker 1962	**C**
13	**The Glimpses of the Moon** (novel)	Gollancz 1977	**C**
		Walker 1978	**C**
14	**Fen Country** (stories)	Gollancz 1979	**C**

Crispin edited the following:
Best SF (7 volumes, 1955–1970, Faber) **Best Detective Stories** (2 volumes, 1959 & 1964, Faber) **Best Tales of Terror** (2 volumes, 1962 & 1965, Faber) **The Stars and Under: A Selection of Science Fiction** (Faber 1968) **Best Murder Stories 2** (Faber 1973) **Outwards from Earth: A Selection of Science Fiction** (Faber 1974)

Crompton, Richmal Born in Lancashire, 1890. Died 1969. Full name Richmal Crompton Lamburn.

They say that collectors are very big on gathering up all that meant anything during their far-flung youth, particularly if there is an element of identification. Well, if the number of gentlemen after *William* books today is anything to go by, there must have been – forty or so years ago – one hell of a lot of tikes and tearaways. But I see signs of Anthony Buckeridge's *Jennings* catching up (q.v.), which may not be an encouraging sign: he was, after all, much *nicer*. Anyway, for those *aficionados* of catapults and grazed knees, here are the novels:

1	**Just William**	1922	N
2	**More William**	1922	L
3	**William Again**	1923	J
4	**William the Fourth**	1924	J
5	**Still William**	1925	J
6	**William the Conqueror**	1926	I
7	**William in Trouble**	1927	I
8	**William the Outlaw**	1927	I
9	**William the Good**	1928	I
10	**William**	1929	I
11	**William the Bad**	1930	I
12	**William's Happy Days**	1930	I
13	**William's Crowded Hours**	1931	H
14	**William the Pirate**	1932	H
15	**William the Rebel**	1933	H
16	**William the Gangster**	1934	H
17	**William the Detective**	1935	H
18	**Sweet William**	1936	H
19	**William the Showman**	1937	H
20	**William the Dictator**	1938	H
21	**William and A.R.P.** (title later changed to *William's Bad Resolution*)	1939	I
22	**William and the Evacuees** (later title *William the Film Star*)	1940	I
23	**William Does His Bit**	1941	G
24	**William Carries On**	1942	G
25	**William and the Brains Trust**	1945	G
26	**Just William's Luck**	1948	G
27	**William the Bold**	1950	F
28	**William and the Tramp**	1952	F
29	**William and the Moon Rocket**	1954	F
30	**William and the Space Animal**	1956	F
31	**William's Television Show**	1958	F
32	**William the Explorer**	1960	E
33	**William's Treasure Trove**	1962	E
34	**William and the Witch**	1964	E
35	**William and the Ancient Briton***	1965	B
36	**William and the Monster***	1965	B
37	**William the Globetrotter***	1965	B
38	**William the Cannibal***	1965	B
39	**William and the Pop Singers**	1965	E
40	**William and the Masked Ranger**	1966	D

| 41 **William the Superman** | 1968 | D |
| 42 **William the Lawless** | 1970 | E |

The four marked * above were published by Mayfair, the rest by Newnes

---

cummings, e.e.   Born in Massachusetts, 1894. Died 1962.

In Britain, cummings has always held steady: he has never fallen from favour, though nor has he ever soared to the heights. Not easy to collect seriously over here, though – and expensive across the Atlantic.

No, I don't know why he spelt his name with little letters either.

cummings published quite a few strictly limited editions and signed pamphlets which I have not been able to list within this book, though details of these may be found in: George J. Firmage *e.e. cummings: A Bibliography* (Wesleyan University Press 1960).

1	**The Enormous Room** (novel)	Boni & Liveright 1922	S
	The 1st Eng. edition has an Intro. by	Cape 1928	J
	Robert Graves		
2	**Tulips and Chimneys** (verse)	Seltzer 1923	Q
3	**XLI Poems**	Dial Press 1925	N
4	**Is 5** (verse)	Boni & Liveright 1926	M
5	**Him** (prose)	Boni & Liveright 1927	L
6	**Vi Va** (verse)	Liveright Inc. 1931	K
7	**Tom** (ballet)	Arrow Editions (NY)	J
	Limited to 1500 copies	1935	
8	**1/20** (verse)	Contemporary Poetry	
		& Prose Editions,	
		London 1936	J
9	**Collected Poems**	Harcourt Brace 1938	H
10	**One Times One** (verse)	Holt (NY) 1944	H
		Horizon 1947	F
11	**Santa Claus** (prose)	Holt 1946	G
12	**XAIRE** (verse)	OUP (NY) 1950	H
13	**i: Six Nonlectures**	Harvard University	G
		Press 1953	
14	**Poems 1923–1954**	Harcourt Brace 1954	F
15	**95 Poems**	Harcourt Brace 1958	N
	300 copies limited and signed, 5000		
	ordinary (**D**).		
16	**100 Selected Poems**	Grove Press 1959	E
17	**Selected Poems**	Faber 1960	D
18	**73 Poems**	Faber 1964	D
19	**Collected Poems** (2 vols)	MacGibbon & Kee 1968	F
20	**Selected Letters**	Harcourt Brace 1969	D
		Deutsch 1972	D
21	**Complete Poems**	Harcourt Brace 1972	D

22 **Etcetera: The Unpublished Poems**	Norton 1984	**C**
23 **Hist Whist and Other Poems for Children**	Norton 1948	**D**

Dahl, Roald   Born in South Wales, 1916. Died 1990.

A sad day when the most popular children's writer on the planet finally hands in his dinner pail – especially so when he had, with such books as *Matilda* and *The Minpins*, quite recovered his grand old style. My own children were not so much sad at the new of Dahl's death as positively *bereaved* – a pattern, I gather, repeated across the country. So, the only thing you have to square with your conscience is how to spend oodles of cash on mint firsts of the following, and then deny access to them to anything even remotely resembling a child: it's the sort of thing that gets collectors a bad name – better buy the Puffins as well.

1	**The Gremlins** (juvenile)	Random House 1943	**O**
	This book is virtually unknown.	Collins 1944	**N**
2	**Over to You** (stories)	Reynal & Hitchcock	**K**
	This first example of his masterly stories	1945	
	is very scarce, and has been out-of-print	Hamilton 1947	**J**
	for a long time.		
3	**Sometime Never** (novel)	Scribner 1948	**K**
		Collins 1949	**J**
4	**Someone Like You** (stories)	Knopf 1953	**J**
	Rare, but Michael Joseph reissued the	Secker & Warburg 1954	**I**
	book in 1961, with two extra stories,		
	and this may be found more easily.		
5	**Kiss, Kiss** (stories)	Knopf 1960	**H**
	This must be Dahl's highlight. The	Joseph 1960	**H**
	great success of this book		
	prompted Joseph to reissue 4		
	the following year (see above) with		
	a similar d/w – red and blue shapes		
	on a background of net curtain.		
6	**James and the Giant Peach**	Knopf 1961	**I**
	(juvenile)	Allen & Unwin 1967	**F**
	Published in the usual way in America		
	in boards and d/w. Allen & Unwin		
	published it in laminated boards, rather		
	like the *Beano Book*. These shiny boards		
	have not stood the test of time, and it		
	will be hard to find good copies.		
7	**Charlie and the Chocolate Factory**	Knopf 1964	**K**
	(juvenile)	Allen & Unwin 1967	**G**
	His best-known children's book.		

8	**The Magic Finger** (juvenile)	Harper 1966	G
		Allen & Unwin 1968	F
9	**Twenty-Nine Kisses**	Joseph 1969	C
	As the title suggests, a collection of past stories.		
10	**Selected Stories**	Random House 1970	C
11	**Fantastic Mr Fox** (juvenile)	Knopf 1970	F
		Allen & Unwin 1970	E
12	**Charlie and the Great Glass Elevator** (juvenile)	Knopf 1972	G
		Allen & Unwin 1973	F
	Successful, because of the word 'Charlie', though less successful in England, because of the word 'Elevator'.		
13	**Switch Bitch** (stories)	Knopf 1974	C
	Only his third collection of stories, this time on the theme of sex.	Joseph 1974	C
14	**Danny: The Champion of the World** (juvenile)	Knopf 1975	D
		Cape 1975	D
15	**The Wonderful Story of Henry Sugar** (novel)	Knopf 1977	C
		Cape 1977	C
16	**The Best of Roald Dahl**	Vintage (US) 1978	C
17	**The Enormous Crocodile** (juvenile)	Knopf 1978	C
	Illus. Quentin Blake.	Cape 1978	C
18	**Tales of the Unexpected** (stories)	Joseph 1979	C
		Vintage 1979	C
19	**My Uncle Oswald** (novel)	Joseph 1979	C
		Knopf 1980	C
20	**More Tales of the Unexpected**	Joseph 1980	C
	Including four new stories.		
21	**The Twits** (juvenile)	Cape 1980	D
	Illus. Quentin Blake.	Knopf 1981	C
22	**George's Marvellous Medicine** (juvenile)	Cape 1981	D
		Knopf 1982	C
	Illus. Quentin Blake.		
23	**Roald Dahl's Revolting Rhymes**	Cape 1982	C
	Illus. Quentin Blake.	Knopf 1983	C
24	**The BFG** (juvenile novel)	Cape 1982	C
		Farrar Straus 1982	C
25	**Dirty Beasts** (juvenile)	Cape 1983	C
	Illus. Rosemary Fawcett.	Farrar Straus 1983	C
26	**The Best of Roald Dahl** (stories)	Joseph 1983	B
27	**Roald Dahl's Book of Ghost Stories**	Cape 1983	B
	A misleading title; Dahl is merely the editor, and not the author, of these stories.		
28	**The Witches** (juvenile)	Cape 1983	D
	Illus. Quentin Blake.	Farrar Straus 1983	C

Davies, Robertson

29 **Boy: Tales of Childhood** (memoir)   Cape 1984   C
Farrar Straus published simultaneously   Farrar Straus 1984   C
a signed, limited edition at $30

30 **The Giraffe, the Pelly and Me**   Cape 1985   C
(juvenile)   Farrar Straus 1985   C
Illus. Quentin Blake.

31 **Going Solo** (memoir)   Cape 1986   C
32 **Two Fables** (fiction)   Viking 1986   C
33 **Matilda** (juvenile novel)   Cape 1988   C
    Viking Kestrel 1988   C

34 **Ah, Sweet Mystery of Life**   Joseph 1989   B
(story)   Knopf 1990   B
35 **Rhyme Stew** (juvenile)   Cape 1989   C
    Viking Penguin 1990   C

36 **Esio Trot** (juvenile)   Cape 1990   C
Illus. Quentin Blake.   Viking Penguin 1990   C
37 **The Minpins** (juvenile)   Cape 1991   C
    Viking Penguin 1991   C

38 **The Vicar of Nibbleswicke**   Century 1991   C
39 **Roald Dahl's Guide to**   British Railways Board   A
Railway Safety   1991
Illus. Quentin Blake.

40 **Collected Short Stories**   Joseph 1991   B
41 **Boy** and **Going Solo**   Cape 1992   B
(contains nos. 29 & 31)

Davies, Robertson   Born in Ontario, 1913. Canadian.

Davies has long been a national institution in his native Canada, but although his wonderful trilogies have been a well-kept secret among the intelligentsia in this country for years, it is only very recently – thanks to a fairly energetic sales campaign by Penguin – that this grand old man's peerless prose is reaching a wider audience. The trilogies are highly addictive, and not easy to find (particularly *The Salterton Trilogy*). I confine the listing below to the fiction, although Davies has published dozens and dozens of plays and volumes of literary criticism.

1 **Tempest-Tost** (novel)   Clarke Irwin, Canada   I
    1951
    Chatto & Windus 1952   H
    Rinehart 1952   H
2 **Leaven of Malice** (novel)   Clarke Irwin, Canada   H
    1954
    Chatto & Windus 1955   G
    Scribner 1955   G
3 **A Mixture of Frailties** (novel)   Macmillan, Canada   G
    1958

	Weidenfeld & Nicolson 1958	F
	Scribner 1958	F

Nos 1–3 form *The Salterton Trilogy*, published in one volume by Penguin in 1986

4 **Fifth Business** (novel)	Macmillan, Canada 1970	E
	Viking Press US 1970	D
	Macmillan UK 1971	D
5 **The Manticore** (novel)	Macmillan, Canada 1972	F
	Viking Press US 1972	D
	Macmillan UK 1973	D
6 **World of Wonders** (novel)	Macmillan, Canada 1975	D
	Viking Press UK 1976	C
	W.H. Allen 1977	C

Nos 4–6 form *The Deptford Trilogy*, published in one volume by Penguin in 1983

7 **The Rebel Angels** (novel)	Macmillan, Canada 1981	D
	Viking Press US 1982	C
	Allen Lane 1982	C
8 **What's Bred in the Bone** (novel)	Macmillan, Canada 1985	C
	Viking US 1985	C
	Viking UK 1986	C
9 **The Lyre of Orpheus** (novel)	Viking UK 1988	C
	Viking US 1989	C

Nos 7–9 form *The Cornish Trilogy*

Davies has also published:

10 **High Spirits: A Collection of Ghost Stories**	Penguin 1982	C
	Viking Press US 1983	C
11 **Murther and Walking Spirits**	McClelland & Stewart Canada 1991	C
	Viking US 1991	C
	Sinclair-Stevenson 1991	C

Davies, W.H.   Born in Monmouthshire, 1871. Died 1940.

The most famous tramp ever, mainly for his highlight, recorded below. Davies became a near-compulsive writer, publishing over fifty books in his lifetime, mostly verse.

The Autobiography of a Super-Tramp	Fifield 1908	I
	Knopf 1917	E

Day-Lewis, C. Born in Ireland, 1904. Poet Laureate 1968. Died 1972.

Day-Lewis published about fifty books under his own name, occasionally omitting the hyphen, as well as the detective novels under the pseudonym Nicholas Blake. A checklist may be found in *The New Cambridge Bibliography of English Literature* vol. 4. For fuller details, an excellent bibliography is G. Handley-Taylor and Timothy d'Arch Smith *C. Day-Lewis: The Poet Laureate* (St James Press 1968).

Apart from his tranlsations of Virgil, Day-Lewis is probably best remembered for *The Poetic Image* Cape 1947; 1st Amer. Oxford 1947. This is Grade C.

Of late, the Blake novels have come to the fore, and these are listed below:

1	**A Question of Proof**	Collins 1935	O
		Harper 1935	M
2	**Thou Shell of Death**	Collins 1936	N
	The American edition omits *Thou* from the title.	Harper 1936	L
3	**There's Trouble Brewing**	Collins 1937	K
		Harper 1937	I
4	**The Beast Must Die**	Collins 1938	K
		Harper 1938	I
5	**The Smiler with the Knife**	Collins 1939	K
		Harper 1939	I
6	**Malice in Wonderland**	Collins 1940	J
7	**Summer Camp Mystery**	Harper 1940	H
	(same as 6)		
8	**The Case of the Abominable Snowman**	Collins 1941	J
9	**Corpse in the Snowman**	Harper 1944	H
10	**Minute for Murder**	Collins 1947	I
		Harper 1948	G
11	**Head of a Traveller**	Collins 1949	I
		Harper 1949	G
12	**The Dreadful Hollow**	Collins 1953	H
		Harper 1953	E
13	**The Whisper in the Gloom**	Collins 1954	H
		Harper 1954	E
14	**A Tangled Web**	Collins 1956	G
		Harper 1956	D
15	**End of Chapter**	Collins 1957	G
		Harper 1957	D
16	**A Penknife in my Heart**	Collins 1958	G
		Harper 1958	D
17	**The Widow's Cruise**	Collins 1959	G
		Harper 1959	D

18	**The Worm of Death**	Collins 1961	F
		Harper 1961	C
19	**The Deadly Joker**	Collins 1963	E
		Harper 1963	C
20	**The Sad Variety**	Collins 1964	E
		Harper 1964	C
21	**The Morning after Death**	Collins 1966	E
		Harper 1966	C
22	**The Nicholas Blake Omnibus** (incl. Nos 4, 12 and 14)	Collins 1966	D
23	**The Private Wound**	Collins 1968	D
		Harper 1968	C

Deighton, Len   Born in London, 1929.

Still very popular with readers, although I do not see a mad scramble among collectors eager for his later work. The trilogy idea has become a bit of a formula where the titles, one feels sure, came first, and the books followed. Nor is the frisson of excitement there any more when Deighton publishes – as it still is in the case of, say, John le Carré and Frederick Forsyth. That said, Deighton will always be remembered (and collected) for that really excellent agent Harry Palmer – the *Ipcress* trilogy and the cook books remaining his finest work: his first four books, in fact.

1	**The Ipcress File** (novel) Only 4000 of the Hodder ed. printed	Hodder & Stoughton 1962	L
		Simon & Schuster 1963	H
2	**Horse Under Water** (novel)	Cape 1963	I
		Putnam 1968	C
3	**Funeral in Berlin** (novel)	Cape 1964	F
		Putnam 1965	C
4	**Action Cook Book: Len Deighton's Guide to Eating** (food)	Cape 1965	F
5	**Où Est le Garlic: Or, Len Deighton's French Cook Book** (food)	Penguin 1965	D
6	**Cookstrip Cook Book** (same as 4)	Geis (NY) 1966	D
7	**The Billion Dollar Brain** (novel) The English version omits *The* from the title.	Putnam 1966	F
		Cape 1966	D
8	**An Expensive Place to Die** (novel) *Must* have buff 'Top Secret' wallet laid in.	Putnam 1967	E
		Cape 1967	D
9	**Len Deighton's London Dossier** (non-fiction) Publication was simultaneous, but only	Cape 1967	E
		Penguin 1967	C

Deighton

5600 hardbacks were produced, against 75 000 Penguins.

10	**Only When I Larf** (novel)	Joseph 1968	H
	Preceded by a privately printed ring-bound ed. of only 150 (**K**), 9000 hardbacks, and a staggering 250 000 from Sphere.	Sphere 1968	C
11	**Len Deighton's Continental Dossier** (non-fiction)	Joseph 1968	D
12	**Bomber** (novel)	Cape 1970	D
		Harper & Row 1970	C
13	**Declarations of War** (stories)	Cape 1971	E
14	**Close-Up** (novel)	Cape 1972	C
		Atheneum 1972	B
15	**Spy Story** (novel)	Cape 1974	C
		Harcourt Brace 1974	B
16	**Yesterday's Spy** (novel)	Cape 1975	C
		Harcourt Brace 1975	B
17	**Eleven Declarations of War** (same as 13, omitting two stories)	Harcourt Brace 1975	C
18	**Twinkle, Twinkle, Little Spy** (novel)	Cape 1976	C
		Harcourt Brace 1976	B
19	**Fighter: The True Story of the Battle of Britain**	Cape 1977	C
		Knopf 1978	B
20	**SS-GB** (novel)	Cape 1978	C
		Knopf 1979	B
21	**Airshipwreck** (non-fiction)	Cape 1978	E
		Holt Rinehart 1979	D
22	**Basic French Cooking**	Cape 1979	C
	A revised and enlarged edition of 5.		
23	**Blitzkrieg** (non-fiction)	Cape 1979	C
		Knopf 1980	B
24	**Battle of Britain** (non-fiction)	Cape 1980	C
		Coward McCann 1980	B
25	**The Orient Flight L.Z 127-Graf Zeppelin** (pseud. Cyril Deighton, with Fred F. Blau)	Germany Philatelic Society 1980	F
26	**The Egypt Flight L.Z 127-Graf Zeppelin** (pseud. Cyril Deighton, with Fred F. Blau)	Germany Philatelic Society 1981	F
	Nos 25 and 26 are a pair of recently discovered non-fictional oddities.		
27	**XPD** (novel)	Hutchinson 1981	C
		Knopf 1981	B
28	**Goodbye Mickey Mouse** (novel)	Hutchinson 1982	B
		Knopf 1982	B
29	**Berlin Game** (novel)	Hutchinson 1983	B
		Knopf 1984	B

30 **Mexico Set** (novel)	Hutchinson 1984	B
	Knopf 1985	B
31 **London Match** (novel)	Hutchinson 1985	B
	Knopf 1986	B

Nos 29–31 form the *Game, Set and Match* trilogy, published in one volume by Hutchinson in 1985, and by Knopf US in 1989.

32 **Winter: A Berlin Family 1899–1945** (novel)	Century Hutchinson 1987	B
	Knopf 1987	B
33 **Spy Hook** (novel)	Century Hutchinson 1988	B
	Knopf 1988	B
34 **Spy Line** (novel)	Century Hutchinson 1989	B
	Knopf 1989	B
35 **Spy Sinker** (novel)	Hutchinson 1990	B
	HarperCollins US 1990	B

Nos 33–35 form the *Hook, Line and Sinker* trilogy, published in one volume by Hutchinson in 1991

36 **Mamista** (novel)	Hutchinson 1991	B
	HarperCollins 1991	B
37 **City of Gold** (novel)	Century 1992	B

Bibliography:
(Len Deighton: An Annotated Bibliography 1954–1985 by Edward Milward-Oliver, with a foreword by Julian Symons. It contains a 4000-word interview with Deighton, and of the first edition 375 copies were numbered and signed by Deighton, and carry a signed page proof from **London Match**

Delaney, Shelagh   Born in Lancashire, 1939.

Although she has published several books and plays, Delaney remains notable for one – an important work for collectors of modern drama, and a key of the late fifties and early sixties, made more so by the quality of the ensuing film, with the wonderful Rita Tushingham.

A Taste of Honey (play)	Methuen 1959	D
	Grove Press 1959	C

DeLillo, Don   Born in New York, 1936. American.

Not for everyone, this gutsy American writer, but if you like these powerful explorations of subcultures, you had better start acquiring them without delay, for DeLillo is becoming formidably trendy.

93

Dexter

1 **Americana** (novel)	Houghton Mifflin 1971	**H**
	Penguin 1990	**B**
2 **End Zone** (novel)	Houghton Mifflin 1972	**F**
	Deutsch 1973	**E**
3 **Great Jones Street** (novel)	Houghton Mifflin 1973	**E**
	Deutsch 1974	**D**
4 **Ratner's Star** (novel)	Knopf 1976	**D**
5 **Players** (novel)	Knopf 1977	**D**
6 **Running Dog** (novel)	Knopf 1978	**D**
	Gollancz 1979	**D**
7 **The Names** (novel)	Knopf 1982	**C**
	Harvester Press 1983	**C**
8 **White Noise** (novel)	Viking 1985	**C**
	Picador 1986	**C**
9 **The Day Room** (play)	Knopf 1987	**C**
10 **Libra** (novel)	Viking US 1988	**C**
	Viking UK 1988	**C**
11 **Mao II** (novel)	Viking US 1991	**C**
	Viking UK 1991	**C**

Dexter, Colin   Born in Lincolnshire, 1930.

An enormous number of readers have discovered Dexter through the inordinately successful TV series, *Inspector Morse*. Morse, you will recall, is played by the vagabond from *The Sweeney* with a sort of posh voice, and he drinks real ale, solves real crosswords, drives a real car, investigates real crimes and talks to his sidekick, Lewis, who seems rather artificial... These novels seem to be here to stay, though – I have even heard of members of the Sherlock Holmes Society re-enacting the plots, than which I can say little more.

All the following novels feature Morse:

1 **Last Bus to Woodstock** (novel)	Macmillan 1975	**I**
	St. Martin's Press 1975	**G**
2 **Last Seen Wearing** (novel)	Macmillan 1976	**G**
	St. Martin's Press 1976	**E**
3 **The Silent World of Nicholas Quinn** (novel)	Macmillan 1977	**G**
	St. Martin's Press 1977	**E**
4 **Service of all the Dead** (novel)	Macmillan 1979	**E**
	St. Martin's Press 1980	**D**
5 **The Dead of Jericho** (novel)	Macmillan 1981	**E**
	St Martin's Press 1981	**D**
6 **The Riddle of the Third Mile** (novel)	Macmillan 1983	**D**
7 **The Secret of Annexe 3** (novel)	Macmillan 1986	**D**
	St. Martin's Press 1987	**C**

8 **The Wench is Dead** (novel)	Macmillan 1989	**C**
	St. Martin's Press 1990	**C**
9 **The Way Through the Woods** (novel)	Macmillan 1992	**C**

Donleavy, J.P. Born in New York, 1926. Irish citizen 1967.

Squire Donleavy continues to produce his quirky and idiosyncratic concoctions – always readable, and always bearing lovably loony titles. Never a huge noise in the collecting world – if you simply want a representation, you have to go for *The Ginger Man* – but great fun all the same.

1 **The Ginger Man** (novel)	Olympia Press (Paris) 1955	**J**
	Spearman 1956	**H**
	McDowell Obolensky 1958	**F**
	1st complete ed.:	
	Corgi 1963	**C**
	Delacorte 1965	**C**
2 **Fairy Tales of New York** (play)	Penguin 1961	**C**
	Random House 1961	**C**
3 **The Ginger Man** (play)	Random House 1961	**C**
4 **What They Did in Dublin with the Ginger Man** (same as 3)	McGibbon & Kee 1962	**C**
5 **A Singular Man** (novel)	Little, Brown 1963	**D**
	Bodley Head 1964	**C**
6 **Meet My Maker the Mad Molecule** (stories)	Little, Brown 1964	**C**
	Bodley Head 1965	**C**
7 **A Singular Man** (play)	Bodley Head 1965	**C**
8 **The Saddest Summer of Samuel S** (novel)	Delacorte 1966	**B**
	Eyre & Spottiswoode 1967	**B**
9 **The Beastly Beatitudes of Balthazar B** (novel)	Delacorte 1968	**B**
	Eyre & Spottiswoode 1969	**B**
10 **The Onion Eaters** (novel)	Delacorte 1971	**C**
	Eyre & Spottiswoode 1971	**B**
11 **The Plays of J.P. Donleavy** (inc. 3, 2, 7 and the play of 8)	Delacorte 1972	**B**
	Penguin 1974	**B**
12 **A Fairy Tale of New York** (novel)	Delacorte 1973	**B**
	Eyre Methuen 1973	**B**
13 **The Unexpurgated Code: A Complete Manual of Survival and Manners**	Delacorte 1975	**B**
	Wildwood House 1975	**B**
14 **The Destinies of D'Arcy Dancer**	Delacorte 1977	**B**

Gentleman (novel)	Lane 1978	**B**
15 **Schultz** (novel)	Delacorte 1979	**B**
	Lane 1980	**B**
16 **Leila** (novel)	Delacorte 1983	**B**
Sequel to 14.	Lane 1983	**B**
17 **J.P. Donleavy's de Alfonce**	Weidenfeld 1984	**B**
Tennis: The Superlative Game	Dutton 1985	**B**
of Eccentric Champions. Its		
History, Accoutrements, Rules,		
Conduct and Regimen		
18 **J.P. Donleavy's Ireland: In Some**	Joseph 1986	**B**
of Her Graces and All of Her Sins	Viking 1986	**B**
19 **Are You Listening Rabbi Low**	Viking UK 1987	**B**
(novel)	Atlantic Monthly	**B**
	Press 1988	
20 **A Singular Country** (non-fiction)	Ryan 1989	**B**
	Norton 1990	**B**
21 **That Darcy, That Dancer,**	Viking UK 1990	**B**
That Gentleman (novel)	Atlantic Monthly	**B**
	Press 1991	

Douglas, Keith   Born in Tunbridge Wells, 1920. Died 1944.

Among the millions, many poets and artists were killed at the front during the Great War. During the Second World War, many more were to lose their lives. Keith Douglas was one of these.

Nothing was published during his lifetime. His war journals, entitled *Alamein to Zem-Zem*, were published in 1946. These contained a few poems, which were reprinted in:

1 **Collected Poems**	Editions Poetry	**K**
This is scarce.	(London) 1951	
Almost half the poems in the above were		
reprinted in:		
2 **Selected Poems**	Faber 1964	**E**
This is edited and has an Introduction	Chilmark Press 1964	**E**
by Ted Hughes, and is also sought after		
by Hughes collectors.		
3 **Complete Poems**	OUP 1977	**D**

Biography:
Desmond Graham **Keith Douglas 1920–1944** OUP 1974

Doyle, Arthur Conan   Born in Edinburgh, 1859. Died 1930.

I am sometimes asked why I include Conan Doyle in this book, and omit his nineteenth-century contemporaries. The answer is perfectly simple, my dear whatnot: Doyle created Sherlock Holmes, and the others did not. It would be an impossible *impertinence* to ignore the greatest detective the world has ever known.

I must say I believed that every interpretation of Holmes had been explored, but this recent TV adaptation sent me back to the books. Jeremy Brett is quite simply the Best Holmes *ever*. No – even that's not right; just as Sean Connery *is* James Bond, so Brett is Holmes. I have spake.

A complete checklist of Conan Doyle may be found in *The New Cambridge Bibliography of English Literature* vol. 3, and some valuable information in: John Dickson Carr *The Life of Sir Arthur Conan Doyle* Murray 1949.

Below are all the Sherlock Holmes books.

1 **A Study in Scarlet**
The wrappered annual which ushered Holmes into the world is fantastically scarce. The book is also very scarce.

28th Beeton's **Z**
Christmas Annual
1887
1st book form
Ward Lock 1887 **T**

2 **The Sign of Four**
Very, very scarce.

Lippincott's **R**
Magazine 1890
1st book
form Blackett **S**
1890

3 **The Adventures of Sherlock Holmes**
The Strand Magazine, which began in 1891, issued bound volumes of six months' issues, and Newnes (who owned the *Strand*) published the *Adventures* in a similar format – pale blue bevelled boards, with gold blocking. It is strange that there is so much difference between the prices of the bound magazines and the 1st book forms. This is true also of many of the following titles, but it is apparent now that bound *Strands* are not as common as they used to be, and a marked rise in price seems inevitable.

Strand Magazine **D**
1891–92 (per volume)

1st book
form Newnes 1892 **Q**

4 **The Memoirs of Sherlock Holmes**
Same situation as in 3. Identical format, but in dark blue cloth.

Strand Magazine **D**
1892–93 (per volume)

1st book form
Newnes 1894 **Q**

5 **The Hound of the Baskervilles**

Strand Magazine **D**

Newnes ed. has an attractively decorated red cover.	1901–02 (per volume)	
	1st book form Newnes 1902	O
6 **The Return of Sherlock Holmes** The Newnes 1st is one of the most difficult to find. Blue cloth.	Strand Magazine 1903–04 (per volume)	D
	1st book form Newnes 1905	P
7 **The Valley of Fear** 1st book in red cloth.	Strand Magazine 1914–15 (per volume)	D
	1st book form Smith, Elder 1915	L
8 **His Last Bow** These stories were scattered throughout *The Strand Magazine* over the period 1893–1917.	Murray 1917	K
9 **The Case-Book of Sherlock Holmes** These too were scattered in the *Strand* over many years.	Murray 1927	J

There have been a vast number of books on Holmes, each specializing in putting forward theories more fantastic than the last, and indicating flaws in their predecessors' deductions, hopefully in the manner of the great man himself. Two works that strike me as essential are: William S. Baring-Gould (ed.) **The Annotated Sherlock Holmes** (2 vols) Murray 1968   Michael and Mollie Hardwick **The Sherlock Holmes Companion** Murray 1962

Drabble, Margaret   Born in Yorkshire, 1939.

Drabble is back to her prolific self, but her novels, I think, are now appealing to an increasingly narrow audience, whereas her political and feminist stuff ranges from the wearisome to the unreadable. But there will always be a collector's market for her classics – i.e. the pre-1970 novels.

1 **A Summer Bird-Cage** (novel)	Weidenfeld 1963	J
	Morrow 1964	E
2 **The Garrick Year** (novel)	Weidenfeld 1964	H
	Morrow 1965	D
3 **The Millstone** (novel)	Weidenfeld 1965	F
	Morrow 1966	C
4 **Wordsworth** (non-fiction)	Evans 1966	D
5 **Jerusalem the Golden** (novel)	Weidenfeld 1967	E
	Morrow 1967	C
6 **The Waterfall** (novel)	Weidenfeld 1969	C
	Knopf 1969	B

7 **The Needle's Eye** (novel)	Weidenfeld 1972	**C**
	Knopf 1972	**B**
8 **Virginia Woolf: A Personal Debt** (essay)	Aloe Editions 1973	**D**
9 **Arnold Bennett: A Biography**	Weidenfeld 1974	**B**
	Knopf 1974	**B**
10 **The Realms of Gold** (novel)	Weidenfeld 1975	**C**
	Knopf 1975	**B**
11 **The Genius of Thomas Hardy** (ed.)	Weidenfeld 1976	**C**
	Knopf 1976	**C**
12 **The Ice Age** (novel)	Weidenfeld 1977	**B**
	Knopf 1977	**B**
13 **For Queen and Country: Britain in the Victorian Age** (juvenile)	Deutsch 1978	**C**
	Seabury Press 1979	**B**
14 **A Writer's Britain: Landscape in Literature** (non-fiction)	Thames & Hudson 1979	**B**
	Knopf 1979	**B**
15 **The Middle Ground** (novel)	Weidenfeld 1980	**B**
	Knopf 1980	**B**
16 **The Oxford Companion to English Literature** (ed.)	OUP 1985	**C**
17 **The Tradition of Women's Fiction: Lectures in Japan**	OUP, Tokyo 1985	**C**
18 **The Radiant Way** (novel)	Weidenfeld & Nicolson 1987	**B**
	Knopf 1987	**B**
19 **Case for Equality** (non-fiction)	Fabian Society 1988	**B**
20 **Stratford Revisited: A Legacy of the Sixties** (non-fiction)	Celandine Press 1989	**B**
21 **A Natural Curiosity** (novel)	Viking UK 1989	**B**
	Viking US 1989	**B**
22 **Safe As Houses: An Examination of Home Ownership and Mortgage Tax Relief** (non-fiction)	Chatto & Windus 1990	**A**
23 **The Gates of Ivory** (novel)	Viking UK 1991	**B**
	Viking US 1992	**B**

Du Maurier, Daphne Born in London, 1907. Died 1989.

Author of nearly forty books, only the highlights appealing to collectors. These appear below.

1 **The Loving Spirit** (novel) Her first book.	Heinemann 1931	**H**
	Doubleday 1931	**F**
2 **Jamaica Inn** (novel)	Gollancz 1936	**I**
	Doubleday 1936	**F**

Dunn, Douglas

3 **Rebecca** (novel)	Gollancz 1938	**K**
	Doubleday 1938	**G**
4 **Frenchman's Creek** (novel)	Gollancz 1941	**E**
	Doubleday 1942	**C**
5 **The Breaking Point** (stories)	Gollancz 1959	**D**
Incl. 'The Birds'.	Doubleday 1959	**C**

Dunn, Douglas Born in Renfrewshire, 1942.

Dunn has been quietly publishing with Britain's most prestigious poetry publisher (still) for quite a time, as may be seen below. Always respected among a small élite, his winning of the Whitbread Prize in 1985 for *Elegies* (scooping a vast political biography and no less than Peter Ackroyd's *Hawksmoor* for the grand prize) quite rightly brought his name to a much wider audience. Anyone impressed by the extraordinary sensitivity, sadness and cadence of *Elegies* will, I think, wish to gather the early work. Scarce for the usual reason with poetry: very few were printed.

1 **Terry Street** (verse)	Faber 1969	**H**
2 **Backwaters** (verse pamphlet)	The Review 1971	**D**
3 **The Happier Life** (verse)	Faber 1972	**E**
4 **Love or Nothing** (verse)	Faber 1974	**D**
5 **Barbarians** (verse)	Faber 1979	**D**
6 **St Kilda's Parliament** (verse)	Faber 1981	**C**
7 **Europa's Lover** (verse pamphlet)	Bloodaxe 1982	**C**
8 **Secret Villages** (stories)	Faber 1985	**D**
	Dodd Mead 1985	**C**
9 **Elegies** (verse)	Faber 1985	**C**
10 **Selected Poems 1964–1983**	Faber 1986	**C**
11 **Under the Influence: Douglas Dunn on Philip Larkin** (prose)	Edinburgh University Library 1987	**C**
12 **Northlight** (verse)	Faber 1988	**C**
13 **New and Selected Poems 1966–1988**	Ecco Press US 1989	**C**
14 **Poll Tax, the Fiscal Fake: Why We Should Fight the Community Charge** (prose)	Chatto & Windus 1990	**A**

Dunn has also edited **The Faber Book of Twentieth Century Scottish Poetry** (Faber, 1992)

Dunn, Nell Born in London, 1936.

Rather quiet since her stage success *Steaming*, though still notable for a couple of 'sixties period pieces:

1 **Up the Junction** (stories)	MacGibbon & Kee 1963	**D**
	Lippincott 1966	**B**
2 **Poor Cow** (novel)	MacGibbon & Kee 1967	**D**
	Doubleday 1967	**B**

Durrell, Lawrence   Born in India, 1912. British. Died
1990.

The only context in which Durrell's name seems to have arisen since his death is for allegedly abusing his daughter, Sappho, during her childhood; Sappho committed suicide when still quite young – a very miserable tale indeed. From a critical point of view, however, Durrell's reputation seems not to have suffered, although a certain slackeninging off of interest on the part of collectors is discernible. A few of the more usual items – *Bitter Lemons*, say – might now be acquired for less than ten years ago. But Durrell will be back.

A clean set of *The Alexandria Quartet* remains the prize. *Spirit of Place* and Durrell's private correspondence with Henry Miller (see below) will fill in a good deal of biographical information. (S.S. Fraser *Lawrence Durrell: A Study* Faber 1968 is also essential reading, and contains a bibliography by Alan G. Thomas.)

1 **Quaint Fragment** (poems)	Cecil Press 1931	**Y**
Durrell says that this was never published; but Thomas (see above) says that several have passed through the salerooms, though it is extremely scarce. Very difficult to grade such an item, as it would seem to be on a par with Auden's *Poems* (1928).		
2 **Ten Poems**	Caduceus Press 1932	**U**
Very limited, and very rare – the remaining stock having been destroyed in the Blitz. Again, difficult to grade.		
3 **Bromo Bombasts**	Caduceus Press 1933	**U**
This parody of Shaw's *Black Girl* is far more scarce than the original, and was limited to 100 copies.		
4 **Transition** (poems)	Caduceus Press 1934	**U**
The same situation as 2.		
5 **Pied Piper of Lovers** (novel)	Cassell 1935	**T**
The first commercially published work, with d/w by Nancy Myers, Durrell's first wife. Very scarce. The spine of the case misprints the title as *Pied Pipers of Lovers*.		
6 **Panic Spring** (novel)	Faber 1937	**S**

Durrell

Although Durrell's first book with Faber, it was published under the pseudonym Charles Norden at their request, because 5 had sold so badly. This item is very scarce. It was also the first Durrell book to be published in America.

	Covici-Friede 1937	Q

7 **The Black Book** (novel)
For the publication of the work in England, Durrell held a signing session in London, and so autographed copies might turn up.

Obelisk Press (Paris) 1938	Q
Dutton 1960	H
Faber 1973	C

8 **A Private Country** (verse)
Grey boards, grey d/w with red lettering. First poetry published by Faber, and scarce.

| Faber 1943 | I |

9 **Prospero's Cell** (non-fiction)
Although quite an early work, it seems to come up fairly often.

| Faber 1945 | H |
| Dutton 1960 | C |

10 **Cities, Plains and People** (verse)
Quite scarce.

| Faber 1946 | G |

11 **Cefalû** (novel)
Scarce. It was apparently issued in both brown and green cloth, but either is particularly difficult in the d/w.

| Editions Poetry (London) 1947 | H |

12 **On Seeming to Presume** (verse)
Red boards, with cream d/w printed in black and red.

| Faber 1948 | E |

13 **Sappho** (play)
Grey boards with purple d/w.

| Faber 1950 | E |
| Dutton 1958 | C |

14 **Key to Modern Poetry** (lectures)
This is particularly scarce, though quite recent.

| Nevill 1952 | I |

15 **A Key to Modern British Poetry** (same as 14)

| Oklahoma Press 1952 | G |

16 **Reflections on a Marine Venus** (travel)

| Faber 1953 | G |
| Dutton 1960 | C |

17 Emmanuel Royidis **Pope Joan**
Translated from the Greek by L.D. Quite scarce, particularly in the d/w.

| Verschoyle 1954 | G |
| Dutton 1961 | D |

18 **The Tree of Idleness** (verse)
Quite difficult, although there is an abundance of second impressions around!

| Faber 1955 | E |

19 **Selected Poems**

| Faber 1956 | C |
| Grove Press 1956 | C |

20 **Bitter Lemons** (travel)
His best-known travel work, this book

| Faber 1957 | D |
| Dutton 1958 | C |

on Cyprus has become quite a classic.
The d/w can be hard to find. Be careful
of the Book Society editions, of which
there are plenty around, as they are not
the true 1st, although printed by Faber.

21	**Esprit de Corps** (stories)	Faber 1957	**D**
	The first of the Antrobus trilogy.	Dutton 1958	**B**
22	**Justine** (novel)	Faber 1957	**N**
	The 1st edition has always been very	Dutton 1957	**I**

difficult, and many are the Alexandria
Quartets lacking the first volume!
Durrell says there were about '250
errors which were put right in the 2nd',
An important work – see *Balthazar*,
Mountolive and *Clea* below.

23	**White Eagles over Serbia** (novel)	Faber 1957	**G**
	Durrell thought it a detective story;	Criterion 1957	**D**

Faber thought it a juvenile, and as such
was it published. Quite scarce.

24	**The Dark Labyrinth** (same as 11)	Ace (NY) 1958	**D**

Faber published it under this title in
1961 (**C**).

25	**Balthazar** (novel)	Faber 1958	**H**
	The second of the Quartet.	Dutton 1958	**E**
26	**Mountolive** (novel)	Faber 1958	**G**
	The third of the Quartet.	Dutton 1959	**D**
27	**Stiff Upper Lip** (stories)	Faber 1958	**C**
	The second of the Antrobus trilogy (see	Dutton 1959	**C**

21). Nicolas Bentley drew the pictures.

28	**Art and Outrage**	Putnam 1959	**D**
	A correspondence about Henry Miller	Dutton 1960	**C**

between Alfred Perles and Lawrence
Durrell.

29	**Clea** (novel)	Faber 1960	**F**
	The completion of the Quartet. The	Dutton 1960	**D**

four look dynamic together, with their
bold, graphic d/ws – yellow, grey, green
and off-white, respectively, with red
and black designs and lettering.

30	**Collected Poems**	Faber 1960	**D**
		Dutton 1960	**C**
31	**The Alexandria Quartet**	Faber 1962	**H**
	This one-volume edition was issued in	Dutton 1962	**F**

an ordinary trade edition and one
limited to 500 copies, signed by L.D.
This is Grade **L**.

32	**Lawrence Durrell and Henry**	Dutton 1963	**E**
	Miller: A Private Correspondence	Faber 1963	**E**

33	**Beccafico Le Becfigue** (verse) Limited to 150 copies, signed.	La Licorne (France) 1963	**K**
34	**An Irish Faustus** (play)	Faber 1963 Dutton 1964	**D** **C**
35	**La Descente du Styx** (verse) Limited to 250 copies, signed.	La Murène (France) 1964	**J**
36	**Selected Poems 1935–1963** Paper-covered edition.	Faber 1964	**B**
37	**Acte** (play)	Faber 1965 Dutton 1965	**C** **C**
38	**Sauve Qui Peut** (stories) The final Antrobus (see 21 and 27). Nicolas Bentley drew the pictures.	Faber 1966 Dutton 1967	**C** **C**
39	**The Ikons** (poems)	Faber 1966 Dutton 1967	**D** **C**
40	**Tunc** (novel) The first of the *Revolt of Aphrodite* duet.	Faber 1968 Dutton 1968	**C** **B**
41	**Spirit of Place** (travel) Essays edited by Alan G. Thomas.	Faber 1969 Dutton 1969	**D** **C**
42	**Nunquam** (novel) The completion of the duet (see 40).	Faber 1970 Dutton 1970	**C** **B**
43	**The Red Limbo Lingo** (poetry notebook) An unusual venture for Faber. Limited edition, 100 of which signed (**J**). Red cloth in slipcase.	Faber 1971	**H**
44	**On the Suchness of the Old Boy** (verse) Illustrated by Sappho Durrell. Limited.	Turret 1972	**I**
45	**Vega and Other Poems** Very quickly replaced by a paperback edition, and may prove quite hard to find.	Faber 1973	**D**
46	**The Big Supposer** A dialogue with Marc Alyn. First published in French as *Le Grand Suppositoire* by Editions Pierre Belfond (Paris) 1972.	Abelard-Schuman 1973 Grove Press 1974	**B** **B**
47	**The Revolt of Aphrodite** 40 and 42 in one volume.	Faber 1974	**D**
48	**The Best of Antrobus** A selection from 21, 27 and 38.	Faber 1974	**C**
49	**Monsieur: or, The Prince of Darkness** (novel) The publication of this work saw a signing session with Durrell in London, so check title pages!	Faber 1974 Viking 1974	**C** **B**
50	**Prospero's Cell**	Faber 1975	**C**

A reissue of 9, with a new Preface.

51	**Sicilian Carousel** (travel)	Faber 1977	C
	Possibly the slightest of the travel	Viking 1977	B
	books.		
52	**The Greek Islands** (travel)	Faber 1978	C
	A fine book, this. Large format, and	Viking 1978	C
	beautifully illustrated. Reprinted very		
	quickly.		
53	**Livia or Buried Alive** (novel)	Faber 1978	C
	The second in the Avignon 'quincunx'.	Viking 1979	B
54	**Collected Poems: 1931–1974**	Faber 1980	C
		Viking 1980	C
55	**A Smile in the Mind's Eye** (essay)	Wildwood House	C
	An odd little essay, from an untypical	1980	
	publisher.		
56	**Literary Lifelines: The Richard**	Faber 1981	C
	Aldington/Lawrence Durrell	Viking 1981	C
	Correspondence (letters)		
57	**Constance or Solitary Practices**	Faber 1982	B
	(novel)	Viking 1982	B
58	**Sebastian or Ruling Passions**	Faber 1983	B
	(novel)	Viking 1984	B
59	**Quinx** or **The Ripper's Tale** (novel)	Faber 1985	B
	(49, 53, 57, 58 & 59 make up the	Viking 1985	B
	Avignon 'quincunx')		
60	**The Durrell/Miller Letters**	Faber 1988	C
		Viking 1988	C
61	**Caesar's Vast Ghost: Aspects**	Faber 1990	C
	of Provence (travel)		
62	**The Avignon Quintet**	Faber 1992	C
	(contains nos. 49, 53, 57, 58, 59).		

Durrell also edited many works, including, most notably: **A Henry Miller Reader** New Directions 1959 (**D**) **The Best of Henry Miller** (same as above) Heinemann 1960 (**D**) **New Poems 1963: A PEN Anthology** Hutchinson 1963 (**B**) **Wordsworth** Penguin 1973 (**B**)

Eliot, T.S. Born in Missouri, 1888. British. Died 1965.

There has been no marked rise in collectors' interest in Eliot since the lull of about five years ago – although prices in the earliest items continue to rise steeply. This is indicative of the fact that both collectors and dealers alike will always recognize the immense significance of Eliot, despite the fact that the later, run-of-the-mill stuff fails to quicken the pulse. But among the more common items, there are bargains to be had. We have finally got some Eliot letters, having waited God knows how long for them, but if this is the speed of publication, a good many collectors will be dead by the time we get the rest.

Eliot

From the collector's point of view, the essential book is: Donald Gallup *T.S. Eliot: A Bibliography* Faber 1969. This extremely fine bibliography lists absolutely everything, though I must limit myself to a checklist of his books. He wrote many Introductions and the like, all of which are in Gallup.

1 **Prufrock and Other Observations**	Egoist Ltd 1917	**U**
2 **Ezra Pound: His Metric and Poetry**	Knopf (NY) 1917	**R**
Published anonymously.		
3 **Poems**	Hogarth Press 1919	**P**
4 **Ara Vos Prec** (verse)	Ovid Press 1920	
	(unsigned)	**O**
	(signed)	**R**
5 **Poems** (same as 4)	Knopf 1920	**M**
6 **The Sacred Wood** (essays)	Methuen 1920	**J**
	Knopf 1921	**H**
7 **The Waste Land** (verse)	Boni & Liveright (NY) 1922	**Q**
	Hogarth Press 1923	**Q**
8 **Homage to John Dryden** (verse)	Hogarth Press 1924	**N**
9 **Poems 1909–1925**	Faber & Gwyer 1925	**J**
	Harcourt Brace 1932	**H**
10 **Journey of the Magi** (poem)	Faber & Gwyer 1927	**I**
Faber ed.: 5000 copies printed. Rudge ed.: 27 copies printed.	Rudge 1927	**R**
11 **Shakespeare and the Stoicism of Seneca** (address)	OUP 1927	**I**
12 **A Song for Simeon** (poem)	Faber & Gwyer 1928	**H**
13 **For Lancelot Andrewes** (essays)	Faber & Gwyer 1928	**J**
	Doubleday 1929	**G**
14 **Dante** (essay)	Faber 1929	**H**
15 **Animula** (poem)	Faber 1929	**G**
400 signed. (**L**)		
16 **Ash-Wednesday** (verse)	Faber 1930	**I**
Slightly preceded by limited, signed edition. (**M**)	Putnam 1930	**F**
17 **Anabasis: A Poem by St J. Perse**	Faber 1930	**I**
Translated by T.S.E.	Harcourt Brace 1938 1st rev. eds	**E**
	Harcourt Brace 1949	**E**
	Faber 1959	**E**
18 **Marina** (poem)	Faber 1930	**G**
19 **Thoughts After Lambeth** (*Criterion* miscellany)	Faber 1931	**E**
20 **Triumphal March** (poem)	Faber 1931	**G**
21 **Charles Whibley: A Memoir**	OUP 1931	**I**
22 **Selected Essays 1917–1932**	Faber 1932	**H**
	Harcourt Brace 1932	**F**
23 **John Dryden: The Poet, the**	Holliday (NY) 1932	**H**

Dramatist, The Critic (criticism)

24 **Sweeney Agonistes** (drama)	Faber 1932	I
25 **The Use of Poetry and the Use of**	Faber 1933	H
Criticism	Harvard University	F
	Press 1933	
26 **After Strange Gods** (lectures)	Faber 1934	I
	Harcourt Brace 1934	G
27 **The Rock** (play)	Faber 1934	F
	Harcourt Brace 1934	D
28 **Elizabethan Essays**	Faber 1934	F
29 **Murder in the Cathedral** (play) **E**	Goulden 1935	M
	1st complete eds.	
	Faber 1935	I
	Harcourt Brace 1935	G
30 **Essays Ancient and Modern**	Faber 1936	D
	Harcourt Brace 1936	D
31 **Collected Poems 1909–1935**	Faber 1936	I
Cont. first appearance of *Burnt Norton*.	Harcourt Brace 1936	G
32 **The Family Reunion** (play)	Faber 1939	E
	Harcourt Brace 1939	C
33 **Old Possum's Book of Practical**	Faber 1939	O
Cats	Harcourt Brace 1939	M
1939 ed.: d/w by T.S.E. 1940 ed.:	Illus. ed. Faber 1940	J
Nicolas Bentley drew the pictures.		
34 **The Idea of a Christian Society**	Faber 1939	D
(lectures)	Harcourt Brace 1940	C
35 **The Waste Land and Other Poems**	Faber 1940	E
	Harcourt Brace 1955	D
36 **East Coker** (poem)	Faber 1940	E
Published previously in *The New English*		
Weekly Easter no. of the same year.		
37 **Burnt Norton** (poem)	Faber 1941	E
1st separate ed. See 31.		
38 **Points of View** (essays)	Faber 1941	D
Contains no new material.		
39 **The Dry Salvages** (poem)	Faber 1941	E
40 **The Classics and the Man of**	OUP 1942	E
Letters (address)		
41 **The Music of Poetry** (lecture)	Jackson (Glasgow)	H
	1942	
42 **Little Gidding** (poem)	Faber 1942	E
This, with 36, 37 and 39, completes the		
Four Quartets.		
43 **Four Quartets**	Harcourt Brace 1943	E
	Faber 1944	E
44 **What is a Classic?** (address)	Faber 1945	D
45 **On Poetry** (address)	Concord	K
750 copies printed, and distributed gratis	(Massachusetts) 1947	

46 **Milton** (lecture) 500 copies printed.	Cumberlege (London) 1947	**J**
47 **A Sermon** 300 copies printed, and distributed gratis.	CUP 1948	**K**
48 **Selected Poems**	Penguin 1948	**C**
	Harcourt Brace 1967	**B**
49 **Notes Towards the Definition of** **Culture**	Faber 1948	**E**
	Harcourt Brace 1949	**D**
50 **From Poe to Valéry** (lecture) 1500 copies printed for distribution to friends of publisher.	Harcourt Brace 1948	**I**
51 **The Undergraduate Poems** Unauthorized publication, 1000 copies printed.	Harvard Advocate, (Massachusetts) 1949	**K**
52 **The Aims of Poetic Drama**	Poets' Theatre Guild 1949	**G**
53 **The Cocktail Party** (play)	Faber 1950	**E**
	Harcourt Brace 1950	**C**
54 **Poetry and Drama** (lecture)	Cambridge (Massachusetts) 1951	**E**
55 **The Value and Use of Cathedrals** **in England Today**	Chichester 1952	**J**
56 **An Address to the Members of the** **London Library** 500 copies printed.	London 1952	**G**
57 **The Complete Poems and Plays** (**1909–1950**)	Harcourt Brace 1952	**D**
58 **Selected Prose**	Penguin 1953	**C**
59 **American Literature and the** **American Language** 500 copies printed.	Washington University 1953	**I**
60 **The Three Voices of Poetry** (lecture)	NBL 1953	**D**
	CUP (US) 1954	**C**
61 **The Confidential Clerk** (play)	Faber 1954	**D**
	Harcourt Brace 1954	**C**
62 **Religious Drama: Mediaeval and** **Modern** 326 copies printed. 300 numbered, 26 lettered and signed (**L**).	House of Books (NY) 1954	**I**
63 **The Cultivation of Christmas** **Trees** (poem) Illus. David Jones	Faber 1954	**E**
	Farrar Straus 1956	**C**
64 **The Literature of Politics** (address)	Conservative Centre 1955	**C**
65 **The Frontiers of Criticism** (lecture) 10,050 copies printed, and distributed gratis.	Minnesota 1956	**D**

66 **On Poetry and Poets** (essays)	Faber 1957	**F**
	Farrar Straus 1957	**D**
67 **The Elder Statesman** (play)	Faber 1959	**D**
	Farrar Straus 1959	**C**
68 **Geoffrey Faber 1889–1961** (memoir)	Faber 1961	**L**
Limited to 100 copies, distributed gratis.		
69 **Collected Plays**	Faber 1962	**D**
70 **George Herbert** (essay)	NBL 1962	**C**
71 **Collected Poems 1909–1962**	Faber 1963	**D**
	Harcourt Brace 1963	**D**
72 **Knowledge and Experience in the**	Faber 1964	**D**
Philosophy of F.H. Bradley	Farrar Straus 1964	**C**
73 **To Criticize the Critic**	Faber 1965	**D**
(essays)	Farrar Straus 1965	**C**
74 **Poems Written in Early Youth**	Faber 1967	**C**
Preceded only by a privately printed edition in 1950, which was limited to 12 copies. (**T**).	Farrar Straus 1967	**C**
75 **The Complete Poems and Plays**	Faber 1968	**D**
76 **The Waste Land: A Facsimile and**	Faber 1971	**E**
Transcript	Harcourt Brace 1971	**D**
77 **The Letters of T.S. Eliot:**	Faber 1988	**C**
Volume 1. 1898–1922		

Eliot edited and introduced a vast number of books, a few of the more important being:

Ezra Pound: Selected Poems	Faber & Gwyer 1928	**I**
A Choice of Kipling's Verse	Faber 1941	**E**
	Scribner 1943	**D**
Introducing James Joyce	Faber 1942	**D**
Literary Essays of Ezra Pound	Faber 1954	**D**
	New Directions 1954	**D**

Biography:
Peter Ackroyd **T.S. Eliot** Hamilton 1984 Simon & Schuster 1984

Ellis, Alice Thomas   Born in Liverpool, 1932.

Suddenly one of the most admired and fashionable writers in London, her slim novels having become very collectable indeed. Because of this, I list Mrs Haycraft (wife of the chairman of Duckworth) in full for the first time – even down to her odd little cookbooks.

1 **Natural Baby Food: A Cookery Book**	Duckworth 1977	**B**
(pseud. Brenda O'Casey)		
2 **The Sin Eater** (novel)	Duckworth 1977	**F**

3	**The Birds of the Air** (novel)	Duckworth 1980	D
		Viking Press 1981	C
4	**Darling, You Shouldn't Have Gone to So Much Trouble** (cookery) (as Anna Haycraft, with Caroline Blackwood)	Cape 1980	B
5	**The 27th Kingdom** (novel)	Duckworth 1982	C
6	**The Other Side of the Fire** (novel)	Duckworth 1983	C
7	**Unexplained Laughter** (novel)	Duckworth 1985	C
		Harper 1987	B
8	**Home Life** (columns)	Duckworth 1986	B
9	**Secrets of Strangers** (non-fiction) With Tom Pitt-Aikens.	Duckworth 1986	B
10	**The Clothes in the Wardrobe** (novel)	Duckworth 1987	B
11	**More Home Life** (columns)	Duckworth 1987	B
12	**The Skeleton in the Cupboard** (novel)	Duckworth 1988	B
13	**Home Life 3** (columns)	Duckworth 1988	B
14	**The Fly in the Ointment** (novel) Nos 10, 12 and 14 form a trilogy	Duckworth 1989	B
15	**Loss of the Good Authority: The Cause of Delinquency** (non-fiction) With Tom Pitt-Aikens.	Viking 1989	B
16	**Home Life 4** (columns)	Duckworth 1989	B
17	**A Welsh Childhood** (non-fiction)	Joseph 1990	B
18	**The Inn at the Edge of the World** (novel)	Viking 1990	B
19	**Pillars of Gold** (novel)	Viking 1992	B

Farrell, J.G.   Born in Liverpool, 1935. Died 1979.

Although not as posthumously famous as he was, Farrell's short list remains stubbornly difficult to lay one's hands on. *The Siege of Krishnapur* remains the highlight.

1	**A Man from Elsewhere** (novel)	Hutchinson 1963	J
2	**The Lung** (novel)	Hutchinson 1965	G
3	**A Girl in the Head** (novel)	Cape 1967	E
		Harper 1969	C
4	**Troubles** (novel)	Cape 1970	C
		Knopf 1971	C
5	**The Siege of Krishnapur** (novel)	Weidenfeld 1973	F
		Harcourt Brace 1974	D
6	**The Singapore Grip** (novel)	Weidenfeld 1978	D
		Knopf 1979	B
7	**The Hill Station** (novel)	Weidenfeld 1981	C

Faulkner, William Born in New Albany, Mississippi, 1867. Died 1962.

In America, Faulkner is hugely regarded – he has been since he was awarded the Nobel Prize in 1949 – and first editions change hands for fortunes. His reputation is high in Britain, too, but even English firsts are not easy to come by, and Faulkner is a difficult man to collect. It ought to be remembered (and this is true of all American literary lions) that the US firsts are worth *very much* more than their English counterparts.

1	**The Marble Faun** (verse)	Privately printed 1924	U
2	**Soldier's Pay** (novel)	Liveright 1926	S
		Chatto & Windus 1930	M
3	**Mosquitoes** (novel)	Privately printed 1927	R
	A revised ed. was published by Garden City in 1937 (**H**), and in England by Chatto & Windus in 1964 (**D**).		
4	**Sartoris** (novel)	Harcourt Brace 1929	N
		Chatto & Windus 1933	J
5	**The Sound and the Fury** (novel)	H. Smith 1929	M
		Chatto & Windus 1931	K
6	**As I Lay Dying** (novel)	H. Smith 1930	N
		Chatto & Windus 1935	I
7	**Sanctuary** (novel)	H. Smith 1930	N
		Chatto & Windus 1931	K
8	**These 13** (stories)	H. Smith 1930	K
		Chatto & Windus 1933	H
9	**Light in August** (novel)	Random House 1932	M
		Chatto & Windus 1933	I
10	**A Green Bough** (verse)	H. Smith 1933	I
11	**Doctor Martino and Other Stories**	H. Smith 1934	N
		Chatto & Windus 1934	J
12	**Pylon** (novel)	H. Smith 1935	J
		Chatto & Windus 1936	H
13	**Absalom, Absalom!** (novel)	Random House 1936	I
		Chatto & Windus 1937	G
14	**The Unvanquished** (novel)	Random House 1938	I
		Chatto & Windus 1938	G
15	**The Wild Palms** (stories)	Random House 1939	I
		Chatto & Windus 1939	F
16	**The Hamlet** (novel)	Random House 1940	I
		Chatto & Windus 1940	F
17	**Go Down, Moses** (novel)	Random House 1942	I
		Chatto & Windus 1942	H
18	**Intruder in the Dust** (novel)	Random House 1948	H
		Chatto & Windus 1949	G
19	**Knight's Gambit** (stories)	Random House 1949	H

	Chatto & Windus 1951	**F**
20 **Collected Stories**	Random House 1950	**E**
	Chatto & Windus 1951	**D**
21 **Requiem for a Nun** (novel)	Random House 1951	**G**
	Chatto & Windus 1953	**F**
22 **A Fable** (novel)	Random House 1954	**F**
	Chatto & Windus 1954	**D**
23 **Faulkner's Country** (stories)	Chatto & Windus 1955	**D**
24 **The Town** (novel)	Random House 1957	**F**
	Chatto & Windus 1958	**D**
25 **New Orleans Sketches**	Rutgers University Press 1958	**E**
	Sidgwick & Jackson 1959	**D**
26 **The Collected Stories** (3 vols)	Chatto & Windus 1958	**G**
27 **The Mansion** (novel)	Random House 1959	**E**
With 16 and 24, this forms a trilogy.	Chatto & Windus 1960	**D**
28 **The Reivers** (novel)	Random House 1962	**E**
	Chatto & Windus 1962	**E**
29 **Selected Short Stories**	Random House 1962	**D**
30 **Early Prose and Poetry**	Little, Brown 1962	**D**
	Cape 1962	**C**
31 **Essays, Speeches, and Public Letters**	Random House 1966	**C**
	Chatto & Windus 1966	**C**

Biography:
Joseph Blotner **Faulkner: A Biography** (2 vols) Chatto & Windus 1974

Feinstein, Elaine   Born in Lancashire, 1930.

Elaine Feinstein has been quietly publishing highly regarded poetry and novels for twenty-five years, yet only recently has she come to the critical fore – her latest novel, *Loving Brecht*, quite rightly drawing reviews that were not much short of rave. Such reviews, however, by no means guarantee huge sales, and so Feinstein is neither what we term a bestseller nor – yet – truly collectable. Both of these situations could change, however, and so if you appreciate her verse and fiction, now would be the right time to gather them up.

1 **In a Green Eye** (verse)	Goliard Press 1966	**E**
2 **The Circle** (novel)	Hutchinson 1970	**E**
3 **The Magic Apple Tree** (verse)	Hutchinson 1971	**C**
4 **The Amberstone Exit** (novel)	Hutchinson 1972	**D**
5 **At the Edge** (verse)	Sceptre Press 1972	**D**
6 **Matters of Chance** (story)	Covent Garden Press 1972	**D**
7 **The Celebrants and Other Poems**	Hutchinson 1973	**C**

8 **The Glass Alembic** (novel)	Hutchinson 1973	C
9 **The Crystal Garden** (same as 8)	Dutton US 1974	C
10 **Children of the Rose** (novel)	Hutchinson 1975	C
11 **The Ecstasy of Dr. Miriam Garner** (novel)	Hutchinson 1976	C
12 **Some Unease and Angels: Selected Poems**	Hutchinson 1977	C
	Green River Press US 1977	C
13 **The Shadow Master** (novel)	Hutchinson 1978	C
	Simon & Schuster 1979	C
14 **The Feast of Euridice** (verse)	Faber 1980	C
15 **The Survivors** (novel)	Hutchinson 1982	B
	Penguin US 1991	B
16 **The Border** (novel)	Hutchinson 1984	B
	Boyars US 1989	B
17 **Bessie Smith** (non-fiction)	Penguin 1985	B
18 **Badlands** (verse)	Century Hutchinson 1986	B
19 **A Captive Lion: The Life of Marina Tsvetayeva** (biography)	Century Hutchinson 1987	B
	Dutton 1987	B
20 **Mother's Girl** (novel)	Century Hutchinson 1988	B
	Dutton 1988	B
21 **City Music** (verse)	Hutchinson 1990	B
22 **All You Need** (novel)	Century Hutchinson 1989	B
	Viking 1991	B
23 **Loving Brecht** (novel)	Hutchinson 1992	B

Firbank, Ronald   Born in London, 1886. Died 1926.

Had Firbank been born earlier, he most certainly would have been with Wilde and the Aesthetes. Osbert Sitwell tells us that Firbank wrote his books not in an exercise book, not on loose leaves, but upon an interminable succession of azure blue postcards. Any man so disposed would have been at no loss as to what he might do with a green carnation.

1 **Odette d'Antrevernes and A Study in Temperament** (stories)	Elkin Mathews 1905	N
2 **Vainglory** (novel) Frontis. by Felicien Rops.	Grant Richards 1915	K
3 **Odette** (same as in 1)	Grant Richards 1916	H
4 **Inclinations**	Grant Richards 1916	K
5 **Caprice** Frontis. by Augustus John.	Grant Richards 1917	K

Fitzgerald, F. Scott

6	**Valmouth: A Romantic Novel** Frontis. by Augustus John.	Grant Richards 1919	K
7	**The Princess Zoubaroff: A Comedy**	Grant Richards 1920	I
8	**Santal** (story)	Grant Richards 1921	I
9	**The Flower Beneath the Foot** (biog.) Portraits by Augustus John and Wyndham Lewis.	Grant Richards 1923	I
10	**Prancing Nigger** (novel)	Brentano's (NY) 1924	L
11	**Sorrow in Sunlight** (same as 10)	Brentano's (UK) 1925	I
12	**Concerning the Eccentricities of** **Cardinal Pirelli** (novel) Portrait by Augustus John.	Grant Richards 1926	I
13	**The Artificial Princess** (novel)	Duckworth 1934	G

Details of the works may be found in: M.J. Benkowitz **A Bibliography of Ronald Firbank** Soho Bibliographies, Hart-Davis 1963   Brigid Brophy **Prancing Novelist: A Defence of Fiction in the Form of a Critical Biography in Praise of Ronald Firbank** Cape 1972; Barnes & Noble 1973.

Two of the several collected editions are: **The Collected Works of Ronald Firbank** (6 vols) Duckworth 1929. Intro. by Arthur Waley, with an essay by Osbert Sitwell   **Five Novels** (6, 10, 9, 13 and 12) Duckworth 1949. Intro. By Osbert Sitwell, portrait by Augustus John.

Fitzgerald, F. Scott   Born in Minnesota, 1896. Died 1940.

I think it might be something to do with the recent fashion revival of peg-top trousers, short haircuts and jackets cut on the lines of a grocery box that has occasioned yet another wave of fondness in Britain for all things American. This could be bilge. Either way, Fitzgerald and his contemporaries do seem to be more popular than they were a few years ago, and although this is reflected in the (relatively moderate) rise in prices, it must be borne in mind that first editions in this country (even the American ones) will never ever reach the vertiginous heights achieved in the USA. Fitzgerald and Hemingway are the nearest they get to a formal religion.
   Collected editions and anthologies have been òmitted.

1	**This Side of Paradise** (novel)	Scribner 1920	T
		Grey Walls Press 1948	I
2	**Flappers and Philosophers** (stories)	Scribner 1920	P
		Collins 1922	L
3	**The Beautiful and Damned** (novel)	Scribner 1922	P
		Collins 1922	M
4	**Tales of the Jazz Age** (stories)	Scribner 1922	L
		Collins 1923	J
5	**The Great Gatsby** (novel)	Scribner 1925	Q
		Chatto & Windus 1925	M

6 **All the Sad Young Men** (stories)	Scribner 1926	**K**
7 **John Jackson's Arcady** (stories)	Baker (NY) 1928	**K**
8 **Tender is the Night** (novel)	Scribner 1934	**L**
	Chatto & Windus 1934	**I**
9 **Taps at Reveille** (stories)	Scribner 1935	**I**
10 **The Last Tycoon** (unfinished novel)	Scribner 1941	**I**
	Grey Walls Press 1949	**F**
11 **The Crack-Up** (letters and essays)	New Directions 1945	**G**
	Grey Walls Press 1947	**E**
12 **Afternoon of an Author** (stories)	Scribner 1957	**D**
	Bodley Head 1958	**D**

Bibliography:
Charles E. Shane **Scott Fitzgerald** University of Minnesota American Authors Pamphlet

Biography:
André le Vot *Scott Fitzgerald: A Biography* Doubleday 1983, Lane 1984

Fitzgerald, Penelope   Born in Lincoln, 1916.

Still a largely unrecognized writer, despite her having won several literary prizes, including the Booker. The novels should not be too hard to gather, but her first two books – both biographies – could be elusive. Unusual for a novelist to commence his or her writing career with non-fiction, but there is a notable precedent in Muriel Spark.

1 **Edward Burne-Jones: A Biography**	Joseph 1975	**D**
2 **The Knox Brothers** (biography)	Macmillan 1977	**C**
	Coward McCann 1977	**C**
3 **The Golden Child** (novel)	Duckworth 1977	**E**
	Scribner 1978	**C**
4 **The Bookshop** (novel)	Duckworth 1978	**D**
5 **Offshore** (novel)	Collins 1979	**C**
6 **Human Voices** (novel)	Collins 1980	**C**
7 **At Freddie's** (novel)	Collins 1982	**C**
	Godine 1983	**B**
8 **Charlotte Mew and Her Friends: With a Selection of Her Poems**	Collins 1984	**B**
	Addison Wesley 1988	**B**
9 **Innocence** (novel)	Collins 1986	**B**
	Holt 1987	**B**
10 **The Beginning of Spring** (novel)	Collins 1988	**B**
	Holt 1989	**B**
11 **The Gate of Angels**	Collins 1990	**B**

Fleming, Ian   Born in London, 1908. Died 1964.

Every so often, some misguided oaf floats the opinion that James Bond is yesterday's man: in the age of the super-hero, they sneer, who has time for a mere secret agent? They really don't get it, do they? Bond has transcended, become dateless and timeless – like Sherlock Holmes (like The Beatles, if it comes to it, but that is a little out of context). Anyway, this view may partially explain why dealers keep expecting the Fleming thing to wear off; it doesn't, of course – although people do realize now that first editions of the latest books were printed in enormous quantities, and so fancy prices are hardly in order (and nor should one accept much less than perfect copies). On the other hand, I recently heard of a collector who paid £1000 for *Casino Royale*, *Live and Let Die* and *Moonraker* – none of which had a dust wrapper. This demonstrates not only the comparative rarity, but also the expense people are prepared to run to for copies that will never *truly* delight them.

1	**Casino Royale** (Bond novel) Black boards, as are all the Bond books, with red heart motif. Grey (gunmetal?) d/w, repeating heart motif, devised by I.F. This is the very first appearance of Bond, and it is very, very scarce. 4750 copies were printed of the 1st edition, many of these going to public libraries.	Cape 1953 Macmillan 1954	R K
2	**Live and Let Die** (Bond novel) Medallion motif on boards. Scarlet d/w with yellow lettering, devised by I.F. Very difficult.	Cape 1954 Macmillan 1955	P J
3	**Moonraker** (Bond novel) Silver titling on boards, yellow and orange flame design on d/w, with black lettering, devised by I.F. Very difficult.	Cape 1955 Macmillan 1955	O I
4	**Diamonds Are Forever** (Bond novel) Blind-stamped diamond-pane motif on boards. Black, tan, pink and white d/w lettered in black and white.	Cape 1956 Macmillan 1956	L H
5	**From Russia, with Love** (Bond novel) Gun and rose motif on boards, repeated on the superb Chopping d/w, depicting a sawn-off Smith and Wesson and a red rose against a pale wood ground. The famous stencil lettering appears to be inked onto the wood, but beneath the rose stem. This is the first of Richard Chopping's *trompe l'oeuil* d/ws, which continued, with the	Cape 1957 Macmillan 1957	K G

exception of 7, to the end of the Bond saga.

6	**The Diamond Smugglers** (non-fiction)	Cape 1957 Macmillan 1958	**H** **E**

Black boards, red, black and grey d/w. Quite scarce.

7	**Dr No** (Bond novel)	Cape 1958 Macmillan 1958	**J** **E**

Brown and black d/w with a girl's silhouette, repeated on boards. One feels Cape might have compared this d/w with that of 5, and recalled Chopping quickly!

8	**Goldfinger** (Bond novel) .	Cape 1959 Macmillan 1959	**I** **E**

Skull motif with gold coins on boards, repeated on Chopping d/w.

9	**For Your Eyes Only** (Bond stories)	Cape 1960 Viking 1960	**H** **D**

Matisse-like eye motif on boards. Chopping d/w.

10	**Thunderball** (Bond novel)	Cape 1961 Viking Press 1961	**F** **D**

Blind-stamped skeletal hand motif, repeated on Chopping d/w.

11	**The Spy Who Loved Me** (Bond novel)	Cape 1962 Viking 1962	**D** **C**

Silver dagger motif on boards, repeated on Chopping d/w. t/p reads: by Ian Fleming with Vivienne Michel. This is not a genuine collaboration: Fleming wrote this novel as Vivienne Michel in the first person. Hence, the 'Spy' in the title is none other than 007.

12	**On Her Majesty's Secret Service** (Bond novel)	Cape 1963 NAL 1963	**C** **C**

White gunsmoke motif on boards. Chopping d/w.

12a	**On Her Majesty's Secret Service** (ltd ed.)	Cape 1963	**S**

Same motif on black boards, as in 12, but with white vellum spine. Coloured frontis. portrait of I.F. by Amherst Villiers. t/p printed in red and black. Verso of t/p reads: 'This special edition is limited to 250 numbered copies only for sale, each signed by the author. Copy number...', followed by IF.'s signature. As is apparent from the limitation, this book is very, very scarce.

13	**Thrilling Cities** (non-fiction)	Cape 1963	**F**

Grey mottled boards with white cloth spine. Daliesque d/w by Paul Davis in monochrome with shocking-pink spine and lettering. Quite scarce.	NAL 1964	**D**
14 **You Only Live Twice** (Bond novel)	Cape 1964	**C**
Chinese characters motif on boards. Chopping d/w.	NAL 1964	**C**
15 **Chitty-Chitty-Bang-Bang** (juveniles) There are three of these books, all admirably illustrated by John Burningham. The pictorial boards are also by Burningham, the identical designs being reproduced on the laminated d/ws. The first has 'Adventure Number 1' within a red disc on the cover (1964), the second (1964) bears a turquoise disc reading 'Adventure Number 2', and the third (1965) had 'Adventure Number 3' on a lilac disc. They are very difficult, particularly in fine condition – as is the case with all children's books.	Cape 1964–5 (individually) (set) Random House 1964	**E** **K** **G**
16 **The Man with the Golden Gun** (Bond novel) The only Bond to lack a motif on the boards. The blurbs, which used to be very newsy, have grown simpler now. This one reads: The New James Bond. Enough said. Chopping d/w.	Cape 1965 NAL 1965	**C** **C**
17 **Ian Fleming Introduces Jamaica** (non-fiction) Rust cloth, laminated photographic d/w. Despite the two-inch-high lettering of 'Ian Fleming' on the d/w, it contains only an 11-page Intro. by him. Nonetheless, a handsome book, with many fine coloured photographs. The second impression was remaindered, but the 1st remains elusive.	Deutsch 1965 Hawthorne 1965	**C** **C**
18 **Octopussy** and **The Living Daylights** (Bond stories) Intended to be a sequel (i.e. a book of short stories) to 9, but sadly, Fleming died having completed only these two. Chopping d/w.	Cape 1966 NAL 1966	**C** **C**

A James Bond story (*The Property of a Lady*) appeared in **The Ivory Hammer: The Year at Sotheby's** Longman 1963 (**I**)

Fleming wrote introductions to the following, all of which are scarce:

Herbert O. Yardley **The Education of a Poker Player**	Cape 1959	**H**
Donald Fish **Airline Detective**	Collins 1962	**G**
Hugh Edwards **All Night at Mr Stanyhurst's**	Cape 1963	**F**

The essential sourcework on Fleming is still:

John Pearson **The Life of Ian Fleming**	Cape 1966 McGraw Hill 1966

Pearson has also written the amusing, and very convincing:

James Bond: The Authorized Biography	Sidgwick & Jackson 1973 Morrow 1973

Forester, C.S.   Born in Cairo, 1899. Died 1966.

Apart from the Hornblower series, listed below, Forester is best remembered for *The African Queen*, everyone having seen the film and few realizing that Forester wrote it. One always recalls Bogart dragging that boat through the filthy swamp – two of the most disgusting moments being when he emerges from the silage covered in leeches, and when a still evangelical Katharine Hepburn pours all that gin over the side. Horrific. (In the last edition of this book, I wrote *whisky* instead of gin. Of all the hundreds and hundreds of letters I received about all sorts of things on first publication, mentions of this error outnumbered the lot. What *that* tells one about collectors, I have no idea at all.)

1 **A Pawn Among Kings** (novel) This is his first book. Scarce.	Methuen 1924	**L**
2 **The African Queen** (novel) Not a title always associated with Forester, but a highlight of his work.	Little, Brown 1935 Heinemann 1935	**J** **I**

Herewith follows the Hornblower series, in entirety, but omitting collections, anthologies, omnibus volumes and extracts – of which there seem to have been an amazing number.

3 **Beat to Quarters**	Little, Brown 1937	**H**

Forster, E.M.

4 **The Happy Return** (same as 3)	Joseph 1937	G
5 **A Ship of the Line**	Little, Brown 1938	G
	Joseph 1938	F
6 **Flying Colours**	Little, Brown 1938	G
	Joseph 1938	F
7 **Commodore Hornblower**	Little, Brown 1945	E
8 **The Commodore** (same as 7)	Joseph 1945	D
9 **Lord Hornblower**	Little, Brown 1946	E
	Joseph 1946	D
10 **Mr Midshipman Hornblower**	Little, Brown 1950	D
	Joseph 1950	D
11 **Lieutenant Hornblower**	Grosset (NY) 1952	D
	Joseph 1952	D
12 **Hornblower and the Atropos**	Little, Brown 1953	D
	Joseph 1953	D
13 **Admiral Hornblower in the West Indies**	Little, Brown 1958	D
14 **Hornblower in the West Indies** (same as 13)	Joseph 1958	D
15 **Hornblower and the Hotspur**	Little, Brown 1962	C
	Joseph 1962	C
16 **Captain Hornblower R.N.**	Joseph 1965	C

Forster, E.M.   Born in London, 1879. Died 1970.

Although *A Passage to Indian* retains a secure place as a classic – as does, to a slightly lesser extent, *Howard's End* – Forster is now quite as famous for having been an artistically repressed homosexual, having endlessly and puzzlingly referred to 'personal relationships' in his books, feeling unable to be frank. The publication of *Maurice* in 1971 (the year after his death) made things clearer, but it seems extraordinary now that such a book should have been (voluntarily) suppressed for fifty-seven years after it was written. Unlike many such books, though, it does not end in sourness and despair, but happily – even in triumph.

The recent film versions of his novels have added immeasurably to Forster's popularity; he is now a Penguin bestseller – all over again.

1 **Where Angels Fear to Tread** (novel)	Blackwood 1905	O
	Knopf 1920	J
2 **The Longest Journey** (novel)	Blackwood 1907	M
	Knopf 1922	H
3 **A Room with a View** (novel)	Arnold 1908	N
	Putnam 1911	I
4 **Howard's End** (novel)	Arnold 1910	L
	Putnam 1910	H

5 **The Celestial Omnibus** (stories)	Sidgwick & Jackson 1911	I
	Knopf 1923	E
6 **The Story of the Siren**	Hogarth Press 1920	J
7 **Egypt** (non-fiction)	Labour Research Dept. 1920	K
8 **Alexandria** (history)	Whitehead Morris 1922	L
	Doubleday 1961	C
9 **Pharos and Pharillon** (essays)	Hogarth Press 1923	I
	Knopf 1923	F
10 **A Passage to India** (novel)	Arnold 1924	N
	Harcourt Brace 1924	J
11 **Anonymity** (essay)	Hogarth Press 1925	F
12 **Aspects of the Novel** (prose)	Arnold 1927	F
	Harcourt Brace 1927	D
13 **The Eternal Moment** (stories)	Sidgwick & Jackson 1928	F
	Harcourt Brace 1928	D
14 **A Letter to Madan Blanchard** (essay)	Hogarth Press 1931	C
	Harcourt Brace 1932	B
15 **Goldsworthy Lowes Dickinson** (non-fiction)	Arnold 1934	C
	Harcourt Brace 1934	C
16 **Abinger Harvest** (essays)	Arnold 1936	E
	Harcourt Brace 1936	C
17 **What I Believe** (essay)	Hogarth Press 1939	C
18 **Reading as Usual** (lecture)	Tottenham Public Libraries 1939	C
19 **England's Pleasant Land** (prose)	Hogarth Press 1940	D
20 **Nordic Twilight** (essay)	Macmillan 1940	D
21 **Virginia Woolf** (lecture)	CUP 1942	E
	Harcourt Brace 1942	D
22 **The Development of English Prose** (lecture)	Jackson (Glasgow) 1945	D
23 **The Collected Tales**	Knopf 1947	D
24 **Collected Short Stories** (same as 23)	Sidgwick & Jackson 1948	D
25 **Two Cheers for Democracy** (essays)	Arnold 1951	C
	Harcourt Brace 1951	C
26 **Billy Budd** (libretto for Britten's opera)	Boosey & Hawkes 1951	E
27 **The Hill of Devi** (prose)	Arnold 1953	C
	Harcourt Brace 1953	C
28 **Marianne Thornton** (biography)	Arnold 1956	C
	Harcourt Brace 1956	C
29 **Maurice** (novel)	Arnold 1971	C
	Norton 1971	B
30 **The Life to Come** (stories)	Arnold 1972	C
	Norton 1973	B

Forster, Margaret

31 **Selected Letters** (Volume 1)	Collins 1983	C
	Harvard University Press 1983	C
32 **Selected Letters** (Volume 2)	Collins 1984	C
	Harvard University Press 1984	C

There is now a standard, authorized biography: P.N. Furbank **E.M. Forster: A Life** (2 vols) Secker & Warburg 1977, 1978 Further bibliographical details may be found in: B.J. Kirkpatrick **A Bibliography of E.M. Forster** Soho bibliographies, Hart-Davis 1968

Forster, Margaret   Born in Carlisle, 1938.

A stylish, thoughtful and ever more prolific author of both novels and biographies (she is currently working on Daphne du Maurier) and that rare thing – a novelist who actually *reads* newly published novels. In fact she consumes them voraciously; I have long been of the opinion that if Margaret Forster became a judge for the Booker (a task for which she is amply qualified) her daily routine would hardly be altered at all.

1 **Dames' Delight** (novel)	Cape 1964	E
2 **Georgy Girl** (novel)	Secker & Warburg 1965	F
3 **The Bogeyman** (novel)	Secker & Warburg 1965	D
	Putnam 1966	C
4 **The Travels of Maudie Tipstaff** (novel)	Secker & Warburg 1967	D
	Stein & Day 1967	C
5 **The Park** (novel)	Secker & Warburg 1968	C
6 **Miss Owen Owen is at Home** (novel)	Secker & Warburg 1969	C
	Simon & Schuster 1969	B
7 **Fenella Phizackerley** (novel)	Secker & Warburg 1970	C
	Simon & Schuster 1970	B
8 **Mr Bone's Retreat** (novel)	Secker & Warburg 1971	C
	Simon & Schuster 1971	B
9 **The Rash Adventurer: The Rise and Fall of Chas. Ed. Stuart** (non-fiction)	Secker & Warburg 1973	C
	Stein & Day 1973	B
10 **The Seduction of Mrs Pendlebury**	Secker & Warburg 1974	C
11 **William Makepeace Thackeray: Memoirs of a Victorian Gentleman** (biography)	Secker & Warburg 1978	C
	Morrow 1979	C
12 **Mother Can You Hear Me?** (novel)	Secker & Warburg 1980	C
13 **The Bride of Lowther Fell** (novel)	Secker & Warburg 1981	C
	Athenaeum 1981	B
14 **Marital Rites** (novel)	Secker & Warburg 1982	B
	Athenaeum 1982	B

15 **Significant Sisters: Grassroots of Active Feminism 1839–1939** (non-fiction)	Secker & Warburg 1984 Knopf 1985	**B** **B**
16 **Private Papers** (novel)	Chatto & Windus 1986	**B**
17 **Elizabeth Barrett Browning: A Biography**	Chatto & Windus 1988 Doubleday 1989	**B** **B**
18 **Have the Men Had Enough?** (novel)	Chatto & Windus 1989	**B**
19 **Lady's Maid** (novel)	Chatto & Windus 1990 Doubleday 1991	**B** **B**
20 **The Battle for Christabel** (novel)	Chatrto & Windus 1991	**B**

Forsyth, Frederick Born in Kent, 1938.

A dependable, bankable and *improving* author who always delivers. He is also becoming much more collectable, partially because of his small output. *The Day of the Jackal* remains the highlight, but do glance at the newly discovered item, number 10 – for which I have no explanation whatever, and I shall quite understand if you do not rush out to claim it for your own.

1 **The Biafra Story** (non-fiction)	Penguin 1969	**E**
2 **The Day of the Jackal** (novel)	Hutchinson 1971 Viking 1971	**I** **F**
3 **The Odessa File** (novel)	Hutchinson 1972 Viking 1972	**D** **C**
4 **The Dogs of War** (novel)	Hutchinson 1974 Viking 1974	**C** **C**
5 **The Shepherd** (story)	Hutchinson 1975 Viking 1976	**C** **C**
6 **The Novels of Frederick Forsyth** Includes 2, 3 and 4.	Hutchinson 1978	**C**
7 **The Devil's Alternative** (novel)	Hutchinson 1979 Viking 1980	**C** **B**
8 **No Comebacks** (stories)	Hutchinson 1982 Viking 1982	**C** **B**
9 **The Four Novels of Frederick Forsyth** Includes 2, 3, 4 and 7, together with a new intro.	Hutchinson 1982	**C**
10 **Emeka** (a biography – of Chukwuemeka Odumegu-Ojukwu)	Spectrum, Ibadan 1982	**B**
11 **The Fourth Protocol** (novel)	Hutchinson 1984 Viking Press 1984	**B** **B**
12 **The Negotiator** (novel)	Bantam 1989 Bantam US 1989	**B** **B**

13 **The Deceiver** (novel)	Bantam 1991	**B**
	Bantam US 1991	**B**

Fowles, John   Born in Essex, 1926.

One hears rumours that due to ill health, it is possible that Fowles will never again write a novel; this would be a great shame, for at his peak (although it must be said that that peak was during the 1970s) he truly was one of the great literary forces. And it is these gems that the collector wants – mainly, of course, *The Collector* – but prices remain high.

1 **The Collector** (novel)	Cape 1963	**N**
	Little, Brown 1963	**J**
2 **The Aristos** (prose)	Little, Brown 1964	**N**
	Cape 1965	**M**
(a revised edition was published in paperback by Pan in 1968, and by Little, Brown in 1970) (**E**)		
3 **The Magus** (novel)	Little, Brown 1965	**K**
	Cape 1966	**J**
(a revised edition was published by Cape in 1977, and Little, Brown in 1978) (**D**)		
4 **The French Lieutenant's Woman** (novel)	Cape 1969	**I**
	Little, Brown 1969	**G**
5 **Poems**	Ecco Press US 1973	**F**
6 **The Ebony Tower** (novellas)	Cape 1974	**F**
	Little, Brown 1974	**D**
7 **Shipwreck** (photographic essay)	Cape 1974	**E**
	Little, Brown 1975	**D**
8 **Daniel Martin** (novel)	Little, Brown 1977	**D**
	Cape 1977	**C**
9 **Islands** (photographic essay)	Cape 1978	**C**
	Little, Brown 1979	**C**
10 **Conditional** (verse)	Lord John Press US 1979	**G**
11 **The Tree** (photographic essay)	Aurum Press 1979	**E**
	Little, Brown 1980	**D**
12 **The Enigma of Stonehenge** (photographic essay)	Cape 1980	**D**
	Summit 1980	**D**
13 **A Brief History of Lyme** (non-fiction)	Friends of the Lyme Regis Museum 1981	**E**
14 **A Short History of Lyme Regis** (non-fiction)	Dovecote Press 1982	**D**
	Little, Brown 1983	**C**
15 **Mantissa** (novel)	Cape 1982	**C**
	Little, Brown 1982	**C**

16 **Land** (photographic essay)	Heinemann 1985	**C**
	Little, Brown 1985	**C**
17 **A Maggot** (novel)	Cape 1985	**C**
	Little, Brown 1985	**C**

In addition to the above, Fowles has translated *Cinderella* by Perrault (Cape 1974, Little, Brown 1975) and *Ourika* by Claire du Durfort (Taylor US 1977). Fowles contributed a nine-page foreword to Harold Pinter's *The Screenplay of the French Lieutenant's Woman* (Cape 1981, Little, Brown 1981)

Francis, Dick   Born in Pembrokeshire, 1920.

The standard very rarely dips below excellent in Francis's annual treats. What can one say? Terrific – and ever more collectable (as well as – you guessed it – expensive).

1	**The Sport of Queens: The Autobiography of Dick Francis**	Joseph 1957	**J**
		Harper 1969	**D**
2	**Dead Cert** (novel)	Joseph 1962	**M**
		Holt Rinehart 1962	**H**
3	**Nerve** (novel)	Joseph 1964	**L**
		Harper 1964	**I**
4	**For Kicks** (novel)	Joseph 1965	**J**
		Harper 1965	**G**
5	**Odds Against** (novel)	Joseph 1965	**H**
		Harper 1966	**E**
6	**Flying Finish** (novel)	Joseph 1966	**G**
		Harper 1967	**D**
7	**Blood Sport** (novel)	Joseph 1967	**G**
		Harper 1968	**D**
8	**Forfeit** (novel)	Joseph 1968	**F**
		Harper 1969	**C**
9	**Enquiry** (novel)	Joseph 1969	**F**
		Harper 1969	**C**
10	**Rat Race** (novel)	Joseph 1970	**D**
		Harper 1971	**C**
11	**Bonecrack** (novel)	Joseph 1971	**D**
		Harper 1972	**C**
12	**Smokescreen** (novel)	Joseph 1972	**D**
		Harper 1972	**C**
13	**Slay-Ride** (novel)	Joseph 1973	**D**
		Harper 1974	**C**
14	**Knock-Down** (novel)	Joseph 1974	**D**
		Harper 1975	**C**
15	**Across the Board** (incl. 6, 7 and 9).	Harper 1975	**C**

16 **High Stakes** (novel)	Joseph 1975	**D**
	Harper 1976	**C**
17 **In the Frame** (novel)	Joseph 1976	**D**
	Harper 1977	**C**
18 **Risk** (novel)	Joseph 1977	**D**
	Harper 1978	**C**
19 **Trial Run** (novel)	Joseph 1978	**C**
	Harper 1979	**B**
20 **Whip Hand** (novel)	Joseph 1979	**C**
	Harper 1980	**B**
21 **Reflex** (novel)	Joseph 1980	**C**
	Putnam 1981	**B**
22 **Twice Shy** (novel)	Joseph 1981	**C**
	Putnam 1982	**B**
23 **Banker** (novel)	Joseph 1982	**C**
	Putnam 1983	**B**
24 **The Danger** (novel)	Joseph 1983	**C**
	Putnam 1984	**B**
25 **Proof** (novel)	Joseph 1984	**C**
	Putnam 1985	**B**
26 **Break In** (novel)	Joseph 1985	**C**
	Putnam 1986	**B**
27 **Bolt** (novel)	Joseph 1986	**C**
	Putnam 1987	**B**
28 **Lester: The Official Biography**	Joseph 1986	**C**
29 **A Jockey's Life: The Biography of Lester Piggott** (same as 28)	Putnam 1986	**C**
30 **Hot Money** (novel)	Joseph 1987	**C**
	Putnam 1988	**B**
31 **The Edge** (novel)	Joseph 1988	**C**
	Putnam 1989	**B**
32 **Straight** (novel)	Joseph 1989	**C**
	Putnam 1989	**B**
33 **Longshot** (novel)	Joseph 1990	**C**
	Putnam 1990	**B**
34 **Comeback** (novel)	Joseph 1991	**C**
	Putnam 1991	**B**
35 **Driving Force** (novel)	Joseph 1992	**B**

Fraser, George Macdonald   Born in Carlisle, 1925.

Although his books – and in particular his *Flashman* books – sell very well on publication and in paperback, Fraser seems to be underrated by collectors (as opposed to *just* readers) and hence the books – although not common – are low in price. They are great fun, these *Flashman* books – and anyway, an author who can make a hero (kind of) out of the school bully in an essentially sentimental children's classic deserves considerable investigation.

Below are listed all the *Flashman* titles to date:

1	**Flashman** (novel)	Barrie & Jenkins 1969	**G**
2	**Royal Flash** (novel)	Barrie & Jenkins 1970	**D**
3	**Flash for Freedom** (novel)	Barrie & Jenkins 1971	**D**
4	**Flashman at the Charge** (novel)	Barrie & Jenkins 1973	**C**
5	**Flashman in the Great Game** (novel)	Barrie & Jenkins 1975	**C**
6	**Flashman's Lady** (novel)	Barrie & Jenkins 1977	**C**
7	**Flashman and the Redskins** (novel)	Collins 1982	**C**
8	**Flashman and the Dragon**	Collins 1985	**C**
9	**Flashman and the Mountain of Light** (novel)	Collins 1990	**C**
		Knopf 1991	**B**

Frayn, Michael   Born in London, 1933.

Tricky to collect (particularly the plays) but in most cases worth the effort. Frayn has returned to writing novels lately (and they tend to win prizes) but the most rewarding firsts to track down are still the collected *Guardian* and *Observer* columns (nos 1, 2, 4 and 9).

1	**The Day of the Dog** (articles)	Collins 1962	**E**
		Doubleday 1963	**C**
2	**The Book of Fub** (articles)	Collins 1963	**D**
3	**Never Put Off to Gomorrah** (same as 2)	Pantheon (NY) 1964	**C**
4	**On the Outskirts** (articles)	Collins 1964	**D**
5	**The Tin Men** (novel)	Collins 1965	**D**
		Little, Brown 1966	**C**
6	**The Russian Interpreter** (novel)	Collins 1966	**D**
		Viking 1966	**C**
7	**Towards the End of Morning** (novel)	Collins 1967	**C**
8	**Against Entropy** (same as 7)	Viking 1967	**C**
9	**At Bay in Gear Street** (articles)	Fontana 1967	**C**
10	**A Very Private Life** (novel)	Collins 1968	**C**
		Viking 1968	**B**
11	**The Two of Us** (play)	Fontana 1970	**B**
12	**Sweet Dreams** (novel)	Collins 1974	**C**
		Viking 1974	**B**
13	**Constructions** (philosophy)	Wildwood House 1974	**B**
14	**Alphabetical Order, Donkey's Years and Clouds** (plays)	Eyre Methuen 1977	**C**
15	**The Cherry Orchard** (play) (adaptation from Chekhov)	Eyre Methuen 1978	**B**
16	**The Fruits of Enlightenment** (play) (adaptation from Tolstoy)	Eyre Methuen 1979	**B**
17	**Make and Break** (play)	Methuen 1980	**B**

18 **Noises Off** (play)	Methuen 1982	**D**
	French US 1985	**C**
19 **Three Sisters** (play)	Methuen 1983	**B**
(adaptation from Chekhov)		
20 **Wild Honey** (play)	Methuen 1984	**B**
(adaptation from Chekhov)		
21 **Benefactors** (play)	Methuen 1984	**B**
22 **Number One** (play)	French 1985	**B**
(adaptation from Jean Anouilh)		
23 **Clockwise** (screenplay)	Methuen 1986	**C**
24 **The Seagull** (play)	Methuen 1986	**B**
(adaptation from Chekhov)		
25 **Plays I**	Methuen 1986	**B**
(includes nos 14, 17 and 18)		
26 **Balmoral** (play)	Methuen 1987	**B**
27 **Uncle Vanya** (play)	Methuen 1987	**B**
(adaptation from Chekhov)		
28 **Chekhov: Plays**	Methuen 1988	**B**
(includes nos 15, 19, 24 and 27)		
29 **The Sneeze** (play)	Methuen 1989	**B**
(adaptation from Chekhov)	French US 1989	**B**
30 **First and Last** (play)	Methuen 1989	**B**
31 **Exchange** (play)	Methuen 1990	**B**
(adaptation from Trifonov)		
32 **The Trick of It** (novel)	Viking UK 1989	**B**
	Viking US 1989	**B**
33 **Look Look** (play)	Methuen 1990	**B**
34 **Listen to this: 21 Short Plays and Sketches**	Methuen 1991	**B**
35 **A Landing on the Sun** (novel)	Viking UK 1991	**B**
	Viking US 1992	**B**
36 **Now You Know** (novel)	Viking UK 1992	**B**

Frost, Robert   Born in San Francisco, 1874. Died 1963.

Frost is still the Grand Old Man of American poetry, and hugely respected and collected in that country. I am aware of few collectors in Britain – and indeed, it must be admitted that assembling Frost in any quantity here has never been an easy task, as so much was published only in America, and even then in limited and private press editions. In recognition of Frost's importance, however, there follows a listing of his commercially published works.

1 **A Boy's Will** (verse)	Holt 1913	**L**
2 **North of Boston** (verse)	Holt 1914	**K**
3 **Mountain Interval** (verse)	Holt 1916	**I**
4 **New Hampshire** (verse)	Holt 1923	**H**
5 **Selected Poems**	Heinemann 1923	**F**

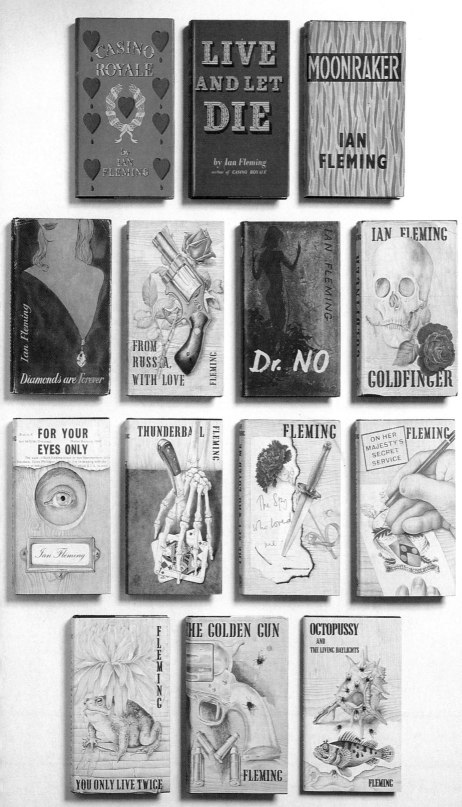

Ian Fleming's 'James Bond' books, complete

The three most famous fictional schoolboys. The *Jennings* is the first in the series, while the two *Bunters* are explained by the fact that one version was issued free as a Christmas gift by the Butlin's holiday camps, while the other is the standard edition

A selection of early Wodehouse school stories, two of them rewrites of the 1950s

Thrillers from Christie and Chandler, with artwork in sympathy

The complete sequence: Anthony Powell's
'A Dance to the Music of Time'. Designs by Broom-Lynne

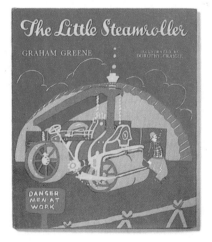

Graham Greene's first juvenile (published anonymously) and a couple of sequels

Ted Hughes's four early juveniles

The Alexandria Quartet, in the four separate first editions

6 **West-Running Brook** (verse)	Holt 1928	**F**
7 **Collected Poems**	Holt 1930	**E**
	Longman 1930	**E**
8 **The Lone Striker** (verse)	Holt 1933	**E**
9 **A Further Range** (verse)	Holt 1936	**E**
	Cape 1937	**D**
10 **From Snow to Snow** (verse)	Holt 1936	**D**
11 **A Witness Tree** (verse)	Holt 1942	**D**
	Cape 1943	**C**
12 **A Masque of Reason** (verse)	Holt 1945	**D**
	Cape 1948	**C**
13 **Steeple Bush** (verse)	Holt 1947	**D**
14 **A Masque of Mercy** (verse)	Holt 1947	**C**
15 **In the Clearing** (verse)	Holt (NY) 1962	**C**
	Holt (UK) 1962	**C**
16 **The Poetry of Robert Frost**	Holt 1969	**C**
	Cape 1971	**C**

In addition to 5, a further **Selected Poems** was published in England by Cape in 1936, with several introductory essays, including one by W.H. Auden (**E**).
Very many of the above were issued simultaneously with a limited, signed edition, but the prices here refer to the ordinary trade editions.

Gibbons, Stella   Born in London, 1902.

The author of more than thirty books, including one all-time classic. *Still* an underrated book – but not by collectors. There are many who would love to get their hands on a good copy – or even a not-so-good copy: it is extremely scarce.

Cold Comfort Farm (novel)	Longman 1932	**M**
	Longman (US) 1933	**J**

Ginsberg, Allen   Born in New Jersey, 1926.

Despite the resurgence of the Beats among the young, none of them is truly *collected* in this country, as they are in America. This is largely due to the old reason of availability, for during the sixties there were many more bookshops in London specializing in imported books (particularly American) than there are now. Ginsberg remains popular, though – the most popular of the Beats, probably – and there follows a selection of highlights.

1 **Howl and Other Poems**	City Lights 1956	**I**
Ginsberg's first book.		
2 **Kaddish and Other Poems**	City Lights 1961	**F**
3 **Penguin Modern Poets 5**	Penguin 1963	**B**
This book, shared with Gregory Corso and Lawrence Ferlinghetti, established the Beat Poets in this country.		

Golding, William   Born in Cornwall, 1911.

Sir William Golding is extremely highly regarded, and his early (and best) work continues to be rare and expensive. Anything published in the last twelve or so years is pretty affordable – but these, of course, are not *really* what people are after. The recent Sea Trilogy is worth having, though.

1 **Poems**	Macmillan 1934	**U**
Very, very scarce: one of these books that is worth what a collector is willing to pay!	Macmillan (NY) 1935	**R**
2 **Lord of the Flies** (novel)	Faber 1954	**R**
Not only Golding's highlight, but one of the key novels of recent years. It is a small volume, with a d/w bearing fine artwork and the magnificent Faber Albertus type, as do most of his works. It is very scarce. E.M. Forster singled it out for special attention on publication, and the second and third impressions came swiftly. By now, the editions are beyond count, and it has long been a 'set book' in schools. Very satisfying, then, to have the 1st and, although it is rising fast, any price is a good price, as a collection of modern fiction would never be complete without it.	Coward McCann 1955	**M**
3 **The Inheritors** (novel)	Faber 1955	**K**
Similar in format to 2. Quite scarce.	Harcout Brace 1962	**D**
4 **Pincher Martin** (novel)	Faber 1956	**I**
5 **The Two Deaths of Christopher Martin** (same as 4)	Harcourt Brace 1957	**F**
6 **The Brass Butterfly** (play)	Faber 1958	**L**
	NAL 1962	**D**
7 **Free Fall** (novel)	Faber 1959	**H**
	Harcourt Brace 1960	**D**
8 **The Spire** (novel)	Faber 1964	**F**
	Harcourt Brace 1965	**C**

9 **The Hot Gates** (occasional pieces)	Faber 1965	F
	Harcourt Brace 1965	D
10 **The Pyramid** (novel)	Faber 1967	E
	Harcourt Brace 1967	C
11 **The Scorpion God** (stories)	Faber 1971	C
One of the stories – *Envoy Extraordinary* –	Harcourt Brace 1972	C
was first published in **Sometime,**		
Never – Three Tales of		
Imagination Eyre & Spottiswoode		
1956; Ballantine 1956 (**K,I**)		
12 **Darkness Visible** (novel)	Faber 1979	C
	Farrar Straus 1979	C
13 **Rites of Passage** (novel)	Faber 1980	C
	Farrar Straus 1980	C
14 **A Moving Target** (essays)	Faber 1982	C
	Farrar Straus 1982	C
15 **Nobel Lecture**	Sixth Chamber Press	
500 copies in wraps (**D**) and 50	1983	
bound in goatskin, signed and		
slipcased (**M**).		
16 **The Paper Men** (novel)	Faber 1984	C
	Farrar Straus 1984	B
17 **An Egyptian Journal** (travel)	Faber 1985	C
	Farrar Straus 1985	C
18 **Close Quarters** (novel)	Faber 1987	C
	Farrar Straus 1987	B
19 **Fire Down Below** (novel)	Faber 1989	C
	Farrar Straus 1989	B
20 **To the Ends of the Earth:**	Faber 1991	B
A Sea Trilogy		
(contains nos 13, 18 and 19)		

Bibliography:
R.A. Gekoski and David Hughes **William Golding: A Bibliography**,
Deutsch 1991. Published at £75, de luxe edition £150.

Gordimer, Nadine   Born in Transvaal, 1923. South
African.

A highly respected author, whose early novels and short stories *are* sought
after by collectors, though I would not describe Gordimer as a hotly collected author – and I feel that if this situation was to change, it probably would
have done already. But I could be wrong.

1 **Face to Face** (stories)	Silver Leaf Books	J
	(Johannesburg) 1949	

2	**The Soft Voice of the Serpent and Other Stories**	Simon & Schuster 1952	**H**
		Gollancz 1953	**G**
3	**The Lying Days** (novel)	Gollancz 1953	**G**
		Simon & Schuster 1953	**D**
4	**Six Feet of the Country** (stories)	Gollancz 1956	**F**
		Simon & Schuster 1956	**D**
5	**A World of Strangers** (novel)	Gollancz 1958	**E**
		Simon & Schuster 1958	**D**
6	**Friday's Footprint and Other Stories**	Gollancz 1960	**D**
		Viking Press 1960	**C**
7	**Occasion for Loving** (novel)	Gollancz 1963	**D**
		Viking Press 1963	**C**
8	**Not for Publication and Other Stories**	Gollancz 1965	**D**
		Viking Press 1965	**C**
9	**The Late Bourgeois World** (novel)	Gollancz 1966	**C**
		Viking Press 1966	**B**
10	**A Guest of Honour** (novel)	Viking Press 1970	**C**
		Cape 1971	**C**
11	**Livingston's Companions** (stories)	Viking Press 1971	**C**
		Cape 1972	**C**
12	**The Conservationist** (novel)	Cape 1974	**C**
		Viking Press 1975	**C**
13	**Selected Stories**	Cape 1975	**C**
14	**Burger's Daughter** (novel)	Cape 1979	**C**
		Viking Press 1979	**B**
15	**A Soldier's Embrace** (stories)	Cape 1980	**C**
		Viking Press 1980	**B**
16	**July's People** (novel)	Cape 1981	**C**
		Viking Press 1981	**B**
17	**Something Out There** (novel)	Cape 1984	**C**
		Viking Press 1984	**B**
18	**Lifetimes: Under Apartheid** (non-fiction)	Cape 1986	**B**
		Knopf 1986	**B**
19	**A Sport of Nature** (novel)	Cape 1987	**B**
		Knopf 1987	**B**
20	**The Essential Gesture: Writing, Politics and Places** (edited by Stephen Clingman)	Cape 1988	**B**
		Knopf 1988	**B**
21	**My Son's Story** (novel)	Bloomsbury 1990	**B**
		Farrar Straus 1990	**B**
22	**Conversations with Nadine Gordimer**	University Press of Mississippi 1990	**B**
23	**Jump and Other Stories**	Bloomsbury 1991	**B**
		Farrar Straus 1991	**B**

Grahame, Kenneth Born in Edinburgh, 1859. Died 1932.

Grahame published few works, and three of the most notable – including the absolute highlight – are listed below.

1 **The Golden Age** (juvenile)	Lane 1895	**G**
	Stone & Kimball 1895	**E**
2 **Dream Days** (juvenile)	Lane 1898	**G**
	Lane (US) 1898	**E**
3 **The Wind in the Willows** (juvenile)	Methuen 1908	**L**
	Scribner 1908	**I**

Grass, Günter Born in Danzig, 1927.

I don't often list works that have first been published in a language other than English, but even in translation the author's first book is an important addition to a collection of modern fiction, and a desirable item.

The Tin Drum (novel)	Random House 1963	**H**
This was, of course, originally published	Secker & Warburg	**H**
in Germany as *Die Blechtrommel* in 1959.	1963	
The English language editions, however,		
are by no means common.		

Graves, Robert Born in London, 1895. Died 1985.

During his lifetime, Graves produced over one hundred and thirty books, less than half of them poetry. There must be collectors anxious to obtain every single item (there always are) but in my experience I find it is more usual for collectors to restrict themselves to just the areas of greatest interest to them – say, just the novels and maybe a *Collected Poems*, or so. Amongst the vast *œuvre*, there are a couple of highlights – very fine and very famous books (indeed, the first of these is *essential*) and these I find are usually the most wanted items. For the serious collector, however, I recommend: Fred H. Higgison *A Bibliography of the Works of Robert Graves* Vane 1966

1 **Good-bye to All That: An**	Cape 1929	**M**
Autobiography		(see below)
This is Graves' best-known work, though	Cape & Smith 1930	**G**
there is an important issue point which		
greatly affects the value. In the first issue		
(**M**) there is a long poem by Siegfried		
Sassoon, beginning on page 341. This is		
replaced in the second issue (**H**) by		
asterisks. The title pages are identical.		

Both, however, are very scarce in the
d/w, which is a black-and-white
montage of artwork and photographs

2 **I, Claudius** (novel)	Barker 1934	**H**
	Smith & Haas 1934	**E**
3 **Claudius the God** (novel)	Barker 1934	**G**
Sequel to 2.	Smith & Haas 1935	**D**

Although the prose works are the best
known, the poetry is very desirable –
particularly the very early books. Many
are called simply **Poems**, followed by
the relevant dates. The first was **Over
the Brazier** Poetry Bookshop 1916; the
seemingly definitive **Collected Poems
1975** was published by Cassell.

Gray, Alasdair Born in Glasgow, 1934.

A unique and very weird writer indeed – indescribable prose, so I won't even
try. Damn good, though. Here is Gray himself, then, to give you an insight
into the genesis of some of his work: '*Lanark* was planned as a whale, *1982
Janine* as an electric eel, *The Fall of Kelvin Walker* as a tasty sprat.' And there
we have it.

1	**The Comedy of the White Dog** (story)	Print Studio Press 1979	**H**
2	**Lanark** (novel)	Canongate 1981	**F**
		Harper 1981	**D**
3	**Unlikely Stories, Mostly** (stories)	Canongate 1983	**D**
		Penguin US 1984	**C**
4	**1982 Janine** (novel)	Cape 1984	**D**
		Viking 1984	**C**
5	**The Fall of Kelvin Walker** (novel)	Canongate 1985	**C**
		Braziller 1986	**C**
6	**Lean Tales** (stories)	Cape 1985	**C**
	With James Kelman & Agnes Owens.		
7	**Self-portrait** (autobiography)	Saltire Society 1988	**C**
8	**The Anthology of Prefaces** (prose)	Canongate 1989	**C**
9	**Old Negatives: Four Verse Sequences**	Cape 1989	**C**
10	**Something Leather** (novel)	Cape 1990	**C**
		Random House 1991	**C**
11	**McGrotty and Ludmilla** (novel)	Dog and Bone 1990	**C**
12	**Poor Things** (novel)	Bloomsbury 1992	**B**

Green, Henry
Born in England. 1905. Died 1973.
Pseudonym for Henry Vincent Yorke.

Very sought after by collectors, and very elusive – almost impossible in dust-wrapper. Dust-wrappers are particularly important here, actually, as because all the books came from The Hogarth Press, the artists employed were of the calibre you might expect: Vanessa Bell, Lynton Lamb, John Piper, etc.

1	**Blindness** (novel)	Dutton 1926	L
		Dent 1926	K
2	**Living** (novel)	Dutton 1929	K
		Dent 1929	J
3	**Party Going** (novel)	Hogarth Press 1939	K
		Longman (Toronto) 1939	I
4	**Pack My Bag** (autobiog.)	Hogarth Press 1940	J
		Macmillan (Toronto) 1940	H
5	**Caught** (novel)	Hogarth Press 1943	I
		Macmillan (Toronto) 1943	G
6	**Loving** (novel)	Hogarth Press 1945	H
		Macmillan (Toronto) 1945	E
7	**Back** (novel)	Hogarth Press 1946	G
		Oxford (Toronto) 1946	D
8	**Concluding** (novel)	Hogarth Press 1948	G
		Viking 1950	D
9	**Nothing** (novel)	Hogarth Press 1950	F
		Viking 1950	D
10	**Doting** (novel)	Hogarth Press 1952	F
		Viking 1952	D

Greene, Graham
Born in Hertfordshire, 1904. Died 1992.

Greene never did receive the Nobel prize or a knighthood – but everyone instinctively knew he was the best anyway. One cannot report a surge in collectors' interest since his death, because interest has been at fever pitch for decades, and can only become more intense.

1	**Babbling April: Poems**	Blackwell (Oxford)	S
	Of legendary scarcity, despite the fact that it appears at sales not irregularly.	1925	

2	**The Man Within** (novel)	Heinemann 1929	**R**
	Very scarce, particularly in d/w.	Doubleday 1929	**P**
3	**The Name of Action** (novel)	Heinemann 1930	**R**
	Same situation as 2.	Doubleday 1931	**P**
4	**Rumour at Nightfall** (novel)	Heinemann 1931	**R**
	Again, very scarce.	Doubleday 1932	**P**
5	**Stamboul Train** (novel)	Heinemann 1932	**I**

Classed by Greene as 'An entertainment', this was published in America as *Orient Express* by Doubleday in 1933, anticipating Agatha Christie's *Murder* ... by just one year. This is the easiest of the early Greenes, though difficult in d/w and correspondingly more expensive than the grade given.

6	**It's a Battlefield** (novel)	Heinemann 1934	**M**
	Again, scarce and more expensive in d/w.	Doubleday 1934	**J**
7	**England Made Me** (novel)	Heinemann 1935	**Q**
	Scarce.	Doubleday 1935	**O**
8	**The Basement Room** (stories)	Cresset Press 1935	**P**
	Very scarce.		
9	**A Gun for Sale** (novel)	Heinemann 1936	**N**
	This Gun for Hire	Doubleday 1936	**L**
	An entertainment.		
10	**Journey Without Maps** (travel)	Heinemann 1936	**N**
		Doubleday 1936	**J**
11	**Brighton Rock** (novel)	Heinemann 1938	**L**
		Viking 1938	**J**

Greene's highlight. Not only scarce in d/w, this, but legendary. I know several ardent Greene collectors who despair of ever seeing it, let alone acquiring it. If one came up in d/w, the price could be **T**. In America only it was classed as 'An entertainment'.

12	**The Confidential Agent** (novel)	Heinemann 1939	**L**
	Scarce.	Viking 1939	**J**
13	**Twenty-Four Stories**	Cresset Press 1939	**I**
	With James Laver and Sylvia Townsend Warner. An unusual item.		
14	**The Lawless Roads** (travel)	Longman 1939	**Q**
	Another Mexico	Viking 1939	**O**
15	**The Power and the Glory** (novel)	Heinemann 1940	**S**
	The Labyrinthine Ways	Viking 1940	**Q**
16	**British Dramatists** (non-fiction)	Collins 1942	**D**

One of the Britain in Pictures series. Not published separately in America, but included in *The Romance of English Literature* Hastings House 1944.

17 **The Ministry of Fear** (novel)	Heinemann 1943	**I**
	Viking 1943	**G**
18 **The Little Train** (juvenile)	Eyre & Spottiswoode	**P**
Published anonymously while Greene	1946	
was a director at E. & S. Scarce.	Lothrop 1958	**F**
19 **Nineteen Stories**	Heinemann 1947	**G**
Heinemann published a supplemented	Viking 1949	**C**
edition as **Twenty-One Stories** in		
1954 (**C**).		
20 **The Heart of the Matter** (novel)	Heinemann 1948	**E**
One of the easy Greenes, but beware	Viking 1948	**C**
the Book Society edition – these are		
very common (**B**).		
21 **Why Do I Write?: An Exchange of**	Marshall 1948	**E**
Views Between Elizabeth Bowen,		
Graham Greene, and V.S. Pritchett		
22 **The Little Fire Engine** (juvenile)	Parrish 1950	**N**
Scarce.		
The Little Red Fire Engine	Lothrop 1952	**K**
23 **The Third Man** (novel)	Viking Press 1950	**K**
24 **The Third Man** and **The Fallen Idol**	Heinemann 1950	**H**
(novels)		
25 **The End of the Affair** (novel)	Heinemann 1951	**F**
	Viking 1951	**D**
26 **The Lost Childhood**	Eyre & Spottiswoode	**E**
(essays)	1951	
	Viking 1952	**D**
27 **The Little Horse Bus** (juvenile)	Parrish 1952	**M**
Scarce.	Lothrop 1954	**I**
28 **The Little Steam Roller** (juvenile)	Parrish 1953	**M**
Scarce.	Lothrop 1955	**I**
29 **The Living Room** (play)	Heinemann 1953	**I**
His first play, and not common.	Viking 1954	**F**
30 **Loser Takes All** (novel)	Heinemann 1955	**F**
	Viking Press 1957	**C**
31 **The Quiet American** (novel)	Heinemann 1955	**D**
	Viking 1956	**C**
32 **The Potting Shed** (play)	Viking 1957	**F**
	Heinemann 1958	**F**
33 **Our Man in Havana**	Heinemann 1958	**D**
(novel)	Viking 1958	**C**
An entertainment.		
34 **The Complaisant Lover**	Heinemann 1959	**E**
(play)	Viking 1961	**C**
35 **In Search of a Character: Two**	Bodley Head 1961	**E**
African Journals	Viking 1961	**D**

One of the journals, *Convoy to West Africa*, was first published in Geoffrey Grigson (ed.) *The Mint* Routledge 1946

36	**A Burnt-Out Case** (novel)	Heinemann 1961	**D**
		Viking Press 1961	**C**
37	**A Sense of Reality** (stories)	Bodley Head 1963	**E**
		Viking 1963	**C**
38	**Carving a Statue** (play)	Bodley Head 1964	**E**
39	**The Comedians** (novel)	Bodley Head 1966	**D**
		Viking 1966	**C**
40	**May We Borrow Your Husband?** (stories)	Bodley Head 1967	**C**
		Viking 1967	**C**

There is also a signed, limited British Edition (**I**).

41	**The Third Man: A Film** (screenplay)	Lorrimer 1969	**D**

With Carol Reed.

42	**Collected Essays**	Bodley Head 1969	**D**
		Viking 1969	**C**
43	**Travels with My Aunt** (novel)	Bodley Head 1969	**C**
		Viking 1970	**C**
44	**A Sort of Life** (autobiog.)	Bodley Head 1971	**C**
		Simon & Schuster 1971	**C**
45	**The Pleasure Dome: The Collected Film Criticism 1935–40**	Secker & Warburg 1972	**D**
		Simon & Schuster 1972	**C**
46	**The Collected Stories**	Bodley Head/ Heinemann 1972	**C**
		Viking 1973	**C**
47	**The Honorary Consul** (novel)	Bodley Head 1973	**C**
		Viking 1973	**C**
48	**The Portable Graham Greene**	Viking 1973	**C**
49	**Lord Rochester's Monkey** (biog.)	Bodley Head 1974	**C**
		Viking 1974	**C**
50	**Shades of Greene** (stories)	Bodley Head/ Heinemann 1975	**B**
51	**The Return of A.J. Raffles** (play)	Bodley Head 1975	**D**
		Simon & Schuster 1978	**C**

250 copies of the first edition were specially bound in boards and signed by the author. Only numbers 81–250 were for sale, at £25 (**I**).

52	**The Human Factor** (novel)	Bodley Head 1978	**C**
		Simon & Schuster 1978	**C**
53	**Dr Fischer of Geneva or The Bomb Party** (novel)	Bodley Head 1980	**C**
		Simon & Schuster 1980	**C**
54	**Ways of Escape** (autobiog.)	Lester & Orpen Dennys (Canada) 1980	**G**
		Bodley Head 1980	**C**

	Simon & Schuster 1981	C
55 **The Great Jowett** (play)	Bodley Head 1981	I

Published *only* as a limited, signed edition of 500.

56 **Monsignor Quixote** (novel) Lester & Orpen
  Dennys (Canada) 1982 **H**
  Bodley Head 1982 **C**
  Simon & Schuster 1982 **C**

57 **J'Accuse: The Darker Side of Nice** Bodley Head 1982 **C**
  (non-fiction) Simon & Schuster 1982 **C**
Greene's rather brave exposé of corruption in Nice, published in wrappers with both an English and a French text.

58 **The Other Man: Conversations** Bodley Head 1983 **C**
  with Graham Greene Simon & Schuster 1983 **C**
  With Marie-Françoise Allain. **C**

59 **For Whom the Bell Chimes** and **Yes** Bodley Head 1983 **I**
  and No (plays)
Again issued solely as a limited, signed edition, the limitation this time having risen to 775 copies.

60 **Getting to Know the General** Bodley Head 1984 **C**
  (non-fiction) Simon & Schuster 1984 **C**

61 **The Tenth Man** (novel) Bodley Head/Blond **C**
  1985
  Simon & Schuster 1985 **C**

62 **The Captain and the Enemy** (novel) Reinhardt 1988 **C**
  Viking 1988 **C**

63 **Why the Epigraph?** (prose) Nonesuch 1989 **H**
  (limited to 1000 signed copies, published at £30)

64 **Yours, etc: Letters to the Press** Reinhardt 1989 **C**
  Viking 1990 **C**

65 **The Last Word and Other Stories** Reinhardt 1990 **C**
  Viking 1991 **C**

66 **Reflections 1923–1988** (prose) Reinhardt 1990 **C**
  Viking 1990 **C**

67 **A World of My Own** (dreams) Reinhardt 1992 **C**
Greene has edited the following:

The Old School: Essays by Divers Cape 1934 **I**
Hands Smith 1934 **G**
Greene also has an essay in this. Scarce.

The Spy's Bedside Book Hart-Davis 1957 **H**
With Hugh Greene.

An Impossible Woman: The Bodley Head 1975 **C**
Memories of Dottoressa Moor of Viking Press 1976 **C**
Capri

Greenwood

Also of interest:
Graham Greene Country (Pavilion 1986) Paintings by Paul Hogarth of scenes mentioned in the novels, with comments by Greene

It should be noted that from the nineteen-sixties onwards, Greene has quite regularly published maddening little bookettes, in very limited quantities, apparently for the purpose of giving away, selling at a high price, or driving collectors further round the bend. For details consult:

R.A. Woobe **Graham Greene: A Bibliography and Guide to Research** (Garland, US, 1980)
A.F. Cassis **Graham Greene: An Annotated Bibliography** (1981)

Greenwood, Walter   Born in Lancashire, 1903. Died 1974.

Author of several books, though notable for one in particular – destined for revival, one would think, in these dark days of rife unemployment. Love is, after all, free. It was declared so in the sixties, and will remain so until the Government subjects it to VAT.

Love on the Dole	Cape 1933	**I**
It is scarce.	Doubleday 1934	**G**

Grossmith, George and Weedon
George, 1847–1912. Weedon, 1854–1919.

They wrote only one book, and I *know* it's not a twentieth-century work, but it's going in anyway – for its influence on modern journalism, if you like; but really because it's so funny, and it has never been bettered.

The Diary of a Nobody	Arrowsmith 1892	**M**

Originally a series of contributions to *Punch*, and then enlarged and developed for this book. Illustrated by Weedon, and published in Arrowsmith's Three-and-sixpenny series.

Biography:
Tony Joseph **George Grossmith** published by the author, and printed by none other than J.W. Arrowsmith of Bristol (1982).

Gunn, Thom   Born in Kent, 1929.

Not an easy poet to collect (a lot of largely American Private Press stuff) and few of the mainstream early Faber volumes tend to come up. Worthwhile, though – but it must be admitted that Gunn does not seem to command the position that he did in the sixties, when he was seen to be more or less on a par with Ted Hughes – indeed, at times they appeared almost to be partners.

1 **Poetry from Cambridge 1951–1952**   Fortune Press 1952   **I**
An anthology introduced by Gunn, and containing four of his poems.

2 **The Fantasy Poets No. 16**   Fantasy Press 1953   **J**
There were about 300 copies of this pamphlet.

3 **Fighting Terms** (verse)   Fantasy Press 1954   **J**
Again, around 300 copies. The first   Hawk's Well Press   **F**
state contains a printing error on   1958
page 38, where the last letter of the word 'thought' is omitted.

4 **The Sense of Movement** (verse)   Faber 1957   **G**
   University of
   Chicago Press 1959   **D**

5 **My Sad Captains** (verse)   Faber 1961   **F**
   University of
   Chicago Press 1961   **C**

6 **Selected Poems** (verse)   Faber 1962   **D**
With Ted Hughes.

7 **A Geography** (verse)   Stone Wall Press   **G**
Limitation of 220 copies, but   (Iowa) 1966
apparently only 216 were printed.

8 **Positives** (verse)   Faber 1966   **E**
Large format, illustrated with   University of
photographs by Ander Gunn,   Chicago Press 1967   **D**
Thom's brother.

9 **Touch** (verse)   Faber 1967   **F**
   University of
   Chicago Press 1968   **D**

10 **The Garden of the Gods** (verse)   Pym-Randall 1968   **H**
A limitation of 200 numbered, 26 lettered. A first impression was destroyed (save 10 copies) as production was deemed to be inadequate.

11 **The Explorers** (verse)   Gilbertson 1969   **K**
Only 6 copies of this were published (at £60 each), and bound to order. Later issues do not add very many to the total: 'deluxe issue' (10 copies), 'special issue' (20 copies) and 'ordinary issue' (64 copies).

12 **The Fair in the Woods** (verse) Single-sheet folded broadside. 500 printed.	Sycamore Press 1969	**C**
13 **Poems 1950–1966: A Selection**	Faber 1969	**C**
14 **Sunlight** (verse) Only 150 numbered copies for sale.	Albondocani Press 1969	**C**
15 **Moly** (verse)	Faber 1971	**E**
	Farrar Straus 1973	**C**
16 **Last Days at Teddington** (verse) Single-sheet broadside. 1000 copies.	John Roberts Press 1971	**C**
17 **Poem After Chaucer** Christmas greeting from the publisher. 320 printed, none for sale.	Albondocani Press 1971	**F**
18 **The Spell** (verse) Single-sheet broadside (500 copies) published at 20p.	Steane 1973	**C**
19 **Songbook** (verse) 230 copies, 200 for sale.	Albondocani Press 1973	**F**
20 **To the Air** (verse)	Godine 1974	**E**
21 **Mandrakes** (verse) 150 copies, numbered and signed.	Rainbow Press 1974	**I**
22 **Jack Straw's Castle** (verse) 300 paperbound copies for sale. 100 hardbound (signed) copies were on sale the following year (**H**).	Hallman 1975	**F**
23 **The Missed Beat** (verse) 50 copies. An English edition of 'about 70 copies' was published in the same year by the Gruffyground Press (**E**).	Janus Press 1976	**G**
24 **Jack Straw's Castle and Other** **Poems** Of the English edition. 750 hardback (**D**) and 4000 paper (**B**).	Faber 1976 Farrar Straus 1976	**D** **C**
25 **A Crab** (verse) A pirated, freely distributed poem. 30 copies.	The Pirates 1978	**E**
26 **Games of Chance** (verse)	Abattoir 1979	**D**
27 **Selected Poems 1950–1975**	Faber 1979	**C**
	Farrar Straus 1979	**C**
28 **The Passages of Joy** (verse)	Faber 1982	**C**
	Farrar Straus 1982	**C**
29 **Sidewalks** (verse)	Albondocani Press US 1985	**D**
30 **Lament** (verse)	Doe Press US 1985	**D**
31 **The Hurtless Trees** (verse)	Privately Printed 1986	**E**
32 **Night Sweats** (verse)	Barth US 1987	**C**
33 **Undesirables** (verse)	Pig Press UK 1988	**C**

34 **At the Barriers** (verse)	NADJA 1989	**C**
35 **Death's Door** (verse)	Red Hydra 1989	**C**
36 **The Man with Night Sweats** (verse)	Faber 1992	**C**
Gunn has edited the following:		
Five American Poets	Faber 1963	**E**
With Ted Hughes.		
Selected Poems of Fulke Greville	Faber 1968	**D**
	University of	
	Chicago Press 1968	**C**
Ben Jonson	Penguin 1974	**B**

An excellent bibliography exists: Jack W.C. Hagstrom and George Bixby **Thom Gunn: A Bibliography 1940–1978** Rota 1979. This contains an introductory biographical essay by Thom Gunn.

Hamilton, Patrick   Born in Sussex, 1904. Died 1962.

A brilliant and rather overlooked writer whom I myself have only quite recently discovered – much to my joy. Very English, very understated, extraordinarily observant, wickedly and snobbishly funny and really rather mesmeric. *Hangover Square* is the acknowledged classic, but my own favourites are the novels that make up the *Gorse* trilogy: Ralph Gorse really is the most unputdownable bounder, while the superb second volume – *Mr Stimpson and Mr Gorse* – offers in addition delightful cameos on such as the compulsive idiocies of prize crossword solving and the facility of the amateur poet.

1 **Monday Morning** (novel)	Constable 1925	**I**
	Houghton Mifflin 1925	**G**
2 **Craven House** (novel)	Constable 1926	**H**
	Houghton Mifflin 1927	**F**
3 **Twopence Coloured** (novel)	Constable 1928	**G**
	Houghton Mifflin 1928	**E**
4 **The Midnight Bell: A Love Story** (novel)	Constable, 1929	**G**
	Little, Brown 1930	**D**
5 **Rope** (play)	Smith US 1930	**H**
6 **The Siege of Pleasure** (novel)	Constable 1932	**F**
	Little, Brown 1932	**D**
7 **The Plains of Cement** (novel)	Constable 1934	**F**
	Little, Brown 1935	**D**
8 **Twenty Thousand Streets Under The Sky: A London Trilogy** (contains nos 4, 6 and 7)	Constable 1935	**D**
9 **Impromptu in Moribundia** (novel)	Constable 1939	**E**
10 **Money with Menaces** and **To the Public Danger: Two Radio Plays**	Constable 1939	**D**
	Constable 1939	**D**

11 **Hangover Square; or, The Man with Two Minds: A Story of Darkest Earl's Court in the Year 1939** (novel)	Constable 1941 Random House 1942	J G
12 **This is Impossible** (play)	French 1942	C
13 **Gas Light: A Victorian Thriller** (play)	French 1942	C
14 **The Duke in Darkness** (play)	Constable 1943	C
15 **The Slaves of Solitude** (novel)	Constable 1947	C
16 **Riverside** (same as 15)	Random House 1947	C
17 **The West Pier** (novel)	Constable 1951 Doubleday 1952	E C
18 **Mr. Stimpson and Mr. Gorse** (novel)	Constable 1953	F
19 **The Man Upstairs** (play)	Constable 1954	C
20 **Unknown Assailant** (novel) (nos 17, 18, and 20 form *The Gorse Trilogy*)	Constable 1955	D
21 **The Gorse Trilogy**	Penguin 1992	B

Hammett, Dashiell   Born in Maryland, 1894. Died 1961.

Along with Chandler, classic American tough-guy stuff – for men who (à la Mailer) don't dance, and wouldn't be seen dead with a quiche. The classic remains *The Maltese Falcon*, the John Huston debut film always memorable, and ever incomprehensible; not that it matters.

1 **Red Harvest** (novel)	Knopf 1929 Cassell 1929	S Q
2 **The Dain Curse** (novel)	Knopf 1929 Cassell 1929	Q O
3 **The Maltese Falcon** (novel) The highlight, this.	Knopf 1930 Cassell 1930	T R
4 **The Glass Key** (novel)	Knopf 1931 Cassell 1931	O L
5 **The Thin Man** (novel)	Knopf 1934 Barker 1934	S Q
6 **$106,000 Blood Money** (novel) This was republished the same year by World as *Blood Money*, and reissued in 1948 by Spivak as *The Big Knock-over.*	Spivak (NY) 1943	M
7 **The Adventures of Sam Spade** (stories) Ed. Ellery Queen. This was reissued in 1949 as *They Can Only Hang You Once.*	Spivak 1944	M
8 **The Continental Op** (stories) Ed. Ellery Queen.	Spivak 1945	I

9 **The Return of the Continental Op** (stories) Ed. Ellery Queen.	Spivak 1945	**H**
10 **Hammett Homicides** (stories) Ed. Ellery Queen.	Spivak 1946	**I**
11 **Dead Yellow Women** (stories) Ed. Ellery Queen.	Spivak 1947	**H**
12 **Nightmare Town** (stories) Ed. Ellery Queen.	Spivak 1948	**H**
13 **The Creeping Siamese** (stories) Ed. Ellery Queen.	Spivak 1950	**H**
14 **Women in the Dark** (stories) Ed. Ellery Queen.	Spivak 1951	**H**
15 **A Man Named Thin and Other Stories** Ed. Ellery Queen.	Ferman (NY) 1952	**H**
16 **The Big Knockover: Selected Stories and Short Novels** Ed. Lillian Hellman.	Random House 1966	**D**
17 **The Hammett Story Omnibus** (same as 16)	Cassell 1966	**C**

Bibliography:
Richard Layman **Dashiell Hammett: A Descriptive Bibliography** University of Pittsburgh Press 1979

Biography:
Diane Johnson **The Life of Dashiell Hammett** Chatto & Windus 1984

Harris, Thomas   Born in Missouri, 1940. American.

This very occasional author became prominent as a result of the ghoulish and terrifying *The Silence of the Lambs* – although it is true to say that almost no-one had heard of him or it until the film. Destined to be a cult, this man; there follows the works to date.

1 **Black Sunday** (novel)	Putnam 1975	**E**
	Hodder & Stoughton 1975	**D**
2 **Red Dragon** (novel) (this was republished as *Manhunter* by Bantam US in 1986)	Putnam 1981 Bodley Head 1982	**D** **C**
3 **The Silence of the Lambs** (novel)	St Martin's Press 1988 Heinemann 1989	**H** **G**
4 **Black Sunday R/I** (novel)	Hodder & Stoughton 1992	**B**

Hartley, L.P. Born in Cambridgeshire, 1895. Died 1972.

Never a 'popular' success with readers or collectors, Hartley is still very much followed by a select band who are very determined to complete their collections. It is not easy – all the books that come up tend to be post-1950.

1	**Night Fears and Other Stories**	Putnam (UK) 1924	**L**
2	**Simonetta Perkins** (novel)	Putnam 1925	**K**
		Putnam (US) 1925	**I**
3	**The Killing Bottle** (stories)	Putnam 1932	**I**
4	**The Shrimp and the Anemone** (novel)	Putnam 1944	**I**
5	**The West Window** (same as 4)	Doubleday (NY) 1945	**F**
6	**The Sixth Heaven** (novel)	Putnam 1946	**F**
		Doubleday 1947	**D**
7	**Eustace and Hilda** (novel)	Putnam 1947	**E**
	4, 6 and 7 form a trilogy.		
8	**The Travelling Grave** (stories)	Arkham House (US) 1948	**E**
		Barrie 1951	**D**
9	**The Boat** (novel)	Putnam 1950	**D**
		Doubleday 1950	**C**
10	**My Fellow Devils** (novel)	Barrie 1951	**C**
11	**The Go-Between** (novel)	Hamilton 1953	**D**
		Knopf 1954	**C**
12	**A White Wand and Other Stories**	Hamilton 1954	**C**
13	**A Perfect Woman** (novel)	Hamilton 1955	**C**
		Knopf 1956	**B**
14	**The Hireling** (novel)	Hamilton 1957	**C**
		Rinehart 1958	**B**
15	**Facial Justice** (novel)	Hamilton 1960	**C**
		Doubleday 1961	**B**
16	**Two for the River** (stories)	Hamilton 1961	**C**
17	**The Brickfield** (novel)	Hamilton 1964	**C**
18	**The Betrayal** (novel)	Hamilton 1966	**C**
19	**Poor Clare** (novel)	Hamilton 1968	**C**
20	**The Collected Stories**	Hamilton 1968	**C**
		Horizon Press 1969	**B**
21	**The Love-Adept** (novel)	Hamilton 1969	**B**
22	**My Sister's Keeper** (novel)	Hamilton 1970	**B**
23	**The Harness Room** (novel)	Hamilton 1971	**B**
24	**Mrs Carteret Receives** (stories)	Hamilton 1971	**B**
25	**The Will and the Way** (novel)	Hamilton 1973	**B**

Heaney, Seamus   Born in County Derry, 1939.

Still one of the most popular poets of all, among readers and collectors – and one who can guarantee a packed auditorium at a reading. Maybe it is because there are very few *rising* young poets that one can put a name to, that such as Heaney and Ted Hughes are increasingly revered and collected. Certainly the prices continue to go up and up – a smugly pleasant thought if you've got the highlights, and again time to discover an overlooked genius if you haven't.

1 **Eleven Poems**	Festival (Belfast) 1965	**O**
2 **Death of a Naturalist** (verse)	Faber 1966	**L**
	OUP (US) 1966	**G**
3 **A Lough Neagh Sequence**	Phoenix Pamphlet Poets Press 1969	**J**
4 **Door into the Dark** (verse)	Faber 1969	**J**
	OUP (US) 1969	**F**
5 **Night Drive: Poems** Limited to 100 copies, signed, 25 of which contain a poem in the author's hand (**N**).	Gilbertson (Crediton) 1970	**J**
6 **Boy Driving His Father to Confession** Limited to 150 numbered copies, 50 signed (**M**).	Sceptre Press 1970	**K**
7 **Wintering Out** (verse)	Faver 1972	**H**
	OUP (US) 1973	**D**
8 **The Fire i' the Flint: Reflections on the Poetry of Gerard Manley Hopkins** (lecture)	OUP (US) 1975	**E**
9 **North** (verse)	Faber 1975	**F**
	OUP (US) 1976	**C**
10 **Bog Poems**	Rainbow Press 1975	**M**
11 **Stations** (verse)	Ulsterman (Belfast) 1975	**G**
12 **Robert Lowell: A Memorial Lecture and an Eulogy**	Privately printed 1978	**J**
13 **The Makings of Music: Reflections on the Poetry of Wordsworth and Yeats** (lecture)	University of Liverpool 1978	**F**
14 **Field Work** (verse)	Faber 1979	**F**
	Farrar Straus 1979	**D**
15 **Ugolino** (verse)	Carpenter, Dublin 1979	**K**
16 **Selected Poems 1965–1975**	Faber 1980	**D**
17 **Preoccupations: Selected Prose 1968–1978**	Faber 1980	**D**

18 **The Rattle-Bag** (anthol.) Ed. with Ted Hughes.	Faber 1982	D
19 **An Open Letter** (verse)	Field Day, Derry 1983	F
20 **Sweeney Astray** (verse)	Field Day, Derry 1983	F
21 **Among the Schoolchildren** (lecture)	Queen's University, Belfast 1983	E
22 **Sweeney Astray** (verse) (an augmented edition of 20)	Faber 1984 Farrar Straus 1984	D C
23 **Station Island** (verse)	Faber 1984 Farrar Straus 1984	D C
24 **Verses for a Fordham Commencement** 200 numbered copies, signed (**J**). 26 lettered copies on hand-made paper, signed (**O**).	Nadja, New York 1984	D
25 **Place and Displacement** (lecture)	Dove Cottage 1984	D
26 **Hailstones** (verse) 250 copies signed (**I**). 500 copies unsigned (**E**).	Gallery Press, Dublin 1984	
27 **The Haw Lantern** (verse)	Faber 1987 Farrar Straus 1987	C C
28 **The Government of the Tongue** (prose)	Faber 1988 Farrar Straus 1988	C C
29 **New Selected Poems 1966–87**	Faber 1990 Farrar Straus 1990	C C
30 **The Place of Waiting** (verse)	Scholars Press US 1990	C
31 **The Tree Clock** (verse)	Faber 1990	C
32 **Sweeney's Flight** (verse)	Faber 1992 Farrar Straus 1992	C C

Heller, Joseph   Born in Brooklyn, 1923.

As may be seen from the following list, Heller has published very little and it's all fairly available, and fairly cheap – all, that is, except one: *Catch-22*. Which tends to be the only one people want: Catch-22.

1 **Catch-22** (novel)	Simon & Schuster 1961 Cape 1962	K I
2 **We Bombed in New Haven** (play)	Knopf 1968 Cape 1969	C C
3 **Catch-22** (play)	French (NY) 1971	C
4 **Clevinger's Trial** (play)	French (NY) 1973	B
5 **Something Happened** (novel)	Knopf 1974 Cape 1974	C C
6 **Good as Gold** (novel)	Simon & Schuster 1979 Cape 1979	C C

7 **God Knows** (novel)	Knopf 1984	C
	Cape 1984	C
8 **No Laughing Matter** (non-fiction)	Knopf 1986	C
With Speed Vogel.	Cape 1986	B
9 **Picture This** (novel)	Putnam 1988	C
	Macmillan 1988	C

Hemingway, Ernest   Born in Illinois, 1899. Died 1961.

England has always had a rather love-hate relationship with Hemingway – collectors have, anyway. His importance is recognized – some even find him readable – but there is a sort of a feeling that one would not care to make him too prominent a feature of one's collection; we maybe feel that all that macho and all that gore are not quite *nice*. Americans, of course, have no such mealy-mouthed doubts – they deify him. It is true, of course, that Hemingway is not easy to collect in this country, and nor are the early items by any means cheap. *The Old Man and the Sea* (an atypical work) seems the favourite in this country, and it is not too hard to find. If, however, a *serious* collection of Hemingway is contemplated, one ought to be forewarned that American first editions are very pricey – and the prices asked in America! Well, you'd have to be American to pay them.

1 **Three Stories and Ten Poems**	Privately printed (Paris 1923)	U
2 **In Our Time** (stories)	Boni & Liveright 1924	Q
	Cape 1924	N
3 **The Torrents of Spring** (novel)	Scribner 1926	P
4 **The Sun Also Rises** (novel)	Scribner 1926	Q
5 **Fiesta** (same as 4)	Cape 1927	N
6 **Men Without Women** (stories)	Scribner 1927	L
	Cape 1927	J
7 **A Farewell to Arms** (novel)	Scribner 1929	L
	Cape 1929	F
8 **Death in the Afternoon** (non-fiction)	Scribner 1932	N
	Cape 1932	J
9 **Winner Take Nothing** (stories)	Scribner 1933	J
	Cape 1934	H
10 **Green Hills of Africa** (non-fiction)	Scribner 1935	L
	Cape 1936	H
11 **To Have and Have Not** (novel)	Scribner 1937	L
	Cape 1937	H
12 **The Fifth Column and the First Forty-Nine Stories** (play and stories)	Scribner 1938	H
	Cape 1941	E
13 **For Whom the Bell Tolls** (novel)	Scribner 1940	J
	Cape 1941	D
14 **Across the River and into the Trees** (novel)	Cape 1950	E
	Scribner 1950	E

15	**The Old Man and the Sea** (novel)	Scribner 1952	**D**
		Cape 1952	**C**
16	**A Moveable Feast** (non-fiction)	Scribner 1964	**D**
		Cape 1964	**C**
17	**Islands in the Stream** (novel)	Scribner 1970	**C**
		Collins 1970	**C**
18	**Selected Letters 1916–1961**	Granada 1981	**C**
		UK & US	
19	**The Dangerous Summer** (non-fiction)	Hamilton 1985	**C**
		Scribner 1985	**C**

In 1947 Cape published **The Essential Hemingway**, which contains extracts from his works.

Highsmith, Patricia   Born in Fort Worth, Texas, 1921.

It is not hard to see why Highsmith continues to be the queen of strange and weird and downright *disturbing* 'psychological' crime. She's been doing it for so long, for a start – and so well – but when you read an interview with her, or see a photograph of her in her dark, rather depressing room in Switzerland, it is quite impossible to imagine her producing any *other* sort of book. Apparently, she enjoys carpentry; makes her own furniture. I really do not know what to say about this.

1	**Strangers on a Train** (novel)	Harper 1950	**L**
		Cresset Press 1951	**K**
2	**The Price of Salt** (novel) (pseud. Claire Morgan)	Coward McCann (NY) 1952	**K**
3	**The Blunderer** (novel)	Coward McCann 1954	**J**
		Cresset Press 1956	**H**
4	**The Talented Mr Ripley** (novel)	Coward McCann 1955	**J**
		Cresset Press 1957	**I**
5	**Deep Water** (novel)	Harper 1957	**I**
		Heinemann 1958	**H**
6	**A Game for the Living** (novel)	Harper 1958	**H**
		Heinemann 1959	**F**
7	**Miranda the Panda is on the Verandah** (juvenile) With Doris Sanders.	Coward McCann 1958	**G**
8	**This Sweet Sickness** (novel)	Harper 1960	**G**
		Heinemann 1961	**E**
9	**The Cry of the Owl** (novel)	Harper 1962	**G**
		Heinemann 1963	**E**
10	**The Two Faces of January** (novel)	Doubleday 1964	**F**
		Heinemann 1964	**D**

11	**The Glass Cell** (novel)	Doubleday 1964	**F**
		Heinemann 1965	**D**
12	**The Story-Teller** (novel)	Doubleday 1965	**F**
13	**A Suspension of Mercy** (same as 12)	Heinemann 1965	**E**
14	**Plotting and Writing Suspense Fiction**	Writer (Boston) 1966	**D**
15	**Those Who Walk Away** (novel)	Doubleday 1967	**E**
		Heinemann 1967	**D**
16	**The Tremor of Forgery** (novel)	Doubleday 1969	**D**
		Heinemann 1969	**C**
17	**Ripley Under Ground** (novel)	Doubleday 1970	**F**
		Heinemann 1971	**E**
18	**The Snail-Watchers** (stories)	Doubleday 1970	**D**
19	**Eleven** (same as 18)	Heinemann 1970	**C**
20	**A Dog's Ransom** (novel)	Knopf 1972	**C**
		Heinemann 1972	**C**
21	**Ripley's Game** (novel)	Knopf 1974	**D**
		Heinemann 1974	**C**
22	**The Animal Lover's Book of Beastly Murder** (stories)	Heineman 1975	**C**
23	**Edith's Diary** (novel)	Heinemann 1977	**C**
24	**Little Tales of Misogyny** (stories) First published in German, Zürich 1974 (**D**).	Heinemann 1977	**C**
25	**Slowly, Slowly in the Wind** (stories)	Heinemann 1979	**C**
26	**The Boy Who Followed Ripley** (novel)	Heinemann 1980	**C**
		Lippincott 1980	**C**
27	**The Black House** (novel)	Heinemann 1981	**C**
28	**The People Who Knock on the Door** (novel)	Heinemann 1983	**C**
		Mysterious Press 1985	**C**
29	**Mermaids on the Golf Course** (stories)	Heinemann 1985	**C**
30	**Found in the Street** (novel)	Heinemann 1986	**B**
31	**Tales of Natural and Unnatural Catastrophes** (stories)	Bloomsbury 1987	**B**
		Atlantic Monthly Press 1989	**B**
32	**Carol** (novel)	Bloomsbury 1990	**B**
33	**Ripley Under Water** (novel)	Bloomsbury 1991	**B**
		Knopf 1992	**B**

Hill, Susan   Born in Yorkshire, 1942.

Once one of the most admired novelists of her generation, Hill now seems content to pour forth a pretty constant stream of children's books and illustrated books and picture books – pretty non-books, generally. True she finally published another two novels, but they failed to set the literary world alight. Anyway, there have been about a dozen of these oddities during the past five years, as against the one novel in a decade: in view of this, I limit the following to the fiction only.

1 **The Enclosure** (novel)	Hutchinson 1961	**I**
2 **Do Me a Favour** (novel)	Hutchinson 1963	**H**
3 **Gentlemen and Ladies** (novel)	Hamilton 1968	**G**
	Walker 1969	**D**
4 **A Change for the Better** (novel)	Hamilton 1969	**F**
5 **I'm the King of the Castle** (novel)	Hamilton 1970	**E**
	Saturday Review Press 1970	**C**
6 **Strange Meeting** (novel)	Hamilton 1971	**D**
	Saturday Review Press 1972	**C**
7 **The Albatross and Other Stories**	Hamilton 1971	**D**
8 **The Bird of Night** (novel)	Hamilton 1972	**D**
	Saturday Review Press 1972	**C**
9 **The Custodian** (story)	Covent Garden Press 1972	**D**
10 **A Bit of Singing and Dancing** (stories)	Hamilton 1973	**D**
11 **In the Springtime of the Year** (novel)	Hamilton 1974	**D**
	Saturday Review Press 1974	**C**
12 **The Woman in Black** (novel)	Hamilton 1983	**C**
	Godine 1986	**B**
13 **Lanterns Across the Snow** (story)	Joseph 1987	**B**
	Potter 1988	**B**
14 **Air and Angels** (novel)	Sinclair-Stevenson 1991	**B**
15 **The Mist in the Mirror** (novel)	Sinclair-Stevenson 1992	**B**

Household, Geoffrey Born in Bristol, 1900. Pseudonym for Edward West. Died 1988.

Still collected in a sort of a way – though much more avidly by crime buffs. *Rogue Male* remains the extremely elusive highlight – and if one simply wants a representation of the author, this, I'm afraid, just has to be it.

1 **The Terror of Villadonga** (juvenile)	Hutchinson 1936	**K**
2 **The Spanish Cave** (same as 1, revised)	Little, Brown 1936	**J**
3 **The Third Hour** (novel)	Chatto & Windus 1937	**I**
	Little, Brown 1938	**H**
4 **The Salvation of Pisco Gabar** (stories)	Chatto & Windus 1938	**G**
	Little, Brown 1940	**F**

5	**Rogue Male** (novel)	Chatto & Windus 1939	L
		Little, Brown 1939	J
6	**Arabesque** (novel)	Chatto & Windus 1948	G
		Little, Brown 1948	E
7	**The High Place** (novel)	Joseph 1950	E
		Little, Brown 1950	D
8	**A Rough Shoot** (novel)	Joseph 1951	E
		Little, Brown 1951	D
9	**A Time to Kill** (novel)	Little, Brown 1951	E
		Joseph 1952	D
10	**Tales of Adventurers** (stories)	Joseph 1952	D
		Little, Brown 1952	D
11	**Fellow Passenger** (novel)	Joseph 1955	D
		Little, Brown 1955	C
12	**The Exploits of Xenophon** (juvenile)	Random House 1955	D
	Xenophon's Adventure	Bodley Head 1961	C
13	**The Brides of Solomon** (stories)	Joseph 1958	D
		Little, Brown 1958	C
14	**Watcher in the Shadows** (novel)	Joseph 1960	D
		Little, Brown 1960	C
15	**Thing to Love** (novel)	Joseph 1963	D
		Little, Brown 1963	C
16	**Olura** (novel)	Joseph 1965	D
		Little, Brown 1965	C
17	**Sabres on the Sand** (stories)	Joseph 1966	D
		Little, Brown 1966	C
18	**Prisoner of the Indies** (juvenile)	Bodley Head 1967	C
		Little, Brown 1967	C
19	**The Courtesy of Death** (novel)	Joseph 1967	C
		Little, Brown 1967	C
20	**Dance of the Dwarfs** (novel)	Joseph 1968	C
		Little, Brown 1968	C
21	**Doom's Caravan** (novel)	Joseph 1971	C
		Little, Brown 1971	C
22	**The Three Sentinels** (novel)	Joseph 1972	C
		Little, Brown 1972	C
23	**The Lives and Times of Bernardo Brown** (novel)	Joseph 1973	C
		Little, Brown 1974	C
24	**Red Anger** (novel)	Joseph 1975	C
		Little, Brown 1976	C
25	**Escape Into Daylight** (juvenile)	Bodley Head 1976	C
26	**Hostage: London** (novel)	Joseph 1977	C
		Little, Brown 1977	B
27	**The Last Two Weeks of George Rivac** (novel)	Joseph 1978	C
		Little, Brown 1978	B
28	**The Europe That Was** (stories)	David & Charles 1979	C
		St Martin's 1979	B

29 **The Sending** (novel)	Joseph 1980	C
	Little, Brown 1980	B
30 **Summon the Bright Water** (novel)	Joseph 1981	B
	Little, Brown 1981	B
31 **Capricorn and Cancer** (stories)	Joseph 1981	B
32 **Rogue Justice** (novel)	Joseph 1982	C
	Little, Brown 1983	B
33 **Arrows of Desire** (stories)	Joseph 1985	B
	Little, Brown 1986	B
34 **The Days of Your Fathers** (stories)	Joseph 1987	B
	Little, Brown 1987	B
35 **Face to the Sun** (novel)	Joseph 1988	B

Howard, Elizabeth Jane   Born in London, 1923.

The latest novels received tremendous reviews, and yet best-sellerdom stubbornly eludes Elizabeth Jane Howard. And nor, it must be said, is she one of the most collected authors – this reflected in the low prices: good news for her admirers, anyway.

1 **The Beautiful Visit** (novel)	Cape 1950	F
	Random House 1950	D
2 **We Are for the Dark: Six Ghost Stories**	Cape 1951	D
With Robert Aickman.		
3 **The Long View** (novel)	Cape 1956	D
	Reynal 1956	C
4 **The Sea Change** (novel)	Cape 1959	D
	Harper 1960	C
5 **After Julius** (novel)	Cape 1965	D
	Viking 1965	C
6 **Something in Disguise** (novel)	Cape 1969	C
	Viking 1970	C
7 **Odd Girl Out** (novel)	Cape 1972	C
	Viking 1972	C
8 **Mr Wrong** (stories)	Cape 1975	C
	Viking 1975	C
9 **The Lover's Companion** (verse)	David & Charles 1978	B
An anthology of other people's poetry, selected and introduced by E.J.H., to coincide with Valentine's Day.		
10 **Getting it Right** (novel)	Hamilton 1982	B
	Viking 1982	B
11 **Howard and Maschler on Food**	Joseph 1987	B
(cookery) With Fay Maschler.		
12 **The Light Years** (novel)	Macmillan 1990	B
	Pocket Books 1990	B

13 **Making Time** (novel)	Macmillan 1991	**B**
	Pocket Books 1991	**B**

Hughes, Richard   Born in Surrey, 1900. Died 1976.

It is rather sad that Richard Hughes embarked so late in life upon his *Human Predicament* – the umbrella title for what was to have been an epic sequence of novels, the exact number unspecified. Not that sixty-one is a terribly great age to publish the first volume – but he was seventy-three when he published the second, which was to be the last. It is, however, his very early works which are rare and command the high prices, while a representative work would be *A High Wind in Jamaica* – still the highlight, and still reasonably priced.

Hughes published a fair amount of private press material which does not appear here. A list may be found in *The New Cambridge Bibliography of English Literature* vol. 4, and the Golden Cockerel Press items may be found in their own checklist of publications.

1 **The Sister's Tragedy** (play)	Blackwell 1922	**J**
2 **The Sister's Tragedy and Other Plays**	Heinemann 1924	**H**
Incl. *The Man Born to be Hanged*, *A Comedy of Good and Evil* and *Danger*.		
A Rabbit and a Leg: Collected Plays	Knopf 1924	**F**
3 **Confessio Juvenis: Collected Poems**	Chatto & Windus 1925	**H**
4 **A Moment of Time** (stories)	Chatto & Windus 1926	**H**
5 **A High Wind in Jamaica** (novel)	Chatto & Windus 1929	**E**
Also limited ed. of 150 copies (**J**).		
6 **The Innocent Voyage** (same as 5)	Harper (NY) 1929	**D**
7 **Richard Hughes: An Omnibus** (stories, plays and poems)	Harper 1931	**D**
8 **The Spider's Palace** (juvenile stories)	Chatto & Windus 1931	**K**
	Harper 1932	**H**
9 **In Hazard** (novel)	Chatto & Windus 1938	**D**
	Harper 1938	**D**
10 **Don't Blame Me and Other Stories** (juvenile)	Chatto & Windus 1940	**F**
	Harper 1940	**D**
11 **The Fox in the Attic** (novel)	Chatto & Windus 1961	**C**
	Harper 1961	**C**
12 **Gertrude's Child** (juvenile)	Harlin Quist (NY) 1966	**D**
13 **The Wooden Shepherdess** (novel)	Chatto & Windus 1973	**C**
	Harper 1973	**C**
14 **The Wonder-Dog: The Collected Stories** (juvenile)	Chatto & Windus 1977	**C**

15 **In the Lap of Atlas: Stories of Morocco**	Chatto & Windus 1979	**C**
	Merrimack 1980	**C**

Ed. Richard Poole.

Hughes, Ted Born in Yorkshire, 1930.

A lot of collectors have become fairly thoroughly sick of our Poet Laureate's limited editions, many of which have – despite their notional value – become virtually unsaleable. Of course the early Faber stuff, including the children's books, are still immensely desirable (and pricey) but care should be taken before spending too much on the recent offerings.

1 **The Hawk in the Rain** (verse)	Faber 1957	**M**
	Harper 1957	**J**
2 **Pike** (poem)	Gehenna Press 1959	**J**
A single-sheet broadside in an edition of 150.		
3 **Lupercal** (verse)	Faber 1960	**K**
	Harper 1960	**H**
4 **Meet My Folks!** (juvenile)	Faber 1961	**H**
	Bobbs-Merrill 1973	**C**
5 **Selected Poems** With Thom Gunn.	Faber 1962	**D**
6 **How the Whale Became** (juvenile)	Faber 1963	**G**
	Atheneum 1964	**E**
7 **The Earth-Owl and Other Moon-People** (juvenile)	Faber 1963	**F**
8 **Nessie the Mannerless Monster** (juvenile)	Faber 1964	**G**
	Bobbs-Merrill 1974	**C**
The American edition omits the word 'mannerless' from the title.		
9 **The Burning of the Brothel** (verse)	Turret Books 1966	**I**
300 copies, 75 numbered and signed (**L**).		
10 **Recklings** (verse)	Turret Books 1966	**L**
150 copies, numbered and signed.		
11 **Scapegoats and Rabies** (verse)	Poet & Printer 1967	**H**
400(ish) copies.		
12 **Wodwo** (miscellany)	Faber 1967	**E**
	Harper 1967	**C**
13 **Animal Poems**	Gilbertson 1967	
100 copies, as follows:		
1–6: poems hand-written by T.H. next to text: (**Q**).		
7–16: with 3 manuscript poems (**P**).		
17–36: with 1 manuscript poem (**N**)		
37–100: signed (**J**).		

14	**Poetry in the Making** (prose)	Faber 1967	**G**
	The American edition was entitled	Doubleday 1970	**F**
	Poetry Is.		
15	**Gravestones** (verse)	Bartholemew 1967	**K**
	A set of six broadsides; linocuts by Gavin		
	Robbins. 40 sets printed.		
16	**Seneca's Oedipus** (play)	Faber 1969	**E**
		Doubleday 1972	**C**
17	**The Iron Man** (juvenile)	Faber 1968	**G**
18	**The Iron Giant**	Harper 1968	**D**
	The American edition of 17.		
19	**Five Autumn Songs for Children's Voices** (verse)	Gilbertson 1968	
	500 copies, as follows (for sale):		
	3–11: a verse in manuscript & a		
	watercolour (**O**).		
	12–37: a verse in manuscript (**M**).		
	38–188: signed (**I**).		
	189–500: numbered (**D**).		
20	**I Said Goodbye to Earth** (poem)	Turret Books 1969	**H**
	Broadside. 75 copies, signed.		
21	**A Crow Hymn** (poem)	Sceptre Press 1970	
	21 signed (**J**), 64 unsigned (**E**) for sale.		
22	**The Martyrdom of Bishop Farrar**	Gilbertson 1970	**J**
	100 copies. signed.		
23	**The Coming of the Kings and Other Plays**	Faber 1970	**D**
	The Tiger's Bones and Other Plays for Children.	Viking 1974	**D**
24	**A Few Crows** (verse)	Rougemont Press 1970	**G**
	150 copies, 75 signed (**K**).		
25	**Crow** (verse)	Faber 1970	**E**
		Harper 1971	**D**
26	**Fighting for Jerusalem** (poem)	Northumberland Arts	**E**
	Broadside, number of copies unknown.	1970	
27	**Crow Wakes** (verse)	Poet & Printer 1971	**H**
	100 for sale.		
28	**Poems**	Rainbow Press 1971	**L**
	With Ruth Fainlight and Alan Sillitoe.		
	300 copies, numbered and signed by the		
	three poets.		
29	**Shakespeare's Poem**	Lexham Press 1971	**J**
	150 copies, 75 (signed) for sale.		
30	**Eat Crow** (verse)	Rainbow Press 1971	**L**
	150 copies, signed and numbered.		
31	**Selected Poems 1957–1967**	Faber 1972	**C**
		Harper 1973	**C**

Hughes, Ted

32 **Orpheus** (play)   Dramatic Publishing
1023 copies.   Company (US) 1973   **E**
33 **Prometheus on His Crag** (verse)   Rainbow Press 1973   **L**
160 copies signed by T.H. and Leonard
Baskin.
34 **Spring Summer Autumn Winter**   Rainbow Press 1974   **L**
(verse)
140 copies, numbered and signed.
35 **Season Songs**   Doubleday 1975   **C**
First trade editions of 34.   Faber 1976   **C**
36 **Cave Birds** (verse)   Scolar Press 1975
Ten sheets in a box, illustrated by
Leonard Baskin. 125 copies printed, at
£125 each (**M**). *Sensible* editions were
published by Faber in 1978 (**D**) and the
Viking Press in 1979 (**C**).
37 **Earth-Moon** (verse)   Rainbow Press 1976   **K**
226 signed and numbered copies, 200 for
sale.
38 **Eclipse** (verse)   Sceptre Press 1976   **E**
250 copies, 50 signed (**I**).
·39 **Moon-Whales and Other Poems**   Viking 1976   **C**
Previously published verse, but new to
America.
40 **Gaudete** (verse)   Faber 1977   **C**
                                                      Harper 1977   **C**
41 **Chiasmadon** (verse)   Janus Press (US) 1977 **K**
175 signed copies, 120 for sale.
42 **Sunstruck** (verse)   Sceptre Press 1977
300 copies, as follows:
100 signed (50 for sale) (**J**).
200 numbered (**E**).
43 **A Solstice** (verse)   Sceptre Press 1978
350 copies, as follows:
100 signed (50 for sale) (**I**).
250 numbered (**D**).
44 **Orts** (verse)   Rainbow Press 1978   **K**
200 copies, numbered and signed.
45 **Moortown Elegies** (verse)   Rainbow Press 1978
175 copies, as follows:
6 author's copies.
26 lettered A–Z (£175) (**N**).
143 numbered (£140) (**K**).
46 **The Threshold** (poem)   Steam Press 1979   **L**
12 leaves, illustrated by Ralph
Steadman. Signed by R.S.and T.H.
100 copies at £105 each.

47 **Adam and the Sacred Nine** (verse)   Rainbow Press 1979   **K**
200 copies, numbered and signed.

48 **Remains of Elmet** (verse)   Rainbow Press 1979
With photographs by Fay Godwin.
180 copies, as follows:
1–70: bound, signed by T.H. and F.G.
(£140) (**N**).
71–80: ordinary binding, signed by T.H.
(£48) (**I**).
Attainable editions were published by
Faber and Harper & Row later in the
year (**D**).

49 **Night Arrival of Sea-Trout, The**   Morrigu Press 1979   **G**
Iron Wolf, Puma (verse)
Three broadsides. 30 sets printed at £15
each. The Press is owned by Hughes's
son Nicholas.

50 **Brooktrout** (poem)   Morrigu Press 1979   **F**
Broadside. 60 copies printed.

51 **Four Tales Told by an Idiot**   Sceptre Press 1979   **D**
450 numbered copies, 100 signed (**H**).

52 **Pan** (poem)   Morrigu Press 1979   **F**
Broadside. 60 copies printed.

53 **Woodpecker** (poem)   Morrigu Press 1979   **F**
Broadside. 60 copies printed.

54 **Moortown** (verse)   Faber 1979   **C**
                             Harper 1980   **C**

55 **Henry Williamson** (tribute)   Rainbow Press 1979   **I**
200 copies, 125 for sale.

56 **Wolverine** (poem)   Morrigu Press 1979   **E**
Broadside. 75 copies.

57 **Eagle** (poem)   Morrigu Press 1980   **E**
Broadside. 75 copies.

58 **Mosquito** (poem)   Morrigu Press 1980   **E**
Broadside. 60 copies.

59 **Catadrome** (poem)   Morrigu Press 1980   **E**
Broadside. 75 copies.

60 **Caddis** (poem)   Morrigu Press 1980   **E**
Broadside. 75 copies.

61 **Visitation** (poem)   Morrigu Press 1980   **E**
Broadside. 75 copies.

62 **Under the North Star** (verse)   Faber 1981   **C**
                                        Viking 1981   **C**

63 **The Rattle-bag**   Faber 1982   **D**
An anthology of everyone, edited by
T.H. and Seamus Heaney.

64 **Selected Poems 1957–1981**   Faber 1982   **C**

	The Harper edition was entitled	Harper 1982	**C**
	New Selected Poems:		
65	**River** (verse)	Faber 1983	**D**
	With photographs by Peter Keen,	Harper 1984	**C**
	which the American edition omits.		
66	**Weasels at Work** (poem)	Morrigu Press 1983	**E**
67	**Fly Inspects** (poem)	Morrigu Press 1983	**E**
68	**Mice are Funny Little Creatures**	Morrigu Press 1983	**E**
	(nos 66–68 are booklets printed in an		
	edition of 75 copies each)		
69	**What is the Truth?** (juvenile)	Faber 1984	**C**
		Harper 1984	**C**
70	**Ffangs the Vampire Bat and**	Faber 1986	**C**
	the Kiss of Truth (juvenile)		
71	**Flowers and Insects: Some Birds**	Faber 1986	**C**
	and a Pair of Spiders (verse)	Knopf 1986	**C**
	Illustrated by Leonard Baskin.		
72	**T.S. Eliot: A Tribute**	Faber 1987	**J**
	(Private printing of 25 copies)		
73	**Tales of the Early World** (verse)	Faber 1988	**C**
74	**The Cat and the Cuckoo**	Wykeham Press 1988	**G**
	(juvenile)		
75	**Wolfwatching** (verse)	Faber 1989	**C**
76	**Shakespeare and the Goddess**	Faber 1992	**C**
	of Complete Being (prose)		
77	**Rain-Charm for the Duchy** (verse)	Faber 1992	**C**
	(published simultaneously in hardback,		
	paperback and a limited edition priced		
	at £75)		
78	**Dancer to God** (lecture)	Faber 1992	**C**

Huxley, Aldous   Born in Surrey, 1894. Died 1963.

A lot of interest in Huxley from both old and new collectors. The scope attracts a lot of people, I think, although as will be seen below, prices fluctuate pretty dramatically. The highlight remains *Brave New World* – a fairly common book *without* the dust-wrapper, it might be noted, and worth only one-eighth of the value of a fine dust-wrapper copy: most were destroyed, we understand.

1	**The Burning Wheel** (verse)	Blackwell 1916	**P**
2	**Jonah** (verse)	Holywell 1917	**Q**
	Approximately 50 signed copies.		
3	**The Defeat of Youth and Other**	Blackwell 1918	**O**
	Poems		
	250 copies only.		
4	**Leda** (verse)	Chatto & Windus 1920	**K**

In addition to the trade edition, Chatto put out 160 numbered and signed editions (**N**). The Doran edition contained only the title poem, and was illustrated by Eric Gill. — Doran 1920 — **I**

5 **Limbo** (6 stories and a play) — Chatto & Windus 1920 **I** / Doran 1920 **G**

6 **Crome Yellow** (novel) — Chatto & Windus 1921 **M** / Doran 1922 **J**

7 **Mortal Coils** (stories) — Chatto & Windus 1922 **J** / Doran 1922 **G**
Includes Huxley's most celebrated story 'The Gioconda Smile'.

8 **Antic Hay** (novel) — Chatto & Windus 1923 **H** / Doran 1923 **F**

9 **On the Margin** (essays) — Chatto & Windus 1923 **F** / Doran 1923 **D**

10 **Little Mexican and Other Stories** — Chatto & Windus 1924 **H** / Doran 1924 **F**

11 **Along the Road** (essays) — Chatto & Windus 1925 **F** / Doran 1925 **D**
As well as the trade edition, Doran issued 250 signed numbered copies (**L**).

12 **Selected Poems** — Blackwell 1925 **H** / Appleton 1925 **F**

13 **Those Barren Leaves** (novel) — Chatto & Windus 1925 **G** / Doran 1925 **D**
Doran edition: as with 11.

14 **Essays New and Old** — Chatto & Windus 1926 **L** / Doran 1927 **E**
The Chatto edition comprised 650 signed, numbered copies.

15 **Jesting Pilate** (travel) — Chatto & Windus 1926 **G** / Doran 1926 **D**

16 **Two or Three Graces and Other Stories** — Chatto & Windus 1926 **F** / Doran 1926 **D**

17 **Proper Studies** (essays) — Chatto & Windus 1927 **E** / Doubleday Doran 1928 **C**

18 **Point Counter Point** (novel) — Chatto & Windus 1928 **H** / Doubleday Doran 1928 **F**

19 **Arabia Infelix** (verse) — Fountain Press (NY) 1929 **J**
Comprising 692 signed, numbered copies. — Chatto & Windus 1929 **J**

20 **Do What You Will** (essays) — Chatto & Windus 1929 **E** / Doubleday Doran 1929 **D**

21 **Holy Face and Other Essays** — The Fleuron Press 1929 **K**
Drawings by Albert Rutherston. 300 numbered copies.

22 **Apennine** (verse) — Slide Mountain Press (US) 1930 **L**
91 signed, numbered copies.

23 **Brief Candles** (stories) — Chatto & Windus 1930 **F**

		Doubleday Doran 1930	**D**
24	**Vulgarity in Literature** (essay) Published as 260 signed, numbered copies (**K**), and also as No. 1 in Chatto's 'Dolphin's Books' series (**C**).	Chatto & Windus 1930	
25	**The Cicadas and Other Poems** Chatto published 160 signed, numbered copies simultaneously (**K**).	Chatto & Windus 1931 Doubleday Doran 1931	**F** **D**
26	**Music at Night and Other Essays** By now the simultaneous publication of signed, numbered editions was established, and for this book – between Britain and America – no less than 1684 such numbered copies were published (**H**).	Chatto & Windus 1931 Doubleday Doran 1931	**E** **C**
27	**The World of Light** (play) Chatto also published 160 signed, numbered copies (**I**).	Chatto & Windus 1931 Doubleday Doran 1931	**D** **C**
28	**Brave New World** (novel) Of this classic, both Chatto and Doubleday issued a signed numbered edition, of 324 and 250, respectively (**Q**).	Chatto & Windus 1932 Doubleday Doran 1932	**P** **J**
29	**Rotunda** (essays A selection of previously published work.	Chatto & Windus 1932	**D**
30	**T.H. Huxley as a Man of Letters** 28 pages. The Huxley Memorial Lecture.	Macmillan 1932	**D**
31	**Texts and Pretexts** (essays)	Chatto & Windus 1932 Harper 1933	**D** **C**
32	**Retrospect: An Omnibus of Aldous Huxley's Books**	Doubleday Doran 1933	**D**
33	**Beyond the Mexique Bay** (essays) In addition to the trade edition, Chatto issued 210 signed, numbered copies (**J**).	Chatto & Windus 1934 Harper 1934	**D** **C**
34	**Eyeless in Gaza** (novel) Chatto also issued 200 signed, numbered copies (**K**).	Chatto & Windus 1936 Harper 1936	**E** **D**
35	**The Olive Tree and Other Essays**	Chatto & Windus 1936 Harper 1937	**C** **C**
36	**What Are You Going to do About It? The Case for Constructive Peace** 35-page pamphlet.	Chatto & Windus 1936 Harper 1937	**C** **C**
37	**Ends and Means** (essays) Chatto also issued 160 signed,	Chatto & Windus 1937 Harper 1937	**D** **C**

numbered copies (**I**).

38	**Stories, Essays and Poems**	Dent 1937	**C**
	An anthology of previously published material, in the Everyman's Library.		
39	**After Many a Summer**	Chatto & Windus 1939	**D**
	(novel)	Harper 1939	**C**
40	**Grey Eminence** (non-fiction)	Chatto & Windus 1941	**C**
		Harper 1941	**C**
41	**The Art of Seeing** (non-fiction)	Chatto & Windus 1942	**C**
		Harper 1942	**C**
42	**Time Must Have a Stop** (novel)	Chatto & Windus 1944	**D**
		Harper 1944	**C**
43	**The Perennial Philosophy**	Chatto & Windus 1945	**C**
		Harper 1945	**C**
44	**Science, Liberty and Peace**	Chatto & Windus 1946	**C**
	(non-fiction)	Harper 1946	**C**
45	**Verses and a Comedy**	Chatto & Windus 1946	**C**
46	**Ape and Essence** (novel)	Chatto & Windus 1948	**C**
		Harper 1948	**C**
47	**The Gioconda Smile** (play)	Chatto & Windus 1948	**C**
	Dramatized version of the story in 7.	Harper 1948	**C**
48	**The Prisons** (essay)	Trianon Press 1949	
	The English (Trianon) edition comprised 1000 unsigned copies (**D**) and 212 signed and numbered (**I**), and the American just 212 signed and numbered (**I**).	Zeitlin & Ver Brugge 1949	
49	**Themes and Variations** (essays)	Chatto & Windus 1950	**C**
		Harper 1950	**B**
50	**The Devils of Loudun**	Chatto & Windus 1952	**C**
	(non-fiction)	Harper 1952	**B**
51	**The Doors of Perception**	Chatto & Windus 1954	**D**
	A seminal work, revived in the sixties at the height of the drug culture.	Harper 1954	**C**
52	**The Genius and the Goddess**	Chatto & Windus 1955	**C**
	(novel)	Harper 1955	**C**
53	**Adonis and the Alphabet** (essays)	Chatto & Windus 1956	**C**
54	**Tomorrow and Tomorrow and Tomorrow** (essays)	Harper 1956	**C**
	Same as 53.		
55	**Heaven and Hell** (non-fiction)	Chatto & Windus 1956	**C**
		Harper 1956	**C**
56	**Collected Short Stories**	Chatto & Windus 1957	**C**
		Harper 1957	**C**
57	**Brave New World Revisited**	Chatto & Windus 1958	**D**
	(essays)	Harper 1958	**C**
58	**Collected Essays**	Harper 1959	**C**

59 **Island**	Chatto & Windus 1961	**C**
	Harper 1961	**C**

Bibliography:
Claire John Eschelbach & Joyce Lee Shober **Aldous Huxley:
A Bibliography 1916–1959** University of California Press 1961

Biography:
The essential and definitive biography: Sybille Bedford **Aldous Huxley**
Vol. 1: **1894–1939** Chatto/Collins 1973; Vol. 2: **1939–63** Chatto/Collins
1974

Isherwood, Christopher   Born in Cheshire, 1904. Died 1986.

Nothing much after *A Single Man* is of huge interest to collectors, though the all-time classics are ever rarer and more expensive – particularly nos 1, 2, 3, 7 and 10.

1	**All the Conspirators** (novel)	Cape 1928	**O**
		New Directions 1958	**E**
2	**The Memorial** (novel)	Hogarth Press 1932	**N**
		New Directions 1946	**E**
3	**Mr Norris Changes Trains** (novel)	Hogarth Press 1935	**N**
4	**The Last of Mr Norris** (same as 3)	Morrow (NY) 1935	**J**
5	**The Dog Beneath the Skin** (play)	Faber 1935	**I**
	With W.H. Auden.	Random House 1935	**G**
6	**The Ascent of F6** (play)	Faber 1936	**H**
	With W.H. Auden.	Random House 1937	**F**
7	**Sally Bowles** (novel)	Hogarth Press 1937	**N**
8	**On The Frontier** (play)	Faber 1938	**F**
	With W.H. Auden	Random House 1939	**D**
9	**Lions and Shadows** (prose)	Hogarth Press 1938	**J**
		New Directions 1948	**E**
10	**Goodbye to Berlin** (novel)	Hogarth Press 1939	**N**
		Random House 1939	**K**
11	**Journey to a War** (non-fiction)	Faber 1939	**H**
	With W.H. Auden.	Random House 1939	**G**
12	**Prater Violet** (novel)	Random House 1945	**H**
		Methuen 1946	**H**
13	**The Berlin Stories**	New Directions 1946	**D**
	Cont. 3, 7 and 10.		
14	**The Condor and the Cows**	Random House 1949	**E**
	(travel)	Methuen 1949	**E**
15	**The World in the Evening** (novel)	Random House 1954	**D**
		Methuen 1954	**D**
16	**Down There on a Visit** (novel)	Simon & Schuster 1962	**D**
		Methuen 1962	**D**

17 **A Single Man** (novel)	Simon & Schuster 1964	**C**
	Methuen 1964	**C**
18 **Ramakrishna and His Disciples** (non-fiction)	Simon & Schuster 1965	**C**
	Methuen 1965	**C**
19 **Exhumations** (miscellany)	Simon & Schuster 1966	**C**
	Methuen 1966	**C**
20 **A Meeting by the River** (novel)	Simon & Schuster 1967	**C**
	Methuen 1967	**C**
21 **Kathleen and Frank** (biog.)	Simon & Schuster 1971	**C**
	Methuen 1971	**C**
22 **Frankenstein: The True Story** (screenplay)	Avon (NY) 1973	**C**
23 **The Berlin of Sally Bowles** (same as 13)	Hogarth Press 1975	**C**
24 **Christopher and His Kind** (autobiog.)	Simon & Schuster 1977	**C**
	Eyre Methuen 1977	**C**
25 **My Guru and His Disciple** (non-fiction)	Farrar Straus 1980	**C**
	Eyre Methuen 1980	**C**
26 **October** (prose)	Twelvetrees Press (US) 1980	**N**
The American limited edition was printed on hand-made paper, leather bound, and $400 on publication. The Methuen edition was paperback, limited to 1000 copies, and priced at £12.50.	Methuen 1982	**D**
27 **People One Ought to Know** (verse) Nonsense verse, illustrated by Sylvain Mangeot.	Doubleday 1982	**C**
	Macmillan 1982	**C**

Isherwood's interest in Vedanta is shown by the two books he wrote – **An Approach to Vedanta** and **Essentials of Vedanta** Vedanta Press (USA) 1963 and 1969, as well as the two books he edited: **Vedanta and the Western World** Rodd 1946; Allen & Unwin 1948, **Vedanta for Modern Man** Harper 1951; Allen & Unwin 1952

Ishiguro, Kazuo   Born in Nagasaki, Japan, 1954.

One of the larger reputations among our younger writers, and one of the smallest (possibly *the* smallest) of outputs. Spare, cool, elegant and fine – very well worth collecting, but the first of the novels won't be easy.

1 **A Pale View of Hills** (novel)	Faber 1982	**H**
	Putnam 1982	**E**
2 **An Artist of the Floating World** (novel)	Faber 1986	**D**
	Putnam 1986	**C**
3 **The Remains of the Day** (novel)	Faber 1989	**C**
	Knopf 1989	**C**

James, P.D. Born in Oxford, 1920.

Phyllis Dorothy James was created a Baroness in 1991 – not a lot of crime
writers (not a lot of *any* sort of writers) are so honoured. James has anyway
been the aristocrat of the literary whodunnit for many years now, publishing
occasionally, and never disappointing her growing throng of admirers.
Never easy to collect, and currently damned hard indeed.

1	**Cover Her Face** (novel)	Faber 1962	O
		Scribner 1966	G
2	**A Mind to Murder** (novel)	Faber 1963	M
		Scribner 1967	E
3	**Unnatural Causes** (novel)	Faber 1967	K
		Scribner 1967	E
4	**Shroud for a Nightingale** (novel)	Faber 1971	H
		Scribner 1971	E
5	**An Unsuitable Job for a Woman** (novel)	Faber 1972	H
		Scribner 1972	E
6	**The Black Tower** (novel)	Faber 1975	F
		Scribner 1975	D
7	**Death of an Expert Witness** (novel)	Faber 1977	E
		Scribner 1977	C
8	**Innocent Blood** (novel)	Faber 1980	E
		Scribner 1980	C
9	**P.D. James Omnibus** Includes 3, 4 and 5.	Faber 1982	C
10	**The Skull Beneath the Skin** (novel)	Faber 1982	D
		Scribner 1982	C
11	**A Taste for Death** (novel)	Faber 1986	C
		Knopf 1986	C
12	**Devices and Desires** (novel)	Faber 1989	C
		Knopf 1990	B
13	**The Omnibus P.D. James** (contains nos 5, 7 and 8)	Faber 1990	C
14	**Children of Men** (novel)	Faber 1992	C

Jerome, Jerome K. Born in Walsall, 1859. Died 1927.

As may be seen from the following bibliography, Jerome *did* write more than
Three Men in a Boat, although of course this remains the highlight, not to say
one of the funniest books ever written, as I am sure you do not need me to tell
you. A lot of his writing would be seen to be too simplistic and – not so much
sentimental as unsophisticated; but much more is unjustly ignored, or simply
not known about. Buy them when you see them, and discover a true original.

1 **On the Stage – And Off** (pieces)	Field & Tuer 1885	**H**
This tiny book (about four inches by three) was soon followed by an illustrated edition, Leadenhall Press, illus. by Kenneth M. Skeaping (**D**).		
2 **Barbara** (play)	Lacy 1886	**C**
3 **The Idle Thoughts of an Idle Fellow** (essays)	Field & Tuer 1886	**G**
The earliest editions make no mention of 'edition' on cover.		
4 **Sunset** (play)	Fitzgerald (NY) n.d. (1888)	**C**
5 **Fennel** (play)	French n.d. (1888)	**C**
6 **Woodbarrow Farm** (play)	French n.d. (1888)	**C**
7 **Stage-Land** (satire)	Chatto & Windus 1889	**F**
8 **Three Men in a Boat** (novel)	Arrowsmith 1889	**L**

8 **Three Men in a Boat** (novel)

The famous novel, bound in Thames-green cloth, the front bearing a silhouette and black lettering, while the spine is lettered in gold. Subsequent issues may easily be mistaken for the very first edition, as superficially all are similar. The basic distinction remains that the publisher's address at the foot of the title page should read 'Quay Street' and *not* '11 Quay Street'. The heading over the advertisements on the front fixed endpaper, however, should read 'J.W. Arrowsmith, Bristol' and *not* '11 Quay Street, Bristol'. Questions have been raised as to the relevance of inverted ornamental capitals opening chapters, but the above two points remain the only really reliable guides. The book is illustrated by A. Fredrics, and the title page bears the date of publication.

9 **Told After Supper** (essays)	Leadenhall Press 1891	**F**
10 **The Diary of a Pilgrimage** (novel)	Arrowsmith 1891	**E**

Earliest editions also contain six essays, and make no mention of edition on cover.

11 **Novel Notes** (articles)	Leadenhall Press 1893	**E**
12 **John Ingerfield** (stories)	McClure 1894	**E**
13 **My First Book** (essays, with other writers)	Chatto & Windus 1894	**E**

Blue cloth. The 1897 red-bound edition is often mistaken for the 1st.

14	**The Prude's Progress** (play)	French 1895	**C**
15	**Sketches in Lavender, Blue and Green** (stories)	Longman 1897	**F**
16	**The Second Thoughts of an Idle Fellow**	Hurst & Blackett 1898	**E**
17	**Three Men on the Bummel** (novel)	Arrowsmith 1900	**G**
18	**The Observations of Henry** (stories)	Arrowsmith 1901	**E**
19	**Miss Hobbs** (play)	French 1902	**C**
20	**Paul Kelver** (novel)	Hutchinson 1902	**F**
21	**Tea-Table Talk** (essays)	Hutchinson 1903	**E**
22	**Tommy and Co.** (novel)	Hutchinson 1904	**E**
23	**American Wives and Others** (essays)	Stokes 1904	**E**
	A miscellany published only in USA.		
24	**Idle Ideas in 1905** (essays)	Hurst & Blackett 1905	**D**
25	**The Passing of the Third Floor Back** (essays, stories)	Hurst & Blackett 1907	**E**
26	**The Angel and the Author** (essays)	Hurst & Blackett 1908	**D**
27	**They and I** (novel)	Hutchinson 1909	**D**
28	**Fanny and the Servant Problem** (play)	Lacy 1909	**C**
29	**The Passing of the Third Floor Back** (play)	Hurst & Blackett 1910	**D**
30	**The Master of Mrs Chilvers** (play)	T. Fisher Unwin 1911	**C**
31	**Robina in Search of a Husband** (play)	Lacy 1914	**C**
32	**Malvina of Brittany** (stories)	Cassell 1916	**C**
33	**All Roads Lead to Calvary** (novel)	Hutchinson 1919	**C**
34	**Anthony John** (novel)	Cassell 1923	**C**
35	**A Miscellany of Sense and Nonsense**	Arrowsmith 1923	**D**
36	**The Celebrity** (play	Hodder & Stoughton 1926	**C**
37	**My Life and Times** (autobiog.)	Hodder & Stoughton 1926	**G**
38	**The Soul of Nicholas Synders** (play)	Hodder & Stoughton 1927	**C**

The list above is of English first editions, though it should be noted that in America 17 was published as **Three Men on Wheels**, 32 as **The Street of the Blank Wall**, 28 as **Lady Bantock** and 36 as **Cook**.

In addition to the above, the following works should be noted:
Playwriting: A Handbook for Would-Be Dramatic Authors This booklet, published by the Stage Office in 1888 by 'A Dramatist' is almost certainly by J.K.J., as has been reasonably established in Arnott & Robinson, **English Theatrical Literature, 1559–1900**. **K** Arrowsmith 1892. The story 'K' was published by a writer cloaked beneath the

pseudonym 'McK'. Jerome never owned to having written the piece, but a letter written to Arrowsmith and auctioned by Sotheby's in 1968 revealed that McK was none other than Jerome. It appears that the story was to have been entitled *Weeds*, and it is not at all certain that any copies went on sale.   **Humours of Cycling** Bowden 1897. Jerome contributes an essay entitled 'Women on Wheels'. The volume was reissued in 1905 by Chatto & Windus.   **Songs From the Heart of England: An Anthology of Walsall Poetry** T. Fisher Unwin 1920. Jerome contributed a short foreword to this, compiled by Alfred Moss. Jerome also edited two magazines, *The Idler* and *Today*. *The Idler* was founded in 1892 by Robert Barr, who offered Jerome the joint editorship. They edited it until 1898, although the magazine ran until 1911. *The Idler* was issued in bound volumes. (**D** each). *Today* was a weekly founded by Jerome himself in 1893. He edited it until 1898 and the magazine ran until 1905, when it merged with *London Opinion*. Bound volumes of *Today* were also published, but these are much more scarce than *The Idler (***E** each).

Biography (including bibliography):
Joseph Connolly **Jerome K. Jerome: A Critical Biography** Orbis 1982

Jhabvala, Ruth Prawer   Born in Cologne, 1927. American.

Still greatly respected, though still *not* very avidly collected. That explains the relatively low prices – good news if this somewhat idiosyncratic writer appeals.

1	**To Whom She Will** (novel)	Allen & Unwin 1955	J
2	**Amrita** (same as 1)	Norton (US) 1956	D
3	**The Nature of Passion** (novel)	Allen & Unwin 1956	H
		Norton 1957	D
4	**Esmond in India** (novel)	Allen & Unwin 1957	G
		Norton 1958	D
5	**The Householder** (novel)	Murray 1960	E
		Norton 1960	C
6	**Get Ready for Battle** (novel)	Murray 1962	E
		Norton 1963	C
7	**Like Birds, Like Fishes and Other Stories**	Murray 1963	E
		Norton 1964	C
8	**A Backward Place** (novel)	Murray 1965	D
		Norton 1965	C
9	**A Stronger Climate: 9 stories**	Murray 1968	D
		Norton 1969	C
10	**An Experience of India** (stories)	Murray 1971	C
		Norton 1972	C
11	**A New Dominion** (novel)	Murray 1973	C
12	**Travelers** (same as 11)	Harper & Row 1973	C

13	**Heat and Dust** (novel)	Murray 1975	F
		Harper 1976	C
14	**How I Became a Holy Mother** (stories)	Murray 1976	C
		Harper 1976	C
15	**In Search of Love and Beauty** (novel)	Murray 1983	C
		Morrow 1983	C
16	**Out of India: Selected Stories**	Morrow 1986	C
		Murray 1987	C
17	**Three Continents** (novel)	Murray 1987	C
		Morrow 1987	C

Johns, W.E. Born in Hertfordshire, 1893. Died 1968.

In previous editions of this book, I contented myself with listing only Johns' first book, and the first with the redoubtable Biggles in the title: this was clearly not enough for the diehard enthusiasts – a growing band – and so, in Johns' centenary year, there follows Biggles In Toto (which sounds like one of the very few places he has never been).

1	**The Camels Are Coming**	Hamilton 1932	J
2	**The Cruise of the Condor: A Biggles Story**	Hamilton 1933	J
3	**Biggles of the Camel Squadron**	Hamilton 1934	J
4	**Biggles Flies Again**	Hamilton 1934	H
5	**Biggles Learns to Fly**	Boys' Friend Library 1935	F
6	**Biggles Flies East**	OUP 1935	G
7	**Biggles Hits the Trail**	OUP 1935	G
8	**Biggles in France**	Boys' Friend Library 1935	F
9	**The Black Peril: A Biggles Story**	Hamilton 1935	G
10	**Biggles in Africa**	OUP 1936	F
11	**Biggles & Co**	OUP 1936	F
12	**Biggles – Air Commodore**	OUP 1937	F
13	**Biggles Flies West**	OUP 1937	F
14	**Biggles Flies South**	OUP 1938	F
15	**Biggles Goes to War**	OUP 1938	F
16	**Champion of the Main**	OUP 1938	F
17	**Biggles Flies North**	OUP 1939	F
18	**Biggles in Spain**	OUP 1939	F
19	**The Rescue Flight: A Biggles Story**	OUP 1939	F
20	**Biggles in the Baltic**	OUP 1940	E
21	**Biggles in the South Seas**	OUP 1940	E
22	**Biggles – Secret Agent**	OUP 1940	E
23	**Worrals of the W.A.A.F.**	Lutterworth Press 1941	D

Johns

52	**Biggles Breaks the Silence**	Hodder & Stoughton 1949	C
53	**Biggles Takes a Holiday**	Hodder & Stoughton 1949	C
54	**Gimlet Lends a Hand**	Brockhampton Press 1949	C
55	**Worrals Goes Afoot**	Lutterworth Press 1949	C
56	**Worrals in the Wastelands**	Lutterworth Press 1949	C
57	**Worrals Investigates**	Lutterworth Press 1950	C
58	**Biggles Gets His Men**	Hodder & Stoughton 1950	C
59	**Gimlet Bores In**	Brockhampton Press 1950	C
60	**Another Job for Biggles**	Hodder & Stoughton 1951	C
61	**Biggles Goes to School**	Hodder & Stoughton 1951	C
62	**Biggles Works It Out**	Hodder & Stoughton 1951	C
63	**Gimlet Off the Map**	Brockhampton Press 1951	C
64	**Biggles – Air Detective**	Latimer 1952	C
65	**Biggles Follows On**	Hodder & Stoughton 1952	C
66	**Biggles Takes the Case**	Hodder & Stoughton 1952	C
67	**Gimlet Gets the Answer**	Brockhampton Press 1952	C
68	**Biggles and the Black Raider**	Hodder & Stoughton 1953	C
69	**Biggles in the Blue**	Brockhampton Press 1953	C
70	**Biggles of the Special Air Police**	Thames 1953	C
71	**Biggles in the Gobi**	Hodder & Stoughton 1953	C
72	**Biggles and the Pirate Treasure**	Brockhampton Press 1954	C
73	**Biggles Cuts it Fine**	Hodder & Stoughton 1954	C
74	**Biggles, Foreign Legionnaire**	Hodder & Stoughton 1954	C
75	**Biggles, Pioneer Airfighter**	Thames 1954	C
76	**Gimlet Takes a Job**	Brockhampton Press 1954	C
77	**Kings of Space**	Hodder & Stoughton 1954	C
78	**Adventure Bound**	Nelson 1955	C

79	**Biggles' Chinese Puzzle**	Brockhampton Press 1955	C
80	**Biggles in Australia**	Hodder & Stoughton 1955	C
81	**Return to Mars**	Hodder & Stoughton 1955	C
82	**Biggles of 266**	Thames 1956	C
83	**Biggles Takes Charge**	Brockhampton Press 1956	C
84	**No Rest For Biggles**	Hodder & Stoughton 1956	C
85	**Now to the Stars**	Hodder & Stoughton 1956	C
86	**Biggles Makes Ends Meet**	Hodder & Stoughton 1957	C
87	**Adventure Unlimited**	Nelson 1957	C
88	**Biggles of the Interpol**	Brockhampton Press 1957	C
89	**Biggles on the Home Front**	Hodder & Stoughton 1957	C
90	**The Outer Space**	Hodder & Stoughton 1957	C
91	**Biggles Buries a Hatchet**	Brockhampton Press 1958	C
92	**Biggles on Mystery Island**	Hodder & Stoughton 1958	C
93	**Biggles Presses On**	Brockhampton Press 1958	C
94	**The Edge of Beyond**	Hodder & Stoughton 1958	C
95	**Biggles at World's End**	Brockhampton Press 1959	C
96	**Biggles' Combined Operation**	Hodder & Stoughton 1959	C
97	**Biggles in Mexico**	Brockhampton Press 1959	C
98	**The Death Rays of Ardilla**	Hodder & Stoughton 1959	C
99	**Adventures of the Junior Detection Club**	Parrish 1960	B
100	**Biggles and the Leopards of Zinn**	Brockhampton Press 1960	C
101	**Biggles Goes Home**	Hodder & Stoughton 1960	C
102	**To Worlds Unknown**	Hodder & Stoughton 1960	C
103	**Where the Golden Eagle Soars**	Hodder & Stoughton 1960	B

Johns

128	**Biggles Sorts It Out**	Brockhampton Press 1967	B
129	**Biggles and the Dark Intruder**	Knight 1967	A
130	**Biggles in the Underworld**	Brockhampton Press 1968	B
131	**The Boy Biggles**	Dean 1968	A
132	**Biggles and the Deep Blue Sea**	Brockhampton Press 1968	B
133	**Biggles and the Little Green God**	Brockhampton Press 1969	B
134	**Biggles and the Noble Lord**	Brockhampton Press 1969	B
135	**Biggles Sees Too Much**	Brockhampton Press 1970	B

Also of interest:
Biggles: The Authorised Biography by John Pearson (Sidgwick & Jackson 1979)

By Jove, Biggles: The Life of Captain W.E. Johns by Peter Beresford Ellis & Piers Williams (Allen 1981)

Jones, David   Born in Kent, 1895. Died 1974.

I had *heard* of *In Parenthesis* and *The Anathemata* – this mainly because of Auden's enthusiasm for it – but I hadn't read them. My first awareness of David Jones was as an artist, when I was devastated by the beauty of an ordination certificate he had done for Peter Levi. The lettering is as easy to feel as the poetry can be difficult to understand, so chock full of learning and allusion is it – recalling, in this respect, Auden and Pound. Jones's main work is worth the struggle. The later stuff – and the posthumous pieces – might always remain a conundrum understood fully only by its creator.

1	**In Parenthesis**	Faber 1937	N
	Although the Amer. ed. is 24 years after the English, it contains an Intro. by T.S. Eliot, reprinted in the first English paperback edition, Faber 1963	Chilmark 1961	I
2	**The Anathemata**	Faber 1952	L
		Chilmark 1963	D
3	**Epoch and Artist**	Faber 1959	H
		Chilmark 1964	D
4	**The Tribune's Visitation**	Fulcrum Press 1969	E
5	**The Sleeping Lord**	Faber 1974	E
6	**The Kensington Mass**	Agenda Editions 1975	C
7	**Letters to Vernon Watkins**	University of Wales Press 1976	C

8 **The Dying Gaul and Other Writings**	Faber 1978	**D**
9 **Introducing David Jones: A Selection of His Writings** Ed. John Matthias	Faber 1980	**C**
10 **Dai Greatcoat: A Self-Portrait in His Letters** Ed. René Hague.	Faber 1980	**D**
11 **The Painted Inscriptions of David Jones** By Nicolette Gray	Gordon Fraser 1980	**G**
12 **The Roman Quarry and Other Sequences**	Agenda 1981 Sheap Meadow (US) 1982	**C** **C**

D/ws are extremely important with David Jones, as those of 2, 3, 4 and 5 bear his exquisite typography. There have been two *Agenda* special numbers devoted to David Jones, Vol. 5 Nos 1–3 1967, and Vol. 11 No. 4–Vol. 12 No. 1 1973/74; and one slight book on his art, Penguin Modern Painters 1949; it is one of the most scarce of the series, and Grade **C**. One book of literary criticism has appeared: David Blamires **David Jones, Artist and Writer** Manchester University Press 1971, Grade **D**. In 1975, *The Tablet* published Peter Levi **In Memory of David Jones.** The d/w and frontis. of Peter Levi **Fresh Water, Sea Water** Black Raven Press 1966 reproduces Jones's superb design for Levi's ordination certificate.

It should be noted that in addition to the above, there has been published a considerable number of opulently bound and otherwise upholstered things, published at vast sums and now fetching about the same or, in a few cases, a bit more.

Joyce, James   Born in Ireland, 1882. Died 1941.

Joyce is scarce. There is really no such thing as a common or easy Joyce first edition; even the three volumes of his letters issued in the sixties have gone to ground. To collect Joyce seriously, then, you need to have a lot of luck in coming across the items, and a whole lot more money with which to pay for them. And Joyce's signature too, incidentally – whether upon a limited edition, or a trade edition, or a letter – is very valuable and rare.

1 **Chamber Music** (poems) The American first was unauthorized. The authorized edition was published later in the same year by Huebsch (**Q**)	Elkin Mathews 1907 Cornhill Co. 1918	**X** **R**
2 **Dubliners** (stories)	Grant Richards 1914 Huebsch 1916	**Q** **M**

3 **A Portrait of the Artist as a Young Man**   Huebsch 1916   **P**
Egoist Ltd 1917   **N**
The 1st English was American sheets.
In the following year The Egoist Ltd
published a 2nd edition, printed in
England.

4 **Exiles** (play)   Grant Richards 1918   **M**
This play was reissued in 1951 by the   Huebsch 1918   **K**
Viking Press 'with hitherto unpublished
notes by the author' (**H**). It was
published in this form in England by
Cape in 1952 (**H**)

5 **Ulysses** (novel)   Shakespeare Press   **U**
Limited to 1000 copies, 100 signed (**V**)   (Paris) 1922
Published in France.

6 **Ulysses**   Egoist Press 1922   **R**
This was the 1st English edition,
though printed in France. Limited to
2000 numbered copies.

7 **Ulysses**   Shakespeare Press   **P**
This was the 1st American edition,   (Paris) 1929
though unauthorized. The 1st
authorized American edition was
published in 1934 by Random House,
though set up from the Shakespeare
edition. The first printing of the
Random House ed., due to copyright,
was only 100 copies (**R**), and the
second printing 10 300 (**L**)

8 **Ulysses**   Bodley Head 1936   **L**
This was the 1st English edition
actually printed in England. 100 were
signed (**R**).

9 **Ulysses**   Bodley Head 1986   **E**
This is seen to be the definitive and   Penguin 1986   **C**
authorized text. Publication of the   Random House 1986   **D**
Bodley Head and Penguin editions was
simultaneous, the earliest copies
carrying an inserted leaf reading: 'This
edition of *Ulysses* was purchased on
Bloomsday, 16th June 1986.
Publication day of the new correct
text.'

10 **Pomes Penyeach**   Shakespeare & Co   **N**
100 were signed (**S**). The 1st American   (Paris) 1927
edition was published by Sylvia Beach
in 1931 (**M**). The 1st English edition –
but printed in France – was by the

Obelisk Press in 1932 (**K**) and the 1st
English edition printed in England was
by Faber in 1933 (**I**).

11 **Anna Livia Plurabelle** (fragment) The American ed. was limited to 850 signed copies, but the Faber ed. was in the Criterion Miscellany series, and unlimited.	Crosby Gaige (NY) 1928 Faber 1930	O F
12 **Tales Told of Shem and Shaun** Limited to 650 copies, 100 signed (**R**).	Black Sun Press (Paris) 1929	P
13 **Two Tales of Shem and Shaun** Extract from 11; 1st English.	Faber 1932	H
14 **Haveth Childers Everywhere** (fragment) Printed in France, but published in America. Limited to 685 copies, 100 signed (**Q**). The 1st English edition was published by Faber in the following year, in an unlimited edition (**E**).	Fountain Press 1930	L
15 **Collected Poems** Limited to 800 copies, 540 signed (**P**). A trade edition followed in 1937 from Viking (**H**).	Black Sun Press 1936	K
16 **Finnegans Wake**	Faber 1939 Viking 1939	L J
17 **Stephen Hero** (draft)	Cape 1944 New Directions 1944	J H
18 **The Essential James Joyce** (extracts)	Cape 1948	D
19 **The Letters** Vol.I	Faber 1957	H
20 **The Critical Writings**	Faber 1959	E
21 **The Cat and the Devil** (juvenile)	Faber 1965	F
22 **The Letters** Vol. II	Faber 1966	E
23 **The Letters** Vol. III	Faber 1966	E
24 **Giacomo Joyce**	Viking 1968 Faber 1968	G F

Bibliography:
John J. Slocum & Herbert Cahoon **A Bibliography of James Joyce**
Yale University Press 1953
There have been a vast number of books on Joyce, but below appears a
selection of the best:
T.S. Eliot **Introducing James Joyce** Faber 1942   Harry Levin **James
Joyce: A Critical Introduction** Faber 1944   Richard Ellmann **James
Joyce** OUP 1959; new edition OUP 1983.   Anthony Burgess **Here
Comes Everybody** Faber 1965   John Gross **Joyce** Fontana 1971   A
good deal of information is also given in Stanislaus Joyce **My Brother's**

Keeper Faber 1958. This was edited by Richard Ellmann, and has a Preface by T.S. Eliot.

Kästner, Erich Born in Germany, 1899. Died 1974.

Although a translation, a children's classic, and one that seems to be remembered by all with fondness. Kästner wrote other books, and the character Emil appears again, but none captures the great appeal of the following:

Emil and the Detectives (juvenile)	Cape 1930	**F**
This was first published in Germany in	Doubleday 1930	**D**
1929 as *Emil und die Detektive*. The 1st		
English edition is scarce.		

Kazantzakis, Nikos Born in Greece, 1885. Died 1957.

The author of quite a few novels, but still remembered for the one – and damnably hard to find it is, too.

Zorba the Greek (novel)	Lehmann 1952	**H**
The novel was originally published in	Simon & Schuster 1953	**E**
Greek in 1946. The Lehmann edition		
spells his name Kazantzaki. It is scarce.		

Keillor, Garrison Born in Midwest America, 1942.

Keillor has captivated millions on radio, and with his published funny/sad and accurate portrayals of small town American life. You either love it or loath it, actually – *Wobegon* was marvellous, certainly, but I think that even the most diehard fans were a little disappointed by *Radio Romance*.

1 **Lake Wobegon Days** (novel)	Viking US 1985	**F**
	Faber 1986	**D**
2 **Leaving Home** (novel)	Viking US 1988	**D**
	Faber 1988	**C**
3 **We Are Still Married** (novel)	Viking US 1989	**C**
	Faber 1989	**C**
4 **Radio Romance** (novel)	Viking US 1991	**C**
	Faber 1991	**C**

Kelman, James   Born in Glasgow, 1946.

Sombre, compelling and totally uncompromising – one of the more convincing new voices to have emerged recently; not to everyone's taste, to be sure – the sometimes Beckett-like language within the context of realist fiction can be brilliant, and grate like the devil – but fairly easy to gather at the moment.

1	**An Old Pub Near the Angel** (story)	Puckerbush Press US 1973	E
2	**Three Glasgow Writers** (stories) With Tom Leonard and Alex Hamilton.	Molendinar Press UK 1976	C
3	**Short Tales From the Nightshift** (stories)	Print Studio Press 1978	D
4	**Not Not While the Giro** (stories)	Polygon Press 1983	D
5	**The Busconductor Hines** (novel)	Polygon Press 1984	D
6	**A Chancer** (novel)	Polygon Press 1985	D
7	**Lean Tales** (stories) With Alasdair Gray and Agnes Owens.	Cape 1985	C
8	**Greyhound for Breakfast** (stories)	Secker & Warburg 1987	C
		Farrar Straus 1987	C
9	**A Disaffection** (novel)	Secker & Warburg 1989	C
		Farrar Straus 1989	C
10	**The Burn** (stories)	Secker & Warburg 1991	C
11	**Hardie and the Baird: The Last Days** (play)	Secker & Warburg 1991	B

Keneally, Thomas   Born in Sydney, 1935. Australian.

A very prolific author, still on the borderlines of being seriously collected – although, naturally enough, this is far from being true in his native Australia, where native literary heroes are cherished. Still good value, then.

The first seven of Keneally's books were published in Britain and Australia simultaneously.

1	**The Place at Whitton** (novel)	Cassell 1964	H
		Walker 1965	D
2	**The Fear** (novel)	Cassell 1965	F
3	**Bring Larks and Heroes** (novel)	Cassell 1967	E
		Viking 1968	D
4	**Three Cheers for the Paraclete** (novel)	Angus & Robertson 1968	D
		Viking 1969	C
5	**The Survivor** (novel)	Angus & Robertson 1969	D

6 **A Dutiful Daughter** (novel)	Angus & Robertson 1971	C
	Viking 1971	C
7 **The Chant of Jimmie Blacksmith** (novel)	Angus & Robertson 1972	C
	Viking 1972	C
8 **Blood Red, Sister Rose** (novel)	Collins 1974	C
	Viking 1974	C
9 **Moses the Lawgiver** (novelization)	Harper 1975	C
	Collins 1976	C
10 **Gossip from the Forest** (novel	Collins 1975	C
	Harcourt Brace 1976	C
11 **Season in Purgatory** (novel)	Collins 1976	C
	Harcourt Brace 1977	C
12 **A Victim of the Aurora** (novel)	Collins 1977	C
	Harcourt Brace 1978	C
13 **Ned Kelly and the City of Bees** (juvenile)	Cape 1978	C
	Godine 1981	C
14 **Passenger** (novel)	Collins 1979	C
	Harcourt Brace 1979	C
15 **The Confederates** (novel)	Collins 1979	C
	Harcourt Brace 1980	C
16 **The Cut-Rate Kingdom**	Wild Cat Press (Australia; periodical) 1980	C
	1st book form Penguin (Australia) 1984	B
	Allen Lane (UK) 1984	C
17 **Schindler's Ark** (novel)	Hodder & Stoughton 1982	D
18 **Schindler's List** (same as 16)	Simon & Schuster 1982	D
19 **Outback** (non-fiction)	Hodder & Stoughton 1983	C
20 **A Family Madness** (novel)	Hodder & Stoughton 1985	C
	Simon & Schuster 1986	C
21 **The Playmaker** (novel)	Hodder & Stoughton 1987	B
	Simon & Schuster 1987	B
22 **Australia: Beyond the Dreamtime** (non-fiction) With Patsy Adam-Smith and Robyn Davidson	BBC 1987	B
	Facts on File US 1989	B
23 **Towards Asmara** (novel)	Hodder & Stoughton 1989	B
24 **To Asmara** (same as 23)	Warner 1989	B
25 **Flying Hero Class** (novel)	Hodder & Stoughton 1991	B

		Warner 1991	**B**
26	**The Place Where Souls are Born**	Prentice-Hall 1991	**B**
	(non-fiction)	Hodder & Stoughton 1992	**B**
27	**A Woman of the Inner Sea**	Hodder & Stoughton 1992	**B**
	(novel)	Doubleday 1992	**B**

Kerouac, Jack   Born in Massachussets, 1922. Died 1969.

Kerouac has a following, and is hard to gather. The novels are, I think, infinitely more desirable than the verse, and the highlight is *On the Road*.

1	**The Town and the City** (novel)	Harcourt Brace 1950	**L**
	(Author's name appears as *John* Kerouac)	Eyre & Spottiswoode 1951	**K**
2	**On the Road** (novel)	Viking 1957	**N**
		Deutsch 1958	**L**
3	**The Subterraneans** (novel)	Grove Press 1958	**J**
		Deutsch 1960	**H**
4	**The Dharma Bums** (novel)	Viking 1958	**J**
		Deutsch 1959	**H**
5	**Mexico City Blues** (verse)	Grove Press 1959	**G**
6	**Hymn – God Pray For Me** (verse)	Privately printed 1959	**I**
7	**Doctor Sax: Faust Part Three** (novel)	Grove Press 1959	**G**
		Evergreen 1961	**D**
8	**Maggie Cassidy** (novel)	Avon 1959	**F**
		Panther 1960	**D**
9	**Excerpts from 'Visions of Cody'** (novel)	New Directions 1959	**E**
10	**Tristessa** (novel)	Avon 1960	**E**
11	**Rimbaud** (verse)	City Lights 1960	**E**
12	**Book of Dreams** (verse)	City Lights 1960	**E**
13	**The Scripture of the Golden Eternity** (verse)	Totem-Corinth (US) 1960	**D**
14	**Lonesome Traveler** (prose)	McGraw Hill 1960	**E**
	Drawings by Larry Rivers.	Deutsch 1962	**D**
15	**Big Sur** (novel)	Farrar Straus 1962	**E**
		Deutsch 1963	**D**
16	**Poem**	Privately printed 1962	**H**
17	**Visions of Gerard** (novel)	Farrar Straus 1963	**E**
	The Deutsch edition includes 10.	Deutsch 1964	**D**
18	**Desolation Angels** (novel)	Coward McCann 1965	**E**
		Deutsch 1966	**D**
19	**Satori in Paris** (novel)	Grove Press 1966	**E**
		Deutsch 1967	**D**

20 **Hugo Weber** (verse)	Portents (US) 1967	**E**
21 **Someday You'll be Lying** (verse)	Privately printed 1968	**H**
22 **Vanity of Duluoz:**	Coward McCann 1968	**E**
An Adventurous Education 1935–46	Deutsch 1969	**D**
(novel)		
23 **A Last Haiku** (verse)	Privately printed 1969	**H**
24 **Pic** (novel)	Grove Press 1971	**D**
The Deutsch edition includes 3.	Deutsch 1973	**C**
25 **Scattered Poems**	City Lights 1971	**F**
26 **Trip, Trap** (verse)	Grey Fox Press 1973	**F**
27 **Heaven and Other Poems**	Grey Fox Press 1977	**F**
28 **Baby Driver: A Story about Myself**	St Martin's 1981	**D**
Ed. Jan Kerouac.	Deutsch 1982	**C**

Bibliography:
Ann Charters **A Bibliography of Works by Jack Kerouac (Jean Louis de Kerouac) 1939–1967** Phoenix Bookshop 1967; revised edition 1975.

Kesey, Ken   Born in Colorado, 1935. American.

A zestful and sparing author – the classic, of course, remains *Cuckoo*, but pretty much the whole of the oeuvre is well worthwhile.

1 **One Flew over the Cuckoo's Nest**	Viking 1962	**M**
(novel)	Methuen 1963	**I**
2 **Sometimes a Great Notion** (novel)	Viking 1964	**G**
	Methuen 1966	**E**
3 **Kesey's Garage Sale** (prose)	Viking 1973	**D**
4 **The Day Superman Dies** (story)	Lord John Press US 1980	**F**
5 **Demon Box** (novel)	Viking US 1986	**C**
	Methuen 1986	**C**
6 **Little Tricker the Squirrel Meets Big Double the Bear** (juvenile)	Viking US 1990	**C**
7 **The Further Inquiry** (novel)	Viking 1990	**C**

Koestler, Arthur   Born in Hungary, 1905. Died 1983.

Quite a few of Koestler's highlights are surprisingly easy to find – including his very first, due to the enormous quantities printed for the Left Book Club – although the absolute highlight (*Darkness at Noon*) remains elusive. Koestler is neither avidly collected nor entirely ignored at the moment: a representation contents most people.

Koestler

1	**Spanish Testament** (autobiog.) This is the orange-wrapped Left Book Club edition. An abridged edition was published in America by Macmillan in 1942 as **Dialogue with Death**.	Gollancz 1937	C
2	**The Gladiators** (novel)	Cape 1939 Macmillan (US) 1939	E C
3	**Darkness at Noon** (novel)	Cape 1940 Macmillan 1941	L H
4	**Scum of the Earth** (autobiog.)	Cape 1941 Macmillan 1941	E C
5	**Arrival and Departure** (novel)	Cape 1943 Macmillan 1943	D C
6	**The Yogi and the Commissar** (essays)	Cape 1945 Macmillan 1945	D C
7	**Thieves in the Night** (novel)	Macmillan (UK) 1946 Macmillan (US) 1946	D C
8	**Insight and Outlook** (essay)	Macmillan (UK) 1949 Macmillan (US) 1949	C C
9	**Promise and Fulfilment** (non- fiction)	Macmillan (UK) 1949 Macmillan (US) 1949	C C
10	**The Age of Longing** (novel)	Collins 1951 Macmillan 1951	C C
11	**Arrow in the Blue** (autobiog.)	Collins/Hamilton 1952 Macmillan 1952	C C
12	**The Invisible Writing** (autobiog.)	Collins/Hamilton 1954 Macmillan 1954	C C
13	**The Trail of the Dinosaur** (essays)	Collins 1955 Macmillan 1955	C C
14	**Reflections on Hanging** (essay)	Gollancz 1957 Macmillan 1957	C C
15	**The Sleepwalkers** (non-fiction)	Hutchinson 1959 Macmillan 1959	C C
16	**The Lotus and the Robot** (essays)	Hutchinson 1960 Macmillan 1961	C C
17	**Hanged by the Neck** (essay)	Penguin 1961	B
18	**The Act of Creation** (non-fiction)	Hutchinson 1964 Macmillan 1964	C C
19	**The Ghost in the Machine** (non- fiction)	Hutchinson 1967 Macmillan 1968	C C
20	**Drinkers of Infinity: Essays 1955–1967**	Hutchinson 1968 Macmillan 1969	C C
21	**The Case of the Midwife Toad** (non-fiction)	Hutchinson 1971 Random House 1972	C C
22	**The Call-Girls** (novel)	Hutchinson 1972 Random House 1973	C C
23	**The Roots of Coincidence** (non- fiction)	Hutchinson 1972 Random House 1972	C C

24 **The Lion and the Ostrich** (essay)	OUP 1973	C
25 **The Challenge of Chance** (non-fiction)	Hutchinson 1973	C
With Alister Hardy and Robert Harvie.	Random House 1975	C
26 **The Heel of Achilles: Essays 1968–1973**	Hutchinson 1974	C
	Random House 1975	C
27 **The Thirteenth Tribe** (non-fiction)	Hutchinson 1976	C
	Random House 1976	C
28 **Janus: A Summing Up** (essays)	Hutchinson 1978	C
	Random House 1978	C
29 **Bricks to Babel** (essays)	Hutchinson 1980	C
	Random House 1981	C
30 **Stranger on the Square**	Hutchinson 1984	C
This is the fourth, unfinished, volume of	Random House 1984	C

This is the fourth, unfinished, volume of
autobiography, following 4, 11 and 12.
It is billed as having been written by
Arthur and Cynthia Koestler.

Biography:
Koestler: A Biography Iain Hamilton   Secker & Warburg 1982
Macmillan US 1982

Larkin, Philip   Born in Warwickshire, 1922. Died 1985.

Although Larkin specified in his will that all his remaining letters should be
burned, unread, with the exception of those written to Kingsley Amis,
Robert Conquest and Barbara Pym – these he bequeathed to the Bodleian
Library in Oxford, together with his correspondence with his long-standing
confidante Margaret Jones – 1992 saw the publication of a *Selected Letters*.
The reason for this, apparently, is that the will was 'open to interpretation'.
Well, I *suppose* public interest can *sort* of justify it . . . or maybe not. Anyway,
Larkin's *Collected Poems* of 1988 has sold nearly 80,000 copies in hardback
alone, so the fan club remains as mighty as ever.

1 **The North Ship** (verse)	Fortune Press 1945	R

Black cloth, the maroon d/w describing
it as being one of the Fortune Poets
series. There was an unauthorized
edition published in 1965 (though
stating 'first published 1945' on the verso
of the title page) in maroon cloth (**H**).
About 500 were printed, but the edition
was recalled when Larkin became aware
of its existence. Faber published an
edition in 1966, with a new introduction
and an extra poem (**F**).

2 **Jill** (novel) A revised edition was published in 1964 by Faber, and in America by the St Martin's Press (**H**).	Fortune Press 1946	**P**
3 **A Girl in Winter** (novel)	Faber 1947 St Martin's 1957	**O** **G**
4 **XX Poems** Only 100 printed, all for the author – none for sale.	Privately printed 1951	**R**
5 **The Fantasy Poets No. 21** About 300 copies.	Fantasy Press 1954	**N**
6 **The Less Deceived** (verse)	Marvell Press 1955 St Martin's 1960	**O** **J**
7 **The Whitsun Weddings** (verse)	Faber 1964 Random House 1964	**H** **F**
8 **All What Jazz: A Record Diary** **1961–68**	Faber 1970 St Martin's 1970	**E** **E**
9 **The Explosion** This was a single-sheet poem, in a signed limited edition of 1000 available at five guineas, only on subscription.	Poem-of-the-Mouth Club 1970	**L**
10 **The Oxford Book of Twentieth-** **Century English Verse** This very important book was edited by Larkin.	OUP 1973	**D**
11 **High Windows** (verse)	Faber 1974 Farrar Straus 1974	**E** **C**
12 **Required Writing** (prose)	Faber 1983 Farrar Straus 1983	**E** **C**
13 **Collected Poems**	Faber 1988 Farrar Straus 1988	**D** **C**
14 **Selected Letters** Larkin also wrote the Preface for **The** **Arts Council Collection of Modern** **Literary Manuscripts 1963–72** Turret Books 1974, a fascinating and valuable book in itself (**D**).	Faber 1992	**C**

Also of note:

Larkin at Sixty A tribute, with contributions by Kingsley Amis, John Betjeman, and Seamus Heaney, among others.	Faber 1982

Bibliography:
B.C. Blomfield **Philip Larkin: A Bibliography 1933–76** Faber 1979

Lawrence, D.H.   Born in Nottinghamshire, 1885. Died 1930.

Still very much collected, and at last living down the reputation bestowed upon him by the idiots as having been the man who wrote that dirty book, for to a whole new generation The Trial of Lady Chatterley is ancient history. I do wish they would stop filming Lawrence, though. It is a personal view, of course, but I have never seen any film version of a Lawrence novel or story that has not been in some way *embarrassing* – something the books are not. Certainly, the films do nothing to enhance the author's reputation.

As will be seen from the following valuations, a great deal of the *œuvre* remains scarce and expensive. This position will persist.

Below is all his main work, though I have omitted a few privately printed items, special editions, etc. In some cases, however – notably *Lady Chatterley's Lover* – there are several relevant editions, and these have been included.

1	**The White Peacock** (novel)	Duffield (NY) 1911	Q
		Heinemann 1911	P
2	**The Trespasser** (novel)	Duckworth 1912	O
		Kennerley 1912	M
3	**Love Poems and Others**	Duckworth 1913	M
		Kennerley 1913	J
4	**Sons and Lovers** (novel)	Duckworth 1913	O
		Kennerley 1913	M
5	**The Widowing of Mrs Holroyd** (play)	Kennerly 1914	K
		Duckworth 1914	K
6	**The Prussian Officer** (stories)	Duckworth 1914	K
		Huebsch 1916	I
7	**The Rainbow** (novel)	Methuen 1915	M
		Huebsch 1916	J
8	**Twilight in Italy** (travel)	Duckworth 1916	K
		Huebsch 1916	H
9	**Amores** (verse)	Duckworth 1916	I
		Huebsch 1916	G
10	**New Poems**	Secker 1918	I
		Huebsch 1920	G
11	**The Lost Girl** (novel)	Secker 1920	I
		Seltzer 1921	G
12	**Women in Love** (novel) This was the 1st trade edition, preceded by 50 numbered and signed (**R**).	Secker 1921	L
13	**Sea and Sardinia** (travel)	Seltzer 1921	J
		Secker 1923	H
14	**Aaron's Rod** (novel)	Seltzer 1922	K
		Secker 1922	I
15	**Fantastia of the Unconscious** (non-fiction)	Seltzer 1922	I
		Secker 1923	H

16 **England, My England** (stories)	Seltzer 1922 Secker 1924	I H
17 **The Ladybird** (novelettes) Incl. **The Fox** and **The Captain's** **Doll.**	Secker 1923	I
18 **The Captain's Doll** (as in 17)	Seltzer 1923	G
19 **Kangaroo** (novel)	Secker 1923 Seltzer 1923	J H
20 **Birds, Beasts and Flowers** (verse)	Seltzer 1923 Secker 1923	I H
21 **The Boy in the Bush** (novel)	Secker 1924 Seltzer 1924	K I
22 **Reflections on the Death of a** **Porcupine and Further Essays**	Centaur Press, US 1925 Secker 1934	I H
23 **The Plumed Serpent** (novel)	Secker 1926 Knopf 1926	K H
24 **David** (play)	Secker 1926 Knopf 1926	G F
25 **Mornings in Mexico** (travel)	Secker 1927 Knopf 1927	K I
26 **The Woman Who Rode Away** (stories)	Secker 1928 Knopf 1928	H G
27 **Lady Chatterley's Lover** (novel) Printed and published in Florence.	Privately printed 1928	R
28 **Lady Chatterley's Lover** These are the first English and American *expurgated* editions.	Secker 1932 Knopf 1932	M K
29 **Lady Chatterley's Lover** These are the first American and English *unexpurgated* editions, the Penguin following the infamous trial. The Heinemann edition is really a hardback version of the Penguin.	Grove Press 1959 Penguin 1960 Heinemann 1961	E C D
30 **Collected Poems** (2 vols)	Secker 1928	G
31 **Pornography and Obscenity** (essay)	Faber 1929	D
32 **Pansies** (verse)	Secker 1929	G
33 **Nettles** (verse)	Faber 1930	G
34 **The Virgin and the Gypsy** (novel) These were preceded by a limited edition published by Orioli in Florence (**N**).	Secker 1930 Knopf 1930	I G
35 **The Man Who Died** (novelette) This had been published as **The** **Escaped Cock** in Paris in 1929.	Secker 1931	G
36 **Etruscan Places** (travel)	Secker 1932	G
37 **The Letters** Ed. Aldous Huxley.	Heinemann 1932	E

38 **The Lovely Lady** (stories)	Secker 1933	**F**
	Viking 1933	**E**
39 **Last Poems**	Secker 1933	**E**
40 **The Plays**	Secker 1933	**E**
41 **The Tales**	Secker 1934	**E**
42 **A Collier's Friday Night** (play)	Secker 1934	**F**
43 **Pornography and So On** (essay)	Faber 1936	**D**
44 **Poems** (2 vols)	Heinemann 1939	**E**
45 **The Complete Poems** (3 vols)	Heinemann 1957	**F**
46 **The Complete Poems** (2 vols)	Heinemann 1964	**E**
47 **The Complete Plays**	Heinemann 1965	**D**
48 **The Letters of D.H. Lawrence** Volume I.	CUP 1979	**D**
49 **The Letters of D.H. Lawrence** Volume II.	CUP 1981	**C**
50 **Mr Noon** (novel)	CUP 1984	**C**
51 **The Letters of D.H. Lawrence** Volume III.	CUP 1984	**C**
52 **The Letters of D.H. Lawrence** Volume IV	CUP 1987	**C**
53 **The Letters of D.H. Lawrence** Volume V	CUP 1989	**D**
54 **The Letters of D.H. Lawrence** Volume VI	CUP 1991	**D**
55 **The Letters of D.H. Lawrence** Volume VII	CUP 1993	**D**

Bibliography:
Warren Roberts **A Bibliography of D.H. Lawrence** CUP 1982.

Biography:
Harry T. Moore **The Priest of Love** Heinemann 1974.

Lawrence, T.E.   Born in Caernarvonshire, 1888. Died 1935.

The real rarities by Lawrence remain so (somewhere in editions of single figures and may be seen only in such places as the British Museum or the Bodleian) but first trade editions of his best known works remain quite freely available and are still good value.

Variously known as J.H. Ross, T.E. Shaw and T.E. Lawrence, he is very difficult and expensive to collect seriously, though trade editions of his major works may be acquired quite easily, and usually at surprisingly low prices.

The New Cambridge Bibliography of English Literature vol. 4 lists all of Lawrence's works, and gives a few bibliographies, but these all seem to have been limited editions, or duplicated in small numbers.

Below are the major works.

1 **Revolt in the Desert**	Cape 1927	**G**
There were also simultaneous limited editions – of 315 and 250 copies, respectively, in England and America.	Doran 1927	**E**
2 **Seven Pillars of Wisdom**	Cape 1936	**H**
This, it must be noted, is the first *trade* edition. The 1st edition was privately printed in Oxford in 1922 in an edition of 8 copies. It was printed again in 1925, privately, in a revised edition of 100 copies, and once more, in 1926 – text completely revised, with a new prefatory note – privately printed in England and America in editions of 202 and 22 copies, respectively.	Doubleday 1936	**E**
3 **The Letters of T.E. Lawrence**	Cape 1938	**D**
Edited by David Garnett, who also edited **The Essential T.E. Lawrence**, Cape 1951 (**C**).	Doubleday 1939	**D**
4 **The Mint**	Cape 1955	**D**
Once more, this is the first *trade* edition. It was first published in New York in 1936 in an edition of 50.	Doubleday 1955	**D**

There is a vast number of books on Lawrence, though no definitive biography has yet emerged. One outstanding title is: Robert Graves *Lawrence and the Arabs* Cape 1927. Published by Doubleday in America in 1928 as *Lawrence and the Arabian Adventure*.

Leacock, Stephen   Born in Hampshire, 1859. Died 1944.

Although the author of many serious works – *Elements of Political Science* (1906), to give an example – he is remembered for his humorous stuff. There are a great number of these, and collectors have recently shown fair interest in them. The early titles, such as the two examples quoted below, might reach Grade D, but generally speaking, Grade A–B is the norm.

1 **Literary Lapses**	Dodd 1910	**D**
	Lane 1910	**C**
2 **Moonbeams from the Larger Lunacy**	Lane (US) 1915	**C**
	Lane (UK) 1915	**C**

Le Carré, John   Born in Dorset, 1931. Pseudonym for
David Cornwell.

Still a very collected author, though most collections are dogged by the lack of his first two novels. There are so many people after good copies of these that I think they could very easily fetch twice the values I estimate here. This is an example of how very difficult it is to value a scarce book that is hugely in demand – you can record the price paid for the last copy that arose, but how to project that of the next? Nothing after the mid-sixties will ever be difficult, though, simply because the print runs are so massive – 150,000 copies of a first edition is not uncommon.

1	**Call for the Dead** (novel)	Gollancz 1961	Q
		Walker 1962	K
2	**A Murder of Quality** (novel)	Gollancz 1962	P
		Walker 1963	J
3	**The Spy Who Came in from the Cold** (novel)	Gollancz 1963	K
		Coward McCann 1963	G
4	**The Looking-Glass War** (novel)	Heinemann 1965	E
		Coward McCann 1965	C
5	**A Small Town in Germany** (novel)	Heinemann 1968	E
		Coward McCann 1968	C
6	**The Naive and Sentimental Lover** (novel)	Hodder & Stoughton 1971	D
		Knopf 1971	C
7	**Tinker, Tailor, Soldier, Spy** (novel)	Hodder & Stoughton 1974	C
		Knopf 1974	C
8	**The Honourable Schoolboy** (novel)	Hodder & Stoughton 1977	C
		Knopf 1977	C
9	**Smiley's People** (novel) 7, 8 and 9 form the Smiley trilogy. See also 10.	Hodder & Stoughton 1980	C
		Knopf 1980	C
10	**The Quest for Karla** This is an omnibus, containing 7, 8 and 9.	Hodder & Stoughton 1982	C
		Knopf 1982	C
11	**The Little Drummer Girl** (novel)	Hodder & Stoughton 1983	C
		Knopf 1983	C
12	**A Perfect Spy** (novel)	Hodder & Stoughton 1986	C
		Knopf 1986	C
13	**The Clandestine Muse** (prose)	Seluzicki US 1986	C
14	**Vanishing England** (non-fiction) (with Gareth H. Davies)	Salem House US 1987	C

15 **The Russia House** (novel)	Hodder & Stoughton 1989	C
	Knopf 1989	C
16 **The Secret Pilgrim** (novel)	Hodder & Stoughton 1991	C
	Knopf 1991	C

Lee, Laurie   Born in Gloucestershire, 1914.

One cannot exactly say that the third part of Laurie Lee's autobiography was eagerly awaited, as few were aware that such a volume had even been contemplated. Lee himself once said, indeed, that there would not be a third volume because there was nothing else to write – leading one or two reviewers to wonder whether here was not more fiction than fact; not that it terribly much matters either way – it was good to see a new book at all.

1 **The Sun My Monument** (verse)	Hogarth Press 1944	I
	Doubleday 1947	E
2 **Land at War** (non-fiction) Anonymous.	HMSO 1945	G
3 **We Made a Film in Cyprus** With Ralph Keene.	Longman 1947	F
4 **The Bloom of Candles** (verse)	Lehmann 1947	E
5 **Peasant's Priest** (play)	Goulden (Canterbury) 1947	E
6 **The Voyage of Magellan** (play)	Lehmann 1948	E
7 **My Many-Coated Man** (verse)	Deutsch 1955	E
	Coward McCann 1957	D
8 **A Rose for Winter** (travel)	Hogarth Press 1955	E
	Morrow 1956	D
9 **Cider with Rosie** (autobiog.)	Hogarth Press 1959	E
10 **The Edge of Day** (same as 9)	Morrow 1960	D
11 **Poems**	Studio Vista 1960	D
12 **Man Must Move** (juvenile)	Rathbone 1960	F
13 **The Wonderful World of Transportation** (same as 12)	Doubleday 1961	C
14 **As I Walked Out One Midsummer Morning** (autobiog.)	Deutsch 1969	C
	Atheneum 1969	C
15 **I Can't Stay Long** (pieces)	Deutsch 1975	C
	Atheneum 1975	C
16 **Innocence in the Mirror** (prose)	Morrow 1978	C
17 **Selected Poems**	Deutsch 1983	C
18 **Two Women** (photographic essay)	Deutsch 1983	C
19 **A Moment of War** (autobiog.)	Viking UK 1991	C
	Viking US 1991	C
20 **Red Sky at Sunrise** (contains nos. 9, 14 & 19)	Viking UK 1992	B

A pair from a unique Scottish writer (with artwork by the author), and Dahl's very scarce first book

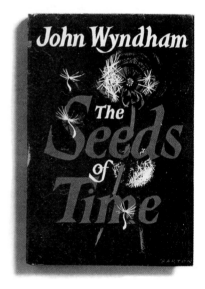

A scarce anthology, with representative works by its three contributors

Dahl's rare novel and his short stories, together with two classic works of fantasy

A scarce Waugh, a representative Green in a John Piper dust-wrapper, a Greene with a film tie-in wrapper, and the English first edition of Bellow's first novel

Murdoch's second and third novels, and two big novels from J. B. Priestley, with whom she collaborated on her dramatized version of *A Severed Head*

The first (pseudonymous) edition of *A Grief Observed* together with the later issue.
The first edition of *Animal Farm* and the curious first illustrated edition

Margaret Drabble's first four novels

Representative works from four of Faber's leading poets

Lehmann, Rosamond   Born in Buckinghamshire, 1901. Died 1990.

Still very popular among a (largely female) elite, but only the earliest stuff is actively sought out – everything published since the war is, as may be seen, pretty reasonably priced.

1	**Dusty Answer** (novel)	Chatto & Windus 1927	K
		Holt 1927	H
2	**A Note in Music** (novel)	Chatto & Windus 1930	J
		Holt 1930	H
3	**Letter to a Sister** (essay)	Hogarth Press 1931	G
		Harcourt Brace 1932	F
4	**Invitation to the Waltz** (novel)	Chatto & Windus 1932	J
		Holt 1932	H
5	**The Weather in the Streets** (novel)	Collins 1936	K
		Reynal Hitchcock 1936	H
6	**No More Music** (play)	Collins 1939	E
		Reynal Hitchcock 1945	C
7	**The Ballad and the Source** (novel)	Collins 1944	E
		Reynal Hitchcock 1945	C
8	**The Gipsy's Baby and Other Stories**	Collins 1946	E
		Reynal Hitchcock 1947	D
9	**The Echoing Grove** (novel)	Collins 1953	C
		Harcourt Brace 1953	C
10	**A Man Seen Afar** (prose) With W. Tudor Pole.	Spearman 1965	D
11	**The Swan in the Evening: Fragments of an Inner Life**	Collins 1967	C
		Harcourt Brace 1967	C
12	**Letters from Our Daughters** 2 vols. With Cynthia Hill Sandys.	College of Psychic Studies 1972	D
13	**The Sea-Grape Tree** (novel)	Collins 1976	C
		Harcourt Brace 1977	C

Lennon, John   Born in Liverpool, 1940. Died 1980.

I still rate highly Lennon's two little books from the sixties – in their own right, as it were. In a way, it's a shame he didn't go on to write more – though thinking about it, he was rather busy doing other things. Anyway, here they are – along with a rather disappointing collection of bits and bobs.

Unless one is a fanatical Beatles collector (in which case all the flimsy, tasteless tin and plastic trash that one's parents said one was mad to spend three-and-eleven on in the sixties, one will now buy all over again at fifty quid a throw), only two extraneous items stand out as relevant – both of which were contemporary – and they are listed below.

Lessing

1 **In His Own Write**	Cape 1964	**E**
	Simon & Schuster 1964	**C**
2 **A Spaniard in the Works**	Cape 1965	**D**
	Simon & Schuster 1965	**C**
3 **Skywriting by Word of Mouth**	Pan 1986	**C**
	Harper and Row 1986	**C**

Also of note:

Brian Epstein **A Cellarful of Noise**	Souvenir Press 1964	**E**
Hunter Davies **The Beatles**	Heinemann 1968	**E**
	(Revised and updated edition, Cape 1985)	**C**

Lessing, Doris   Born in Persia (Iran), 1919. British.

It would be an arduous task – and not always a rewarding one – to attempt to gather the whole of Lessing. Certainly it is still the earlier work that shines out – and that (particularly nos 1, 3, 6 and 14) is exactly what the collectors want.

1 **The Grass is Singing** (novel)	Joseph 1950	**M**
	Crowell 1950	**J**
2 **This was the Old Chief's Country** (stories)	Joseph 1951	**L**
	Crowell 1952	**H**
3 **Martha Quest** (novel)	Joseph 1952	**I**
4 **Five: Short Novels**	Joseph 1953	**H**
5 **Retreat to Innocence** (novel)	Joseph 1953	**I**
6 **A Proper Marriage** (novel)	Joseph 1954	**I**
The American ed. includes 3.	Simon & Schuster 1964	**D**
7 **Going Home** (non-fiction)	Joseph 1957	**G**
	Ballantine 1968	**C**
8 **The Habit of Loving** (stories)	MacGibbon & Kee 1957	**F**
	Crowell 1958	**D**
9 **A Ripple from the Storm** (novel)	Joseph 1958	**E**
10 **Fourteen Poems**	Scorpion Press 1959	**F, J**
	(50 signed)	
11 **In Pursuit of the English:** **A Documentary**	Joseph 1960	**F**
12 **Portrait of the English** (same as 11)	Simon & Schuster 1961	**C**
13 **Play with a Tiger** (play)	Joseph 1962	**G**
14 **The Golden Notebook** (novel)	Joseph 1962	**L**
	Simon & Schuster 1962	**H**
15 **A Man and Two Women: Stories**	MacGibbon & Kee 1963	**F**
	Simon & Schuster 1963	**D**
16 **African Stories**	Joseph 1964	**F**
	Simon & Schuster 1965	**D**

17 **Landlocked** (novel)	MacGibbon & Kee 1965	**D**
The Amer. ed. includes 9.	Simon & Schuster 1966	**C**
18 **Particularly Cats** (non-fiction)	Joseph 1967	**D**
	Simon & Schuster 1967	**C**
19 **Nine African Stories**	Longman 1968	**D**
20 **The Four-Gated City** (novel)	MacGibbon & Kee 1969	**C**
This completes the **Children of Violence** sequence, the other volumes being 3, 6, 9 and 17.	Knopf 1969	**C**
21 **Briefing for a Descent into Hell** (novel)	Cape 1971	**D**
	Knopf 1973	**C**
22 **The Story of a Non-Marrying Man** (stories)	Cape 1972	**D**
23 **The Temptation of Jack Orkney** (same as 22)	Knopf 1972	**C**
24 **The Summer Before the Dark** (novel)	Cape 1973	**C**
	Knopf 1973	**C**
25 **A Small Personal Voice** (pieces)	Knopf 1974	**C**
26 **The Memoirs of a Survivor** (novel)	Octagaon Press 1974	**C**
	Knopf 1975	**C**
27 **A Small Personal Voice: Essays, Reviews and Interviews**	Knopf 1974	**C**
28 **Collected Stories**	Cape 1978	**C**
2 volumes. All the stories appear in the one-volume **Stories**, published by Knopf in the same year (**C**).		
29 **Shikasta** (novel)	Cape 1979	**C**
	Knopf 1979	**C**
30 **The Marriages between Zones Three Four and Five** (novel)	Cape 1980	**C**
	Knopf 1980	**C**
31 **The Sirian Experiments** (novel)	Cape 1981	**C**
	Knopf 1981	**C**
32 **The Making of the Representative for Planet 8** (novel)	Cape 1982	**C**
	Knopf 1982	**C**
33 **The Sentimental Agents in the Volyen Empire** (novel)	Cape 1983	**C**
	Knopf 1983	**C**
34 **The Diary of a Good Neighbour** (novel) (pseud. Jane Somers)	Joseph 1983	**C**
	Knopf 1983	**C**
35 **If the Old Could . . .** (novel) (pseud. Jane Somers)	Joseph 1984	**C**
	Knopf 1984	**C**
36 **The Good Terrorist** (novel)	Cape 1985	**C**
	Knopf 1985	**C**
37 **Prisons We Choose to Live Inside** (non-fiction)	CBC Canada 1986	**C**
	Cape 1987	**C**
	Harper 1987	**C**

38	**The Wind Blows Away Our Words, and Other Documents Relating to Afghanistan** (non-fiction)	Pan 1987	**B**
		Vintage 1987	**B**
39	**The Fifth Child** (novel)	Cape 1988	**B**
		Knopf 1988	**B**
40	**The Doris Lessing Reader**	Cape 1988	**B**
		Knopf 1989	**B**
41	**London Observed: Stories and Sketches**	Cape 1992	**B**
42	**The Real Thing** (same as 41)	HarperCollins US 1992	**B**
43	**African Laughter** (novel)	HarperCollins UK 1992	**B**

Lessing is also the author of several plays, the following having been published:
Each His Own Wilderness (in **New English Dramatists**, Penguin 1959)   **Play with a Tiger** (in **Plays By and About Women**, Random House 1973)   **The Singing Door** (in **Second Playbill 2**, Hutchinson 1973).

Lewis, C.S.   Born in Belfast, 1898. Died 1963.

My old English master at school had been under Lewis at Oxford, and he confirmed my impression that here was indeed a remarkable man. A convert to Anglicanism, much of his writing was given over to religion, but with none of the dullness that this might imply – *The Screwtape Letters* and *Surprised By Joy* (his autobiographical account of his religious conversion) being minor classics. In all other fields of writing he established classics, too – literary criticism, science fiction, philosophy and children's books. Certainly, if all the children of my acquaintance are anything to go by, *The Lion, The Witch, and the Wardrobe* will be around for ever.

In passing, I should like to heartily recommend *Experiment in Criticism* to any student of literature. It is short enough to digest completely, and it really helps one to *understand*, instead of merely confusing the reader or condescending, as do so many works purporting to be its equal.

Lewis published a large number of books, many of them theological, and many of very specific literary criticism. A checklist may be found in *The New Cambridge Bibliography of English Literature* vol. 4, but below are his absolute highlights, of which there are quite a few.

1	**The Allegory of Love** (non-fiction)	OUP 1936	**I**
		OUP (US) 1936	**G**
2	**Out of the Silent Planet** (novel)	Bodley Head, Lane 1938	**N**
		Macmillan (US) 1943	**E**
3	**The Screwtape Letters** (religious)	Bles 1942	**F**
		Saunders 1942	**D**
4	**Perelandra** (novel)	Bodley Head, Lane 1943	**N**
		Macmillan 1944	**I**

5 **That Hideous Strength** (novel) (2, 4 and 5 form his S.F. trilogy)	Bodley Head, Lane 1945 Macmillan 1946	L G
6 **The Lion, the Witch, and the Wardrobe** (juvenile)	Bles 1950 Macmillan 1950	O J
7 **Prince Caspian** (juvenile)	Bles 1951 Macmillan 1951	M I
8 **The Voyage of the Dawn Treader** (juvenile)	Bles 1952 Macmillan 1952	L H
9 **The Silver Chair** (juvenile)	Bles 1953 Macmillan 1953	K H
10 **The Horse and His Boy** (juvenile)	Bles 1954 Macmillan 1954	J G
11 **The Magician's Nephew** (juvenile)	Bodley Head 1955 Macmillan 1955	I G
12 **Surprised by Joy** (autobiog.)	Bles 1955 Harcourt Brace 1956	C C
13 **The Last Battle** (juvenile) 6, 7, 8, 9, 10, 11 and 13 form the **Chronicles of Narnia**.	Bodley Head 1956 Macmillan 1956	H E
14 **The Four Loves** (philosophy)	Bles 1960 Harcourt Brace 1960	D C
15 **Studies in Words** (essay)	CUP 1960 Macmillan 1960	D C
16 **Experiment in Criticism**	CUP 1961 Macmillan 1961	D C
17 **A Grief Observed** (essay) (pseud. N.W. Clerk)	Faber 1961 Seabury 1963	G F

Lewis, Wyndham   Born in 1882. Died 1957.

It is not clear where Wyndham Lewis was born. According to him, it was on board a ship bound for Canada, during a thunderstorm. This is thought to be a less than reliable piece of autobiography, as Lewis was forever inventing for himself more and more glamorous 'pasts' so that art dealers would find the genesis of his paintings more 'interesting'. He always saw himself as a painter first, and in the early days, affected the garb: long hair, cape, wide-brimmed hat. With such trappings *and* so wild and romantic a history, people could not *fail* to accept him as a serious artist, he reasoned. Fortunately, his art – his painting and his writing – was more than equal to his extravagant claims, and Lewis has become a landmark figure of the century.

He published nearly fifty books, many of them from private presses, and in limited editions. An immensely detailed bibliography now exists, and is appended below. I record here the various editions of his highlight.

The Apes of God (novel)   The Arthur Press 1930

This was published in a signed limited edition of 750 copies at the then very high price of three guineas. This is the absolute first edition (**L**). A trade edition was published in 1931 by Nash & Grayson, in a print run of 1900 copies (**H**). The first American edition was published in 1932 by McBride (**F**).

In 1955 a 'twenty-fifth anniversary' edition was published by Arco, in a signed, limited edition of 1000 copies, selling for exactly the same price as the first edition – 3 guineas (**F**).

Bibliography:
Bradford Morrow and Bernard LaFourcade **Wyndham Lewis: A Bibliography** Black Sparrow 1978.

Lodge, David   Born in London, 1935.

A professor, a literary critic, and a very *English* novelist, capable of enormous humour. Only lately of interest to collectors who, I imagine, will mainly be interested in the fiction. I supply a full bibliography here, though, as Lodge's scholarly work is vastly more readable and relevant than most, and some collectors I am sure will be intrigued to hear what he has to say upon the likes of Graham Greene and Evelyn Waugh, as well as on the state of the novel in general.

1 **The Picturegoers** (novel)	MacGibbon & Kee 1960	**K**
2 **Ginger, You're Barmy** (novel)	MacGibbon & Kee 1962	**K**
	Doubleday 1965	**D**
3 **The British Museum is Falling Down** (novel)	MacGibbon & Kee 1965	**I**
	Holt Rinehart 1967	**D**
4 **The Language of Fiction** (non-fiction)	Routledge 1966	**D**
	Columbia University Press 1966	**D**
5 **Graham Greene** (non-fiction)	Columbia University Press 1966	**E**
6 **Out of the Shelter** (novel)	Macmillan 1970	**F**
7 **The Novelist at the Crossroads and Other Essays on Fiction and Criticism**	Routledge 1971	**D**
	Cornell University Press 1971	**D**
8 **Evelyn Waugh** (non fiction)	Columbia University Press 1971	**D**
9 **Twentieth Century Literary Criticism**	Longman 1972	**C**
10 **Changing Places: A Tale of Two Campuses** (novel)	Secker & Warburg 1975	**D**
	Viking 1979	**C**
11 **The Modes of Modern Writing: Metaphor, Metonymy and the Typology of Modern Literature**	Arnold 1977	**C**
12 **How Far Can You Go?** (novel) (**Souls and Bodies** in US)	Secker & Warburg 1980	**C**
	Morrow 1981	**C**

13 **Working with Structuralism:** **Essays and Reviews on Nineteenth** **and Twentieth Century Literature**	Routledge 1981	C
14 **Small World** (novel)	Secker & Warburg 1984	D
	Macmillan 1985	B
15 **Write On** (essays)	Secker & Warburg 1986	B
16 **Nice Work** (novel)	Secker & Warburg 1988	C
	Viking 1989	C
17 **After Bakhtin: Essays on Fiction** **and Criticism**	Routledge 1990	B
18 **The Writing Game** (play)	Secker & Warburg 1991	B
19 **Paradise News** (novel)	Secker & Warburg 1991	B
	Viking US 1992	B

Loos, Anita   Born in California, 1893. Died 1981.

Marilyn Monroe would appear to have borne out the truth of Anita Loos's most famous book title: *everyone* seems to have had a preference for her at one time or another. But such girls end badly, we hear, and the sequel encourages the roaming bachelor to settle down with the dark-haired sort, the quieter, more reliable, unshowy home-making type. Like Jane Russell. Or Elizabeth Taylor, say.

Loos wrote a large number of books, but these will always be the highlights.

1 **Gentlemen Prefer Blondes**	Boni & Liveright 1925	J
Scarce. The sequel seems an attempt to redress the balance. (Note that preference comes more expensive than marriage.)	Brentano's 1926	G
2 **But Gentlemen Marry Brunettes**	Boni & Liveright 1928	E
	Brentano's 1928	D

Lowell, Robert   Born in Boston, 1914. Died 1977.

Popular in Britain, adulated across the Atlantic. An American classic.

1 **The Land of Unlikeness** (verse)	Cummington Press (US) 1944	M
2 **Lord Weary's Castle** (verse)	Harcourt Brace 1946	K
3 **Poems 1938–1949**	Faber 1950	I
4 **The Mills of the Kavanaughs**	Harcourt Brace 1951	J
5 **Life Studies** (verse)	Faber 1959	F
	Farrar Straus 1959	E

Lowry

6	**Imitations** (verse)	Farrar Straus 1961	**E**
		Faber 1962	**E**
7	**Phaedra and Figaro** (plays trans.)	Farrar Straus 1961	**D**
8	**Phaedra** (as in 7)	Faber 1963	**D**
9	**For the Union Dead** (verse)	Farrar Straus 1964	**D**
		Faber 1965	**D**
10	**The Old Glory** (play)	Farrar Straus 1964	**D**

10 An expanded version was published by Faber in 1966, and by Farrar Straus in 1968 (**C**).

11	**Selected Poems**	Faber 1965	**C**
12	**Near the Ocean** (verse)	Farrar Straus 1967	**D**
		Faber 1967	**D**
13	**The Voyage** (Baudelaire trans.)	Farrar Straus 1968	**C**
		Faber 1968	**C**
14	**Notebook 1967–1968**	Farrar Straus 1969	**F**

14 An augmented editon, called simply **Notebook**, was published in 1970 by Faber and Farrar Straus (**E**).

15	**Prometheus Bound** (adapt.)	Farrar Straus 1969	**C**
		Faber 1970	**C**
16	**For Lizzie and Harriet** (verse)	Faber 1973	**C**
		Farrar Straus 1973	**C**
17	**History** (verse)	Faber 1973	**C**
		Farrar Straus 1973	**C**
18	**The Dolphin** (verse)	Faber 1973	**C**
		Farrar Straus 1973	**C**
19	**Poems: A Selection**	Faber 1974	**C**
20	**Day by Day** (verse)	Farrar Straus 1978	**C**
		Faber 1978	**C**
21	**The Oresteia of Aeschylus** (trans.)	Farrar Straus 1979	**C**
		Faber 1979	**C**

Bibliography:
Ian Hamilton **Robert Lowell** Faber 1983.

Lowry, Malcolm   Born in Cheshire, 1909. Died 1957.

A complex, and a rather sad character, who is now assuming the status of a cult figure among younger readers and collectors. He was born of a wealthy family, but sought to be a loner, a tramp, a bum. Several times, he drank himself nearly to death, and was at all times said to be in an alcoholic stupor of varying degree. The pain and the horror of this he anchored well in his highlight *Under the Volcano*. He needed this success (not financially, but psychologically) for his first novel fourteen years earlier had sold only half of its modest print run of 1500, the remaining 750 of which were pulped.

200

1	**Ultramarine** (novel)	Cape 1933	**P**

A revised edition of this novel was
published in 1962 by Lippincott in the
USA and in 1963 by Cape in the UK
(**D**).

2	**Under the Volcano** (novel)	Reynal & Hitchock 1947	**N**
		Cape 1947	**M**
3	**Hear Us O Lord from Heaven Thy Dwelling Place** (stories)	Lippincott 1961	**I**
		Cape 1962	**H**
4	**Selected Poems of Malcolm Lowry**	City Lights 1962	**E**
5	**Selected Letters of Malcolm Lowry**	Lippincott 1965	**E**
		Cape 1967	**D**
6	**Lunar Caustic** (novel)	Grossman 1968	**G**
		Cape 1968	**G**
7	**Dark as the Grave Wherein My Friend is Laid** (stories)	NAL 1968	**E**
		Cape 1969	**E**
8	**October Ferry to Gabriola** (novel)	World 1970	**D**
		Cape 1971	**D**
9	**Notes on a Screenplay for F. Scott Fitzgerald's Tender is the Night**	Bruccoli 1976	**D**
10	**The Collected Poetry of Malcolm Lowry**	University of British Columbia Press 1992	**C**

Biography:
Douglas Day **Malcolm Lowry: A Biography** OUP 1973.

Lurie, Alison   Born in Chicago, 1926. American.

Lurie's constantly entertaining work is still very well reviewed, and appreciated, but she is still not a huge noise in the collecting world – which can only be good news, as the prices for all but the first few novels are still quite low.

1	**Love and Friendship** (novel)	Heinemann 1962	**K**
		Macmillan (US) 1962	**I**
2	**The Nowhere City** (novel)	Heinemann 1965	**H**
		Coward McCann 1966	**G**
3	**Imaginary Friends** (novel)	Heinemann 1967	**F**
		Coward McCann 1967	**E**
4	**Real People** (novel)	Random House 1969	**E**
		Heinemann 1970	**D**
5	**The War Between the Tates** (novel)	Random House 1974	**E**
		Heinemann 1974	**D**
6	**Only Children** (novel)	Random House 1979	**D**
		Heinemann 1979	**D**

7 **The Heavenly Zoo** (juvenile)	Eel Pie 1979	**E**
	Farrar Straus 1980	**E**
8 **Clever Gretchen and Other**	Harper 1980	**D**
Forgotten Folk Tales (juvenile)	Heinemann 1980	**D**
9 **The Language of Clothes** (non-fiction)	Random House 1981	**D**
	Heinemann 1982	**D**
10 **Fabulous Beasts** (juvenile)	Farrar Straus 1981	**C**
	Cape 1981	**C**
11 **Foreign Affairs** (novel)	Random House 1984	**C**
	Joseph 1985	**C**
12 **The Truth About Lorin Jones** (novel)	Little, Brown 1988	**C**
	Joseph 1988	**C**
13 **Don't Tell the Grownups:**	Little, Brown 1990	**C**
Subversive Children's Literature (non-fiction)	Bloomsbury 1990	**C**

Macdonald, Ross Born in California, 1915.
Pseudonym for Kenneth Millar.

In line with the current vogue for detective fiction, Ross Macdonald is of very big interest now, but the early titles are hard to get, particularly with those all-important dust wrappers (with detective novels, it always seems more important than ever, I think because the books look so deliciously lurid *with* them, and so much like any other book without).

Macdonald (or Millar, to give him his real name) wrote under several names. As well as Ross Macdonald we have Kenneth Millar, John Ross Macdonald and John Macdonald. It's the last of these that could cause confusion, as there is *another* writer of detective fiction called John Macdonald – the author of nearly sixty books and the creater of Travis McGee. This is *not* the author under discussion, who was the creator of Lew Archer, as will be seen below.

As Kenneth Millar:
The following feature the character Chet Gordon.

1 **The Dark Tunnel** (novel)	Dodd Mead 1944	**J**
2 **I Die Slowly** (English edition of 1)	Lion 1955	**D**
3 **Trouble Follows Me** (novel)	Dodd Mead 1946	**I**
4 **Night Train** (English edition of 3)	Lion 1955	**D**
5 **Blue City** (novel)	Knopf 1947	**H**
	Cassell 1949	**E**
6 **The Three Roads** (novel)	Knopf 1948	**G**
	Cassell 1950	**E**

As John Ross Macdonald:

7 **The Drowning Pool** (novel)*	Knopf 1950	**I**
	Cassell 1952	**G**

8 **The Way Some People Die** (novel)*	Knopf 1951	H
	Cassell 1953	G
9 **The Ivory Grin** (novel)*	Knopf 1952	H
	Cassell 1953	G
10 **Meet Me at the Morgue** (novel)	Knopf 1953	G
11 **Experience with Evil**	Cassell 1954	F
(English edition of 10)		
12 **Find a Victim** (novel)*	Knopf 1954	G
	Cassell 1955	F
13 **The Name is Archer** (stories)*	Bantam 1955	E

As John Macdonald:

14 **The Moving Target** (novel)	Knopf 1949	H
	Cassell 1951	F

The above, and all those below marked
* feature the character Lew Archer.

As Ross Macdonald:

15 **The Barbarous Coast** (novel)*	Knopf 1956	J
	Cassell 1957	I
16 **The Doomsters** (novel)*	Knopf 1958	G
	Cassell 1958	F
17 **The Galton Case** (novel)*	Knopf 1959	F
	Cassell 1960	E
18 **The Fergusson Affair** (novel)	Knopf 1960	F
	Collins 1961	F
19 **The Wycherley Woman** (novel)	Knopf 1961	F
	Collins 1962	E
20 **The Zebra-Striped Hearse** (novel)*	Knopf 1962	F
	Collins 1963	E
21 **The Chill** (novel)*	Knopf 1964	F
	Collins 1964	E
22 **The Far Side of the Dollar** (novel*)	Knopf 1965	F
	Collins 1965	E
23 **Black Money** (novel)*	Knopf 1966	E
	Collins 1966	D
24 **The Instant Enemy** (novel)*	Knopf 1968	E
	Collins 1968	D
25 **The Goodbye Look** (novel*)	Knopf 1969	D
	Collins 1969	D
26 **The Underground Man** (novel)*	Knopf 1971	C
	Collins 1971	C
27 **Sleeping Beauty** (novel)*	Knopf 1973	C
	Collins 1973	C
28 **The Blue Hammer** (novel)*	Knopf 1976	C
	Collins 1976	C

McEwan

Bibliography:
Matthew J. Broccoli **Kenneth Millar/Ross Macdonald: A Checklist**
Gale US 1971.

McEwan, Ian   Born in Aldershot, 1948.

Rather more prolific than he was a decade ago, McEwan has also recovered critical esteem and collectors' approval after lying fallow for some time. Still seen to be one of the hotter younger British properties, and therefore it is not easy to find the first three books.

1	**First Loves, Last Rites** (stories)	Cape 1975	I
		Random House 1975	E
2	**In Between the Sheets** (stories)	Cape 1978	F
		Simon & Schuster 1978	D
3	**The Cement Garden** (novel)	Cape 1978	E
		Simon & Schuster 1978	C
4	**The Imitation Game: Three Plays for Television** (includes **Solid Geometry** and **Jack Flea's Birthday Celebration**)	Cape 1981	D
5	**The Comfort of Strangers** (novel)	Cape 1981	C
		Simon & Schuster 1981	C
6	**Or Shall We Die?** (oratorio)	Cape 1983	B
7	**The Ploughman's Lunch** (screenplay)	Methuen 1985	C
8	**Rose Blanche** (juvenile)	Cape 1985	C
9	**The Child in Time** (novel)	Cape 1987	C
		Houghton Mifflin 1987	C
10	**Soursweet** (screenplay)	Faber 1988	C
11	**A Move Abroad** (contains nos 6 and 7)	Picador 1989	B
12	**The Innocent** (novel)	Cape 1990	C
		Doubleday 1990	C
13	**Black Dogs** (novel)	Cape 1992	C
		Doubleday 1992	C

McInerney, Jay   Born in Connecticut, 1955. American.

The Salinger of the 1980s? It has been said – but then, a lot of things are said. McInerney is certainly a red hot, whizz-kid, bing-bang, zip-zap, hip-hop ... well, you get the idea. Very culty, very collectable.

1 **Bright Lights, Big City** (novel)	Vintage 1984	**F**
	Cape 1985	**E**
2 **Ransom** (novel)	Vintage 1985	**D**
	Cape 1986	**D**
3 **Story of My Life** (novel)	Bloomsbury 1988	**C**
	Atlantic Monthly Press 1988	**C**
4 **Brightness Falls** (novel)	Knopf 1992	**C**
	Bloomsbury 1992	**C**

MacInnes, Colin   Born in London, 1914. Died 1976.

One of Burne-Jones's grandchildren was the novelist Angela Thirkell. Thirkell's son was Colin MacInnes. MacInnes, in the late fifties and sixties, became a chronicler and a champion of the teenage rebellion, pop music, the plight of blacks in Britain, and the drug scene. In life, MacInnes was seen to be a rebel, a drunk, and a homosexual, who died prematurely. It is little wonder, then, that he has now risen to the level of a cult, and he has an eager following. The ghastly film of *Absolute Beginners* has, I suppose, boosted this – but among a particularly gaudy and vacuous crowd, I fancy.

1 **To The Victors The Spoils** (novel)	MacGibbon & Kee 1950	**H**
2 **June in Her Spring** (novel)	MacGibbon & Kee 1952	**F**
3 **City of Spades** (novel)	MacGibbon & Kee 1957	**E**
	Macmillan (US) 1958	**C**
4 **Absolute Beginners** (novel)	MacGibbon & Kee 1959	**H**
	Macmillan 1960	**D**
5 **Mr Love and Justice** (novel	MacGibbon & Kee 1960	**D**
	Dutton 1961	**C**
6 **England, Half English** (essays)	MacGibbon & Kee 1961	**D**
	Random House 1962	**C**
7 **London: City of Any Dream** (non-fiction)	Thames & Hudson 1962	**D**
8 **Australia and New Zealand** (non-fiction) In collaboration with the editors of **Life**.	Time (US) 1964	**C**
9 **All Day Saturday** (novel)	MacGibbon & Kee 1966	**E**
10 **Sweet Saturday Night** (prose)	MacGibbon & Kee 1967	**D**

11	**Visions of London** An omnibus containing 3, 4 and 5.	MacGibbon & Kee 1969	**C**
12	**The London Novels** (same as 11)	Farrar Straus 1969	**C**
13	**Westward to Laughter** (novel)	MacGibbon & Kee 1969	**C**
		Farrar Straus 1970	**C**
14	**Three Years to Play** (novel)	MacGibbon & Kee 1970	**C**
		Farrar Straus 1970	**C**
15	**Loving Them Both: A Study of** **Bisexuality and Bisexuals** (non-fiction)	Brian & O'Keefe 1973	**C**
16	**Out of the Garden** (novel)	Hart-Davis MacGibbon 1974	**C**
17	**'No Novel Reader'** (non-fiction)	Brian & O'Keefe 1975	**C**
18	**Posthumous Essays**	Brian & O'Keefe 1977	**C**
19	**Out of the Way: Later Essays**	Brian & O'Keefe 1980	**C**

Biography:
Tony Gould **Inside Outsider: The Life and Times of Colin MacInnes** Chatto & Windus 1983.

MacLean, Alistair   Born in Glasgow, 1922. Died 1987.

Although he used to be notable only for his highlight or two (*HMS Ulysses*, *Guns of Navarone*) there seem to be more and more collectors – *aficionados* of the 'good read' variety, nothing wrong with that – eager to gather the whole œuvre. Still very cheap.

1	**HMS Ulysses** (novel)	Collins 1955	**C**
		Doubleday 1956	**B**
2	**The Guns of Navarone** (novel)	Collins 1957	**C**
		Doubleday 1957	**B**
3	**South By Java Head** (novel)	Collins 1958	**B**
		Doubleday 1958	**B**
4	**The Last Frontier** (novel)	Collins 1959	**B**
5	**The Secret Ways** (same as 4)	Doubleday 1959	**B**
6	**Night Without End** (novel)	Collins 1960	**B**
		Doubleday 1960	**B**
7	**Fear is the Key** (novel)	Collins 1961	**B**
		Doubleday 1961	**B**
8	**The Snow on the Ben** (novel) (pseud. Ian Stuart)	Ward Lock 1961	**C**
9	**The Dark Crusader** (novel) (pseud. Ian Stuart)	Collins 1961	**C**
10	**The Black Shrike** (same as 9)	Scribner 1961	**B**

11 **The Golden Rendezvous** (novel)	Collins 1962	B
	Doubleday 1962	B
12 **All About Lawrence of Arabia** (juvenile)	Allen 1962	C
13 **Lawrence of Arabia** (same as 12)	Random House 1962	C
14 **The Satan Bug** (novel) (pseud. Ian Stuart)	Collins 1962	B
	Scribner 1962	B
15 **Ice Station Zebra** (novel)	Collins 1963	B
	Doubleday 1963	B
16 **When Eight Bells Toll** (novel)	Collins 1966	B
	Doubleday 1966	B
17 **Where Eagles Dare** (novel)	Collins 1967	B
	Doubleday 1967	B
18 **Force 10 from Navarone** (novel)	Collins 1968	B
	Doubleday 1968	B
19 **Puppet on a Chain** (novel)	Collins 1969	B
	Doubleday 1969	B
20 **Caravan to Vaccares** (novel)	Collins 1970	B
	Doubleday 1970	B
21 **Bear Island** (novel)	Collins 1971	B
	Doubleday 1971	B
22 **Captain Cook** (non-fiction)	Collins 1971	B
	Doubleday 1972	B
23 **The Way to Dusty Death** (novel)	Collins 1973	B
	Doubleday 1973	B
24 **Breakheart Pass** (novel)	Collins 1974	B
	Doubleday 1974	B
25 **Circus** (novel)	Collins 1975	B
	Doubleday 1975	B
26 **The Golden Gate** (novel)	Collins 1976	B
	Doubleday 1976	B
27 **Death from Disclosure** (novel) Pseud. Ian Stuart.	Hale 1976	B
28 **Flood Tide** (novel) (pseud. Ian Stuart)	Hale 1977	B
29 **Sand Trap** (novel) Pseud. Ian Stuart.	Hale 1977	B
30 **Seawitch** (novel)	Collins 1977	B
	Doubleday 1977	B
31 **Goodbye, California** (novel)	Collins 1978	B
	Doubleday 1978	B
32 **Fatal Switch** (novel) (pseud. Ian Stuart)	Hale 1978	B
33 **A Weekend to Kill** (novel) (pseud. Ian Stuart)	Hale 1978	B
34 **Athabasca** (novel)	Collins 1980	B
	Doubleday 1980	B

35 **River of Death** (novel)	Collins 1981	**B**
	Doubleday 1982	**B**
36 **Partisans** (novel)	Collins 1982	**B**
	Doubleday 1983	**B**
37 **Floodgate** (novel)	Collins 1983	**B**
	Doubleday 1984	**B**
38 **San Andreas** (novel)	Collins 1984	**B**
	Doubleday 1985	**B**
39 **The Lonely Sea** (novel)	Collins 1985	**B**
	Doubleday 1985	**B**
40 **Santorini** (novel)	Collins 1986	**B**

MacNeice, Louis   Born in Belfast, 1907. Died 1963.

One of the great poets of the century – below Auden and Eliot, but above most others. Very collectable – and the larger part of his *œuvre* fairly available. It is, as usual, the early items that are difficult.

1 **Blind Fireworks** (verse)	Gollancz 1929	**N**
2 **Roundabout Way** (novel)	Putman 1932	**O**
(pseud. Louis Malone)		
3 **Poems**	Faber 1935	**J**
	Random House 1937	**H**
4 **The Agamemnon of Aeschylus**	Faber 1936	**E**
(trans.)	Harcourt Brace 1937	**D**
5 **Out of the Picture** (play)	Faber 1937	**G**
	Harcourt Brace 1938	**D**
6 **Letters from Iceland** (non-fiction)	Faber 1937	**I**
With W.H. Auden.	Harcourt Brace 1937	**G**
7 **I Crossed the Minch** (travel)	Longman 1938	**L**
8 **Zoo** (non-fiction)	Joseph 1938	**K**
9 **Modern Poetry: A Personal Essay**	OUP 1938	**F**
10 **The Earth Compels** (verse)	Faber 1938	**F**
11 **Autumn Journal** (verse)	Faber 1939	**E**
	Random House 1939	**C**
12 **The Last Ditch** (verse)	Cuala Press (Dublin) 1940	**K**
13 **Selected Poems**	Faber 1940	**D**
14 **Poems 1925–1940**	Random House 1940	**D**
15 **Plant and Phantom** (verse)	Faber 1941	**F**
16 **The Poetry of W.B. Yeats** (criticism)	OUP 1941	**H**
17 **Meet the U.S. Army** (essay)	Board of Education 1943	**K**
18 **Springboard: Poems 1941–44**	Faber 1944	**E**
	Random House 1945	**C**
19 **Christopher Columbus** (play)	Faber 1944	**F**

20 **The Dark Tower** (plays)	Faber 1947	**E**
21 **Holes in the Sky: Poems 1944–47**	Faber 1948	**E**
	Random House 1949	**D**
22 **Collected Poems 1925–48**	Faber 1949	**E**
	OUP (US) 1949	**D**
23 **Goethe's Faust Parts I & II** (trans.)	Faber 1952	**E**
	OUP 1952	**D**
24 **Ten Burnt Offerings** (verse)	Faber 1952	**F**
	OUP 1953	**D**
25 **Autumn Sequel** (verse)	Faber 1954	**D**
26 **The Other Wing** (Ariel Poem)	Faber 1954	**C**
27 **The Penny That Rolled Away** (juvenile)	Putnam 1954	**I**

This was published in England, no doubt for sound economic reasons, as **The Sixpence That Rolled Away** by Faber in 1956 (**G**).

28 **Visitations** (verse)	Faber 1957	**D**
	OUP 1958	**C**
29 **Eighty-Five Poems**	Faber 1959	**D**
	OUP 1959	**C**
30 **Solstices** (verse)	Faber 1961	**D**
	OUP 1961	**C**
31 **The Burning Perch** (verse)	Faber 1963	**D**
	OUP 1963	**C**
32 **Selected Poems**	Faber 1964	**C**

Ed. and Intro. by W.H. Auden.

33 **The Mad Islands** and **The Administrator** (plays)	Faber 1964	**D**
34 **Astrology** (non-fiction)	Aldus 1964	**C**
	Doubleday 1964	**C**
35 **The Strings are False** (autobiog.)	Faber 1965	**E**
	OUP 1966	**C**
36 **Varieties of Parable** (lecture)	CUP 1965	**D**
37 **Collected Poems**	Faber 1966	**E**
	OUP 1967	**D**
38 **One for the Grave** (play)	Faber 1968	**D**
39 **Persons from Porlock and Other Plays**	BBC 1969	**D**

Intro. by W.H. Auden.

Bibliography:
Christopher Armitage and Neil Clark **A Bibliography of the Works of Louis MacNeice** Kaye & Ward 1973.

Mailer, Norman   Born in New Jersey, 1923.

Mailer is larger than life. He has always been *celebrated* as a personality as much as a writer. His non-fiction, always provocative (*Marilyn, Cannibals and Christians*) took an even more bizarre turn with *The Executioner's Song* – a massive book chronicling the life and last days of Gary Gilmore, a murderer who had requested relief from 'Death Row' in the form of the electric chair. And then Mailer came up with *Ancient Evenings* – a huge novel, and the final entry in Anthony Burgess's *99 Novels*. It concerns Ancient Egypt, and yet it is baroque. It is majestic, funny, powerful, rude, irresistible (but skippable) and it presents the land of the Cleopatras as just as weird as present-day America. Below appears his fictional work, in addition to which Mailer has published about two dozen books.

1	**The Naked and the Dead** (novel)	Rinehart 1948	J
		Wingate 1949	F
2	**Barbary Shore** (novel)	Rinehart 1951	F
		Cape 1952	E
3	**The Deer Park** (novel)	Putnam 1955	E
		Wingate 1957	C
4	**Advertisements for Myself**	Putnam 1959	D
	(miscellany)	Deutsch 1961	C
5	**Deaths for the Ladies and**	Putnam 1962	E
	Other Disasters (verse)	Deutsch 1962	D
6	**An American Dream** (novel)	Dial Press 1965	D
		Deutsch 1965	C
7	**The Deer Park** (play)	Dial Press 1967	C
		Weidenfeld 1970	B
8	**Why are We in Vietnam?** (novel)	Putnam 1967	C
		Weidenfeld 1969	C
9	**Ancient Evenings** (novel)	Little, Brown 1983	C
		Macmillan 1983	C
10	**Tough Guys Don't Dance** (novel)	Random House 1984	C
		Joseph 1984	C
11	**Harlot's Ghost** (novel)	Random House 1991	C
		Joseph 1991	C

Bibliography:
Laura Adams **Norman Mailer: A Comprehensive Bibliography**
Scarecrow Press (New Jersey) 1974.

Manning, Olivia   Born in Portsmouth, 1915. Died 1980.

Always a respected writer, but only quite recently of interest to collectors. It was apparently marriage to a British official in the Balkans that altered her interest, and gave rise to her most celebrated works, now gathered together under the umbrella title 'The Balkan Trilogy' (although now there is a 'Levant Trilogy' as well).

1	**The Wind Changes** (novel)	Cape 1937	**K**
		Knopf 1938	**H**
2	**The Remarkable Expedition: The Story of Stanley's Rescue of Emin Pasha from Equatorial Africa** (non-fiction)	Heinemann 1947	**G**
3	**The Reluctant Rescue** (same as 2)	Doubleday 1947	**E**
4	**Growing Up: A Collection of Short Stories**	Heinemann 1948	**F**
		Doubleday 1948	**D**
5	**Artist Among the Missing** (novel)	Heinemann 1949	**E**
6	**The Dreaming Shore** (travel)	Evans 1950	**E**
7	**School for Love** (novel)	Heinemann 1951	**E**
8	**A Different Face** (novel)	Heinemann 1953	**E**
		Abelard 1957	**C**
9	**Doves of Venus** (novel)	Heinemann 1955	**E**
		Abelard 1958	**C**
10	**My Husband Cartright** (novel)	Heinemann 1956	**E**
11	**The Great Fortune** (novel)	Heinemann 1960	**F**
		Doubleday 1961	**C**
12	**The Spoilt City** (novel)	Heinemann 1962	**E**
		Doubleday 1963	**C**
13	**Friends and Heroes** (novel) 11, 12 and 13 form **The Balkan Trilogy**	Heinemann 1965 Doubleday 1966	**E** **C**
14	**A Romantic Hero and Other Stories**	Heinemann 1967	**D**
15	**Extraordinary Cats** (non-fiction)	Joseph 1967	**E**
16	**The Playroom** (novel)	Heinemann 1969	**D**
17	**The Camperlea Girls** (same as 16)	Coward McCann 1969	**C**
18	**The Rain Forest** (novel)	Heinemann 1974	**D**
19	**The Danger Tree** (novel)	Weidenfeld 1977	**D**
		Atheneum 1977	**C**
20	**The Battle Lost and Won** (novel)	Weidenfeld 1978	**C**
		Atheneum 1979	**C**
21	**The Sum of Things** (novel) 19, 20 and 21 form **The Levant Trilogy**.	Weidenfeld 1980 Atheneum 1981	**C** **C**

Marsh, Ngaio   Born in Christchurch, New Zealand, 1899. Died 1982.

Though not so avidly collected as Agatha Christie or Dorothy L. Sayers (*or* P.D. James), still a grand old lady of crime who retains her following. Still *fairly* good quarry for a beginner...

1	**A Man Lay Dead** (novel)	Bles 1934	L
		Sheridan 1942	I
2	**Enter a Murderer** (novel)	Bles 1935	J
		Sheridan 1942	G
3	**Death in Ecstasy** (novel)	Bles 1936	I
		Sheridan 1941	G
4	**The Nursing Home Murder** (novel) With H. Jellett.	Bles 1936	I
		Sheridan 1941	G
5	**Vintage Murder** (novel)	Bles 1937	I
		Sheridan 1940	G
6	**Artists in Crime** (novel)	Bles 1938	H
		Furman 1938	F
7	**Death in a White Tie** (novel)	Bles 1938	H
		Furman 1938	F
8	**Overture to Death** (novel)	Collins 1939	G
		Little, Brown 1939	D
9	**Death at the Bar** (novel)	Collins 1940	F
		Little, Brown 1940	D
10	**Death of a Peer** (novel)	Little, Brown 1940	F
11	**Surfeit of Lampreys** (same as 10)	Collins 1941	E
12	**Death and the Dancing Footman** (novel)	Collins 1941	F
		Little, Brown 1941	D
13	**Colour Scheme** (novel)	Collins 1943	E
		Little, Brown 1943	D
14	**Died in the Wool** (novel)	Collins 1945	E
		Little, Brown 1945	D
15	**Final Curtain** (novel)	Collins 1947	C
		Little, Brown 1947	C
16	**Swing Brother Swing** (novel)	Collins 1949	C
17	**Wreath for Riviera** (same as 16)	Little, Brown 1949	C
18	**Opening Night** (novel)	Collins 1951	C
19	**Night at the Vulcan** (same as 18)	Little, Brown 1951	C
20	**Spinsters in Jeopardy** (novel)	Little, Brown 1953	D
		Collins 1954	C
21	**Scales of Justice** (novel)	Collins 1955	C
		Little, Brown 1955	C
22	**Death of a Fool** (novel)	Little, Brown 1956	C
23	**Off with His Head** (same as 22)	Collins 1957	C

24	**Singing in the Shrouds** (novel)	Little, Brown 1958	**C**
		Collins 1959	**C**
25	**False Scent** (novel)	Little, Brown 1959	**C**
		Collins 1960	**C**
26	**Hand in Glove** (novel)	Little, Brown 1962	**C**
		Collins 1962	**C**
27	**Dead Water** (novel)	Little, Brown 1963	**C**
		Collins 1964	**C**
28	**Killer Dolphin** (novel)	Little brown 1966	**C**
29	**Death at the Dolphin** (same as 28)	Collins 1967	**C**
30	**Clutch of Constables** (novel)	Collins 1968	**C**
		Little, Brown 1969	**C**
31	**When in Rome** (novel)	Collins 1970	**C**
		Little, Brown 1970	**C**
32	**Tied up in Tinsel** (novel)	Collins 1972	**C**
		Little, Brown 1972	**C**
33	**Black as He's Painted** (novel)	Collins 1974	**B**
		Little, Brown 1974	**B**
34	**Last Ditch** (novel)	Collins 1977	**B**
		Little, Brown 1977	**B**
35	**Grave Mistake** (novel)	Collins 1978	**B**
		Little, Brown 1978	**B**
36	**Photo-Finish** (novel)	Collins 1980	**B**
		Little, Brown 1980	**B**
37	**Light Thickens** (novel)	Collins 1982	**B**
		Little, Brown 1982	**B**

Miller, Arthur   Born in New York, 1915.

Today, more famous for having married Marilyn Monroe than for having written plays. Some years ago, one could have asserted with confidence that his plays would long outlast his sometime-wife's film appearances, but such is the way of the world that this now seems doubtful; shaky, even. But his work is safe – even the title *Death of a Salesman* being famous.

Of his works (about two dozen) the following are stage classics:

1	**All My Sons** (play)	Reynal & Hitchcock 1947	**J**
2	**Death of a Salesman** (play)	Viking 1949	**I**
		Cresset 1949	**G**
3	**The Crucible** (play)	Viking 1953	**F**
		Cresset 1956	**D**
4	**A View from the Bridge** and **A Memory of Two Mondays**	Viking 1955	**F**
5	**A View from the Bridge** (revised)	Cresset 1956	**C**
6	**Collected Plays** Incl. 1, 2, 3 and 4.	Viking 1957	**C**
		Cresset 1958	**C**

Miller, Henry

7 **Incident at Vichy** (play)	Viking 1965	C
	Secker 1966	C

Bibliography:
Tetsumaro Hayashi **Arthur Miller: A Checklist of his Published Works** Kent, Ohio 1967.

Miller, Henry   Born in New York, 1891. Died 1980.

His staying power has been quite remarkable. I detect, however, that although Miller is still avidly *read* (his reputation will always ensure this) there is less interest from collectors than there used to be, say, ten years ago. His classic, though, remains scarce and expensive (in its original form) and still a sought-after book in its subsequent 'firsts', as is its sequel, and these are appended below.

1 **Tropic of Cancer** (novel)	Obelisk Press (Paris)	S
As will be seen, there is a world of	1934	
difference between the Paris edition and	Grove Press 1961	I
the later American and English editions,	Calder 1963	D
and therefore this is reflected in the		
prices.		
2 **Tropic of Capricorn** (novel)	Obelisk Press 1939	R
The same situation applies as in 1.	Grove Press 1961	G
	Calder 1964	C

It ought to be noted that in addition to the above highlights, Miller has published upwards of seventy books.

Bibliography:
Maxine Renken **A Bibliography of Henry Miller 1945–1961** Swallow 1962.

Milne, A. A.   Born in London, 1882. Died 1956.

I suppose that lovers of Winnie the Pooh *et al.* find it difficult to believe that Milne wrote anything else, but in fact he published about sixty books (many of them plays). Only those below pertain to Pooh and all his friends. The other works range from the tolerable to the frankly unreadable.

1 **When We were Very Young** (verse	Methuen 1924	M
	Dutton 1924	J
2 **Winnie the Pooh** (stories)	Methuen 1926	L
	Dutton 1926	H
3 **Now We are Six** (verse)	Methuen 1927	K
	Dutton 1927	G

4 **The House at Pooh Corner** (stories)	Methuen 1928	**J**
	Dutton 1928	**G**
5 **Toad of Toad Hall** (play)	Methuen 1929	**H**
This is an adaptation of Kenneth	Scribner 1929	**E**
Grahame's *The Wind in the Willows*		

Mitchell, Margaret Born in Atlanta, 1900. Died 1949.

For the one and only time, I do not have to say 'author of loads of old rubbish, but notable for just one'. No. Margaret Mitchell was that rare bird who today would have been hard put to resist a publisher's ministrations. But after the success of the film, when she was asked for a sequel, all she said was: 'I know good work and I know good writing, and I didn't think mine good.' The first edition is scarce, and such is the change of mood among collectors since I wrote *Collecting Modern First Editions* that I entirely withdraw what I said in that book – 'It is very uncommon in a first, but would probably never rise above Grade C (then, up to £10) such is its image'. No – it is so popular, kitsch, even, that I can see it fetching £500 today. In America, it could fetch anything between two hundred and a billion dollars; it's part of their heritage.

Gone With the Wind	Macmillan (US) 1936	**Q**
	Macmillan (UK) 1936	**M**

Mitford, Nancy Born in London, 1904. Died 1973.

Best known for having coined the term 'U' and 'non-U'; but apart from that she remains a respected writer, who managed superb economy and wit and she reminds me of Waugh. Author of a few historical works, she is most notable for the following.

1 **The Pursuit of Love** (novel)	Hamilton 1945	**C**
	Random House 1946	**C**
2 **Love in a Cold Climate** (novel)	Hamilton 1949	**C**
	Random House 1949	**C**
3 **The Blessing** (novel)	Hamilton 1951	**C**
	Random House 1951	**C**
4 **Don't Tell Alfred** (novel)	Hamilton 1960	**C**
	Harper 1960	**C**

Also notable is the following volume which she edited, responsible for the whole U and non-U 'controversy' of the fifties:

Noblesse Oblige	Harper 1956	**D**
	Hamilton 1957	**C**

Mo, Timothy   Born in Hong Kong, 1950. British.

An increasingly respected author – not always an easy read, but usually worth the trouble. Mo publishes very occasionally, but the quality remains consistently high; from the collector's point of view, the first book is obstinately difficult, but the rest should not prove to be much trouble.

1 **Monkey King** (novel)	Deutsch 1978	I
	Doubleday 1980	D
2 **Sour Sweet** (novel)	Deutsch 1982	E
	Random House 1985	C
3 **An Insular Possession** (novel)	Chatto & Windus 1986	C
	Random House 1987	C
4 **The Redundancy of Courage** (novel)	Chatto & Windus 1991	C

Moore, Brian   Born in Belfast, 1921.

Quite recently of great interest to collectors – I suspect because of the increasingly adulatory reviews that are conferred upon each new publication. Moore truly is a craftsman and a poet – very well worth reading and possessing, although to possess the lot in fine first editions will not be an easy task.

1 **The Executioners** (novel) (pseud. Michael Bryan)	Harlequin, Canada 1951	M
2 **Wreath for a Redhead** (novel) (pseud. Michael Bryan)	Harlequin, Canada 1951	L
3 **Judith Hearne** (novel)	Collins, Canada 1955	K
	Deutsch 1955	J
4 **The Lonely Passion of Judith Hearne** (same as 3)	Little, Brown 1956	I
5 **Intent to Kill** (novel) (pseud. Michael Bryan)	Dell US 1956	L
	Eyre & Spottiswoode 1956	L
6 **Murder in Majorca** (novel) (pseud. Michael Bryan)	Dell US 1957	I
	Eyre & Spottiswoode 1958	I
7 **The Feast of Lupercal** (novel)	Little, Brown 1957	H
	Deutsch 1958	G
8 **The Luck of Ginger Coffey** (novel)	Little, Brown 1960	H
	Deutsch 1960	G
9 **An Answer from Limbo** (novel)	Little, Brown 1962	G
	Deutsch 1963	F
10 **A Moment of Love** (same as 7)	Panther 1965	D
11 **The Emperor of Ice-cream** (novel)	Viking Press 1965	E
	Deutsch 1966	D

12 **I Am Mary Dunne** (novel)	Viking Press 1968	**D**
	Cape 1968	**C**
13 **Fergus** (novel)	Holt Rinehart 1970	**D**
	Cape 1971	**C**
14 **The Revolution Script** (prose)	Holt Rinehart 1971	**C**
	Cape 1972	**C**
15 **Catholics** (novel)	Cape 1972	**C**
	Harcourt Brace 1973	**C**
16 **The Great Victorian Collection** (novel)	Farrar Straus 1975	**C**
	Cape 1975	**C**
17 **The Doctor's Wife** (novel)	Farrar Straus 1976	**C**
	Cape 1976	**C**
18 **The Mangan Inheritance** (novel)	Farrar Straus 1979	**C**
	Cape 1979	**C**
19 **The Temptation of Eileen Hughes** (novel)	Farrar Straus 1981	**C**
	Cape 1971	**C**
20 **Cold Heaven** (novel)	Holt Rinehart 1983	**C**
	Cape 1983	**C**
21 **Black Robe** (novel)	Dutton 1985	**C**
	Cape 1985	**C**
22 **The Colour of Blood** (novel)	Cape 1987	**C**
	Dutton 1987	**C**
23 **Lies of Silence** (novel)	Bloomsbury 1990	**C**
	Doubleday 1990	**C**

Mortimer, John   Born in Hampstead, London 1923.

It is difficult to get it firmly fixed in one's mind that Mortimer is *not* Rumpole, and that Leo McKern is really an actor who *plays* Rumpole – who, of course, does not exist. But like all really great fictional characters, he is more real than anyone one can think of. When he says 'my old darling', though (he says 'my old darling' a lot) I always think it sounds more actor than barrister, but Mortimer is a QC, so he should know. The Pomeroy's claret is bang on, though, as is Mrs Rumpole (who calls him 'Rumpole') and whom he refers to as 'she who must be obeyed' – the ''er indoors' of the professional classes.

Mortimer has had an unusual publishing history, as will be seen below. Hugely prolific and hardworking (he is an active QC, a journalist, a tireless adaptor for TV – as exemplified by his brilliant *Brideshead Revisited* – and an interviewer, as well as a playwright and novelist), until Rumpole he was best known for his stage work, the bulk of his published *œuvre*. His *A Voyage Round My Father* was autobiographical (memorably televised with Laurence Olivier and Alan Bates) and his actual autobiography, *Clinging to the Wreckage*, was a bestseller. I imagine, though, that it is Rumpole for whom he will be remembered. Rumpole is here to stay.

1 **Charade** (novel)	Lane 1947	**F**
2 **Rumming Park** (novel)	Lane 1948	**F**

Mortimer

3	**Answer Yes or No** (novel)	Lane 1950	**E**
4	**The Silver Hook** (American edition of 3)	Morrow 1950	**D**
5	**Like Men Betrayed** (novel)	Collins 1953	**E**
		Lippincott 1954	**D**
6	**The Narrowing Stream** (novel)	Collins 1954	**D**
7	**Three Winters** (novel)	Collins 1956	**D**
8	**No Moaning at the Bar** (humour) Published under the pseudonym Geoffrey Lincoln.	Bles 1957	**E**
9	**With Love and Lizards** (travel) Written with Penelope Mortimer.	Joseph 1957	**E**
10	**Three Plays**	Elek 1958	**E**
	Includes **The Dock Brief, What Shall We Tell Caroline?** and **I Spy.**	Grove Press 1962	**C**
11	**The Wrong Side of the Park (play)**	Heinemann 1960	**C**
12	**Lunch Hour** (play)	French 1960	**C**
13	**Lunch House** and **Other Plays** Includes **Collect Your Hand Baggage, David and Broccoli,** and **Call Me a Liar**	Methuen 1960	**C**
14	**Two Stars For Comfort** (play)	Methuen 1962	**C**
15	**A Flea in Her Ear** (play) An adaptation of Feydeau.	French (UK) 1967	**B**
		French (US) 1967	**B**
16	**The Judge** (play)	Methuen 1967	**C**
17	**A Choice of Kings** (play) Published in **Playbill Three**, edited by Alan Durband.	Hutchinson 1969	**C**
18	**Cat Among the Pigeons** (play) An adaptation of Feydeau.	French 1970	**B**
19	**Five Plays** Includes **The Dock Brief, What Shall We Tell Caroline?, I Spy, Lunch Hour,** and **Collect Your Hand Baggage**	Methuen 1970	**C**
20	**Come As You Are: Four Short Plays** Includes **Mill Hill, Bermondsey, Gloucester Road,** and **Marble Arch.**	Methuen 1971	**C**
21	**The Captain of Kopenick** (play) An adaptation of Carl Zuckmayer.	Methuen 1971	**B**
22	**A Voyage Round My Father** (play)	Methuen 1971	**D**
23	**Knightsbridge** (play)	French 1973	**B**
24	**Collaborations** (play)	Methuen 1973	**B**
25	**The Lady from Maxim's** (play) An adaptation of Feydeau.	Heinemann 1977	**B**
26	**Will Shakespeare:** **The Untold Story** (novel)	Hodder 1977	**B**
		Delacorte 1978	**B**

27 **The Fear of Heaven** (play)	French 1978	**B**
28 **Heaven and Hell** (plays)	French 1978	**B**
Contains 27 and **The Prince of Darkness.**		
29 **Rumpole of the Bailey** (stories)	Penguin 1978	**D**
	Penguin US 1980	**C**
30 **The Trials of Rumpole** (stories)	Penguin 1979	**C**
	Penguin US 1981	**B**
31 **Rumpole** (contains 29 and 30)	Allen Lane 1980	**C**
32 **Rumpole's Return** (stories)	Penguin 1980	**C**
	Penguin US 1982	**B**
33 **Regina v. Rumpole** (stories)	Allen Lane 1981	**C**
(contains 32 and **Rumpole for the Defence**, published separately by Penguin in 1982)		
34 **Clinging to the Wreckage** (autobiography)	Weidenfeld & Nicolson 1982	**C**
	Ticknor & Fields 1982	**C**
35 **In Character** (interviews)	Allen Lane 1983	**C**
36 **Rumpole and the Golden Thread** (stories)	Penguin US 1983	**B**
37 **The First Rumpole Omnibus** (contains 29, 30 and 32)	Penguin 1983	**B**
38 **Edwin and Other Plays**	Penguin 1984	**B**
39 **Three Boulevard Farces** (plays)	Penguin 1985	**B**
40 **Paradise Postponed** (novel)	Viking UK 1985	**C**
	Viking US 1985	**C**
41 **Character Parts** (interviews)	Viking UK 1986	**C**
42 **Rumpole's Last Case** (stories)	Penguin 1987	**B**
	Penguin US 1988	**B**
43 **The Second Rumpole Omnibus** (contains **Rumpole for the Defence**, 36 and 42)	Viking UK 1987	**B**
	Penguin US 1988	**B**
44 **Summer's Lease** (novel)	Viking UK 1988	**C**
	Viking US 1988	**C**
45 **Rumpole and the Age of Miracles** (stories)	Penguin 1988	**B**
	Penguin US 1989	**B**
46 **Titmuss Regained** (novel)	Viking UK 1990	**C**
	Viking US 1990	**C**
47 **Rumpole à la Carte** (novel)	Viking UK 1990	**C**
	Viking US 1990	**C**
48 **The Rapstone Chronicles** (contains nos 40 and 46)	Viking 1991	**C**
49 **Dunster** (novel)	Viking UK 1992	**C**
	Viking US 1992	**C**
50 **Rumpole on Trial** (stories)	Viking UK 1992	**C**
	Viking US 1992	**C**

Muldoon, Paul   Born in Northern Ireland, 1951.

After Seamus Heaney, probably the best known of the 'Ulster' poets: not hugely collected, but elusive for all that.

1 **Knowing My Place** (verse)	Ulsterman (Belfast) 1971	**G**
2 **New Weather** (verse)	Faber 1973	**G**
3 **Spirit of Dawn** (verse)	Ulsterman (Belfast) 1975	**E**
4 **Mules** (verse)	Faber 1977	**E**
	Wake Forest University Press 1980	**B**
5 **Names and Addresses** (verse)	Ulsterman (Belfast) 1978	**D**
6 **Why Brownlee Left** (verse)	Faber 1980	**D**
	Wake Forest University Press 1980	**B**
7 **Immram** (verse)	Gallery Press 1980	**C**
8 **The O–O's Party** (verse)	Gallery Press 1980	**C**
9 **Out of Siberia** (verse)	Gallery Press 1982	**C**
	Deerfield Press US 1982	**C**
10 **Quoof** (verse)	Faber 1983	**C**
	Wake Forest University Press 1983	**B**
11 **The Wishbone** (verse)	Gallery Press 1984	**C**
12 **Selected Poems 1968–1983**	Faber 1986	**C**
	Ecco Press 1987	**C**
13 **Meeting the British** (verse)	Faber 1987	**C**
	Wake Forest University Press 1987	**C**
14 **Madoc: A Mystery** (verse)	Faber 1990	**C**

Murdoch, Iris   Born in Dublin, 1919.

Dame Iris Murdoch maintains her position as one of the best three or four writers in English today. Always collectable, and becoming scarcer – but still remarkably good value as well.

1 **Sartre: Romantic Rationalist** (non-fiction)	Bowes & Bowes 1953	**J**
	Yale University Press 1953	**G**
2 **Under the Net** (novel)	Chatto & Windus 1954	**O**
	Viking 1954	**H**
3 **The Flight from the Enchanter** (novel)	Chatto & Windus 1956	**L**
	Viking 1956	**G**

4 **The Sandcastle** (novel)	Chatto & Windus 1957	**L**
	Viking 1957	**G**
5 **The Bell** (novel)	Chatto & Windus 1958	**G**
	Viking 1958	**D**
6 **A Severed Head** (novel)	Chatto & Windus 1961	**E**
	Viking 1961	**C**
7 **An Unofficial Rose** (novel)	Chatto & Windus 1962	**E**
	Viking 1962	**C**
8 **The Unicorn** (novel)	Chatto & Windus 1963	**E**
	Viking 1963	**C**
9 **The Italian Girl** (novel)	Chatto & Windus 1964	**E**
	Viking 1964	**C**
10 **A Severed Head** (play)	Chatto & Windus 1964	**G**
With J.B. Priestley.		
11 **The Red and the Green** (novel)	Chatto & Windus 1965	**D**
	Viking 1965	**C**
12 **The Time of the Angels** (novel)	Chatto & Windus 1966	**D**
	Viking 1966	**C**
13 **The Sovereignty of Good** (lecture)	CUP 1967	**G**
14 **The Nice and the Good** (novel)	Chatto & Windus 1968	**D**
	Viking 1968	**C**
15 **Bruno's Dream** (novel)	Chatto & Windus 1969	**D**
	Viking 1969	**C**
16 **The Italian Girl** (play)	French 1969	**D**
With James Saunders.		
17 **A Fairly Honourable Defeat** (novel)	Chatto & Windus 1970	**D**
	Viking 1970	**C**
18 **The Sovereignty of Good** (essays)	Routledge 1971	**E**
Cont. 13. together with other unpublished essays.		
19 **An Accidental Man** (novel)	Chatto & Windus 1971	**C**
	Viking 1972	**C**
20 **The Black Prince** (novel)	Chatto & Windus 1973	**D**
	Viking 1973	**C**
21 **The Three Arrows** and **The Servants and the Snow: Two Plays**	Chatto & Windus 1973	**E**
	Viking 1974	**C**
22 **The Sacred and Profane Love Machine** (novel)	Chatto & Windus 1974	**D**
	Viking 1974	**C**
23 **A Word Child** (novel)	Chatto & Windus 1975	**D**
	Viking 1975	**C**
24 **Henry and Cato** (novel)	Chatto & Windus 1976	**C**
	Viking 1976	**C**
25 **The Fire and the Sun: Why Plato Banished the Artists** (philosophy)	OUP 1977	**D**
26 **The Sea, the Sea** (novel)	Chatto & Windus 1978	**D**
	Viking 1978	**C**

27 **A Year of Birds** (verse)   Compton Press 1978   **K**
A lovely slim volume, and Murdoch's
only published poetry. It is limited to
350 copies, each numbered and signed
by Iris Murdoch and by Reynolds
Stone, who illustrated it (see 30).

28 **Nuns and Soldiers** (novel)   Chatto & Windus 1980 **C**
                                       Viking 1981 **C**

29 **The Servants** (libretto)   OUP 1980 **J**
This was published in an edition of 125
copies for sale by the Music
Department of the OUP. The libretto
is from the opera by William Mathias
based on Murdoch's **The Servants
and the Snow** (see 21).

30 **Reynolds Stone**   Warren Editions 1981 **H**
A four-page address given in St James's
Church, Piccadilly, in memory of
Stone. Limited to 750 copies, but none
is numbered and there is no mention of
whether all or some were signed. My
own copy bears a signature.

31 **The Philosopher's Pupil** (novel)   Chatto & Windus 1983 **C**
                                         Viking 1983 **C**

32 **The Good Apprentice** (novel)   Chatto & Windus 1985 **C**
                                         Viking 1985 **C**

33 **Acastos: Two Platonic Dialogues**   Chatto & Windus 1986 **C**
(plays)   Viking 1987 **C**

34 **The Book and the Brotherhood**   Chatto & Windus 1987 **C**
(novel)   Viking 1988 **C**

35 **Three Plays**   Chatto & Windus 1989 **C**
(contains **The Servants and the
Snow, The Three Arrows** and **The
Black Prince**)

36 **The Existential Political Myth**   Delos Press 1989 **C**
(press)

37 **The Message to the Planet** (novel)   Chatto & Windus 1989 **C**
                                         Viking 1990 **C**

38 **Metaphysics as a Guide to Morals**   Chatto & Windus 1992 **C**
(philosophy)

A story entitled 'Something Special' appears in **Winter's Tales** 3
Macmillan 1957

Bibliography:
Thomas A. Tominaga and Wilma Schneidermeyer **Iris Murdoch and
Muriel Spark: A Bibliography** Scarecrow Press (US) 1976.

Nabokov, Vladimir Born in St Petersburg (now Leningrad), 1899. Died 1977.

Now that the notorious image of *Lolita* has faded, Nabokov is much better known for the power of such novels as *Pale Fire* and *Ada*, and for his recently published lectures on literature.

Nabokov is a difficult author to collect; not least because most collections must probably be compromises, for many of his works were first published in Russian in different countries, sometimes long before the first English editions, although in most cases the translations into English were by Nabokov himself. In the checklist below, I have taken the chronology of the English editions, though stating whether Russian-language publication preceded.

1 **Camera Obscura** (novel) Long (London) 1937 **Q**
A revised edition was published in America by Bobbs Merrill in 1938 as **Laughter in the Dark** (**K**), and by Weidenfeld in 1961 (**H**). First publication, in Russian, was in Paris and Berlin 1933.

2 **Despair** (novel) Long (London) 1937 **O**
A revised edition was published in 1966 in America by Putnam (**F**), and in England by Weidenfeld (**F**). First publication was in Berlin 1936.

3 **The Real Life of Sebastian Knight** (novel) New Directions 1941 **L**
Editions Poetry 1945 **I**

4 **Nikolai Gogol** (non-fiction) New Directions 1944 **I**
Editions Poetry 1947 **H**

5 **Bend Sinister** (novel) Holt 1947 **K**
Weidenfeld 1960 **F**

6 **Nine Stories** New Directions 1947 **H**

7 **Conclusive Evidence: A Memoir** Harper 1951 **K**
Published in England by Gollancz in 1952 as **Speak, Memory: A Memoir** (**H**). A revised edition **Speak, Memory: An Autobiography Revisited** was published in America by Putnam in 1966 (**E**), and in England by Weidenfeld in 1967 (**E**).

8 **Lolita** (novel) Olympia Press (Paris) 1955 **L**
The Paris edition is in two volumes.
Putnam 1958 **F**
Weidenfeld 1959 **E**

9 **Pnin** (novel) Doubleday 1957 **G**
Heinemann 1957 **F**

Nabokov

10 **Nabokov's Dozen** (stories)	Doubleday 1958	E
	Heinemann 1959	E
11 **Invitation to a Beheading** (novel)	Putnam 1959	H
First publication, in Russian, was in	Weidenfeld 1960	F
Paris 1938.		
12 **Poems**	Doubleday 1959	E
	Weidenfeld 1961	E
13 **Pale Fire** (novel)	Putnam 1962	E
	Weidenfeld 1962	E
14 **The Gift** (novel)	Putnam 1963	E
First published, in Russian, in New	Weidenfeld 1963	E
York, 1952.		
15 **The Defense** (novel)	Putnam 1964	E
English title **The Defence**.	Weidenfeld 1964	E
First published, in Russian, in Berlin		
1930.		
16 **Nabokov's Quartet** (stories)	Phaedra 1966	E
	Weidenfeld 1967	E
17 **King, Queen, Knave** (novel)	McGraw-Hill 1968	E
	Weidenfeld 1968	E
18 **Nabokov's Congeries** (anthology)	Viking Press 1968	D
19 **Ada** (novel)	McGraw-Hill 1969	D
	Weidenfeld 1969	C
20 **Mary** (novel)	McGraw-Hill 1970	C
This was, in fact, his first novel,	Weidenfeld 1971	C
and was originally published in Russian		
in Berlin 1926.		
21 **Glory** (novel)	McGraw-Hill 1971	C
First publication, in Russian, was in	Weidenfeld 1972	C
Paris 1932		
22 **Poems and Problems**	McGraw-Hill 1971	C
	Weidenfeld 1972	C
23 **Transparent Things** (novel)	McGraw-Hill 1973	C
	Weidenfeld 1973	C
24 **A Russian Beauty and Other**	McGraw-Hill 1973	C
Stories	Weidenfeld 1973	C
25 **Strong Opinions** (essays)	McGraw-Hill 1973	C
	Weidenfeld 1974	C
26 **Look at the Harlequins!** (novel)	McGraw-Hill 1974	C
	Weidenfeld 1975	C
27 **Lolita: A Screenplay**	McGraw-Hill 1974	C
28 **Tyrants Destroyed and Other**	McGraw-Hill 1975	C
Stories	Weidenfeld 1975	C
29 **Details of a Sunset and Other**	McGraw-Hill 1976	C
Stories	Weidenfeld 1976	C

30	**The Nabokov/Wilson Letters 1940–1971**	Farrar Straus 1978	C
		Weidenfeld 1979	C
	Correspondence between Nabokov and Edmund Wilson.		
31	**Lectures on Literature**	Harcourt Brace 1980	C
		Weidenfeld 1980	C
32	**Lectures on Russian Literature**	Harcourt Brace 1981	C
		Weidenfeld 1982	C
33	**Lectures on Don Quixote**	Harcourt Brace 1983	C
		Weidenfeld 1983	C

Some works – notably the very early verse – did not appear under their original titles in English, but details of these and of his translations of other works, etc., may be found in
Andrew Field **Nabokov: A Bibliography** McGraw-Hill 1974.

Naipaul, Shiva   Born in Trinidad, 1945. Died 1985.

Always a respected author, although not seen to be in the same league as his elder brother V.S., Shiva seemed to have turned away from the novel in favour of travel writing, prior to his untimely death; a shame – *Fireflies* remains his most memorable work. Very many writers mourned the passing of Shiva – not just because he was young and had much work to do, but because they admired his quiet and diligent manner, and his extremely professional approach to his writing, clearly visible in the quality of the product.

1	**Fireflies** (novel)	Deutsch 1970	J
		Knopf 1971	F
2	**The Chip-Chip Gatherers** (novel)	Deutsch 1973	H
		Knopf 1973	E
3	**The Adventures of Gurudeva** (stories)	Deutsch 1976	E
4	**North of South: An African Journey** (travel)	Deutsch 1978	D
		Scribner 1979	D
5	**Black and White** (travel)	Hamilton 1980	D
6	**Journey to Nowhere: A New World Tragedy** (same as 5)	Simon & Schuster 1981	C
7	**A Hot Country** (travel)	Hamilton 1983	C
		Viking 1984	C
8	**Beyond the Dragon's Mouth** (travel)	Hamilton 1984	C
		Viking 1985	C
9	**An Unfinished Journey** (travel)	Hamilton 1986	C

Naipaul, V.S.   Born in Trinidad, 1932. British.

A highly regarded author, the most desirable highlights of whom are still *The*

Naipaul, V.S.

Mystic Masseur (his first book) and *A House for Mr Biswas*. Lately, he has been leaning towards non-fiction, and this is of considerably less interest to the collector.

1 **The Mystic Masseur** (novel)	Deutsch 1957	**M**
	Vanguard Press 1959	**H**
2 **The Suffrage of Elvira** (novel)	Deutsch 1958	**L**
3 **Miguel Street** (novel)	Deutsch 1959	**L**
	Vanguard Press 1960	**G**
4 **A House for Mr Biswas** (novel)	Deutsch 1961	**J**
	McGraw-Hill 1962	**G**
5 **The Middle Passage** (non-fiction)	Deutsch 1962	**H**
	Macmillan (US) 1963	**F**
6 **Mr Stone and the Knights Companion** (novel)	Deutsch 1963	**I**
	Macmillan 1964	**E**
7 **An Area of Darkness** (travel)	Deutsch 1964	**G**
	Macmillan 1965	**D**
8 **The Mimic Men** (novel)	Deutsch 1967	**H**
	Macmillan 1967	**F**
9 **A Flag on the Island** (stories)	Deutsch 1967	**F**
	Macmillan 1968	**D**
10 **The Loss of El Dorado** (history)	Deutsch 1969	**D**
	Knopf 1970	**C**
11 **In a Free State** (novel)	Deutsch 1971	**E**
	Knopf 1971	**C**
12 **The Overcrowded Barracoon** (articles)	Deutsch 1972	**D**
	Knopf 1972	**C**
13 **Guerrillas** (novel)	Deutsch 1975	**D**
	Knopf 1975	**C**
14 **India: A Wounded Civilisation** (non-fiction)	Deutsch 1977	**C**
	Knopf 1977	**C**
15 **A Bend in the River** (novel)	Deutsch 1979	**C**
	Knopf 1979	**C**
16 **The Return of Eva Peron** (essays)	Deutsch 1980	**C**
	Knopf 1980	**C**
17 **Among the Believers: An Islamic Journey** (travel)	Deutsch 1981	**C**
	Knopf 1981	**C**
18 **Finding the Centre: Two Narratives**	Deutsch 1984	**C**
	Knopf 1984	**C**
19 **The Enigma of Arrival** (novel)	Viking UK 1987	**C**
	Knopf 1987	**C**
20 **A Turn in the South** (non-fiction)	Viking UK 1989	**C**
	Knopf 1989	**C**
21 **India: A Million Mutinies Now** (non-fiction)	Heinemann 1990	**C**
	Viking US 1991	**C**

Nash, Ogden   Born in New York, 1902. Died 1971.

What can one say about Nash? One of the great romantic poets of our time – indeed, of any time. He makes Byron seem crass, Shelley inept, and Keats downright insensitive. It is with tears of joy that I bring you the following:

'Many people have asked me what was the most beautiful sight I
   saw during the recent summer,
And I think the most beautiful sight was the day the water
   wouldn't stop running and in came the plumber.'

The master of these unique rhymes has published quite a few volumes, though no one in particular stands out as a highlight. Each seems as delightful as the next, however, and so I print a representative selection.

1 **Hard Lines**	Simon & Schuster 1931	**H**
	Duckworth 1931	**G**
2 **The Primrose Path**	Simon & Schuster 1935	**F**
	Bodley Head 1935	**E**
3 **The Bad Parent's Garden of Verse**	Simon & Schuster 1936	**E**
4 **The Face is Familiar**	Little, Brown 1940	**D**
	Dent 1942	**C**
5 **Verses from 1929 on**	Little, Brown 1961	**C**

5 ... This was published in England as **Collected Verses** by Dent during the same year (**C**).

Naughton, Bill   Born in County Mayo, Ireland, 1910. Died 1992.

Still best known for one key, seminal sixties novel which was in turn made into a key, seminal sixties film notable for Michael Caine and a nasal little ditty by Cilla Black which didn't actually feature in the film at all. Not a lot of people know that.

Alfie	MacGibbon & Kee 1966	**H**
	Ballantine 1966	**D**

O'Brien, Edna   Born in County Clare, Ireland, 1932.

A really excellent and lovely writer – it was good to see a new novel in 1992, but Edna O'Brien's true and wondrous form was on display for the first time in a long time in *Lantern Slides* – unforgettable stories as only she knows how. *Still* underrated by collectors, though.

O'Brien, Edna

1	**The Country Girls** (novel)	Hutchinson 1960	**H**
		Knopf 1960	**D**
2	**The Lonely Girl** (novel)	Cape 1962	**G**
		Random House 1962	**D**
3	**Girls in Their Married Bliss** (novel)	Cape 1964	**E**
		Houghton Mifflin 1968	**C**
	1, 2 and 3 form a trilogy.		
4	**August is a Wicked Month** (novel)	Cape 1965	**D**
		Simon & Schuster 1965	**C**
5	**Casualties of Peace** (novel)	Cape 1966	**C**
		Simon & Schuster 1967	**B**
6	**The Love Object** (stories)	Cape 1968	**D**
		Knopf 1969	**B**
7	**A Pagan Place** (novel)	Weidenfeld 1970	**C**
		Knopf 1970	**B**
8	**Zee & Co** (screenplay)	Weidenfeld 1971	**C**
9	**Night** (novel)	Weidenfeld 1972	**C**
		Knopf 1973	**B**
10	**A Pagan Place** (play)	Faber 1973	**D**
11	**A Scandalous Woman** (stories)	Weidenfeld 1974	**C**
		Harcourt Brace 1974	**B**
12	**Mother Ireland** (autobiog.)	Weidenfeld 1976	**C**
		Harcourt Brace 1976	**C**
13	**Johnnie, I Hardly Knew You** (novel)	Weidenfeld 1977	**C**
		Doubleday 1978	**B**
	The American edition was entitled simply **I Hardly Knew You**.		
14	**Arabian Days** (travel)	Horizon Press (NY) 1977	**C**
		Quartet 1977	**C**
15	**The Collected Edna O'Brien**	Collins 1978	**C**
	Contains 1, 2, 3, 4, 5, 6, 7, 11, together with a new introduction.		
16	**Mrs Reinhardt and Other Stories**	Weidenfeld 1978	**C**
17	**A Rose in the Heart**	Doubleday 1979	**B**
	(American edition of 16)		
18	**Some Irish Loving** (anthology)	Weidenfeld 1979	**B**
	A selection of Irish writing, edited and introduced by E. O'B.	Harper 1979	**B**
19	**Virginia** (play)	Hogarth Press 1981	**C**
		Harcourt Brace 1981	**C**
20	**The Dazzle** (juvenile)	Hodder & Stoughton 1981	**C**
21	**James and Nora** (essay)	Lord John Press (US) 1981	**G**
	Concerning the marriage of Joyce, in a signed edition published at $35.		
22	**Returning** (stories)	Weidenfeld 1982	**C**
23	**A Christmas Treat** (juvenile)	Hodder & Stoughton 1982	**C**

24 **A Fanatic Heart** (previously published stories)	Weidenfeld 1985	B
25 **Tales for Telling: Irish Folk and Fairy Stories** (juvenile)	Pavilion 1986	B
26 **The Country Girls Trilogy and Epilogue**	Farrar Straus 1986	C
	Cape 1987	C
27 **The High Road** (novel)	Weidenfeld 1988	C
	Farrar Straus 1988	B
28 **Lantern Slides** (stories)	Weidenfeld 1990	C
	Farrar Straus 1990	C
29 **Time and Tide** (novel)	Viking UK 1992	C

O'Brien, Flann Pseudonym of Brian O'Nolan, also known as Myles na Gopaleen. Born in Tyrone, Ireland, 1912. Died 1966.

I am not going to even begin to try to explain what sort of a book the following is, but I will say that it is unique, brilliant, funny and very scarce. It remains the highlight.

At-Swim-Two-Birds	Longman 1939	O
	Pantheon 1951	I

Orton, Joe Born in Leicester, 1933. Died 1967.

'Ortonesque' has truly become a fixture in the language – often as a misdirected shorthand for anything grotesque, ribald and more than faintly indecent; maybe not so misdirected, actually. Here is the inimitable body of work that added a new dimension to the English stage – one wonders what on earth Joe might have gone on to write, had he not been cut down (up?) by one lover's tiff too many.

1 **Entertaining Mr. Sloane** (play)	Hamish Hamilton 1964	G
	Grove Press 1965	D
2 **Loot** (play)	Methuen 1967	E
	Grove Press 1968	C
3 **Crimes of Passion** (plays) (contains **The Ruffian on the Stair** and **The Erpingham Camp**)	Methuen 1967	D
	Grove Press 1968	C
4 **What the Butler Saw** (play)	Methuen 1969	C
	Grove Press 1969	C
5 **Funeral Games** and **The Good and Faithful Servant** (plays)	Methuen 1970	C
6 **Head to Toe** (novel)	Blond 1971	C
7 **Joe Orton: The Complete Plays**	Eyre Methuen 1976	C
	Grove Press 1977	C

8 **Up Against It** (screenplay)	Eyre Methuen 1979	**C**
	Grove Press 1979	**C**
9 **The Orton Diaries** (edited by	Methuen 1986	**C**
John Lahr – author of the biography,		
Prick Up Your Ears, Lane 1976,		
Knopf 1976)		

Orwell, George   Born in Bengal, 1903. Died 1950.
Pseudonym for Eric Blair.

Still one of the most sought-after authors of all, but damnably difficult even to gather all the titles in first edition – let alone in fine state. The early stuff almost *never* appears in d/w – even scruffy ones. Tatty copies of *Nineteen Eighty-Four* and *The Road to Wigan Pier* (orange Left Book Club edition) are everywhere, but most other things are uncommon-to-unheard-of – as you will see below.

1 **Down and Out in Paris**	Gollancz 1933	**T**
and London (non-fiction)	Harper 1933	**Q**
2 **Burmese Days** (novel)	Harper 1934	**R**
	Gollancz 1935	**O**
3 **A Clergyman's Daughter** (novel)	Gollancz 1935	**Q**
	Harper 1936	**N**
4 **Keep the Aspidistra Flying** (novel)	Gollancz 1936	**Q**
	Harcourt Brace 1956	**H**
5 **The Road to Wigan Pier** (non-fiction)	Gollancz 1937	**E**
The 1st was published in orange wrpps	Harcourt Brace 1958	**G**
under The Left Book Club imprint.		
A hard-covered trade edition followed.		
6 **Homage to Catalonia** (non-fiction)	Secker 1938	**Q**
	Harcourt Brace 1952	**F**
7 **Coming Up for Air** (novel)	Gollancz 1939	**P**
	Harcourt Brace 1950	**E**
8 **Inside the Whale** (essays)	Gollancz 1940	**I**
9 **The Lion and the Unicorn** (non-	Secker 1941	**G**
fiction)		
This was published as Searchlight Books		
No. 1. Orwell was the editor, with T.R.		
Fyvel, of ten Searchlight Books,		
published between 1941 and 1943.		
Although this was the only one he wrote,		
he contributed Forewords to two more:		
T.C. Worsley **The End of the Old**		
School Tie and J. Cary **The Case for**		
African Freedom.		
10 **Animal Farm** (novel)	Secker 1945	**L**
	Harcourt Brace 1946	**H**

11 **James Burnham and the Managerial Revolution**	Socialist Book Centre 1946	**M**
12 **Critical Essays**	Secker 1946	**F**
13 **Dickens, Dali and Others** (same as 12)	Reynal (NY) 1946	**F**
14 **The English People** (essay) This was No. 100 in the Britain in Pictures series.	Collins 1947	**F**
15 **Nineteen Eighty-Four** Much play is made of the d/w. There are two states – maroon (often faded to pink) and green. No one can say with absolute certainty which preceded, but it is true that the maroon is far scarcer, and therefore, I suppose, the more desirable. It could cost twice as much (**N**).	Secker 1949 Harcourt Brace 1949	**K** **G**

It is also worth acquiring the Oxford rev. ed. if only for the copyright date reading '1984'. The reissued Secker edition also bore this date, actually, but this was quite unjustified as it was an unrevised text.

16 **Shooting an Elephant** (essays)	Secker 1950 Harcourt Brace 1950	**H** **E**
17 **Such, Such Were the Joys** (essays)	Harcourt Brace 1953	**G**
18 **England, Your England** (essays) Substantially the same as 17.	Sekcer 1953	**F**
19 **Animal Farm: Illustrated Edition**	Secker 1954	**F**
20 **Selected Essays**	Penguin 1957	**D**
21 **Selected Writings**	Heinemann 1958	**D**
22 **Collected Essays** Incl. 12, 16 and 18.	Secker 1961	**D**
23 **The Collected Essays, Journalism and Letters** (4 vols)	Secker 1968 Harcourt-Brace 1968	**K** **I**
24 **The War Broadcasts**	BBC/Duckworth 1985	**C**
25 **The War Commentaries**	BBC/Duckworth 1985	**C**

Bibliography:
Z.G. Zeke and W. White **George Orwell: A Selected Bibliography** Boston 1962

Biography:
Bernard Crick **George Orwell: A Life** Secker 1980; revised edition 1982

Osborne, John   Born in London, 1929.

Osborne has always been underrated by collectors (he is almost as important

Osborne

as he says) as well as by critics, as was demonstrated by the on the whole rather sniffy reviews of *Dejavu*. The play is on the long side, it is true, but the dialogue at its best really does crackle in good old Osborne/Porter tradition. The playwright seems to be better known these days for having been beastly to his relations in the course of his two (superb) volumes of autobiography – but he has written many excellent plays in *addition* to *Anger* and *The Entertainer*, and if you see good firsts cheapish, you should pounce; in fact, you should pounce anyway.

1	**Look Back in Anger** (play)	Faber 1957	**G**
		Criterion 1957	**D**
2	**The Entertainer** (play)	Faber 1957	**F**
		Criterion 1958	**C**
3	**Epitaph for George Dillon** (play)	Faber 1958	**E**
	With Anthony Creighton.	Criterion 1958	**C**
4	**The World of Paul Slickey** (play)	Faber 1959	**F**
		Criterion 1961	**C**
5	**A Subject of Scandal and Concern** (play)	Faber 1961	**E**
6	**Luther** (play)	Faber 1961	**E**
		Dramatic Publishing Co. 1961	**C**
7	**Plays for England** Incl. **The Blood of the Bambergs** and **Under Plain Cover**.	Faber 1963	**E**
		Criterion 1964	**C**
8	**Tom Jones: A Film Script**	Faber 1964	**E**
		Grove Press 1964	**C**
9	**Inadmissible Evidence** (play)	Faber 1965	**E**
		Grove Press 1965	**C**
10	**A Bond Honoured** (play)	Faber 1966	**D**
11	**A Patriot for Me** (play)	Faber 1966	**D**
		Random House 1970	**C**
12	**Time Present** and **Hotel in Amsterdam** (plays)	Faber 1968	**C**
13	**The Right Prospectus** (play)	Faber 1970	**C**
14	**Very Like a Whale** (play)	Faber 1971	**C**
15	**West of Suez** (play)	Faber 1971	**C**
16	**Hedda Gabler** (play: adapt. from Ibsen)	Faber 1972	**C**
17	**The Gift of Friendship** (play)	Faber 1972	**C**
18	**A Sense of Detachment** (play)	Faber 1973	**C**
19	**A Place Calling Itself Rome** (play)	Faber 1973	**C**
20	**The Picture of Dorian Gray** (play)	Faber 1973	**C**
21	**The End of Me Old Cigar** (play)	Faber 1975	**C**
22	**Watch It Come Down** (play)	Faber 1975	**C**
23	**You're Not Watching Me, Mummy** and **Try A Little Tenderness** (plays)	Faber 1978	**C**

24 **A Better Class of Person** (autobiog.)	Faber 1981 Dutton 1981	D C
25 **A Better Class of Person** and **God Rot Tunbridge Wells** (plays)	Faber 1985	C
26 **Strindberg's The Father** and **Ibsen's Hedda Gabler** (play adaptations)	Faber 1989	B
27 **Almost a Gentleman: An Auto-biography Vol II: 1955–1966**	Faber 1991	C
28 **Dejavu** (play)	Faber 1992	B

Owen, Wilfred   Born in Shropshire, 1893. Died 1918.

Still the favourite of the war poets, young girls in particular, I have noticed, responding to the sensitivity in his work, as well as the tragic romance of his early death. Although selections of his work have always been readily available, it seems sad that the definitive collected edition had to be published at £55, scholarly two-volume work though it is, when the collected works of almost any other poet one would care to name is available at an infinitely more accessible figure. Maybe soon there will be a compact one-volume edition, minus the annotations.

1 **Poems** Intro. by Siegfried Sassoon.	Chatto & Windus 1920	N
2 **The Poems of Wilfred Owen**	Chatto & Windus 1931 Viking 1931	J G
3 **The Collected Poems of Wilfred Owen** Intro. by C. Day Lewis, memoir by Edmund Blunden.	Chatto & Windus 1963 New Directions 1964	F D
4 **Collected Letters**	OUP 1967	D
5 **The Complete Poems and Fragments** 2 volumes, edited by Jon Stalworthy.	Chatto & Windus 1983	G

Biography:
Jon Stalworthy **Wilfred Owen** OUP/Chatto 1974.

Parkinson, C. Northcote   Born in Durham, 1909.

Parkinson's Law expounds the theory that work will expand to fill the time available. This appears to be a truism, today, but only since Parkinson set it down. This is why the following highlight is collectable, while Parkinson's other (more whimsical, less vital) offerings are not.

Parkinson's Law	Houghton Mifflin	C
	1957	
	Murray 1958	C

Pasternak, Boris   Born in Moscow, 1890. Died 1960.

Not the force he was (he is distinctly unfashionable, these days) but still notable for the one famous novel, made into a highly successful film with a haunting theme tune – or an annoying theme tune, depending upon your outlook. Pasternak is a Russian noun which translated means Parsnip.

| **Dr Zhivago** | Collins/Harvill 1958 | D |
| First publication was in Italy in 1957. | Pantheon 1958 | C |

Peake, Mervyn   Born in China, 1911. Died 1968.

Although there is still very strong collectors' interest in the likes of Peake and Tolkien (people who like one tend to like the other) there is not any more the *passion* that was evident fifteen years ago. The *Gormenghast* trilogy remains a very important and very desirable set, while I find there is still demand for the posthumous fragments. Always an important factor with Peake is the presence of the dust-wrapper, as it was often designed by him – just as the books often carry illustrations by him (all of which, it seems facile to mention, must be present). So I shouldn't say that interest is on the way down, but rather that it has, as it were, peaked.

1	**Captain Slaughterboard Drops Anchor** (juvenile)	Country Life 1939	P
		Macmillan (US) 1967	D
2	**Shapes and Sounds** (verse)	Chatto & Windus 1941	M
3	**Rhymes Without Reason** (verse)	Eyre & Spottiswoode 1944	K
4	**The Craft of the Lead Pencil** (non-fiction)	Wingate 1946	I
5	**Titus Groan** (novel)	Eyre & Spottiswoode 1946	K
		Reynal & Hitchcock 1946	H
6	**Letters from a Lost Uncle from Polar Regions** (stories)	Eyre & Spottiswoode 1948	I
7	**The Drawings of Mervyn Peake**	Grey Walls Press 1949	H
8	**The Glassblowers** (verse)	Eyre & Spottiswoode 1950	H
9	**Gormenghast** (novel)	Eyre & Spottiswoode 1950	I
		Weybright & Talley 1967	C

10	**Mr Pye** (story)	Heinemann 1953	G
11	**Titus Alone** (novel)	Eyre & Spottiswoode	G
	This, with 5, and 9, completes the	1959	
	trilogy. A revised ed. of **Titus Alone**	Weybright & Talley	C
	was published by Eyre & Spottiswoode	1967	
	in 1970.		
12	**The Rhyme of the Flying Bomb**	Dent 1962	E
	(verse)		
13	**Poems and Drawings**	Keepsake Press 1965	J
	Limited to 150 copies.		
14	**A Reverie of Bone** (verse)	Rota 1967	J
	Limited to 300 copies.		
15	**Selected Poems**	Faber 1972	D
16	**A Book of Nonsense**	Owen 1972	C
		Dufour 1975	C
17	**The Drawings of Mervyn Peake**	Davis-Poynter 1974	D
18	**Mervyn Peake: Writings and**	Academy 1974	C
	Drawings	St Martin's 1974	C
19	**Twelve Poems**	Bran's Head 1975	H
20	**Peake's Progress: Selected**	Lane 1979	C
	Writings and Drawings	Overlook Press 1981	C
	Ed. Maeve Gilmore.		

Biography:
John Watney **Mervyn Peake** Joseph 1976

Perelman, S.J.   Born in Brooklyn, 1904. Died 1979.

Perelman has written about thirty books – novels, stories, plays, screenplays, miscellaneous insanities – all in his own inimitable style. There are no highlights as such, though below appears a selection which deserves to be preserved, if only for the titles – or, should I say, not least for the titles.

1	**Keep It Crisp**	Random House 1946	E
		Heinemann 1947	D
2	**Acres and Pains**	Reynal & Hitchcock	D
		1947	
		Heinemann 1948	C
3	**Westward Ha! or, around the**	Simon & Schuster 1947	D
	World in 80 Clichés	Reinhardt & Evans	C
		1949	
4	**The Swiss Family Perelman**	Simon & Schuster 1950	C
		Reinhardt & Evans	C
		1951	
5	**A Child's Garden of Curses**	Heinemann 1951	C
6	**The Rising Gorge**	Simon & Schuster 1961	C
		Heinemann 1962	C

7 **The Last Laugh**	Simon & Schuster 1981	**C**
This – posthumously published – was,	Methuen 1981	**C**
appropriately, his last book.		

Peters, Ellis   Born in Shropshire, 1913.
Pseud. Edith Pargeter.

Edith Pargeter – now eighty years old – is a remarkable lady. She has written dozens of crime novels not only under her own name but also as Peter Benedict, Jolyon Carr, John Redfern and – her most celebrated pseudonym – Ellis Peters. It is, of course, the creation of the twelfth century Benedictine monk extraordinary, Brother Cadfael, that has hurled Ellis Peters to prominence (and the peak of collectability) but it is important to remember that *non* Cadfael novels have also appeared under the Ellis Peters name. Cadfael reigns supreme, however, and there follows the complete saga to date.

1 **A Morbid Taste for Bones: A**	Macmillan 1977	**G**
Mediaeval Whodunnit (novel)	Morrow 1978	**D**
2 **One Corpse Too Many** (novel)	Macmillan 1979	**E**
	Morrow 1980	**C**
3 **Monk's-Hood** (novel)	Macmillan 1980	**E**
	Morrow 1981	**C**
4 **Saint Peter's Fair** (novel)	Macmillan 1981	**E**
	Morrow 1981	**C**
5 **The Leper of Saint Giles** (novel)	Macmillan 1981	**E**
	Morrow 1982	**C**
6 **The Virgin in the Ice** (novel)	Macmillan 1982	**D**
	Morrow 1983	**C**
7 **The Sanctuary Sparrow** (novel)	Macmillan 1983	**D**
	Morrow 1983	**C**
8 **The Devil's Novice** (novel)	Macmillan 1983	**D**
	Morrow 1984	**C**
9 **Dead Man's Ransom** (novel)	Macmillan 1984	**D**
	Morrow 1984	**C**
10 **The Pilgrim of Hate** (novel)	Macmillan 1984	**D**
	Morrow 1984	**C**
11 **An Excellent Mystery** (novel)	Macmillan 1985	**C**
	Morrow 1986	**B**
12 **The Raven in the Foregate** (novel)	Macmillan 1986	**C**
	Morrow 1986	**B**
13 **The Rose Rent** (novel)	Macmillan 1986	**C**
	Morrow 1986	**B**
14 **The Hermit of Eyton Forest** (novel)	Headline 1987	**C**
	Mysterious Press 1988	**B**
15 **The Confession of Brother Haluin**	Headline 1988	**C**
(novel)	Mysterious Press 1989	**B**
16 **The Heretic's Apprentice** (novel)	Headline 1989	**C**

17 **The Potter's Field** (novel)	Headline 1989	**C**
18 **The Summer of the Danes** (novel)	Headline 1991	**C**
19 **The Holy Thief** (novel)	Headline 1992	**C**

Pinter, Harold   Born in London, 1930.

Still politically active (i.e. boring) but increasingly prolific lately on the play front too; I shouldn't think that there are too many completists who rush to buy each new Pinter as it tumbles from the presses, but there will always be a market for the increasingly scarce wonders of the sixties – the like of which, I feel sure, we will never see again.

1 **The Birthday Party** (play)	Encore Publishing 1959	**K**
2 **The Birthday Party and Other Plays** Incl. **The Dumb Waiter** and **The Room.**	Methuen 1960	**H**
3 **The Caretaker** Methuen published an edition later the same year (**D**).	Encore Publishing 1960	**I**
4 **A Slight Ache and Other Plays** Incl. **A Night Out, The Dwarfs** and 5 revue sketches.	Methuen 1961	**E**
5 **The Birthday Party** and **The Room** (same as 2)	Grove Press 1961	**C**
6 **The Collection** (play)	French 1962	**D**
7 **The Caretaker** and **The Room** (plays)	Grove Press 1962	**C**
8 **Three Plays** Incl. **A Slight Ache, The Collection, The Dwarfs**.	Grove Press 1962	**C**
9 **The Lover** (play)	Dramatists Play Service (NY) 1965	**E**
10 **The Dwarfs** and **Eight Revue Sketches**	Dramatists Play Service 1965	**E**
11 **The Homecoming** (play)	Methuen 1965 Grove Press 1966	**E** **C**
12 **The Collection** and **The Lover** (plays) Incl. **The Examination**, a prose piece.	Methuen 1966	**C**
13 **Tea Party** (play)	Grove Press 1966	**C**
14 **Tea Party and Other Plays** Incl. **The Basement** and **Night School.**	Methuen 1967	**C**
15 **Early Plays**	Grove Press 1968	**C**

Pinter

Incl. **A Night Out, Night School**,
revue sketches.

16	**Poems** A revised edition was published in 1971, with extra poems (**D**).	Enitharmon Press 1968	**F**
17	**Mac** (memoir)	Pendragon Press 1968	**F**
18	**Landscape** and **Silence** (plays) Incl. **Night**.	Methuen 1969 Grove Press 1970	**C** **C**
19	**Five Screenplays** Cont. **The Caretaker, The Servant, The Pumpkin Eater, Accident, The Quiller Memorandum**.	Methuen 1971	**D**
20	**Old Times** (play)	Eyre Methuen 1971 Grove Press 1971	**C** **C**
21	**Monologue**	Covent Garden Press 1973	**C**
22	**No Man's Land** (play)	Eyre Methuen 1975 Grove Press 1975	**C** **C**
23	**The Proust Screenplay**	Grove Press 1977 Eyre Methuen 1978	**C** **C**
24	**Poems and Prose 1949–1977**	Grove Press 1978 Eyre Methuen 1978	**C** **C**
25	**Betrayal** (play)	Eyre Methuen 1978 Grove Press 1979	**C** **C**
26	**I Know The Place** (verse)	Greville Press 1979	**E**
27	**The Hothouse** (play)	Eyre Methuen 1980 Grove Press 1989	**C** **C**
28	**The Screenplay of The French Lieutenant's Woman**	Cape 1981 Little, Brown 1981	**C** **C**
29	**The French Lieutenant's Woman and Other Screenplays** Includes **The Last Tycoon** and **Langrishe, Go Down**.	Methuen 1982	**C**
30	**Other Places** (play)	Methuen 1982 Grove Press 1983	**C** **C**
31	**One for the Road** (play)	Methuen 1985	**C**
32	**Mountain Language** (play)	Faber 1988 Grove Weidenfeld 1988	**B** **B**
33	**The Heat of the Day** (play)	Faber 1989 Grove Weidenfeld 1990	**B** **B**
34	**The Comfort of Strangers** and **Other Screenplays**	Faber 1990	**C**
35	**The Dwarfs** (novel)	Faber 1990 Grove Weidenfeld 1990	**C** **C**
36	**100 Poems by 100 Poets** (anthology)	Faber 1991	**B**
37	**Party Time** (play)	Faber 1991	**B**

Plath, Sylvia   Born in Boston, 1932. Died 1963.

There is a danger that Plath will be remembered more for the controversies that surround her life (father hatred, marriage to Ted Hughes, suicide) and for the fact that she was not so much taken up by the feminists as canonized, than for the poetry itself which – at its best – is unforgettable. An awful lot of dross was published too, of course, but nos 2, 3, 4, 14 and 15 are really key.

1 **A Winter Ship** (verse) Published anonymously	Tragara Press (Edinburgh) 1960	**Q**
2 **The Colossus** and **Other Poems** Reissued by Heinemann as **The Colossus** in 1967 (**F**).	Heinemann 1960 Knopf 1962	**N** **I**
3 **The Bell Jar** (novel) Reissued in the Contemporary Fiction series (**I**) and then by Faber – as by Sylvia Plath – in 1966 (**G**), and Harper in the US in 1971 (**D**). The original edition was under the pseudonym Victoria Lucas.	Heinemann 1963	**O**
4 **Ariel** (verse)	Faber 1965 Harper 1966	**G** **D**
5 **Uncollected Poems** Limited to 150 copies.	Turret Books 1965	**J**
6 **Three Women** (play) Limited to 150 copies.	Turret Books 1968	**I**
7 **The Art of Sylvia Plath** A symposium, ed. Charles Newman, containing much new material.	Faber 1970 Indiana University 1970	**F** **D**
8 **Wreath for a Bridal** (verse) Limited to 150 copies.	Sceptre Press 1970	**I**
9 **Million Dollar Month** (verse) Limited to 150 copies.	Sceptre Press 1971	**H**
10 **Fiesta Melons: Poems** Limited to 150 copies.	Rougemont Press 1971	**I**
11 **Child** (verse) Limited to 325 copies.	Rougement Press 1971	**H**
12 **Crystal Gazer** (verse) Limited to 480 copies, 80 specially bound (**K**).	Rainbow Press 1971	**H**
13 **Lyonesse** (verse) Limited to 400 copies, as follows: 10 vellum (**O**). 90 full calf (**M**). 300 quarter leather (**L**).	Rainbow Press 1971	
14 **Crossing the Water** (verse)	Faber 1971 Harper 1971	**F** **D**

Potter, Dennis

15 **Winter Trees** (verse)		Faber 1971	**E**
		Harper 1972	**C**
16 **Pursuit** (verse) Limited to 100 copies.		Rainbow Press 1973	**J**
17 **Letters Home** (letters)		Harper 1975	**D**
		Faber 1976	**C**
18 **The Bed Book** (juvenile)		Faber 1976	**C**
		Harper 1976	**C**
19 **Johnny Panic and the Bible of Dreams and Other Writings** (miscellany)		Faber 1977	**C**
20 **Johnny Panic and the Bible of Dreams: Short Stories, Prose and Diary Excerpts**		Harper 1979	**D**
21 **Collected Poems** Ed. Ted Hughes.		Faber 1981	**D**
		Harper 1981	**C**
22 **Dialogue Over a Ouija Board** (verse) Limited to 140 copies.		Rainbow Press 1981	**J**

Potter, Dennis   Born in Gloucestershire, 1935.

One of the oldest and most widely respected *enfants terribles* in the business – one of the few who has actually made television watchable over the years: an *art* form, even. The *Nigel Barton* plays, *Brimstone and Treacle*, *Pennies from Heaven* – all classics, but the enduring highlight simply has to be *The Singing Detective*.

1 **The Glittering Coffin** (non-fiction)		Gollancz 1960	**D**
2 **The Changing Forest** (non-fiction)		Secker & Warburg 1962	**C**
3 **The Nigel Barton Plays: Stand Up, Nigel Barton** and **Vote Vote Vote For Nigel Barton – Two Television Plays**		Penguin 1968	**C**
4 **Son of Man** (play)		Deutsch 1970	**C**
5 **Follow the Yellow Brick Road** (play) (contained in **The Television Dramatist**, edited Robert Muller)		Elek 1973	**C**
6 **Hide and Seek** (novel)		Deutsch 1973	**C**
7 **Brimstone and Treacle** (play)		Eyre Methuen 1978	**C**
8 **Pennies from Heaven** (novelization)		Quartet 1981	**C**
9 **Sufficient Carbohydrate** (play)		Faber 1983	**C**
10 **Waiting for the Boat: Dennis Potter on Television** (plays) (includes **Joe's Ark, Blue Remembered Hills** and **Cream in My Coffee**)		Faber 1984	**C**

11 **The Singing Detective** (play series)	Faber 1986	D
12 **Ticket to Ride** (novel)	Faber 1986	C
13 **Blackeyes** (novelization)	Faber 1987	C
14 **Christabel** (play)	Faber 1989	B

Potter, Stephen   Born in London, 1900. Died 1969.

Lifemanship – that's the key. The art of always being on top, always being the centre of attention, always winning – without appearing to *try*, and without actually breaking the rules. This was exemplified by Potter himself, while a guest of Roy Plomley on BBC Radio's *Desert Island Discs*:

R.P: Mr Potter, as I've known you for so many years, do you think that on this programme I might call you Stephen?

S.P.:   Well – why not, Plomley?

Potter wrote other books, but it is the quartet below with which we are concerned.

1 **The Theory and Practice of Gamesmanship or The Art of Winning Games Without Actually Cheating**	Hart-Davis 1947	D
2 **Lifemanship, Including Further Researches in Gamesmanship**	Hart-Davis 1950	C
3 **One-Upmanship, Being Some Account of the Activities and Teaching of the Lifemanship Correspondence College of One-Upness and Gameslifemastery**	Hart-Davis 1952	C
4 **Supermanship: How To Try To Continue To Stay Top Without Actually Falling to Pieces** This gorgeous title is how it appears on the dust-wrapper. The title page says... **Without Actually Falling Apart**, but you get the idea.	Hart-Davis 1958	C

Pound, Ezra   Born in Idaho, 1885. Died 1972.

Pound has been accused of being unreadable. This because a great deal of his verse (*The Cantos*, mainly) is so chock-full of allusion, obscurity and foreign words and phrases as to render it impossible unless one is a hyper-educated linguist armed with a battery of classical dictionaries. Such criticism is harsh, and rather silly. Pound is not *easy* (of course not – never was) but most of *The Cantos* is worth the struggle. Young people, I have noticed, seem not at all

Pound

deterred by Pound (possibly because they are taught that anything good *has* to be hard work) and I discern a very definite upturn in collectors' interest – although, of course, Pound has never really fallen from favour, except within pockets of resistance who have never been able to get down his known Fascist sympathies. Not at all easy to collect – most are rare and expensive, as will be seen – but his place in literature as well as in the world of book collecting (not always synonymous) is as solid as a rock. There is a fine bibliography, which I append to the following checklist of Pound's best known works.

1 **A Lume Spento** (verse)	Antonini (Venice) 1908	**Z**
This, Pound's first book, was an edition of only 100 copies. Now extremely rare and near priceless, it was reissued in 1965 by New Directions in the USA (**F**), and by Faber in England (**E**).		
2 **Personae** (verse)	Mathews 1909	**Q**
3 **Exultations** (verse)	Mathews 1909	**P**
4 **The Spirit of Romance** (prose)	Dent 1910	**O**
	Dutton 1910	**L**
5 **Canzoni** (verse)	Mathews 1911	**O**
6 **Ripostes** (verse)	Swift 1912	**O**
	Small Maynard 1913	**M**
7 **Cathay** (translations)	Mathews 1915	**M**
8 **Gaudier-Brzeska** (memoir)	Bodley Head 1916	**O**
	Lane 1916	**O**
9 **Lustra** (verse)	Elkin Matthews 1916	**P**
10 **Quia Pauper Amavi** (verse)	The Egoist 1919	**N**
11 **Hugh Selwyn Mauberley** (verse)	Ovid Press 1920	
165 unsigned copies (**T**). 35 signed (**V**).		
12 **Umbra** (verse)	Elkin Matthews 1920	**P**
13 **Poems 1918–21**	Boni & Liveright 1921	**N**
14 **Selected Poems**	Faber & Gwyer 1928	**M**
Intro. by T.S. Eliot.		
15 **A Draft of XXX Cantos**	Hours Press (Paris) 1930	**P**
The Paris ed. was limited to 210 copies, 10 signed (**R**).	Farrar & Rinehart 1933	**K**
	Faber 1933	**I**
16 **How to Read** (prose)	Harmsworth 1931	**L**
17 **ABC of Economics** (prose)	Faber 1933	**L**
	New Directions 1940	**I**
18 **ABC of Reading** (prose)	Routledge 1934	**K**
	Yale 1934	**J**
19 **Make It New** (essays)	Faber 1934	**J**
	Yale University Press 1935	**H**
20 **Eleven New Cantos: XXXI–XLI**	Farrar & Rinehart 1934	**H**

21 **Draft of Cantos XXXI–XLI** (same as 19)	Faber 1935	**H**
22 **Homage to Sextus Propertius** (verse)	Faber 1934	**K**
23 **Polite Essays**	Faber 1937 New Directions 1940	**I** **F**
24 **The Fifth Decad of Cantos**	Faber 1937 Farrar & Rinehart 1937	**J** **G**
25 **Guide to Kulchur** (prose)	Faber 1938 New Directions 1938	**I** **G**
26 **Cantos LII–LXXI**	Faber 1940 New Directions 1940	**G** **E**
27 **The Pisan Cantos**	New Directions 1948 Faber 1949	**G** **F**
28 **The Cantos** **Seventy Cantos**	New Directions 1948 Faber 1950	**G** **G**
29 **The Cantos of Ezra Pound** This is as above, but including 20. New Collected Editions of the *Cantos* were published by Faber in 1964 and 1976.	Faber 1954	**F**
30 **Patria Mia** (prose)	Seymour 1950 Owen 1962	**H** **G**
31 **The Letters of Ezra Pound**	Harcourt Brace 1950 Faber 1951	**F** **F**
32 **The Translations of Ezra Pound**	Faber 1953 New Directions 1953	**F** **F**
33 **Literary Essays of Ezra Pound** Intro. by T. S. Eliot.	Faber 1954 New Directions 1954	**F** **F**
34 **Section Rock-Drill** (cantos) The Milan edition consisted of 506 copies.	Pesce d'Oro (Milan) 1955 New Directions 1956 Faber 1957	**M** **F** **F**
35 **Thrones** (cantos) The Milan edition consisted of 300 copies.	Pesce d'Oro (Milan) 1959 New Directions 1959 Faber 1960	**K** **F** **F**
36 **Pound/Joyce** (letters)	New Directions 1967 Faber 1968	**E** **E**
37 **Drafts and Fragments of Cantos CX–CXVII**	New Directions 1969 Faber 1970	**D** **D**
38 **Selected Prose 1909–65**	Faber 1973 New Directions 1975	**D** **D**
39 **Collected Early Poems**	Faber 1977	**D**
40 **Pound/Ford** (letters)	Faber 1982	**C**
41 **Eva Pound and Dorothy Shakespeare: Their Letters 1909–1914**	Faber 1985	**C**

Powell

Bibliography:
Donald Gallup **A Bibliography of Ezra Pound** Hart-Davis 1969
Biography:
Noel Stock **The Life of Ezra Pound** Pantheon 1970; Routledge 1970

Powell, Anthony   Born in London, 1905.

From a collector's point of view, the pre-war novels remain far and away the most scarce and expensive, but it is still the wonderful *A Dance to the Music of Time* sequence that continues to seduce, prices of good copies of *all* of them having risen considerably. Kenneth Widmerpool has become the anti pin-up of our age.

1 **Afternoon Men** (novel)	Duckworth 1931	S
	Holt 1932	Q
2 **Venusberg** (novel)	Duckworth 1932	R
	Holliday 1952	F
3 **From a View to a Death** (novel) This was published as *Mr Zouch: Superman* by the Vanguard Press in 1934 (**L**), though the Little, Brown reissue of 1964 mercifully returns to the original title (**D**).	Duckworth 1933	R
4 **Caledonia: A Fragment** Limited to 100 copies.	Privately printed 1945	S
5 **Agents and Patients** (novel)	Duckworth 1936	Q
	Holliday 1952	F
6 **What's Become of Waring** (novel)	Cassell 1939	Q
	Little, Brown 1963	F
7 **John Aubrey and His Friends** (non-fiction) The following comprise **A Dance to the Music of Time:**	Heinemann 1948	H
	Scribner 1949	F
8 **A Question of Upbringing** (novel)	Heinemann 1951	N
	Scribner 1951	J
9 **A Buyer's Market** (novel)	Heinemann 1952	L
	Scribner 1953	G
10 **The Acceptance World** (novel)	Heinemann 1955	K
	Farrar Straus 1956	F
11 **At Lady Molly's** (novel)	Heinemann 1957	H
	Little, Brown 1958	E
12 **Casanova's Chinese Restaurant** (novel)	Heinemann 1960	H
	Little, Brown 1960	E
13 **The Kindly Ones** (novel)	Heinemann 1962	F
	Little, Brown 1962	D

14	**The Valley of Bones** (novel)	Heinemann 1964	**F**
		Little, Brown 1964	**D**
15	**The Soldier's Art (novel)**	Heinemann 1966	**F**
		Little, Brown 1966	**D**
16	**The Military Philosophers** (novel)	Heinemann 1968	**F**
		Little, Brown 1969	**D**
17	**Books Do Furnish a Room** (novel)	Heinemann 1971	**E**
		Little, Brown 1971	**C**
18	**Temporary Kings** (novel)	Heinemann 1973	**D**
		Little, Brown 1973	**C**
19	**Hearing Secret Harmonies** (novel)	Heinemann 1975	**D**
		Little, Brown 1975	**C**

Powell has also published:

20	**The Garden God** and **The Rest I'll Whistle** (plays)	Heinemann 1971	**C**
		Little, Brown 1972	**C**
21	**Infants of the Spring** (autobiography)	Heinemann 1976	**C**
		Holt Rinehart 1976	**C**
22	**Messengers of Day** (autobiography)	Heinemann 1978	**C**
		Holt Rinehart 1978	**C**
23	**Faces in My Time** (autobiography)	Heinemann 1980	**C**
		Holt Rinehart 1981	**C**
24	**The Strangers All Are Gone** (autobiography)	Heinemann 1982	**C**
		Holt Rinehart 1983	**C**

21–24 comprise *To Keep the Ball Rolling*.

25	**O, How the Wheel Becomes It!** (novel)	Heinemann 1983	**C**
		Holt Rinehart 1983	**C**
26	**The Fisher King** (novel)	Heinemann 1986	**C**
		Norton 1986	**C**
27	**Miscellaneous Verdicts: Writings on Writers 1946–1989**	Heinemann 1990	**C**

Powell has edited and introduced the following:

27	**The Barnard Letters 1778–1884**	Duckworth 1928	**K**
28	**Novels of High Society from the Victorian Age**	Pilot 1947	**E**
29	**Brief Lives and Other Selected Writings of John Aubrey**	Cresset 1949	**E**
		Scribner 1949	**D**
30	E.W. Hornung **Raffles** Introduced by A.P.	Eyre & Spottiswoode 1950	**E**
31	**The Complete Ronald Firbank**	Duckworth 1961	**E**
32	Jocelyn Brooke **The Orchid Trilogy** Introduced by A.P.	Secker 1981	**C**

The following work should also be noted:
Hilary Spurling **Handbook to Anthony Powell's Dance to the Music of Time** Heinemann 1977; Little, Brown 1978

The Powys Brothers

As with the Sitwells, there are quite a few collectors who collect all three, which is illogical but neat. Very often too, I find, Powys collectors do not collect anybody else – understandable in a way, for they published a lot of books, most of which are pretty elusive and pricey. Rather limited as a collection, though, I should have thought. Still. I record here only the highlights of each of them (J.C. Powys is still by far the most popular) and I append bibliographies where applicable.

Powys, J.C.   Born in Derbyshire, 1872. Died 1963.

1 **Wolf Solent** (novel)	Simon & Schuster 1929	**M**
The Amer. ed. is in two volumes, the	Cape 1929	**L**
English in one.		
2 **The Meaning of Culture** (prose)	Norton 1929	**H**
	Cape 1930	**G**
3 **In Defense of Sensuality** (philosophy)	Simon & Schuster 1930	**G**
	Gollancz 1930	**F**
4 **A Glastonbury Romance**	Simon & Schuster 1932	**H**
(novel)	Bodley Head 1933	**G**
5 **A Philosophy of Solitude**	Simon & Schuster 1933	**F**
	Cape 1933	**F**
6 **Weymouth Sands** (novel)	Simon & Schuster 1934	**I**
Jobber Skald	Bodley Head 1935	**F**

Bibliography:
L.E. Siberell **A Bibliography to the First Editions of J.C. Powys** Folcroft (Cincinnatti) 1934. Intro. by Powys.

Powys, Llewelyn   Born in Dorchester, 1884. Died 1939.

1 **Apples Be Ripe** (novel)	Harcourt Brace 1930	**G**
	Longman 1930	**F**
2 **Dorset Essays**	Bodley Head 1935	**F**
	Simon & Schuster 1938	**E**
3 **Love and Death** (novel)	Bodley Head 1939	**E**
	Simon & Schuster 1941	**D**

Bibliography:
Kenneth Hopkins **Llewelyn Powys: A Selection** Macdonald 1952. (Contains a checklist.)

Powys, T.F. Born in Dorset, 1875. Died 1953.

1 **Mr Weston's Good Wine** (novel)	Viking 1928	**J**
The American edition was preceded by	Chatto & Windus 1928	**H**
a limited ed. (660 copies) (**K**).		
2 **The White Paternoster** (stories)	Chatto & Windus 1930	**F**
	Viking 1931	**D**

Bibliography:
A.P. Riley **A Bibliography of T.F. Powys** Hastings 1967

Biography:
Kenneth Hopkins **The Powys Brothers** Dickinson (Phoenix) 1967

Price, Anthony Born in Hertfordshire, 1928.

An open secret among collectors of crime for a long time, but now beginning to creep into quite a few mainstream collections. Price is an unusual example of the genre, if only because of the rich historical allusions around which he wraps many of his books – a fine representation would be *Other Paths to Glory*, if you want to test the water, but none but the very most recent is that easy to find.

1 **The Labyrinth Makers** (novel)	Gollancz 1970	**H**
	Doubleday 1971	**E**
2 **The Alamut Ambush** (novel)	Gollancz 1971	**G**
	Doubleday 1972	**D**
3 **Colonel Butler's Wolf** (novel)	Gollanz 1972	**F**
	Doubleday 1973	**C**
4 **October Men** (novel)	Gollancz 1973	**F**
	Doubleday 1974	**C**
5 **Other Paths to Glory** (novel)	Gollancz 1974	**E**
	Doubleday 1975	**C**
6 **Our Man in Camelot** (novel)	Gollancz 1975	**E**
	Doubleday 1976	**C**
7 **War Game** (novel)	Gollancz 1976	**E**
	Doubleday 1977	**C**
8 **The '44 Vintage** (novel)	Gollancz 1978	**D**
	Doubleday 1979	**C**
9 **Tomorrow's Ghost** (novel)	Gollancz 1979	**D**
	Doubleday 1979	**C**
10 **The Hour of the Donkey** (novel)	Gollancz 1980	**D**
11 **Soldier No More** (novel)	Gollancz 1981	**D**
	Doubleday 1982	**B**
12 **The Old Vengeful** (novel)	Gollancz 1982	**C**
	Doubleday 1983	**B**

Priest

13	**Gunner Kelly** (novel)	Gollancz 1983	C
		Doubleday 1984	B
14	**Sion Crossing** (novel)	Gollancz 1985	C
		Mysterious Press 1985	B
15	**Here Be Monsters** (novel)	Gollancz 1985	C
		Mysterious Press 1985	B
16	**For the Good of the State** (novel)	Gollancz 1986	C
		Mysterious Press 1987	B
17	**A New Kind of War** (novel)	Gollancz 1987	C
		Mysterious Press 1988	B
18	**A Prospect of Vengeance** (novel)	Gollancz 1988	B
19	**The Memory Trap** (novel)	Gollancz 1989	B

Priest, Christopher   Born in Manchester, 1943.

Certainly not mainstream, but not a cult either. Priest hovers – quietly, quasi-popular – and therefore a bargain, if he is to your liking.

1	**Introctrinaire** (novel)	Faber 1970	I
		Harper & Row 1970	D
2	**Fugue for a Darkening Island** (novel)	Faber 1972	F
3	**Darkening Island** (same as 2)	Harper & Row 1972	D
4	**Inverted World** (novel)	Faber 1974	D
	The American edition has the word	Harper & Row 1974	C
	The preceding the title.		
5	**Real Time World** (stories)	NEL 1974	C
6	**The Space Machine** (novel)	Faber 1976	D
		Harper & Row 1976	C
7	**A Dream of Wessex** (novel)	Faber 1977	C
8	**The Perfect Lover** (same as 7)	Scribner 1977	C
9	**An Infinite Summer** (stories)	Faber 1979	C
		Scribner 1979	C
10	**The Glamour** (novel)	Cape 1984	C
		Doubleday 1985	C
11	**The Quiet Woman** (novel)	Bloomsbury 1990	C

Priestley, J.B.   Born in Yorkshire, 1894. Died 1984.

The grand old Yorkshireman died just short of his ninetieth birthday, and was paid the tribute of a biography by fellow Yorkshireman, John Braine. Still very much a British institution, but less and less collected, I find. He had published over one hundred and fifty books, but it is the two novels listed below that remain his highlights. They were published in his heyday, when Priestley was, in his mid-thirties, one of the most sought-after authors by collectors of first editions. In the thirties, each of these books would have fetched about fifteen or twenty *pounds* each – indeed, more than they would today, relatively. Be warned – always follow your taste, never fashion; this way, if your collection fails to appreciate in value – or, worse, declines – so what? You still have the books you love.

1	**The Good Companions** (novel)	Heinemann 1929	H
		Harper 1929	E
2	**Angel Pavement** (novel)	Heinemann 1930	G
		Harper 1930	E

Biography:
John Braine **J.B. Priestley** Weidenfeld 1978, Barnes & Noble 1979

Pritchett, V.S.   Born in Suffolk, 1900.

When he turned ninety, there was much talk about Sir Victor being our greatest living writer; whether or no, there is certainly greatly revived interest in the short stories (according to Pritchett, his most important work) while his novels remain largely unknown. I list here all the fiction, in addition to which Pritchett has published about thirty other works.

1	**Clare Drummer** (novel)	Benn 1929	K
2	**The Spanish Virgin and Other Stories**	Benn 1930	K
3	**Shirley Sanz** (novel)	Gollancz 1932	I
4	**Elopement into Exile** (same as 3)	Little, Brown 1932	G
5	**Nothing Like Leather** (novel)	Chatto & Windus 1935	I
		Macmillan US 1935	G
6	**Dead Man Leading** (novel)	Chatto & Windus 1937	H
		Macmillan US 1937	F
7	**You Make Your Own Life** (stories)	Chatto & Windus 1938	G
8	**It May Never Happen and Other Stories**	Chatto & Windus 1945	E
		Reynal 1947	C
9	**Mr Beluncle** (novel)	Chatto & Windus 1951	E
		Harcourt Brace 1951	C
10	**Collected Stories**	Chatto & Windus 1956	D
11	**The Sailor, The Sense of Humour and Other Stories**	Knopf 1956	C
12	**When My Girl Comes Home** (stories)	Chatto & Windus 1961	D
		Knopf 1961	C
13	**The Key to My Heart** (stories)	Chatto & Windus 1963	D
		Random House 1964	C
14	**The Saint and Other Stories**	Penguin 1966	B
15	**Blind Love and Other Stories**	Chatto & Windus 1969	C
		Random House 1970	B
16	**The Camberwell Beauty and Other Stories**	Chatto & Windus 1974	C
		Random House 1974	B

17 **Selected Stories**	Chatto & Windus 1978	**C**
	Random House 1978	**B**
18 **On the Edge of the Cliff** (stories)	Random House 1979	**C**
(stories)	Chatto & Windus 1980	**B**
19 **Collected Stories**	Random House 1982	**C**
	Chatto & Windus 1982	**C**
20 **More Collected Stories**	Random House 1983	**C**
	Chatto & Windus 1983	**C**
21 **A Careless Widow and Other**	Chatto & Windus 1989	**C**
Stories	Random House 1989	**B**
22 **Complete Short Stories**	Chatto & Windus 1990	**C**
23 **Complete Collected Stories**	Random House 1991	
(same as 22)		

Also of note, Pritchett's two volumes of autobiography:

A Cab at the Door: Childhood and	Chatto & Windus 1968	**C**
Youth 1900–1920	Random House 1968	**C**
Midnight Oil	Chatto & Windus 1971	**C**
	Random House 1972	**C**

Puzo, Mario   Born in New York, 1920.

Author of upwards of half a dozen novels, and many screenplays, but notable for the big one.

The Godfather (novel)	Putnam 1969	**G**
	Heinemann 1969	**E**

Pym, Barbara   Born in Shropshire, 1913. Died 1980.

Barbara Pym's is a strange story. She published her first novel in 1950, and five more within the decade. Only one of them was taken by America, and sales declined with each new book. Although the reviews she received were always respectful, it seems as if the book-buying public were simply no longer interested in her view of the world. In the early sixties, she had a novel turned down. The publishers no longer wished to be involved with an uncommercial enterprise. Barbara Pym stopped writing. All her books were out of print. There the matter would no doubt have rested, but in 1977, a clutch of eminent literati was asked by the *TLS* to put forward the names of underrated writers of the century, and two very big names – Lord David Cecil and Philip Larkin – put their full weight behind Barbara Pym. The reaction of most people at the time – whether or not they now care to admit it – was 'Who?' But Cape remembered who, and they reissued her out-of-print novels, selling the American rights while they were about it. More to the point, Macmillan offered her a three-book contract, and Barbara Pym was in print again, writing again and now collected – all after a gap of sixteen years. Barbara Pym wrote the novels, they were published, and she died.

1	**Some Tame Gazelle** (novel)	Cape 1950	K
2	**Excellent Women** (novel)	Cape 1952	I
		Dutton 1978	C
3	**Jane and Prudence** (novel)	Cape 1953	I
		Dutton 1981	C
4	**Less Than Angels** (novel)	Cape 1955	H
		Vanguard 1957	D
5	**A Glass of Blessings** (novel)	Cape 1959	G
		Dutton 1980	C
6	**No Fond Return of Love** (novel)	Cape 1961	F
		Dutton 1982	C
7	**Quartet in Autumn** (novel)	Macmillan 1977	D
		Dutton 1978	C
8	**The Sweet Dove Died** (novel)	Macmillan 1978	C
		Dutton 1979	B
9	**A Few Green Leaves** (novel)	Macmillan 1980	C
		Dutton 1980	B
10	**An Unsuitable Attachment** (novel)	Macmillan 1982	C
		Dutton 1982	B
11	**A Very Private Eye** (journals)	Macmillan 1984	C
		Dutton 1984	B
12	**Crampton Hodnet** (novel)	Macmillan 1985	C
		Dutton 1985	B
13	**An Academic Question** (novel)	Macmillan 1986	C

Pynchon, Thomas   Born in New York, 1937.

Pynchon remains a cult with a devoted following, despite his small output – or maybe *because* of his small output, who knows?

1	**V** (novel)	Lippincott 1963	K
		Cape 1963	J
2	**The Crying of Lot 49** (novel)	Lippincott 1966	H
		Cape 1967	G
3	**Gravity's Rainbow** (novel)	Viking Press 1973	F
		Cape 1973	E
4	**Mortality and Mercy in Vienna** (story)	Aloes 1976	E
5	**Low-lands** (story)	Aloes 1978	E
6	**The Secret Integration** (story)	Aloes 1981	E
7	**The Small Rain** (story) (this item is not dated)	Aloes 1982	E

8 **Slow Learner: Early Stories**	Little, Brown 1984	**C**
	Cape 1985	**C**
9 **Vineland** (novel)	Little, Brown 1990	**C**
	Secker & Warburg 1990	**B**

Raine, Craig Born in County Durham, 1944.

Raine seems to be going in more for adaptations and essays and things – never a good sign from a collector's point of view, because one begins to gather the work of a poet and ends up with all sorts of arcana. At the moment, *Rich* seems to be the highlight.

1 **The Onion, Memory** (verse)	OUP 1978	**F**
2 **A Martian Sends A Postcard Home** (verse)	OUP 1979	**E**
3 **A Journey to Greece** (verse)	Sycamore Press, Oxford 1979	**E**
4 **A Free Translation** (verse)	Salamander Press, Edinburgh 1981	**E**
5 **Rich** (verse)	Faber 1984	**C**
6 **The Electrification of the Soviet Union** (libretto)	Faber 1986	**B**
7 **1953; A Version of Racine's Andromaque**	Faber 1990	**B**
8 **Haydn and the Valve Trumpet** (essays)	Faber 1990	**B**

Raven, Simon Born in London, 1927.

A known author, but possibly rather underrated by collectors. His books do not come up that often (I know of several people trying to complete their *Alms for Oblivion* sequence) but when they do, prices are always surprisingly low.

1 **The Feathers of Death** (novel)	Blond 1959	**F**
	Simon & Schuster 1960	**C**
2 **Brother Cain** (novel)	Blond 1959	**E**
	Simon & Schuster 1960	**C**
3 **Doctors Wear Scarlet** (novel)	Blond 1960	**D**
	Simon & Schuster 1961	**C**
4 **The English Gentleman** (essay)	Blond 1961	**D**
The Decline of the English Gentleman	Simon & Schuster 1962	**C**
5 **Close of Play** (novel)	Blond 1962	**D**
6 **Boys Will Be Boys and Other Essays**	Blond 1963	**C**

The following ten novels form the
Alms for Oblivion sequence:

7 **The Rich Pay Late**	Blond 1964	**F**
	Putnam 1965	**C**
8 **Friends in Low Places**	Blond 1965	**D**
	Putnam 1966	**C**
9 **The Sabre Squadron**	Blond 1966	**C**
	Harper 1967	**B**
10 **Fielding Gray**	Blond 1967	**C**
11 **The Judas Boy**	Blond 1968	**C**
12 **Places Where They Sing**	Blond 1970	**C**
13 **Sound the Retreat**	Blond 1971	**C**
14 **Come Like Shadows**	Blond & Briggs 1972	**C**
15 **Bring Forth the Body**	Blond & Briggs 1974	**C**
16 **The Survivors**	Blond & Briggs 1976	**C**

This completes the sequence.

17 **The Fortunes of Fingel** (stories)	Blond & Briggs 1976	**B**
18 **The Roses of Picardie** (novel)	Blond & Briggs 1980	**B**
19 **An Inch of Fortune** (novel)	Blond & Briggs 1980	**B**

This was the first novel he wrote.

20 **Face of the Waters** (novel)	Blond 1985	**B**
21 **Before the Cock Crow** (novel)	Blond 1986	**B**
22 **The Old School** (non-fiction)	Hamilton 1986	**B**
23 **New Seed for Old** (novel)	Muller 1988	**B**
24 **The Old Gang: A Sporting and Military Memoir**	Hamish Hamilton 1988	**B**
25 **Blood of My Bone** (novel)	Muller 1989	**B**
26 **Bird of Ill Omen** (non-fiction)	Hamish Hamilton 1989	**B**
27 **In the Image of God** (novel)	Muller 1990	**B**
28 **'Is Anybody There?' Said the Traveller: Memories of a Private Nuisance**	Muller 1991	**B**
29 **The Troubadour** (novel)	Hutchinson 1992	**B**

Blond also published, in 1966, **Royal Foundation and Other Plays**.
Raven has written many television and radio plays, though unpublished.

Read, Herbert Born in Yorkshire, 1893. Died 1968.

Most people are surprised by the number of books published by Read – over
100. Most collectable are his art philosophy books, the highlights of which
(see below) have remained in print since publication. As most of his books
were done by Faber, the bold graphics of the case design as well as that of the
dust-wrappers, well becomes the contents – or, at least, it did during Read's
lifetime; the present editions look just like any other books. In the case of
Herbert Read, then, there is very much an aesthetic consideration to collect-

ing the original editions, in addition to all the other reasons for amassing first editions, whatever they may be.

Below are some highlights.

1 **Collected Poems 1913–25**	Faber & Gwyer 1926	**E**
2 **English Prose Style** (criticism)	Bell 1928	**D**
	Holt 1928	**C**
3 **The Meaning of Art**	Faber 1931	**F**
4 **Art Now**	Faber 1933	**G**
A particularly fine piece of book production, with its bold blue and white graphics on black cloth, handsome sans-serif type, and Jean Cocteau frontis.	Harcourt Brace 1937	**D**
5 **Art and Industry**	Faber 1934	**G**
6 **The Green Child** (novel)	Heinemann 1935	**F**
	New Directions 1948	**C**
7 **Surrealism** (ed. by H.R.)	Faber 1936	**G**
8 **Art and Society**	Heinemann 1937	**G**
	Macmillan 1937	**E**
9 **Education Through Art**	Faber 1943	**F**
	Pantheon n.d.	**C**
10 **Collected Poems**	Faber 1946	**D**
A revised edition was published by the Horizon Press in 1966 (**C**).		
11 **The Contrary Experience**	Faber 1963	**D**
(autobiog.)	Horizon Press 1963	**C**

Biography:
George Woodcock **Herbert Read: The Stream and the Source** Faber 1972. This work includes a checklist.

Rendell, Ruth   Born in London, 1930.

Highly popular and collectable – and what scope! Since the last edition of this book, Rendell has published about twenty new things (a few of them collections, admittedly) and – according to her publishers – she has no intention of slowing down. Great news for the library borrower, but maybe less so – what with the price of new novels – for the impecunious collector. (Most book collectors are impecunious, incidentally, for the simple reason that they have spent all their money on books. Obviously.)

1 **From Doon with Death** (novel)	Long 1964	**I**
	Doubleday 1965	**E**
2 **To Fear a Painted Devil** (novel)	Long 1965	**H**
	Doubleday 1965	**E**
3 **Vanity Dies Hard** (novel)	Long 1965	**H**
4 **In Sickness and in Health**	Doubleday 1966	**E**
(same as 3)		

5 **A New Lease of Death** (novel)	Long 1967	**G**
	Doubleday 1967	**D**
6 **Wolf to the Slaughter** (novel)	Long 1967	**F**
	Doubleday 1968	**C**
7 **The Secret House of Death** (novel)	Long 1968	**F**
	Doubleday 1969	**C**
8 **The Best Man to Die** (novel)	Long 1969	**F**
	Doubleday 1970	**C**
9 **A Guilty Thing Surprised** (novel)	Hutchinson 1970	**E**
	Doubleday 1970	**C**
10 **No More Dying, Then** (novel)	Hutchinson 1971	**E**
	Doubleday 1972	**C**
11 **One Across, Two Down** (novel)	Hutchinson 1971	**E**
	Doubleday 1971	**C**
12 **Murder Being Done Once** (novel)	Hutchinson 1972	**D**
	Doubleday 1972	**C**
13 **Some Lie and Some Die** (novel)	Hutchinson 1973	**D**
	Doubleday 1973	**C**
14 **The Face of Trespass** (novel)	Hutchinson 1974	**D**
	Doubleday 1974	**C**
15 **Shake Hands for Ever** (novel)	Hutchinson 1975	**D**
	Doubleday 1975	**C**
16 **A Demon in My View** (novel)	Hutchinson 1976	**D**
	Doubleday 1977	**C**
17 **The Fallen Curtain** and **Other Stories**	Hutchinson 1976	**D**
	Doubleday 1976	**C**
18 **A Judgement in Stone** (novel)	Hutchinson 1977	**D**
	Doubleday 1978	**C**
19 **A Sleeping Life** (novel)	Hutchinsons 1978	**D**
	Doubleday 1978	**C**
20 **Make Death Love Me** (novel)	Hutchinson 1979	**D**
	Doubleday 1979	**C**
21 **Means of Evil** and **Other Stories**	Hutchinson 1979	**D**
22 **The Lake of Darkness** (novel)	Hutchinson 1980	**C**
	Doubleday 1980	**C**
23 **Put on by Cunning** (novel)	Hutchinson 1981	**C**
24 **Death Notes** (same as 23)	Pantheon 1981	**C**
25 **The Fever Tree** and **Other Stories**	Hutchinson 1982	**C**
	Pantheon 1983	**B**
26 **Master of the Moor** (novel)	Hutchinson 1982	**C**
	Pantheon 1982	**B**
27 **The Speaker of Mandarin** (novel)	Hutchinson 1983	**C**
	Pantheon 1983	**B**
28 **The Killing Doll** (novel)	Hutchinson 1984	**C**
	Pantheon 1984	**B**
29 **The Tree of Hands** (novel)	Hutchinson 1984	**C**
	Pantheon 1985	**B**

30 **An Unkindness of Ravens**	Hutchinson 1985	**B**
(novel)	Pantheon 1985	**B**
31 **The New Girlfriend** and **Other**	Hutchinson 1986	**C**
Stories of Suspense	Pantheon 1986	**B**
32 **Live Flesh** (novel)	Hutchinson 1986	**C**
	Pantheon 1986	**B**
33 **A Dark Adapted Eye** (novel)	Viking 1986	**C**
(pseud. Barbara Vine)	Bantam 1986	**C**
34 **A Warning to the Curious** (novel)	Hutchinson 1987	**C**
35 **A Fatal Inversion** (novel)	Viking UK 1987	**C**
(pseud. Barbara Vine)	Bantam 1987	**C**
36 **Heartstones** (novel)	Hutchinson 1987	**C**
	Harper 1987	**C**
37 **Talking to Strange Men** (novel)	Hutchinson 1987	**C**
	Harper 1987	**C**
38 **Collected Short Stories**	Hutchinson 1987	**C**
	Pantheon 1988	**C**
39 **The Veiled One** (novel)	Hutchinson 1988	**C**
	Pantheon 1988	**C**
40 **A Wexford Omnibus**	Hutchinson 1988	**C**
41 **The House of Stairs** (novel)	Viking UK 1989	**C**
(pseud. Barbara Vine)	Crown 1989	**C**
42 **A Second Wexford Omnibus**	Hutchinson 1989	**C**
43 **The Bridesmaid** (novel)	Hutchinson 1989	**C**
	Mysterious Press 1989	**C**
44 **Ruth Rendell's Suffolk**	Muller 1989	**C**
(non-fiction)		
45 **The Third Wexford Omnibus**	Hutchinson 1989	**C**
46 **Gallowglass** (novel)	Viking UK 1990	**C**
(pseud. Barbara Vine)	Crown 1990	**C**
47 **The Fourth Wexford Omnibus**	Hutchinson 1990	**C**
48 **Going Wrong** (novel)	Hutchinson 1990	**C**
	Mysterious Press 1990	**C**
49 **The Copper Peacock** and **Other**	Hutchinson 1991	**C**
Stories		
50 **King Solomon's Carpet** (novel)	Viking UK 1991	**C**
(pseud. Barbara Vine)	Crown 1992	**C**
51 **Wexford Omnibus 5**	Hutchinson 1991	**C**
52 **Kissing the Gunner's Daughter**	Hutchinson 1992	**C**
(novel)	Warner 1992	**C**

Rhys, Jean Born in Dominica, West Indies, 1894. Died 1979.
British.

A small output, but a very big reputation. None of her books is common, but

Four by one of America's more lingering poetic voices

Four novels whose titles have entered the language

Two novels, with their later dramatic adaptations

Middle-period Pound next to a very early translation by him from the Chinese, a selection of stories culled from Connolly's *Horizon*, and David Jones's highlight, in a dust-wrapper designed by the author

Four works by Virginia Woolf, three with Vanessa Bell artwork

The first (1947), second (1956) and third (1964) impressions of Larkin's 'A Girl in Winter', and the first Faber edition of 'Jill' (1964)

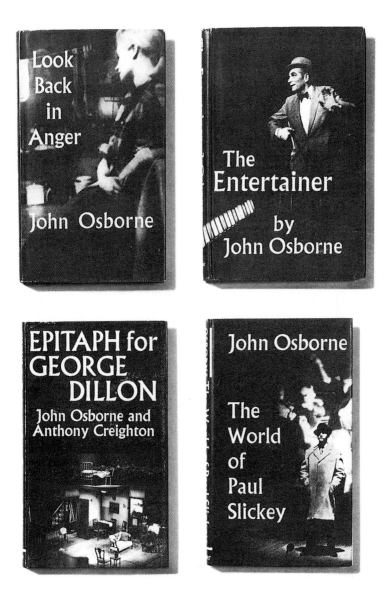

The first four plays from the leading 'angry young man' of the fifties

An early Spark, Keith Waterhouse's first novel, Storey's scarce second novel, and Wyndham's homicidal plant

of course the early titles are far scarcer than the later clutch, for as will be seen from the following checklist, there was a twenty-seven-year gap somewhere in the middle.

1	**The Left Bank** and **Other Stories**	Cape 1927	**M**
		Harper 1927	**J**
2	**Postures** (novel)	Chatto & Windus 1928	**K**
3	**Quartet**	Simon & Schuster 1929	**I**
	Same as 2		
4	**After Leaving Mr Mackenzie** (novel)	Cape 1931	**J**
		Knopf 1931	**G**
5	**Voyage in the Dark** (novel)	Constable 1934	**I**
		Morrow 1935	**G**
6	**Good Morning, Midnight** (novel)	Constable 1939	**I**
7	**Wide Sargasso Sea** (novel)	Deutsch 1966	**F**
		Norton 1966	**C**
8	**Tigers Are Better Looking**	Deutsch 1968	**D**
	(stories)	Harper 1974	**C**
9	**Sleep It Off Lady** (stories)	Deutsch 1976	**D**
		Harper 1976	**C**
10	**Letters 1931–1966**	Deutsch 1984	**C**
		Viking 1984	**C**

Richards, Frank   Born in Middlesex, 1876. Died 1961.
Pseudonym of Charles Hamilton.

Reputed to be the most prolific author *ever*, disputes arising only over the number of million words that he produced. For decades, he singlehandedly wrote every issue of *The Gem* and *The Magnet*, under many pseudonyms – Martin Clifford, Owen Conquest, Hilda Richards and, of course, Frank Richards. Always very moral and upstanding, his books stress the importance of being a clean living gentleman. In the Bunter books, he was particularly down on smoking, drinking and gambling, attributing these habits only to his nasty characters; alas, Richards was very prone to all of these vices himself, but they didn't stop him living 85 years, and bringing delight to millions of boys. And he still does, he still does. When the public libraries withdrew the Bunter books from the shelves for the reason that they discriminated against the overweight child (or fat, as we say) they were missing the point. Bunter was not disliked at Greyfriars because he was *fat*, but because he was a coward, a liar, a cheat, a tuck-thief, a sneak, an egomaniac, a snob and a toady – as well as being ignorant and quite the most insufferably idle child that ever lived. Had he been as skinny as a rake, his demeanour would hardly have endeared him to the Famous Five, would it?

Recently – I can hardly bring myself to write this – a trio of Bowdlerized versions have appeared, no doubt tailored to the requirements of the libraries. You do not need me to tell you to give these leprous articles the very wide berth they deserve.

Richards

But the originals are great – go for them. The collectfulness is terrific!
The following were published by Skilton:

1	**Billy Bunter of Greyfriars School**	1947	J
2	**Billy Bunter's Banknote**	1948	H
3	**Billy Bunter's Barring-Out**	1948	H
4	**Billy Bunter's Christmas Party**	1949	G
5	**Billy Bunter in Brazil**	1949	G
6	**Billy Bunter's Benefit**	1950	F
7	**Billy Bunter among the Cannibals**	1950	F
8	**Billy Bunter's Postal Order**	1951	F
9	**Billy Bunter Butts In**	1951	F
10	**Billy Bunter and the Blue Mauritius**	1952	F

The following were published by
Cassell:

11	**Billy Bunter's Beanfeast**	1952	E
12	**Billy Bunter's Brain-Wave**	1953	E
13	**Billy Bunter's First Case**	1953	E
14	**Billy Bunter the Bold**	1954	E
15	**Bunter Does His Best**	1954	E
16	**Billy Bunter's Double**	1955	E
17	**Backing Up Billy Bunter**	1955	E
18	**Lord Billy Bunter**	1956	E
19	**The Banishing of Billy Bunter**	1956	E
20	**Billy Bunter's Bolt**	1957	E
21	**Billy Bunter Afloat**	1957	E
22	**Billy Bunter's Bargain**	1958	E
23	**Billy Bunter the Hiker**	1958	E
24	**Bunter Out of Bounds**	1959	E
25	**Bunter Comes for Christmas**	1959	E
26	**Bunter the Bad Lad**	1960	D
27	**Bunter Keeps It Dark**	1960	D
28	**Billy Bunter's Treasure-Hunt**	1961	D
29	**Billy Bunter at Butlin's**	1961	D
30	**Bunter the Ventriloquist**	1961	D
31	**Bunter the Caravanner**	1962	D
32	**Billy Bunter's Bodyguard**	1962	D
33	**Big Chief Bunter**	1963	D
34	**Just Like Bunter**	1963	D
35	**Bunter the Stowaway**	1964	D
36	**Thanks to Bunter**	1964	D
37	**Bunter the Sportsman**	1965	D
38	**Bunter's Last Fling**	1965	D

Richards also published:

| 39 | **Bessie Bunter of Cliff House School** (pseud. Hilda Richards) | Skilton 1949 | G |

The only Bessie Bunter novel published.

40 **The Autobiography of Frank**   Skilton 1952   **D**
   Richards

Biography:
W.O. Lofts & D.J. Adley **The World of Frank Richards** Howard Baker
1975

Rosenberg, Isaac   Born in Bristol, 1890. Died 1918.

Another casualty of the Great War – much less known than Brooke and
Owen, but very popular again of late, largely through the publication of his
collected works.

1 **Night and Day** (verse)	Privately printed 1915	**Q**
2 **Moses: A Play**	Privately printed 1916	**O**
3 **Youth** (verse)	Privately printed 1918	**P**
4 **Poems**	Heinemann 1922	**L**
5 **The Collected Works of Isaac Rosenberg**	Chatto & Windus 1937	**I**
6 **Collected Poems**	Chatto & Windus 1949	**G**
	Schocken 1949	**F**
7 **The Collected Works of Isaac Rosenberg: Poetry, Prose, Letters, Paintings and Drawings**	Chatto & Windus 1979 OUP (US) 1979	**C** **C**

Rosten, Leo   Born in Poland, 1908.

Rosten is a genius. Anyone who could create Hyman Kaplan – or
H*Y*M*A*N K*A*P*L*A*N, to give him his full name – would have to
be. The book is very, very, very funny, and so is its sequel. Written largely in
phonetics, you might think the style would weary, the joke stale: not a bit of
it. Rosten *understands* words – he loves them. His books on Yiddish (or, Yin-
glish, as he says) are also well worth looking into, but Kaplan is unmissable.

1 **The Education of Hyman Kaplan** (novel) (pseud. Leonard Q. Ross)	Harcourt Brace 1938 Constable 1938	**I** **G**
2 **The Return of Hyman Kaplan** (novel)	Harper 1959 Gollancz 1969	**E** **C**

Roth, Philip   Born in New Jersey, 1933.

Still a big noise in America, and still viewed as a 'contemporary writer'. In
this country, though, I think Roth is seen to be rather sixties, for better or for

worse. The American writers were rather the thing, then – they seemed to have so much more to offer. Fashions change. The younger, *English* novelist is now the thing, and quite right too.

1	**Goodbye Columbus** and **Five Short Stories**	Houghton Mifflin 1959	H
		Deutsch 1959	G
2	**Letting Go** (novel)	Random House 1962	G
		Deutsch 1962	F
3	**When She Was Good** (novel)	Random House 1967	E
		Cape 1967	D
4	**Portnoy's Complaint** (novel)	Random House 1969	H
		Cape 1970	F
5	**Our Gang** (novel)	Random House 1971	D
		Cape 1971	C
6	**The Breast** (novel)	Holt Rinehart 1972	C
		Cape 1973	C
7	**The Great American Novel** (novel)	Holt Rinehart 1973	C
		Cape 1973	C
8	**My Life as a Man** (novel)	Holt Rinehart 1974	C
		Cape 1974	C
9	**Reading Myself and Others** (prose)	Farrar Straus 1975	C
		Cape 1975	C
10	**The Professor of Desire** (novel)	Farrar Straus 1977	C
		Cape 1978	C
11	**The Ghost Writer** (novel)	Farrar Straus 1979	C
		Cape 1979	C
12	**A Philip Roth Reader** (anthology)	Farrar Straus 1980	C
		Cape 1981	C
13	**Zuckerman Unbound** (novel)	Farrar Straus 1981	C
		Cape 1981	C
14	**The Anatomy Lesson** (novel)	Farrar Straus 1983	C
		Cape 1984	C
15	**The Prague Orgy** (novel)	Farrar Straus 1985	C
		Cape 1985	C
16	**The Counterlife** (novel)	Farrar Straus 1987	C
		Cape 1987	C
17	**The Facts: A Novelist's Autobiography**	Farrar Straus 1988	C
		Cape 1989	C
18	**Deception** (novel)	Simon & Schuster 1990	C
		Cape 1990	C
19	**Patrimony: A True Story**	Simon & Schuster 1991	C
		Cape 1991	C

Bibliography:
Bernard F. Rodgers **Philip Roth: A Bibliography** Scarecrow Press 1974

Rushdie, Salman   Born in Bombay, 1947. British.

When *The Satanic Verses* was published in 1988, the publicity blurb ran thus: 'Wonderful stories and flights of imagination surround the conflict between good and evil.' Well, the conflict has been going on ever since – the Ayatollah's *fatwa* is still in force – rendering Rushdie (among other things) very much more collectable than he ever was before. He really is in an awful position, of course – although life seems better for him than it was, for one sees him all the time these days putting in 'surprise' appearances at just about everything.

And spare a thought too for *Sameen* Rushdie, who also published a book in 1988 (on Indian cookery): it can't have been an easy year.

1 **Grimus** (novel)	Gollancz 1975	H
	Overlook Press 1979	F
2 **Midnight's Children** (novel)	Cape 1981	L
	Knopf 1981	I
3 **Shame** (novel)	Cape 1983	C
	Knopf 1983	C
4 **The Jaguar Smile:**	Picador 1987	C
A Nicaraguan Journey	Viking US 1987	C
5 **The Satanic Verses** (novel)	Viking UK 1988	I
	Viking US 1989	G
6 **Is Nothing Sacred?** (lecture)	Granta 1990	C
7 **Haroun and the Sea of Stories**	Granta 1990	C
(juvenile)	Viking US 1991	C
8 **Imaginary Homelands: Essays and**	Granta 1991	C
Criticism 1981–1991		
9 **The Wizard of Oz** (essay)	BFI 1992	C

Russell, Bertrand   Born in Wales, 1872. Died 1970.

Bertrand Russell is a singular phenomenon in the collecting world, in that although a philosopher and a mathematician, he is collected because he is *literary*. Not that he concerned himself primarily with literature (although his essays as well as his rare forays into the short story are damnably good) but simply because he wrote so utterly lucidly, this quality exemplified, I think, in his three-volume autobiography – a work that could be enjoyed by any right-thinking character. His *History of Western Philosophy* is probably his most popular work today, although here once again we have a book that people talk of 'tackling' or even 'ploughing through'. This is ridiculous. It is a fat book, yes – but as readable as anything on the subject could be. Russell published over 120 books in his long lifetime, and made contributions to 50 more. The more popular titles appear below, though a checklist of his works may be found in *The New Cambridge Bibliography of English Literature* vol. 4.

Sagan

1	**Sceptical Essays**	Allen & Unwin 1928	**E**
		Norton 1928	**C**
2	**Marriage and Morals**	Allen & Unwin 1929	**E**
	(philosophy)	Liveright 1929	**C**
3	**The Conquest of Happiness**	Allen & Unwin 1930	**E**
	(philosophy)	Liveright 1930	**C**
4	**In Praise of Idleness** (philosophy)	Allen & Unwin 1935	**E**
		Norton 1935	**C**
5	**History of Western Philosophy**	Allen & Unwin 1945	**E**
		Simon & Schuster 1946	**C**
6	**Satan in the Suburbs** (stories)	Bodley Head 1953	**E**
		Simon & Schuster 1953	**C**
7	**Nightmares of Eminent Persons** (stories)	Bodley Head 1954	**E**
		Simon & Schuster 1955	**C**
8	**Portraits from Memory** (memoirs)	Allen & Unwin 1956	**D**
		Simon & Schuster 1956	**C**
9	**Fact and Fiction** (miscellany)	Allen & Unwin 1961	**D**
		Simon & Schuster 1962	**C**
10	**Autobiography** (3 vols)	Allen & Unwin 1967–9	**F**
		Little, Brown 1967–9	**E**

Sagan, Françoise   Born in France, 1935. Pseudonym of Françoise Quoirez.

Not a collected author at all, really, but her one key work remains important.

Bonjour Tristesse (novel)	Murray 1955	**D**
This was previously published in France in 1954 (**E**).	Smithers 1955	**C**

Salinger, J.D.   Born in New York, 1919.

The Catcher in the Rye, make no mistake, is a very fine book: everyone talks about it as being in the great American tradition of *Huckleberry Finn*. Published in 1951, it was followed by three volumes of stories published in the next ten years or so, and then – *nothing*. Very big news would be made by a new Salinger, but after thirty years' silence, it looks unlikely.

1	**Catcher in the Rye** (novel)	Little, Brown 1951	**O**
	Later *The Catcher in the Rye*.	Hamilton 1951	**L**
2	**Nine Stories**	Little, Brown 1953	**J**
3	**For Esmé – With Love and Squalour and Other Stories** (same as 2)	Hamilton 1953	**G**
4	**Franny & Zooey** (stories)	Little, Brown 1961	**D**
		Heinemann 1962	**C**

| 5 **Raise High the Roof Beam and** | Little, Brown 1963 | C |
| **Seymour: An Introduction** | Heinemann 1963 | C |

Sandford, Jeremy   Born in England, 1934.

Silly, in one way, to include Sandford in a select band of collected authors, but the works he produced – 'faction', it is now called – were important at the time, and memorable. The two works below were presented as semi-scripted '*cinéma vérité*' TV plays. The paperbacks recorded here are 'novelized' versions of the scripts.

| 1 **Cathy Come Home** | Pan 1967 | D |
| 2 **Edna, The Inebriate Woman** | Pan 1971 | C |

Sapper   Born in England, 1888. Died 1937. Pseudonym of Herman Cyril McNeile.

His first few books met with indifference, and then came Bulldog Drummond. The character was an almost immediate success, and was featured in a long series of novels – but beware, for the series was continued even after McNeile's death by one Gerard T. Fairlie, retaining the Sapper pseudonym.
    Examples of *true* Sapper–Drummond are as follows:

1 **Bulldog Drummond**	Hodder 1920	N
2 **The Return of Bulldog Drummond**	Hodder 1932	G
Bulldog Drummond Returns	Doubleday 1932	D

Sassoon, Siegfried   Born in London, 1886. Died 1967.

There is a steady interest in Sassoon – he attracts little new interest, I think, but the diehard collectors are loyal. The publication of his Diaries recently has brought him back to the fore, though, so maybe the younger set will 'discover' him, as the young are prone to do.
    Sassoon is particularly difficult to collect seriously, as his first fourteen works were either privately printed, or else published by a small press, as were many subsequent books by him. These cannot be listed here, but a bibliography exists, listing them all in some detail:

Below are all the commercially published Sassoon titles.

1 **The Old Huntsman** (verse)	Heinemann 1917	M
	Dutton 1917	K
2 **Counter-Attack** (verse)	Heinemann 1918	J
	Dutton 1918	H
3 **The War Poems of Siegfried**	Heinemann 1919	K
Sassoon		

4	**Selected Poems**	Heinemann 1925	**F**
5	**Satirical Poems**	Heinemann 1926	**J**
		Viking 1926	**H**
6	**Nativity** (Ariel Poem)	Faber 1927	**G**
7	**The Heart's Journey** (verse)	Heinemann 1928	**J**
	This was preceded by a limited edition	Harper 1929	**H**
	in 1927 (**O**).		
8	**To My Mother** (Ariel Poem)	Faber 1928	**D**
9	**Memoirs of a Fox-Hunting Man**	Faber 1928	**K**
	(novel)	Coward McCann 1929	**H**
	This was published anonymously, and 1928 and 1929 also saw a limited edition (**M**) and an illustrated edition (**J**) of the work.		
10	**Memoirs of an Infantry Officer**	Faber 1930	**G**
	(novel)	Coward McCann 1930	**E**
	The initial British print of this title was 20,000, compared with 1500 for 9.		
11	**In Sicily** (Ariel Poem)	Faber 1930	**D**
12	**Poems by Pinchbeck Lyre**	Duckworth 1931	**I**
13	**To the Red Rose** (Ariel Poem)	Faber 1931	**D**
14	**Prehistoric Burials** (poem)	Knopf 1932	**E**
	No. 1 of the Borzoi Chap Books.		
15	**The Road to Ruin** (verse)	Faber 1933	**F**
16	**Vigils** (verse)	Heinemann 1935	**G**
	These trade editions were preceded by	Viking 1936	**E**
	a limited edition (**N**), a large-paper edition (**K**), and also a vellum edition (**J**).		
17	**Sherston's Progress** (novel)	Faber 1936	**D**
	This, with 9 and 10, forms a trilogy.		
18	**The Complete Memoirs of George**	Faber 1937	**E**
	Sherston	Doubleday 1937	**D**
	Contains 9, 10 and 17.		
19	**The Old Century** (prose)	Faber 1938	**D**
	The t/p bears a Gwen Raverat	Viking 1939	**C**
	engraving.		
20	**Rhymed Ruminations** (verse)	Faber 1940	**D**
	A private press edition of 75 copies	Viking 1941	**C**
	appeared in 1939 (**K**).		
21	**Poems Newly Selected**	Faber 1940	**D**
22	**The Flower Show Match** (extracts)	Faber 1941	**C**
23	**The Weald of Youth** (prose)	Faber 1942	**D**
	The d/w and t/p bear an engraving by	Viking 1942	**C**
	Reynolds Stone.		

24	**Siegfried's Journey** (prose)	Faber 1945	D
	As above, this too has a Reynolds Stone engraving.	Viking 1946	C
25	**Collected Poems**	Faber 1947	D
		Viking 1949	C
26	**Meredith** (prose)	Constable 1948	C
		Viking 1948	C
27	**Sequences** (verse)	Faber 1956	C
		Viking 1957	C
28	**Collected Poems 1908–1956**	Faber 1961	C
29	**Diaries 1920–1922**	Faber 1981	C
30	**Diaries 1915–1918**	Faber 1983	C
31	**Diaries 1923–1925**	Faber 1984	C
32	**Siegfried Sassoon: Letters to Max Beerbohm with a Few Answers** (Ed. Rupert Hart-Davis)	Faber 1986	C

Bibliography:
Geoffrey Keynes **A Bibliography of Siegfried Sassoon** Hart-Davis 1962

Sayers, Dorothy L. Born in Oxford, 1893. Died 1957.

Always one of the most popular and collected detective fiction writers of all, and not easy to come by. In later life, Sayers tended towards the religious and the philosophical, but below I list the really good stuff which stretches from 1923 until 1940 – the period during which she still indulged in Wimsey.

1	**Whose Body?** (novel)	Unwin 1923	Q
		Boni & Liveright 1923	N
2	**Clouds of Witness** (novel)	Unwin 1926	P
		Dial Press 1927	M
3	**Unnatural Death** (novel)	Benn 1927	O
	The Dawson Pedigree	Dial Press 1928	L
4	**Lord Peter Views the Body** (stories)	Gollancz 1928	P
		Brewer 1929	M
5	**The Unpleasantness at the Bellona Club** (novel)	Benn 1928	P
6	**Strong Poison** (novel)	Brewer 1928	M
		Gollancz 1930	O
		Harcourt 1930	N
7	**The Documents in the Case** (novel) With Robert Eustace.	Benn 1930	L
		Brewer 1930	J
8	**The Five Red Herrings** (novel)	Gollancz 1931	M
	Suspicious Characters	Harcourt 1931	K
9	**Have His Carcase** (novel)	Gollancz 1932	M
		Harcourt 1932	K

10 **Hangman's Holiday** (stories)	Gollancz 1933	**M**
	Harcourt 1933	**K**
11 **Murder Must Advertise** (novel)	Gollancz 1933	**N**
	Harcourt 1933	**K**
12 **The Nine Tailors** (novel)	Gollancz 1934	**M**
	Harcourt 1934	**K**
13 **Gaudy Night** (novel)	Gollancz 1935	**N**
	Harcourt 1936	**L**
14 **Busman's Honeymoon** (novel)	Gollancz 1937	**M**
	Harcourt 1937	**K**
15 **In the Teeth of the Evidence**	Gollancz 1940	**K**
(stories)	Harcourt 1940	**H**

A checklist of Sayers work may be found in: **The New Cambridge Bibliography of English Literature** vol. 4

Biography:
Janet Hitchman **Such a Strange Lady** NEL 1975

Scott, Paul   Born in India, 1920. Died 1978. British.

A highly successful literary agent, turned highly successful writer, whose colossal standing and fame was largely posthumous. *The Raj Quartet*, of course, is his highlight, but it was the sequel *Staying On* that won him the Booker Prize and triggered a major reappraisal of his work, for before this moment it is true to say that Scott was barely collected at all. *The Raj Quartet* (together with its sequel) now features on most 'best of...' lists, and the recent television adaptation hurled both the reissued hardback omnibus and the separate paperback editions to the top of their relative best-seller lists. Television does indeed sell books, but Scott's reputation was secure before all the razzmatazz.

1 **I Gerontius** (verse)	Favil Press 1941	**N**
2 **Pillars of Salt** (play)	Gollancz 1948	**H**
Contained in *Four Jewish Plays*, edited by H.F. Rubinstein.		
3 **Johnny Sahib** (novel)	Eyre & Spottiswoode 1952	**J**
4 **The Alien Sky** (novel)	Eyre & Spottiswoode 1953	**I**
5 **Six Days in Marapore**	Doubleday 1953	**G**
American edition of 4.		
6 **A Male Child** (novel)	Eyre & Spottiswoode 1956	**H**
	Dutton 1957	**F**
7 **The Mark of the Warrior** (novel)	Eyre & Spottiswoode 1958	**H**
	Morrow 1958	**F**

8	**The Chinese Love Pavilion** (novel)	Eyre & Spottiswoode 1960	**F**
9	**The Love Pavilion** American edition of 8.	Morrow 1960	**D**
10	**The Birds of Paradise** (novel)	Eyre & Spottiswoode 1962	**E**
		Morrow 1962	**C**
11	**The Bender: Pictures From an Exhibition of Middle Class Portraits** (novel) The American edition omits the subtitle.	Secker 1963 Morrow 1963	**D** **C**
12	**The Corrida at San Feliu** (novel)	Secker 1964 Morrow 1964	**D** **C**
13	**The Jewel in the Crown** (novel)	Heinemann 1966 Morrow 1966	**I** **F**
14	**The Day of the Scorpion** (novel)	Heinemann 1968 Morrow 1968	**F** **D**
15	**The Towers of Silence** (novel)	Heinemann 1971 Morrow 1972	**F** **D**
16	**A Division of the Spoils** (novel) 13, 14, 15 and 16 comprise *The Raj Quartet*.	Heinemann 1975 Morrow 1976	**C** **C**
17	**The Raj Quartet** (omnibus) Contains 13, 14, 15 and 16.	Heinemann 1976 Morrow 1976	**C** **C**
18	**Staying On** (novel)	Heinemann 1977 Morrow 1977	**D** **C**
19	**After the Funeral** (story)	Whittington Press 1979	**H**
20	**My Appointment with the Muse** (essays)	Heinemann 1986	**C**

Searle, Ronald   Born in Cambridge, 1920.

Although very much more collected as an artist than as an author (his originals fetch a fortune) Searle's books are very sought after – and so are his dust-wrapper designs, no matter who wrote the book, or what it is about. None the less, it is for St Trinian's that he will be forever remembered and also – hardly to a lesser extent – Nigel Molesworth & Co. Now, credit must be given here to Geoffrey Willans who wrote such wondrous effusions as 'it is peason, he is my grate frend which means we touough each other up continually', to say nothing of all the stuff about fotherington-tomas, who keep dollies at home, sa hullo cloud hullo sky, hav a face like a squished tomato and couldn't hurt a flea. The Searle cartoons, of course, are more than mere illustrations accompanying the text – they make Molesworth *LIVE* (Hem-hem.)

Shaffer

1	**Hurrah for St Trinian's**	Macdonald (UK) 1948	**F**
		Macdonald (US) 1948	**D**
2	**The Terror of St Trinian's**	Parrish 1952	**D**

This was written by 'Timothy Shy'
(D.B. Wyndham Lewis), who wrote the
introduction to 1.

The Molesworth quartet:

3	**Down with Skool!**	Parrish 1953	**D**

The title note deserves quoting:
'Contanes Full Lowdown on Skools,
Swots, Snekes, Cads, Prigs Bulies
Headmasters Criket Foopball, Dirty
Roters Funks, Parents, Masters Wizard
Wheezes, Weeds Aple Pie Beds and
Various other Chizzes – in fact THE
LOT.'

4	**How to be Topp**	Parrish 1954	**D**
5	**Whizz for Atomms**	Parrish 1956	**C**
6	**Back in the Jug Agane**	Parrish 1959	**C**

Shaffer, Peter Born in Liverpool, 1926.

Two of Shaffer's many books stand out – he has written about a score, mainly plays. And damned difficult to find, wouldn't you expect.

1	**Equus** (play)	Deutsch 1973	**G**
		Atheneum 1974	**D**
2	**Amadeus** (play)	Deutsch 1980	**E**
		Harper 1981	**C**

Sharpe, Tom Born in London, 1928.

The early stuff is really very good, and very funny; to my mind, he went off about ten years ago when it all became *so* wild (and rather vulgar) that the humour became lost in belly laughs. Early comparisons with P.G. Wodehouse are now seen to be quite preposterous: Sharpe is not in the same league. Still, all good fun – and the books do have a tremendous following. The bad news for fans, however, is that Sharpe is currently suffering from self-confessed writer's block. He is not at all happy about the situation, by all accounts, and is in fact concerned that he may never again be able to write a comic novel: we must hope that this is not the case.

1 **Riotous Assembly** (novel)	Secker & Warburg 1971	**G**
2 **Indecent Exposure** (novel)	Secker & Warburg 1973	**D**
3 **Porterhouse Blue** (novel)	Secker & Warburg 1974	**D**
4 **Blott on the Landscape** (novel)	Secker & Warburg 1975	**D**
	Random House 1985	**B**
5 **Wilt** (novel)	Secker & Warburg 1976	**D**
	Random House 1984	**B**
6 **The Great Pursuit** (novel)	Secker & Warburg 1977	**C**
	Harper 1978	**B**
7 **The Throwback** (novel)	Secker & Warburg 1978	**C**
	Random House 1985	**B**
8 **The Wilt Alternative** (novel)	Secker & Warburg 1979	**C**
	Random House 1984	**B**
9 **Ancestral Vices** (novel)	Secker & Warburg 1980	**C**
	St. Martin's 1980	**B**
10 **Vintage Stuff** (novel)	Secker & Warburg 1983	**C**
	Random House 1985	**B**
11 **Wilt on High** (novel)	Secker & Warburg 1985	**C**
	Random House 1985	**B**

Sillitoe, Alan   Born in Nottingham, 1928.

Arthur Seaton takes his place among the deathless heroes (?) of fifties fiction – alongside such as Jimmy Porter, Vic Brown, and Joe Lampton.

The characters and strength of such novels aside, isn't it extraordinary that the very *titles* in each case were so well chosen as to have entered the language as phrases, and are endlessly adapted for use in other contexts? *Room at the Top, Look Back in Anger, A Kind of Loving, A Taste of Honey, The L-Shaped Room* – as well as Sillitoe's two, *Saturday Night and Sunday Morning* and *The Loneliness of the Long Distance Runner*. Story's *Live Now, Pay Later* was another one, but that came a few years later.

1 **Without Beer or Bread** (verse)	Outpost Publications	
	1957	**I**
2 **Saturday Night and Sunday Morning** (novel)	Allen 1958	**K**
	Knopf 1958	**G**
3 **The Loneliness of the Long Distance Runner** (stories)	Allen 1959	**I**
	Knopf 1959	**F**
4 **The General** (novel)	Allen 1960	**E**
	Knopf 1960	**C**
5 **The Rats and Other Poems**	Allen 1960	**D**
6 **Key to the Door (novel)**	Macmillan 1961	**C**
	Knopf 1961	**B**
7 **The Ragman's Daughter** (stories)	Allen 1963	**C**
	Knopf 1963	**B**
8 **A Falling out of Love** and **Other Poems**	Allen 1964	**C**

Sillitoe

9	The Road to Volgograd (travel)	Allen 1964	C
		Knopf 1964	B
10	The Death of William Posters (novel)	Macmillan 1965	C
		Knopf 1965	B
11	A Tree on Fire (novel)	Macmillan 1967	C
		Knopf 1967	B
12	The City Adventures of Marmalade Jim (juvenile)	Macmillan 1967	C
13	Guzman Go Home (stories)	Macmillan 1968	C
		Doubleday 1968	B
14	Love in the Environs of Voronezh (verse)	Macmillan 1968	B
		Doubleday 1968	B
15	All Citizens are Soldiers (play) Adaptation with Ruth Fainlight.	Macmillan 1969	B
		Dufour 1969	B
16	A Start in Life (novel)	Allen 1970	C
		Scribner 1971	B
17	Travels in Nihilon (novel)	Allen 1971	C
		Scribner 1972	B
18	Raw Material (novel)	Allen 1972	B
		Scribner 1973	B
19	Men, Women, and Children (stories)	Allen 1973	B
		Doubleday 1974	B
20	Flame of Life (novel)	Allen 1974	B
21	Storm: New Poems	Allen 1974	B
22	Mountains and Caverns (prose)	Allen 1975	B
23	The Widower's Son (novel)	Allen 1976	B
		Harper 1977	B
24	Big John and the Stars (juvenile)	Robson 1977	B
25	The Incredible Fencing Fleas (juvenile)	Robson 1978	B
26	Three Plays	Allen 1978	B
27	Snow on the North Side of Lucifer (verse)	Allen 1979	B
28	The Storyteller (novel)	Allen 1979	B
		Simon & Schuster 1980	B
29	Marmalade Jim at the Farm (juvenile)	Robson 1982	B
30	The Second Chance and Other Stories	Cape 1981	B
		Simon & Schuster 1981	B
31	Her Victory (novel)	Granada 1982	B
		Watts 1982	B
32	The Saxon Shore Way (non-fiction)	Hutchinson 1983	B
33	The Lost Flying Boat (novel)	Granada 1983	B
34	Sun Before Departure: Poems 1974–1984	Granada 1984	B
35	Down from the Hill (novel)	Granada	B

36	**Marmalade Jim and the Fox** (juvenile)	Robson 1984	**B**
37	**Life Goes On** (novel)	Granada 1985	**B**
38	**Tides and Stone Walls** (verse)	Grafton 1986	**B**
39	**Out of the Whirlpool** (novella)	Hutchinson 1987	**B**
		Harper 1988	**B**
40	**Alan Sillitoe's Nottinghamshire** (non-fiction)	Grafton 1987	**B**
41	**Every Day of the Week: An Alan Sillitoe Reader**	W.H. Allen 1987	**B**
42	**Three Poems**	Worlds Press 1988	**D**
43	**The Far Side of the Street** (stories)	W.H. Allen 1988	**C**
44	**The Open Door** (novel)	Grafton 1989	**B**
45	**Lost Loves** (novel)	Grafton 1990	**B**
46	**Snowstop** (novel)	HarperCollins 1992	**B**

Bibliography
Alan Sillitoe: A Bibliography by David E. Gerard (Mansell 1988)

Simenon, Georges   Born in Belgium, 1903. Died 1989.

Well, they said he'd never die. He, of course, *knew* that one day he would, and so packed in as much life as possible in the meantime: thousands of women, mountains of tobacco, rivers of cognac – a lesson for us all. He also wrote books – hundreds of them – the first of which appeared in 1920. I append here the first *Maigret*, the finding of which would truly be a most wonderful thing.

> **The Crime of Inspector Maigret**   Covici 1932   **N**
> The first appearance in England was
> **Introducing Inspector Maigret**, from
> Hurst & Blackett in 1933 (**M**).

The Sitwells

Although there remains considerable interest in the Sitwells, I find that the more common items hang around the shelves for ages – everyone either has them, or doesn't want them. There are collectors who collect nothing but the Sitwells, but in a general collection of literature it seems to me that while they must certainly be represented, the Collected Poems, autobiographies, and one or two selected highlights of each might suffice. It is Edith, of course, who really lives on as a poet, but because my shop was heavily biased in favour of art, I found more demand for Sacheverell than for the others – his architectural travel books, mainly – but this may not be typical of the trend in bookshops generally. Before this (highly selective) listing, then, I shall give

Sitwell, Edith

details of the bibliography, essential reading for anyone with more than a passing interest: Richard Fifoot *A Bibliography of Edith, Osbert and Sacheverell Sitwell* Hart-Davis 1971.

Sitwell, Edith Born in Scarborough, 1887. Died 1964.

1 **Poetry and Criticism** (prose)	Hogarth Press 1925	**H**
	Holt 1926	**E**
2 **Rustic Elegies** (verse)	Duckworth 1927	**F**
	Knopf 1927	**D**
3 **Collected Poems**	Duckworth 1930	**E**
This was preceded by a signed, limited edition published by Duckworth and in America by Houghton Mifflin		
4 **The English Eccentrics** (prose)	Faber 1933	**G**
	Houghton Mifflin 1933	**D**
5 **A Poet's Notebook** (prose)	Macmillan 1943	**C**
6 **Taken Care Of** (autobiog.)	Hutchinson 1965	**C**
	Atheneum 1965	**C**

Sitwell, Osbert Born in London, 1892. Died 1969.

1 **Collected Satires and Poems**	Duckworth 1931	**G**
2 **Left Hand, Right Hand!**	Little, Brown 1944	**C**
(autobiog.)	Macmillan 1945	**C**
3 **The Scarlet Tree** (autobiog.)	Little, Brown 1946	**C**
	Macmillan 1946	**C**
4 **Great Morning** (autobiog.)	Little, Brown 1947	**C**
	Macmillan 1948	**C**
5 **Laughter in the Next Room**	Little, Brown 1948	**C**
(autobiog.)	Macmillan 1949	**C**
6 **Noble Essences** (autobiog.)	Macmillan 1950	**D**
	Little, Brown 1950	**C**

Sitwell, Sacheverell Born in Scarborough, 1897. Died 1988.

1 **Southern Baroque Art**	Grant Richards 1924	**G**
	Knopf 1924	**D**
2 **Collected Poems**	Duckworth 1936	**E**
3 **Conversation Pieces** (art)	Batsford 1936	**E**

	Scribner 1937	D
4 **Edinburgh** (prose)	Faber 1938	D
	Houghton Mifflin 1939	C
5 **British Architects and Craftsmen**	Batsford 1945	D
	Scribner 1946	C
6 **Journey to the Ends of Time**	Cassell 1959	C
Vol. 1 (autobiog.)	Random House 1959	C
Vol. 1 only published.		

Smith, Stevie   Born in Hull, 1902. Died 1971.

Difficult to collect in fine state (in the all-important dust-wrappers, frequently doodled upon by the lady herself) but if anyone's worth it, Stevie is. Good, clean, literate fun – stylish, witty and moving. She is sadly missed – but maybe young Wendy Cope might take up the mantle?

1 **Novel on Yellow Paper** (novel)	Cape 1936	N
	Morrow 1937	J
2 **A Good Time was Had by All**	Cape 1937	M
(verse)		
3 **Over the Frontier** (novel)	Cape 1939	J
4 **Tender Only to One** (verse)	Cape 1938	H
5 **Mother, What is Man?** (verse)	Cape 1942	H
6 **The Holiday** (novel)	Chapman & Hall 1949	H
	Smithers 1950	F
7 **Harold's Leap** (verse)	Chapman & Hall 1950	F
8 **Not Waving but Drowning** (verse)	Deutsch 1957	H
9 **Cats in Colour** (photo essay)	Batsford 1959	D
10 **Selected Poems**	Longman 1962	D
	New Directions 1964	C
11 **The Frog Prince** and **Other Poems**	Longman 1966	E
12 **Two in One**	Longman 1971	C
Cont. 10 and 11.		
13 **Scorpion** and **Other Poems**	Longman 1971	D
14 **Collected Poems**	Lane 1975	C
	OUP (US) 1976	C
15 **Me Again: Uncollected Writings**	Virago 1981	C
	Farrar Straus 1982	C
16 **Stevie Smith: A Selection**	Faber 1983	C
Edited by Hermione Lee.		

Snow, C.P.   Born in Leicester, 1905. Died 1980.

In addition to the celebrated *Strangers and Brothers* sequence, listed below, Snow published about twenty other works, half a dozen of them plays writ-

Solzhenitsyn

ten in collaboration with his wife, Pamela Hansford Johnson. Interest had
flagged after *Last Things*, but Lord Snow's death – as is often rather ghoulish-
ly the way – realerted people to his work, and now I find that the younger
generation of collectors is taking notice, which I should not have foreseen.

1	**Strangers and Brothers**	Faber 1940	**J**
		Scribner 1960	**C**
2	**The Light and the Dark**	Faber 1947	**F**
		Macmillan (US) 1948	**D**
3	**Time of Hope**	Faber 1949	**E**
		Macmillan (US) 1950	**C**
4	**The Masters**	Macmillan (UK) 1951	**D**
		Macmillan (US) 1951	**C**
5	**The New Men**	Macmillan (UK) 1954	**D**
		Scribner 1954	**C**
6	**Homecomings**	Macmillan (UK) 1956	**D**
	The Scribner edition omitted the 's' in the title.	Scribner 1956	**C**
7	**The Conscience of the Rich**	Macmillan (UK) 1958	**D**
		Scribner 1958	**C**
8	**The Affair**	Macmillan (UK) 1960	**C**
		Scribner 1960	**C**
9	**Corridors of Power**	Macmillan (UK) 1964	**C**
		Scribner 1964	**C**
10	**The Sleep of Reason**	Macmillan (UK) 1968	**C**
		Scribner 1969	**C**
11	**Last Things**	Macmillan (UK) 1970	**C**
		Scribner 1970	**C**

Solzhenitsyn, Alexander   Born in Rostov, Russia, 1918.

When I started collecting Solzhenitsyn, he was *it*. His work was not merely
published, it was *smuggled out*. When one of his 'messages' to the West was
published in pamphlet form, it reprinted four, five times within weeks. And
then, to my mind the USSR did a very clever thing: they deported him.
Solzhenitsyn was then accessible, rich (vast royalties had been piling up all
over the world) and no longer had access to the *feel* of his motherland. The
mystique dissolved, and although Solzhenitsyn was – is still – read and
reviewed, we no longer hang upon every syllable. Politics aside, Solzhenitsyn
remains a very fine writer – even in translation – but the sequence of his
published *œuvre* remains confusing and bitty.

Collecting Solzhenitsyn is a task fraught with problems and uncertainties
unless one decides precisely what the aim is. To acquire the *absolute* first
editions in each case would be very difficult, unless one had contacts in
several countries. Assuming that the English-language editions are of most

interest, I list here the English and American details only. Most collectors in England would settle for the complete English first editions, and those in the USA, I imagine, would be satisfied with their American counterparts.

1 **One Day in the Life of Ivan Denisovich** Trans. Max Hayward and Ronald Hingley.	Praeger 1963	G
2 **One Day in the Life of Ivan Denisovich** Trans. Ralph Parker. 1 and 2 appeared simultaneously.	Dutton 1963 Gollancz 1963	E E
3 **We Never Make Mistakes: Two Short Novels** Trans. Paul W. Blackstock.	University of South Carolina 1963	E
4 **The First Circle** Trans. Thomas P. Whitney.	Harper & Row 1968	D
5 **The First Circle** Trans. Michael Guybon.	Collins 1968	D
6 **Cancer Ward** Trans. Nicholas Bethell and David Burg. The English ed. is in two vols, the American in one.	Bodley Head 1968–9 Farrar Straus 1969	F D
7 **The Cancer Ward** Trans. Rebecca Frank.	Dial Press (NY) 1968	C
8 **The Love-Girl and the Innocent** (play) Trans. Nicholas Bethell and David Burg.	Bodley Head 1969 Farrar Straus 1970	C C
9 **Stories and Prose Poems** Trans. Michael Glenny.	Bodley Head 1971 Farrar Straus 1971	C C
10 **August 1914** Trans. Michael Glenny.	Bodley Head 1972 Farrar Straus 1972	C C
11 **'One Word of Truth...'** (Nobel Lecture)	Bodley Head 1972 Farrar Straus 1973	C C
12 **Candle in the Wind** (play) Trans. Keith Armes.	University of Minnesota 1973 Bodley Head/OUP 1973	C C
13 **The Gulag Archipelago** Trans. Thomas P. Whitney.	Harper 1974 Collins 1974	C C
14 **Letter to Soviet Leaders** Trans. Hilary Sternberg.	Index on Censorship 1974 Harper 1974	C C
15 **The Gulag Archipelago (2)** Trans. as 13.	Harper 1975 Collins 1975	C C
16 **From under the Rubble**	Little, Brown 1975	C

Spark

With others. Trans. and ed. by Michael Scammell	Collins 1975	C
17 **Lenin in Zurich**	Farrar Straus 1976	C
Trans. H.T. Willetts.	Bodley Head 1976	C
18 **Warning to the Western World**	Bodley Head/BBC 1976	C
19 **Speeches to the Americans**	Farrar Straus 1976	C
American edition of 18		
20 **The Gulag Archipelago (3)**	Harper 1976	C
Trans. H.T. Willetts.	Collins 1978	C
21 **Prussian Nights** (poem)	Collins/Harvill 1977	C
Trans. Robert Conquest.		
22 **Alexander Solzhenitsyn Speaks to the West**	Bodley Head 1979	C
23 **A World Split Apart**	Harper 1970	C
American edition of 22.		
24 **The Mortal Danger**	Bodley Head 1980	C
	Harper 1980	C
25 **The Oak and the Calf**	Harper 1980	C
	Bodley Head 1980	C
26 **Victory Celebrations** (play)	Bodley Head 1983	C
27 **Prisoners** (play)	Bodley Head 1983	C

Spark, Muriel   Born in Edinburgh, 1918.

The twinkling wit of Muriel Spark is always a joy to behold, and never more so, in my opinion, than in *The Prime of Miss Jean Brodie, The Girls of Slender Means* and the rather underrated novella *The Abbess of Crewe*. This was seen to be an allegorical work pertaining to Watergate (which is either rubbish or not rubbish, it hardly matters) and made into an awful film which they rechristened *Nasty Habits*, which is about as subtle as a bus.

1 **Tribute to Wordsworth** (non-fiction) Ed. with Derek Stanford.	Wingate 1950	F
2 **Child of Light: A Reassessment of Mary Shelley**	Tower Bridge 1951	F
3 **The Fanfarlo and Other Verse** The 1st issue is red-lettered on buff wrpps.	Hand & Flower Press 1952	H
4 **A Selection of Poems by Emily Brontë** (ed. M.S.)	Grey Walls Press 1952	E
5 **Emily Brontë: Her Life and Work** With Derek Stanford.	Owen 1953	F
6 **John Masefield** (non-fiction)	Nevill 1953	E
7 **My Best Mary: The Letters of**	Wingate 1953	F

Mary Shelley	Folcroft Editions 1972	**C**
Ed. with Derek Stanford.		
8 **The Brontë Letters** (ed. M.S.)	Nevill 1954	**F**
9 **Letters of J.H. Newman**	Owen 1957	**D**
Ed. with Derek Stanford.		
10 **The Comforters** (novel)	Macmillan 1957	**I**
	Lippincott 1957	**E**
11 **Robinson** (novel)	Macmillan 1958	**G**
	Lippincott 1958	**D**
12 **The Go-Away Bird and Other Stories**	Macmillan 1958	**D**
	Lippincott 1960	**C**
13 **Memento Mori** (novel)	Macmillan 1959	**G**
	Lippincott 1959	**D**
14 **The Ballad of Peckham Rye** (novel)	Macmillan 1960	**F**
	Lippincott 1960	**C**
15 **The Bachelors** (novel)	Macmillan 1960	**G**
	Lippincott 1961	**D**
16 **Voices at Play** (stories and plays)	Macmillan 1961	**E**
17 **The Prime of Miss Jean Brodie** (novel)	Macmillan 1961	**G**
	Lippincott 1962	**D**
18 **Doctors of Philosophy** (play)	Macmillan 1963	**E**
19 **The Girls of Slender Means** (novel)	Macmillan 1963	**G**
	Knopf 1963	**D**
20 **The Mandelbaum Gate** (novel)	Macmillan 1965	**C**
	Knopf 1965	**C**
21 **Collected Stories I**	Macmillan 1967	**C**
	Knopf 1968	**C**
22 **Collected Poems I**	Macmillan 1967	**C**
23 **The Public Image** (novel)	Macmillan 1968	**C**
	Knopf 1968	**B**
24 **The Very Fine Clock** (juvenile)	Knopf 1968	**E**
	Macmillan 1969	**E**
25 **The Driver's Seat** (novel)	Macmillan 1970	**B**
	Knopf 1970	**B**
26 **Not to Disturb** (novel)	Macmillan 1971	**B**
	Viking Press 1972	**B**
27 **The Hothouse by the East River** (novel)	Macmillan 1972	**B**
	Viking 1972	**B**
28 **The Abbess of Crewe** (novel)	Macmillan 1974	**C**
	Viking 1974	**C**
29 **The Takeover** (novel)	Macmillan 1976	**C**
	Viking 1976	**B**
30 **Territorial Rights** (novel)	Macmillan 1979	**C**
	Coward McCann 1979	**B**
31 **Loitering With Intent** (novel)	Bodley Head 1981	**C**
	Coward McCann 1981	**B**

Spender

32 **Going Up to Sotheby's** and Other Poems	Granada 1982	C
33 **Bang-Bang You're Dead** and Other Stories	Granada 1982	C
34 **The Only Problem** (novel)	Bodley Head 1984	C
	Coward McCann 1984	C
35 **The Stories of Muriel Spark**	Dutton 1985	C
	Bodley Head 1987	C
36 **A Far Cry from Kensington** (novel)	Constable 1988	C
	Houghton Mifflin 1988	C
37 **Symposium** (novel)	Constable 1990	C
	Houghton Mifflin 1990	C
38 **Curriculum Vitae: A Volume** of Autobiography	Constable 1992	C
	Houghton Mifflin 1993	C

Bibliography:
Thomas A. Tominaga and Wilma Schneidermeyer **Iris Murdoch and Muriel Spark: A Bibliography** Scarecrow Press (US) 1976

Spender, Stephen   Born in London, 1909.

There has been a decline in collectors' interest in Spender, but certainly a market remains for the verse and the stories, if not for the prose works and the essays. In addition to his fictional work and poetry listed below, however, I append three non-fictional works which are of importance.

Sir Stephen is now the sole survivor of the thirties set, but there is still much more collectors' interest in Auden, Isherwood and MacNeice – in that order.

1 **20 Poems**	Blackwell 1930	N
2 **Poems**	Faber 1933	J
	Random House 1934	G
3 **Vienna** (verse)	Faber 1934	G
	Random House 1935	E
4 **The Burning Cactus** (stories)	Faber 1936	I
	Random House 1936	F
5 **Trial of a Judge** (play)	Faber 1938	D
	Random House 1938	C
6 **The Still Centre** (verse)	Faber 1939	F
7 **Danton's Death** (play) Adapt. with Goronwy Rees.	Faber 1939	E
8 **Selected Poems**	Faber 1940	C
9 **The Backward Son** (novel)	Hogarth Press 1940	J
10 **Ruins and Visions** (verse)	Faber 1942	E
	Random House 1942	D
11 **Poems of Dedication**	Faber 1946	D
	Random House 1947	C

12	**The Edge of Being** (verse)	Faber 1949	C
		Random House 1949	C
13	**Sirmione Peninsula**	Faber 1954	C
	(Ariel Poem)		
14	**Collected Poems**	Faber 1955	C
		Random House 1955	C
15	**Engaged in Writing and The Fool**	Hamilton 1958	C
	and the Princess (stories)	Farrar Straus 1958	C
16	**Mary Stuart** (play)	Faber 1959	C
	Adapt. from Schiller.		
17	**Selected Poems**	Random House 1964	C
		Faber 1965	C
18	**The Generous Days** (verse)	Faber 1971	C
		Random House 1971	C
19	**Dolphin** (verse)	Faber 1992	C
	Three prose works of importance:		
20	**World Within World**	Hamilton 1951	C
	(autobiography)	Harcourt Brace 1951	C
21	**W.H. Auden: A Tribute**	Weidenfeld 1975	C
		Macmillan 1975	C
22	**Eliot**	Fontana 1975	B
	In the 'Fontana Modern Masters'		
	series.		

Spiegelman, Art   Born in New York, 1948.

Finally – amidst all the flash and the trash – a really first rate graphic 'novel' has been published. Spiegelman is the co-founder/editor of the highly acclaimed avant garde comic book RAW, though his *undoubted* masterpiece is *undoubtedly* **MAUS –** a harrowing tale of the Nazi holocaust in comic strip form, the Jews portrayed as mice, and the Germans as cats. If you do not know the work, I agree it sounds mawkish and dire – but it truly is a work of art: unforgettable.

1	**Maus I: A Survivor's Tale**	Pantheon 1986	F
	My Father Bleeds History	Secker & Warburg 1987	D
		Penguin 1987	C
2	**Maus II: A Survivor's Tale**	Pantheon 1991	D
	And Here My Troubles Began	Secker & Warburg 1992	C
		Penguin 1992	B

(Both volumes were published in Britain simultaneously by Secker & Warburg – in hardback – and by Penguin, in paperback)

Steinbeck, John   Born in California, 1902. Died 1968.

A sort of a semi-cultish god in America, though not hugely collected in this country. A representation seems essential, though – the highlights being nos 6, 10 and 14.

1	**Cup of Gold** (novel)	McBride 1929	M
		Heinemann 1937	I
2	**The Pastures of Heaven** (novel)	Brewer 1932	K
		Allan 1933	I
3	**To a God Unknown** (novel)	Ballou 1933	J
		Heinemann 1935	H
4	**Tortilla Flat** (novel)	Covici Friede 1935	J
		Heinemann 1935	H
5	**In Dubious Battle** (novel)	Covici Friede 1936	I
		Heinemann 1936	H
6	**Of Mice and Men** (novel)	Covici Friede 1937	J
		Heinemann 1937	H
7	**Of Mice and Men** (play)	Covici Friede 1937	E
8	**The Red Pony** (novel) Enlarged edition published by Viking in 1945 (**C**).	Covici Friede 1937	G
9	**The Long Valley** (novel)	Viking 1938	K
		Heinemann 1939	H
10	**The Grapes of Wrath** (novel)	Viking 1939	J
		Heinemann 1939	H
11	**Sea of Cortez: A Leisurely Journal of Travel and Research** This was republished as **The Log from the Sea of Cortez** by Viking and Heinemann (1951 and 1958, respectively) together with a new essay by J.S. on Edward F. Ricketts, the co-writer of the book (**D,C**).	Viking 1941	H
12	**The Moon is Down** (novel)	Viking 1942	D
		Heinemann 1942	C
13	**Bombs Away: The Story of a Bomber Team** (non-fiction)	Viking 1942	G
14	**Cannery Row** (novel)	Viking 1945	E
		Heinemann 1945	D
15	**The Wayward Bus** (novel)	Viking 1947	E
		Heinemann 1947	C
16	**The Pearl** (novel)	Viking 1947	E
		Heinemann 1948	C
17	**A Russian Journal** (non-fiction)	Viking 1948	D
		Heinemann 1949	C

18 **Burning Bright** (novel)	Viking 1950	**D**
	Heinemann 1951	**C**
19 **Viva Zapata!** (screenplay) New edition published by Viking in 1975 (**C**).	Edizioni Filmcritica (Italy) 1952	**D**
20 **East of Eden** (novel)	Viking 1952	**G**
	Heinemann 1952	**D**
21 **Sweet Thursday** (novel)	Viking 1954	**D**
	Heinemann 1954	**C**
22 **The Short Reign of Pippin IV: A Fabrication** (fiction)	Viking 1957	**C**
	Heinemann 1957	**C**
23 **Once There Was a War** (non-fiction)	Viking 1958	**D**
	Heinemann 1959	**C**
24 **The Winter of Our Discontent** (novel)	Viking 1961	**C**
	Heinemann 1961	**C**
25 **Travels With Charley in Search of America** (non-fiction)	Viking 1962	**C**
	Heinemann 1962	**C**
26 **Speech Accepting the Nobel Prize for Literature**	Viking 1962	**D**
27 **America and Americans** (non-fiction)	Viking 1966	**C**
	Heinemann 1966	**C**
28 **The Acts of King Arthur and His Noble Knights**	Farrar Straus 1976	**C**
	Heinemann 1977	**B**

Stevens, Wallace   Born in Pennsylvania, 1879. Died 1955.

That Stevens trained as a lawyer and became vice-president of an insurance company is, perhaps, not in itself amazing – Eliot, as we all know, was a banker. What strikes me as *absolutely* amazing, however, is that throughout his career as a poet – during which he was repeatedly hailed as one of America's greatest – he steadfastly held on to his position on the board of the insurance company! He said – no doubt to the bewildered fury of poets everywhere – that poetry was 'a leisure pursuit'. This remained, as it were, his policy. A checklist of his major work appears below.

1 **Harmonium** (verse) A revised ed. was published by Knopf in 1931.	Knopf 1923	**R**
2 **Ideas of Order** (verse) This was preceded by a limited, signed ed. from Alcestis in 1935 (**Q**).	Knopf 1936	**P**
3 **The Man with the Blue Guitar and Other Poems**	Knopf 1937	**N**
4 **Parts of a World** (verse)	Ryerson Press 1942	**L**
5 **Transport to Summer** (verse)	Knopf 1947	**L**
6 **The Auroras of Autumn** (verse)	Knopf 1950	**J**

7 **The Necessary Angel** (essays)	Knopf 1951	**J**
	Faber 1960	**H**
8 **Selected Poems**	Faber 1953	**G**
	Vintage 1959	**D**
9 **Collected Poems**	Knopf 1954	**I**
	Faber 1955	**G**
10 **Opus Posthumous** (verse)	Knopf 1957	**G**
	Faber 1959	**G**
11 **The Letters**	Knopf 1966	**F**
	Faber 1967	**E**
12 **The Palm at the End of the Mind:**	Knopf 1971	**D**
Selected Poems and a Play		

Bibliography:
J.M. Edelstein **Wallace Stevens: A Descriptive Bibliography**
University of Pittsburgh Press 1973

Stewart, J.I.M. Born in Edinburgh, 1906.

Stewart is better known by his pseudonym, Michael Innes. He has written over seventy books now, but I list here just the first five Innes, and the first five Stewarts.

Michael Innes:

1 **Death at the President's Lodging**	Gollancz 1936	**N**
Seven Suspects	Dodd Mead 1937	**L**
2 **Hamlet, Revenge!**	Gollancz 1937	**L**
	Dodd Mead 1937	**I**
3 **Lament for a Maker**	Gollancz 1938	**K**
	Dodd Mead 1938	**I**
4 **Stop Press**	Gollancz 1939	**K**
The Spider Strikes	Dodd Mead 1939	**H**
5 **The Secret Vanguard**	Gollancz 1940	**H**
	Dodd Mead 1941	**E**

J.I.M. Stewart:

1 **Mark Lambert's Supper**	Gollancz 1954	**I**
2 **The Guardians**	Gollancz 1955	**G**
	Norton 1957	**D**
3 **The Use of Riches**	Gollancz 1957	**F**
	Norton 1957	**D**
4 **The Man Who Wrote Detective**	Gollancz 1959	**E**
Stories and **Other Stories**	Norton 1959	**C**
5 **The Man Who Won the Pools**	Gollancz 1961	**D**
	Norton 1961	**C**

Stoppard, Tom   Born in Czechoslovakia, 1937. British.

Not so prolific, and not *quite* so bing-bang vital as he used to be, Stoppard nonetheless still packs a punch – and the early and most wonderful plays continue to be very hard to find, and ever more expensive.

1 **Lord Malquist and Mr Moon** (novel)	Blond 1966 Knopf 1968	**H** **E**
2 **Rosencrantz and Guildenstern are Dead** (play)	Faber 1967 (Hardback **L**, Paper **G**) Grove Press 1967	**F**
3 **The Real Inspector Hound** (play)	Faber 1968 Grove Press 1969	**I** **D**
4 **Enter a Free Man** (play) This play has an interesting history, for it was originally televised in 1963 as *A Walk on the Water*, and then a revised version was televised the following year as *The Preservation of George Riley*.	Faber 1968 Grove Press 1972	**H** **C**
5 **Albert's Bridge and If You're Glad I'll be Frank: Two Plays for Radio**	Faber 1969	**I**
6 **After Magritte** (play)	Faber 1971 Grove Press 1972	**G** **D**
7 **Jumpers** (play)	Faber 1972 Grove Press 1972	**I** **D**
8 **Artist Descending a Staircase and Where Are They Now?: Two Plays for Radio**	Faber 1973	**F**
9 **Travesties** (play)	Faber 1975 Grove Press 1975	**G** **D**
10 **Dirty Linen and New-Found-Land** (plays) An edition was published by Faber a month later (**C**).	Ambiance/Almost Free Playscript 1976 Grove Press 1976	**E** **C**
11 **The Fifteen Minute Hamlet** (play)	French 1976	**D**
12 **Every Good Boy Deserves Favour and Professional Foul** (plays)	Faber 1978 Grove Press 1978	**E** **C**
13 **Night and Day** (play) A revised edition was published by Faber in 1979 (**C**).	Faber 1978 Grove Press 1979	**F** **D**
14 **Undiscovered Country** A version of Arthur Schnitzler's play.	Faber 1980	**D**
15 **Dogg's Hamlet, Cahoot's Macbeth** (play)	Faber 1980	**D**
16 **On the Razzle** (play)	Faber 1981	**D**
17 **The Real Thing** (play)	Faber 1982	**D**

18	**The Dog It was That Died** and **Other Plays** Includes *The Dissolution of Dominic Boot,* *'M' is for Moon Among Other Things,* *Teeth, Another Moon Called Earth, Neutral* *Ground* and *A Separate Peace.*	Faber 1983	**D**
19	**Four Plays for Radio**	Faber 1984	**D**
20	**Squaring the Circle** (play) Includes the contents of 12.	Faber 1984	**C**
21	**Rough Crossing** (play)	Faber 1985	**C**
22	**Hapgood** (play)	Faber 1988	**C**
23	**Radio Plays 1964–1983**	Faber 1990	**C**
24	**Rosencrantz and Guildenstern Are Dead: The Film**	Faber 1991	**C**

Storey, David   Born in Yorkshire, 1933.

Nearly ten years on, we are still waiting for a new novel from Storey, but his reputation is secure – he really is a first class novelist and playwright, and *This Sporting Life* remains a got-to-have classic.

1	**This Sporting Life** (novel)	Longmans 1960 Macmillan 1960	**L** **H**
2	**Flight into Camden** (novel)	Longmans 1961 Macmillan 1961	**J** **F**
3	**Radcliffe** (novel)	Longmans 1963 Coward McCann 1964	**F** **C**
4	**The Restoration of Arnold Middleton** (play)	Cape 1967	**D**
5	**In Celebration** (play)	Cape 1969 Grove Press 1975	**D** **C**
6	**The Contractor** (play)	Cape 1970 Random House 1971	**D** **C**
7	**Home** (play)	Cape 1970 Random House 1971	**D** **C**
8	**The Changing Room** (play)	Cape 1972 Random House 1972	**D** **C**
9	**Pasmore** (novel)	Longman 1972 Dutton 1974	**C** **C**
10	**Edward** (humour)	Lane 1973	**B**
11	**A Temporary Life** (novel)	Lane 1973 Dutton 1974	**C** **C**
12	**The Farm** (play)	Cape 1973	**C**
13	**Cromwell** (play)	Cape 1973	**C**
14	**Life Class** (play)	Cape 1975	**C**
15	**Saville** (novel)	Cape 1976 Harper 1977	**C** **C**

16 **Mother's Day** (play)	Cape 1977	C
17 **Early Days** (play)	Penguin 1980	B
18 **Sisters** (play)	Penguin 1980	B
19 **A Prodigal Child** (novel)	Cape 1982	C
	Dutton 1983	B
20 **Present Times** (novel)	Cape 1984	B
21 **The March on Russia** (play)	French 1989	B
22 **Storey's Lives: Poems 1951–1991**	Cape 1992	B

Story, Jack Trevor   Born in Hertfordshire, 1917. Died 1991

Jack the lad has spun his last tale: some who knew him thought he was immortal, others were amazed that he had lasted half as long. Anyway, among his scores of novels he leaves us one true classic, the title of which has entered the language:

Live Now, Pay Later (novel)	Secker 1963	H
Unusually for the time, this was	Penguin 1963	C

published simultaneously in hard and
paperback. Both editions are hard to
come by.

Strachey, Lytton   Born in London, 1880. Died 1932.

Interest in the Bloomsbury Group has declined since the heyday of the seventies, but although books on the subject continue to be published, only the ones *really* vital to the thing are taken seriously and, apart from standard biographies, none is of any interest to the collector unless written *by* the person in question, and not *about* him or her. Strachey seems to have been spared being dug and re-dug, but then Holroyd did the job so thoroughly in the sixties that it would be folly to try. Nor do any posthumous writings seem to have emerged recently, and so Strachey's checklist remains the same, as does collectors' interest – it never boomed, but it never went away.

1 **Landmarks in French Literature**	Williams & Norgate	G
This is a very small, fragile item in the	1912	
Home University Library series, but	Holt 1912	D
there are many variant issues,		
chronicled in Percy Muir *Points*.		
2 **Eminent Victorians**	Chatto & Windus 1918	H
	Putnam 1918	F
3 **Queen Victoria**	Chatto & Windus 1921	F
	Harcourt 1921	D
4 **Books and Characters**	Chatto & Windus 1922	D
	Harcourt 1922	C

5	Pope: The Leslie Stephen Lecture	CUP 1925	D
6	Elizabeth and Essex	Chatto & Windus 1928	D
		Harcourt 1928	C
7	Portraits in Miniature	Chatto & Windus 1931	D
		Harcourt 1931	C
8	Characters and Commentaries	Chatto & Windus 1933	D
		Harcourt 1933	C
9	Spectatorial Essays	Chatto & Windus 1964	C
		Harcourt 1965	C
10	Ermyntrude and Esmerelda	Blond 1969	C
	This is illustrated by Erté, and has an Intro. by Michael Holroyd.	Stein & Day 1969	C

A volume of letters between Virginia Woolf and Lytton Strachey was published by the Hogarth Press in 1956, though of course the great work on Strachey is: Michael Holroyd *Lytton Strachey* (2 vols) Heinemann 1967, 1968.

Styron, William   Born in Virginia, 1925.

Sophie's Choice was Styron's fifth novel in thirty years, and something of a *cause célèbre* even before it was published. There were rumblings about 'the new Styron' in America as soon as page proofs were released, and the feeling that here was something 'big' soon spread to this country. It was a fat American novel, to be sure, but it was not to be a blockbuster *à la* Harold Robbins, nor 'big' in the sense that, say, James Michener's novels are big. It was a very literary novel, with too thin a thread, one would have thought, to sustain it. But the power and the intrigue persisted unto the end.

Here is the fiction, in addition to which Styron has produced ten other books.

1	Lie Down in Darkness (novel)	Bobbs-Merrill 1951	I
		Hamilton 1952	G
2	The Long March (novel)	Random House 1956	G
		Hamilton 1962	C
3	Set The House on Fire (novel)	Random House 1960	F
		Hamilton 1961	C
4	The Confessions of Nat Turner (novel)	Random House 1967	D
		Cape 1968	C
5	Sophie's Choice (novel)	Random House 1979	D
		Cape 1979	C

Swift, Graham   Born in London, 1949.

An impressive oeuvre – if rather on the small side – but Swift seems to be having problems recapturing the extraordinary quality of *Waterland*, and the rave reviews that it provoked. We shall wait and see.

1 **The Sweet-Shop Owner** (novel)	Lane 1980	**I**
2 **Shuttlecock** (novel)	Lane 1981	**F**
3 **Learning to Swim** (stories)	London Magazine	**D**
	Editions 1982	
4 **Waterland** (novel)	Heinemann 1983	**E**
	Poseidon 1984	**C**
5 **Out of This World** (novel)	Viking UK 1988	**C**
	Poseidon 1988	**C**
6 **Ever After** (novel)	Picador 1992	**B**
	Knopf 1992	**B**

Symons, Julian   Born in London, 1912.

Julian Symons's eightieth birthday last year occasioned a lot of well-deserved tributes to this undisputed master of his genre – all received with characteristic modesty.

He *is* collected, but he is rarely eagerly pursued. About half his work is non-fiction – essays, criticism, histories, and two very early volumes of verse. It is, of course, his crime fiction that is of the most interest, and that is what is listed below.

1 **The Immaterial Murder Case**	Gollancz 1945	**G**
	Macmillan 1957	**E**
2 **A Man Called Jones**	Gollancz 1947	**F**
3 **Bland Beginning**	Gollancz, 1949	**E**
	Harper 1949	**D**
4 **The 31st of February**	Gollancz 1950	**E**
	Harper 1950	**C**
5 **The Broken Penny**	Gollancz 1952	**D**
	Harper 1953	**C**
6 **The Narrowing Circle**	Gollancz 1954	**D**
	Harper 1954	**C**
7 **The Paper Chase**	Collins 1956	**D**
This was published as *Bogue's Fortune* in America by Harper in 1957 (**C**).		
8 **The Colour of Murder**	Collins 1957	**D**
	Harper 1957	**C**
9 **The Gigantic Shadow**	Collins 1958	**D**
This was published in America by Harper in the same year, with the title		

Pipe Dream (**C**).

10	**The Progress of a Crime**	Collins 1960	D
		Harper 1960	C
11	**Murder, Murder** (stories)	Fontana 1961	B
12	**The Killing of Francie Lake**	Collins 1962	C
	This was published during the same year by Harper in America with the title *The Plain Man* (**C**).		
13	**The End of Solomon Grundy**	Collins 1964	C
		Harper 1964	B
14	**The Belting Inheritance**	Collins 1965	C
		Harper 1965	B
15	**Francis Quarles Investigates** (stories)	Panther 1965	B
16	**The Julian Symons Omnibus**	Collins 1966	C
	Cont. 4, 10 and 13.		
17	**The Man Who Killed Himself**	Collins 1967	C
		Harper 1967	B
18	**The Man Whose Dreams Came True**	Collins 1969	C
		Harper 1969	B
19	**The Man Who Lost His Wife**	Collins 1971	C
		Harper 1971	B
20	**The Players and the Game**	Collins 1972	C
		Harper 1972	B
21	**The Plot Against Roger Rider**	Collins 1973	C
		Harper 1973	B
22	**A Three Pipe Problem**	Collins 1975	C
		Harper 1975	B
23	**The Blackheath Poisonings**	Collins 1978	C
		Harper 1979	B
24	**Sweet Adelaide**	Collins 1980	C
		Harper 1980	B
25	**The Detling Murders**	Macmillan 1982	C
26	**The Detling Secret**	Viking 1983	B
	American edition of 25.		
27	**The Tigers of Subtopia** and **Other Stories**	Macmillan 1982	C
		Viking 1983	B
28	**The Name of Annabel Lee**	Macmillan 1983	C
		Viking 1983	B
29	**The Criminal Comedy of the Contented Couple**	Macmillan 1985	B
30	**A Criminal Comedy** (same as 29)	Viking US 1986	B
31	**The Kentish Manor Murders**	Macmillan 1988	B
		Viking US 1988	B
32	**Death's Darkest Face**	Macmillan 1990	B
		Viking US 1990	B
33	**Something Like a Love Affair**	Macmillan 1992	B
		Mysterious Press 1992	B

Taylor, Elizabeth   Born in Reading, 1912. Died 1976.

She remains of small and limited interest – this perhaps offering scope for someone who wishes to gather the lot, but below are just the three best. I re-read *Mrs Palfrey at the Claremont* recently and was very impressed; it really is a very elegantly paced and stylish novel with more than a touch of vintage Muriel Spark. And as for her treatment of feminine loneliness – it beats the much-vaunted Anita Brookner into a cocked hat.

1	**At Mrs Lippincote's** (novel)	Davies 1945	H
		Knopf 1946	D
2	**Angel** (novel)	Davies 1957	F
		Viking 1957	D
3	**Mrs Palfrey at the Claremont** (novel)	Chatto & Windus 1971	D
		Viking 1971	C

Tennant, Emma   Born in London, 1937.

Suddenly very prolific, rather fashionable and increasingly stylish, Tennant is still not of enormous interest to collectors – and therefore bargains are to be had, particularly with the later work. The first (pseudonymous) novel is a brute to find, however.

1	**The Colour of Rain** (novel) (pseud. Catherine Aydy)	Weidenfeld 1964	I
2	**The Time of the Crack** (novel)	Cape 1973	F
3	**The Last of the Country House Murders** (novel)	Cape 1974	D
		Nelson (US) 1974	C
4	**Hotel de Dream** (novel)	Gollancz 1976	D
5	**The Bad Sister** (novel)	Gollancz 1978	D
		Coward McCann 1978	C
6	**Wild Nights** (novel)	Cape 1979	C
		Harcourt Brace 1980	B
7	**The Boggart** (juvenile)	Granada 1980	C
8	**Alice Fell** (novel)	Cape 1980	C
9	**The Search for Treasure Island** (juvenile)	Puffin 1981	B
10	**Queen of Stones** (novel)	Cape 1982	C
11	**Woman Beware Woman** (novel)	Cape 1983	C
12	**The Ghost Child** (juvenile)	Heinemann 1984	C
13	**The Adventures of Robina, By Herself** (novel)	Faber 1986	C
		Persea 1987	B
14	**The House of Hospitalities** (novel)	Viking UK 1987	C
15	**A Wedding of Cousins** (novel)	Viking UK 1988	C
16	**The Magic Drum** (novel)	Viking UK 1989	C

17 **Two Women of London: The Strange Case of Ms. Jekyll and Mrs. Hyde** (novel)	Faber 1989	C
18 **Sisters and Strangers** (novel)	Grafton 1990	C
19 **Dave's Secret Diary** (juvenile)	Longman 1991	B
20 **Faustine** (novel)	Faber 1991	B
21 **Dave's Secret Pony** (juvenile)	BBC 1992	B
22 **ABC of Writing** (humour)	Faber 1992	A

Theroux, Paul Born in Massachusetts, 1941.

An extremely prolific author – on a par with Updike, almost – and one in whom collectors' interest has erupted quite recently. He writes well and at length, the acute observation that is the hallmark of his novels standing him in very good stead for his popular travel and railway books. He is by no means undiscovered territory, but as will be seen by the following listing, there is a great deal of scope (added to at least annually) and prices remain moderate for the time being.

1 **Waldo** (novel)	Houghton Mifflin 1967	K
	Bodley Head 1968	I
2 **Fong and the Indians** (novel)	Houghton Mifflin 1968	J
	Hamilton 1976	E
3 **Girls at Play** (novel)	Houghton Mifflin 1969	I
	Bodley Head 1969	F
4 **Murder in Mount Holly** (novel)	Ross (London) 1969	J
5 **Jungle Lovers** (novel)	Houghton Mifflin 1971	H
	Bodley Head 1971	E
6 **Sinning with Annie** and **Other Stories**	Houghton Mifflin 1972	H
	Hamilton 1975	D
7 **V.S. Naipaul: An Introduction to his Work** (non-fiction)	Deutsch 1972	G
	Africana 1972	F
8 **Saint Jack** (novel)	Bodley Head 1973	H
	Houghton Mifflin 1973	F
9 **The Black Horse** (novel)	Hamilton 1974	F
	Houghton Mifflin 1974	D
10 **The Great Railway Bazaar: By Train Through Asia** (travel)	Hamilton 1975	E
	Houghton Mifflin 1975	E
11 **The Family Arsenal** (novel)	Hamilton 1976	E
	Houghton Mifflin 1976	D
12 **The Consul's Files** (stories)	Hamilton 1977	D
	Houghton Mifflin 1977	D
13 **Picture Palace** (novel)	Hamilton 1978	D
	Houghton Mifflin 1978	D
14 **A Christmas Card** (juvenile)	Hamilton 1978	D
	Houghton Mifflin 1978	D

15 **The Old Patagonian Express:**   Hamilton 1979   **F**
    By Train Through the Americas   Houghton Mifflin 1979   **D**
    (travel)

16 **World's End** and **Other Stories**   Hamilton 1980   **D**
    Houghton Mifflin 1980   **D**

17 **London Snow** (juvenile)   Hamilton 1980   **C**
    This was preceded by a signed edition,   Houghton Mifflin 1980   **C**
    limited to 450 copies (Russell,
    Salisbury, 1979) (**I**).

18 **The Mosquito Coast** (novel)   Hamilton 1981   **C**
    Houghton Mifflin 1982   **C**

19 **The London Embassy** (stories)   Hamilton 1982   **C**
    Houghton Mifflin 1983   **C**

20 **The Turn of the Years**   Russell (Wilton) 1982   **K**
    Theroux introduces a selection of
    wood engravings by Reynolds Stone,
    V.S. Pritchett contributes an essay.
    Limited to 150 copies, signed by
    Theroux and Pritchett.

21 **The Kingdom of the Sea** (travel)   Hamilton 1983   **C**
    Houghton Mifflin 1983   **C**

22 **Doctor Slaughter** (novel)   Hamilton 1984   **C**

23 **Half Moon Street**   Houghton Mifflin 1984   **C**
    Same as 21, but for the retitling and
    the addition of a story.

24 **Sailing Through China** (travel)   Russell (Salisbury) 1984   **I**
    A signed edition, limited to
    400 copies, although each copy states
    that the limitation is only 150. A trade
    edition followed later.

25 **Patagonia Revisited** (travel)   Russell (Salisbury) 1985   **J**
    With Bruce Chatwin. 250 copies,
    signed by both authors. A trade
    edition followed later.

26 **Sunrise with Seamonsters** (travel)   Hamilton 1985   **C**
    Houghton Mifflin 1985   **C**

27 **The Imperial Way** (travel)   Hamilton 1985   **C**
    With Steve McCurry.   Houghton Mifflin 1985   **C**

28 **The Shortest Day of the Year:**   Sixth Chamber Press
    A Christmas Fantasy   1986
    With the usual unerring feel of
    publishers, this seasonal piece was put
    out in May. Ah well. It comprised:
    26 copies in hand-made paper, signed
    (**M**). 175 copies, signed (**I**).

29 **O-Zone** (novel)   Hamilton 1986   **C**
    Putnam 1986   **C**

30 **Riding the Iron Rooster: By Train Through China** (travel)	Hamish Hamilton 1988	C
	Putnam 1988	C
31 **My Secret History** (novel)	Hamish Hamilton 1989	C
	Putnam 1989	C
32 **Travelling the World** (travel)	Sinclair-Stevenson 1990	C
	Random House 1991	C
33 **Doctor Demarr** (novel)	Hutchinson 1990	C
34 **Chicago Loop** (novel)	Hamish Hamilton 1990	C
	Random House 1991	C

Thomas, D.M.   Born in Cornwall, 1935.

Not nearly as trendy as a decade ago (whatever was all that fuss over *The White Hotel* all about?) and not too seriously collected at all, really; but here is the lot, for the small but loyal body of fans.

1 **Personal and Possessive** (verse)	Outposts 1964	H
2 **Penguin Modern Poets 11**	Penguin 1968	B
With D.M. Black and Peter Redgrove.		
3 **Two Voices** (verse)	Cape Goliard 1968	E
	Grossman 1968	C
4 **The Lover's Horoscope** (verse)	Purple Sage (US) 1970	E
5 **Logan Stone** (verse)	Cape Goliard 1971	D
	Grossman 1971	C
6 **The Shaft** (verse)	Arc 1973	D
7 **Lilith-Prints** (verse)	Second Aeon (Cardiff) 1974	D
8 **Symphony in Moscow** (verse)	Keepsake Press (UK) 1974	D
9 **Love and Other Deaths** (verse)	Elek 1975	C
10 **The Rock** (verse)	Sceptre Press (UK) 1975	E
11 **Orpheus in Hell** (verse)	Sceptre Press (UK) 1977	E
12 **In the Fair Field** (verse)	Five Seasons Press (UK) 1978	E
13 **The Honeymoon Voyage** (verse)	Secker & Warburg 1978	C
14 **The Devil and the Floral Dance** (juvenile)	Robson 1978	D
15 **The Flute-Player** (novel)	Gollancz 1979	D
	Dutton 1979	C
16 **Protest** (poem)	Privately printed 1980	D
17 **Birthstone** (novel)	Gollancz 1980	D
	Viking Press 1980	C
18 **Dreaming in Bronze** (verse)	Secker & Warburg 1981	D
19 **The White Hotel** (novel)	Gollancz 1981	G
	Viking Press 1981	F

20 **Selected Poems**	Secker & Warburg 1983	C
	Viking Press 1983	C
21 **News From the Front** (verse)	Arc 1983	C
With Sylvia Kantaris.		
22 **Ararat** (novel)	Gollancz 1983	B
	Viking Press 1983	B
23 **Swallow** (novel)	Gollancz 1984	B
	Viking Press 1984	B
24 **Sphinx** (novel)	Gollancz 1986	B
	Viking 1987	B
25 **Summit** (novel)	Gollancz 1987	B
	Viking 1988	B
26 **Memories and Hallucinations:**	Gollancz 1988	B
An Autobiographical	Viking 1988	B
Excursion		
27 **Lying Together** (novel)	Gollancz 1990	B
	Viking 1990	B
28 **Flying in to Love** (novel)	Bloomsbury 1992	B
	Scribner 1992	B

Thomas, Dylan   Born in Swansea, 1914. Died 1953.

Dylan Thomas remains one of the really great writers of the century, and this is reflected in the scarceness and high prices of most of his work. This situation will not alter: he will always be collected – isn't it?

1 **18 Poems** — Sunday Referee & The Parton Bookshop 1934 — U

Black cloth, lettered in gold, with grey d/w. The second issue is distinguishable in many ways, two being the rounded spine, as opposed to the flat spine of the first issue, and the advert on the verso for slim volumes by George Barker, Dylan Thomas and David Gascoyne, not present in first issue. The spine lettering tends to discoloration on the second issue, due to inferior gold. The 1st issue is Grade **U** and over now, though the 2nd issue is Grade **Q** in fine condition. A 2nd edition was published by the Fortune Press in, it is thought, 1942, the first issue of this having red boards, and a yellow d/w. Subsequent issues retain the yellow d/w, but have various coloured boards (**H**).

2 **Twenty-Five Poems** — Dent 1936 — M
Grey boards, grey d/w.

3 **The Map of Love**   Dent 1939   **L**
(verse and prose)
Mauve cloth, grey and purple d/w.
Three subsequent issues exist, the first
identifiable by its smooth-grained cloth,
and gold lettering.

4 **The World I Breathe**   New Directions 1939   **H**
This American anthology was bound in
brown, with cream d/w. It contains
selections from 1, 2 and 3, though two
stories appear for the first time.

5 **Portrait of the Artist as a Young**   Dent 1940   **L**
Dog   New Directions 1940   **I**
English ed. is green cloth with scarlet
d/w, American ed. is red cloth with
cream d/w.

6 **New Poems**   New Directions 1943   **H**
Mauve boards in mauve d/w.

7 **Deaths and Entrances**   Dent 1946   **H**
$5\frac{1}{2}$ in. × $4\frac{1}{2}$ in. only. Orange cloth,
vermilion d/w.

8 **Selected Writings**   New Directions 1946   **G**
Pinkish cloth in pinkish d/w.

9 **Twenty-six Poems**   Dent/New Directions   **N**
This consisted of 150 signed copies, the   1950
first ten on Japanese vellum (**Q**), the
remainder on handmade paper, divided
between Dent and New Directions, all
printed in Italy.

10 **In Country Sleep**   New Directions 1952   **G**
100 signed copies (**O**), and 5000
ordinary copies.

11 **Collected Poems**   Dent 1952   **G**
Published simultaneously with the   New Directions 1953   **E**
English ed. was a signed, limited issue
of 65 copies, 60 for sale (**P**).

12 **The Doctor and the Devils**   Dent 1953   **F**
The American ed. was printed off from   New Directions 1953   **D**
the English 2nd impression.

13 **Under Milk Wood**   Dent 1954   **I**
     New Directions 1954   **F**

14 **Quite Early One Morning**   Dent 1954   **E**
     New Directions 1954   **D**

15 **Conversation About Christmas**   New Directions 1954   **F**
2000 printed for distribution by the
publisher.

16 **Adventures in the Skin Trade** and   New Directions 1955   **F**

Other Stories
The title story was published alone
by Putnam in 1955, with a Foreword
by Vernon Watkins (**F**).

17 **A Prospect of the Sea**	Dent 1955	E
18 **Letters to Vernon Watkins**	Faber/Dent 1957	D
	New Directions 1957	C
19 **The Beach of Falesa**	Stein & Day 1963	D
	Cape 1964	D
20 **Twenty Years A-Growing**	Dent 1964	C
21 **Rebecca's Daughters**	Triton 1965	C
	Little, Brown 1965	C
22 **Me and My Bike**	McGraw-Hill 1965	C
	Triton 1965	C
23 **Selected Letters of Dylan Thomas**	Dent 1966	D
	New Directions 1967	C
24 **The Notebooks of Dylan Thomas**	New Directions 1967	D
Poet in the Making	Dent 1968	C
25 **Early Prose Writings**	Dent 1971	C
	New Directions 1972	C
26 **The Death of the King's Canary**	Hutchinson 1976	B
With John Davenport.		
27 **The Collected Letters of**	Dent 1985	C
Dylan Thomas		

Bibliography:
Ralph Maud **Dylan Thomas in Print: A Bibliographical History**
Dent 1970; University of Pittsburgh Press 1970

Thomas, R.S.   Born in Cardiff, 1913.

A surprisingly large oeuvre for a poet who is lately spoken of hardly at all –
and now eighty years old. The early stuff remains difficult, though it is
certainly that which you should be after. *Poetry for Supper* and *Tares* might
well be seen to be the highlights.

1 **The Stones of the Field** (verse)	Druid Press 1946	O
2 **An Acre of Land** (verse)	Printing Company 1952	M
3 **The Minister** (verse)	Printing company 1953	L
4 **Song at the Year's Turning** (verse)	Hart Davis 1955	H
5 **Poetry for Supper** (verse)	Hart Davis 1958	G
	Dufour 1961	D
6 **Judgement Day** (verse)	Poetry Book Society 1960	F
7 **Tares** (verse)	Hart Davis 1961	F
	Dufour 1961	D

8 **The Bread of Truth** (verse)	Hart Davis 1963	**F**
	Dufour 1963	**D**
9 **Words and the Poet** (lecture)	University of Wales Press 1964	**D**
10 **Pieta** (verse)	Hart Davis 1966	**F**
11 **Not That He Brought Flowers** (verse)	Hart Davis 1968	**E**
12 **Pergamon Poets 1** (with Roy Fuller)	Pergamon Press 1968	**D**
13 **The Mountains** (verse)	Chilmark Press US 1968	**E**
14 **H'm** (verse)	Macmillan 1972	**D**
	St Martin's Press 1972	**C**
15 **Young and Old** (juvenile)	Chatto & Windus 1972	**C**
16 **Selected Poems 1946–1968**	Hart Davis MacGibbon 1973	**C**
	St Martin's Press 1973	**C**
17 **What is a Welshman?** (poem)	Davies 1974	**D**
18 **Laboratories of the Spirit** (verse)	Macmillan 1975	**D**
	Godine 1976	**C**
19 **The Way Of It** (verse)	Ceolfrith Press 1977	**D**
20 **Frequencies** (verse)	Macmillan 1978	**C**
21 **Between Here and Now** (verse)	Macmillan 1981	**C**
22 **Poet's Meeting** (verse)	Celandine 1983	**D**
23 **Later Poems: A Selection**	Macmillan 1983	**C**
24 **Selected Prose**	Poetry Wales Press 1983	**C**
	Dufour 1984	**C**
25 **The Poems of R.S. Thomas**	University of Arkansas Press 1985	**C**
26 **Destinations** (verse)	Celandine 1985	**C**
27 **Ingrowing Thoughts** (prose)	Poetry Wales Press 1985	**C**
28 **NEB** (prose)	Gwasg Gwynedd 1985	**C**
29 **Experimenting with an Amen** (verse)	Macmillan 1986	**C**
30 **Welsh Airs** (verse)	Poetry Wales Press 1987	**C**
	Dufour 1987	**C**
31 **The Echoes Return Slow** (verse)	Macmillan 1988	**C**
32 **Three Poems**	Words Press 1988	**C**
33 **Counterpoint** (verse)	Bloodaxe 1990	**C**

Thubron, Colin   Born in London, 1939.

Thubron is gaining a considerable reputation for his novels (despite, or maybe because of, the pretty dismal subject matter – pain, generally, in one form or another) and I think it is these in which the collector would be most interested. However, as he started out as a travel writer – and he is, these days, a travel writer of considerable acclaim – I have listed the entire oeuvre.

1 **Mirror to Damascus** (travel)	Heinemann 1967	**F**
	Little, Brown 1968	**D**

2 **The Hills of Adonis: A Quest** **In Lebanon** (travel)	Heinemann 1968 Little, Brown 1969	**E** **D**
3 **Jerusalem** (travel)	Heinemann 1969 Little, Brown 1969	**D** **C**
4 **Journey into Cyprus** (travel)	Heinemann 1975	**D**
5 **The God in the Mountain** (novel)	Heinemann 1977 Norton 1977	**E** **D**
6 **Istanbul** (travel, with others)	Time-Life 1978	**C**
7 **Emperor** (novel)	Heinemann 1978	**D**
8 **The Venetians** (travel, with others)	Time-Life 1980	**C**
9 **The Ancient Mariners** (travel, with others)	Time-Life 1981	**C**
10 **The Royal Opera House, Covent Garden** (non-fiction)	Hamish Hamilton 1982	**D**
11 **Among the Russians** (travel)	Heinemann 1983	**C**
12 **Where the Nights are Longest: Travels by Car Through Western Russia** (same as 11)	Random House 1984	**C**
13 **A Cruel Madness** (novel)	Heinemann 1984 Atlantic Monthly Press 1985	**C** **C**
14 **Behind the Wall: A Journey Through China** (travel)	Heinemann 1987 Atlantic Monthly Press 1988	**C** **C**
15 **Falling** (novel)	Heinemann 1989 Atlantic Monthly Press 1990	**C** **C**
16 **The Silk Road – China: Beyond the Celestial Kingdom** (travel)	Pyramid 1990	**C**
17 **Turning Back the Sun** (novel)	Heinemann 1991	**C**

Thurber, James Born in Ohio, 1894. Died 1961.

The cynical, world-wise, off-beat American humorist, *par excellence*. Quite apart from his writing, his cruelly economical cartoons would have assured him of a place in the history of humour. His dogs are not nearly as funny (or as grotesque) as his women. All these women are shaped like a cardboard box, bear expressions of unyielding malevolence (unless they are drunk) and their hair resembles a charred and sparse floor mop. It was to escape such harridans that Walter Mitty entered his dream world, and who can blame him. The wonderful Danny Kaye film, it might be noted here, was spun out of the original short story of only nine pages.

1 **Is Sex Necessary? Or: Why You Feel the Way You Do** With E.B. White.	Harper 1929 Heinemann 1930	**J** **H**

2	**The Owl in the Attic and Other**	Harper (US) 1931	I
	Perplexities	Harper (UK) 1931	G
3	**The Seal in the Bedroom and Other**	Harper (US) 1932	I
	Predicaments	Harper (UK) 1932	G
4	**My Life and Hard Times**	Harper (US) 1933	G
		Harper (UK) 1933	G
5	**The Middle-Aged Man on the**	Harper 1935	G
	Flying Trapeze	Heinemann 1935	E
6	**Let Your Mind Alone! and Other**	Harper 1937	D
	More or Less Inspirational Pieces	Hamilton 1937	D
7	**Cream of Thurber**	Hamilton 1939	D
	(anthology)		
8	**The Last Flower: A Parable in**	Harper 1939	E
	Pictures	Hamilton 1939	D
9	**Fables of Our Time and Famous**	Harper 1940	D
	Poems Illustrated	Hamilton 1940	D
10	**The Male Animal** (play)	Random House 1940	C
	With Elliott Nugent.	Hamilton 1940	C
11	**My World – and Welcome to It**	Harcourt Brace 1942	H
	This contains the story *The Secret Life of*	Hamilton 1942	G
	Walter Mitty.		
12	**Many Moons** (juvenile)	Harcourt Brace 1943	G
		Hamilton 1945	F
13	**Men, Women and Dogs**	Harcourt Brace 1943	D
		Hamilton 1945	D
14	**The Great Quillow** (juvenile)	Harcourt Brace 1944	G
15	**The White Deer** (juvenile)	Harcourt Brace 1945	F
		Hamilton 1945	E
16	**The Thurber Carnival**	Harper 1945	D
	(anthology)	Hamilton 1945	C
17	**The Beast in Me and Other**	Harcourt Brace 1948	D
	Animals	Hamilton 1949	C
18	**The 13 Clocks** (juvenile)	Simon & Schuster 1950	F
		Hamilton 1951	F
19	**The Thurber Album**	Simon & Schuster 1952	C
		Hamilton 1952	C
20	**Thurber Country**	Simon & Schuster 1953	D
		Hamilton 1953	C
21	**The Wonderful O** (juvenile)	Simon & Schuster 1955	D
		Hamilton 1955	C
22	**Thurber's Dogs**	Simon & Schuster 1955	D
		Hamilton 1955	C
23	**A Thurber Garland** (anthology)	Hamilton 1955	C
24	**Further Fables of Our Time**	Simon & Schuster 1956	C
		Hamilton 1956	C
25	**Alarms and Diversions**	Harper 1957	C
		Hamilton 1957	C

26	**The Years with Ross** (non-fiction)	Little, Brown 1959	C
		Hamilton 1959	C
27	**Lanterns and Lances**	Harper 1961	C
		Hamilton 1961	C
28	**A Thurber Carnival** (play)	French (US) 1962	C
29	**Credos and Curios**	Harper 1962	C
		Hamilton 1962	C
30	**Vintage Thurber** (anthology, 2 vols)	Hamilton 1963	E
31	**Thurber and Company**	Harper 1967	C
		Hamilton 1967	C

Bibliography:
Edwin T. Bowden **James Thurber: A Bibliography** Ohio State
University Press 1968

Tolkien, J.R.R. Born in Birmingham, England 1892.
Died 1973.

The Hobbit and *The Lord of the Rings* remain the (expensive) prizes, though there is much else to enjoy in the canon. A little thing like death, nearly twenty years ago, hasn't slowed up the old boy in the slightest – the books just keep on coming.

1	**A Middle English Vocabulary**	OUP 1922	M
		OUP (US) 1922	J
2	**Sir Gawain and the Green Knight** Ed. with E.V. Gordon.	OUP 1925	L
		OUP (US) 1925	J
3	**Songs for the Philologists** (verse)	Privately printed 1936	S
4	**Beowulf: The Monsters and the Critics** (lecture)	OUP 1936	J
		Folcroft Editions 1972	C
5	**The Hobbit** (novel)	Allen & Unwin 1937	V
		Houghton Mifflin 1938	S
6	**Farmer Giles of Ham** (novel)	Allen & Unwin 1949	H
		Houghton Mifflin 1950	F
7	**The Fellowship of the Ring** (novel)	Allen & Unwin 1954	P
		Houghton Mifflin 1954	L
8	**The Two Towers** (novel)	Allen & Unwin 1954	O
		Houghton Mifflin 1955	K
9	**The Return of the King** (novel)	Allen & Unwin 1955	N
		Houghton Mifflin 1956	K

7, 8 and 9 form the trilogy *The Lord of the Rings*. Revised editions of these three volumes were published by the same publishers, in 1966 and 1967 respectively

Tolkien

10 **The Adventures of Tom Bombadil** (verse)	Allen & Unwin 1962	G
	Houghton Mifflin 1963	E
11 **Tree and Leaf** (essay)	Allen & Unwin 1964	F
	Houghton Mifflin 1965	D
12 **The Tolkien Reader**	Ballantine (NY) 1966	D
13 **Smith of Wootton Major** (novelette)	Allen & Unwin 1967	F
	Houghton Mifflin 1967	D
14 **The Road Goes Ever On** (verse) Music by Donald Swann.	Houghton Mifflin 1967	E
	Allen & Unwin 1968	D
15 **Bilbo's Last Song** (poster poem)	Houghton Mifflin 1974	D
	Allen & Unwin 1974	D
16 **Sir Gawain and the Green Knight, Pearl, and Sir Orfeo** (trans.)	Allen & Unwin 1975	C
	Houghton Mifflin 1975	C
17 **The Homecoming of Beorhtnoth** (poem) Published together with reprints of 11 and 13.	Allen & Unwin 1975	C
18 **The Father Christmas Letters**	Allen & Unwin 1976	C
	Houghton Mifflin 1976	C
19 **The Silmarillion** (novel)	Allen & Unwin 1977	C
	Houghton Mifflin 1977	C
20 **Pictures by J.R.R. Tolkien** **The Pictures of J.R.R. Tolkien**	Allen & Unwin 1979	C
	Houghton Mifflin 1979	C
21 **Poems and Stories**	Allen & Unwin 1980	C
	Houghton Mifflin 1980	C
22 **Unfinished Tales**	Allen & Unwin 1980	C
	Houghton Mifflin 1980	C
23 **Letters**	Allen & Unwin 1981	C
	Houghton Mifflin 1981	C
24 **Mr Bliss** (juvenile)	Allen & Unwin 1982	C
	Houghton Mifflin 1983	C
25 **Finn and Hengest: The Fragment and the Episode**	Allen & Unwin 1983	C
	Houghton Mifflin 1983	C
26 **The Monsters and the Critics**	Allen & Unwin 1983	C
	Houghton Mifflin 1983	C
27 **The Book of Lost Tales Part I**	Allen & Unwin 1983	C
	Houghton Mifflin 1984	C
28 **The Book of Lost Tales Part 2**	Allen & Unwin 1984	C
	Houghton Mifflin 1984	C
29 **The Book of Lost Tales Part 3: The Lays of Beleriand**	Allen & Unwin 1985	C
	Houghton Mifflin 1985	C
30 **The Book of Lost Tales Part 4: The Shaping of Middle-Earth**	Allen & Unwin 1986	C
	Houghton Mifflin 1986	C
31 **The Lost Road** and **Other Writings**	Unwin Hyman 1987	C
	Houghton Mifflin 1987	C

32 **The Return of the Shadow**	Unwin Hyman 1988	C
	Houghton Mifflin 1988	C
33 **Treason in Isengard**	Unwin Hyman 1989	C
	Houghton Mifflin 1989	C
34 **Lord of the Rings**	HarperCollins 1991	D
	Houghton Mifflin 1991	D

(New one-volume edition, illustrated by Alan Lee)

Tremain, Rose   Born in London, 1943.

Not desperately collected, but maybe one to gather in now while her name is still relatively low-profile (to say nothing of the prices). Tremain is a very strong writer, though the subject matter tends to the grim and dismal, it has to be said.

1 **The Fight for Freedom for Women** (non-fiction)	Ballantine US 1973	D
2 **Stalin: An Illustrated Biography** (non-fiction)	Ballantine US 1975	D
3 **Sadler's Birthday** (novel)	Macdonald 1976	E
	St. Martin's Press 1977	C
4 **Letter to Sister Benedicta** (novel)	Macdonald 1978	D
	St. Martin's Press 1979	C
5 **The Cupboard** (novel)	Macdonald 1981	C
	St. Martin's Press 1982	C
6 **The Colonel's Daughter** and **Other Stories**	Hamish Hamilton 1984	C
	Summit 1984	B
7 **Journey to the Volcano** (juvenile)	Hamish Hamilton 1985	C
8 **The Swimming Pool Season** (novel)	Hamish Hamilton 1985	C
	Summit 1985	B
9 **The Garden of the Villa Mollini** and **Other Stories**	Hamish Hamilton 1987	C
10 **Restoration** (novel)	Hamish Hamilton 1989	C
	Viking 1990	B
11 **Sacred Country** (novel)	Sinclair-Stevenson 1992	C

Trevor, William   Born in Cork, 1928.

Now regarded as a grand old man, Trevor continues to produce his colourful and evocative novels and short stories – a firm favourite with collectors, these days, although prices are not too alarming – with the exception, as ever, of the very earliest items.

Trevor

1	**A Standard of Behaviour** (novel)	Hutchinson 1958	**J**
2	**The Old Boys** (novel)	Bodley Head 1964	**H**
		Viking 1964	**E**
3	**The Boarding House** (novel)	Bodley Head 1965	**F**
		Viking 1965	**D**
4	**The Love Department** (novel)	Bodley head 1966	**E**
		Viking 1967	**C**
5	**The Day We Got Drunk on Cake** (novel)	Bodley Head 1967	**E**
		Viking 1968	**C**
6	**The Girl** (play)	French 1968	**C**
7	**Mrs Eckdorf in O'Neill's Hotel** (novel)	Bodley Head 1969	**E**
		Viking 1970	**C**
8	**The Old Boys** (play)	Poynter 1971	**C**
9	**Miss Gomez and the Brethren** (novel)	Bodley Head 1971	**D**
10	**A Night With Mrs Da Tonka** (play)	French 1972	**C**
11	**The Ballroom of Romance** (novel)	Bodley Head 1972	**D**
		Viking 1972	**C**
12	**Going Home** (play)	French 1972	**C**
13	**Elizabeth Alone** (novel)	Bodley Head 1973	**D**
		Viking 1974	**C**
14	**Marriages** (play)	French 1973	**C**
15	**Angels at the Ritz** and **Other Stories**	Bodley Head 1975	**D**
		Viking 1976	**C**
16	**The Children of Dynmouth** (novel)	Bodley Head 1976	**D**
		Viking 1977	**C**
17	**Old School Ties** (story)	Lemon Tree Press 1976	**H**
18	**Lovers of Their Time** and **Other Stories**	Bodley Head 1978	**D**
		Viking 1978	**C**
19	**Other People's Worlds** (novel)	Bodley Head 1980	**C**
		Viking 1981	**C**
20	**Beyond the Pale** (stories)	Bodley Head 1981	**C**
		Viking 1982	**C**
21	**Fools of Fortune** (novel)	Bodley Head 1983	**C**
		Viking 1983	**C**
22	**A Writer's Ireland** (non-fiction)	Viking 1984	**C**
		Thames & Hudson 1984	**C**
23	**The News From Ireland** and **Other Stories**	Bodley head 1986	**C**
		Viking 1986	**C**
24	**Nights at the Alexandria** (story)	Hutchinson 1987	**C**
		Harper 1987	**C**
25	**The Silence in the Garden** (novel)	Bodley Head 1988	**C**
		Viking 1988	**C**
26	**Family Sins and Other Stories**	Bodley Head 1990	**C**
		Viking 1990	**C**

| 27 | **Two Lives** (novels)
(contains **Reading Turgenev**
and **My House in Umbria**) | Viking UK 1991
Viking US 1991 | C
C |

Trevor has edited **The Oxford Book of Irish Short Stories** (OUP 1989)

Tyler, Anne   Born in Minneapolis, 1941. American.

Far better known in her native America than in this country, Tyler nonetheless has an ever-widening circle of admirers – particularly since the success of the film *The Accidental Tourist*, based upon her novel. Anne Tyler *might* be cheap and easy to collect, but you will have to move fast.

1	**If Morning Ever Comes** (novel)	Knopf 1964	G
		Chatto & Windus 1965	E
2	**The Tin Can Tree** (novel)	Knopf 1965	F
		Macmillan 1966	D
3	**A Slipping-Down Life** (novel)	Knopf 1970	D
		Severn House 1983	C
4	**The Clock Winder** (novel)	Knopf 1972	D
		Chatto & Windus 1973	C
5	**Celestial Navigation** (novel)	Knopf 1974	C
		Chatto & Windus 1975	C
6	**Searching for Caleb** (novel)	Knopf 1976	C
		Chatto & Windus 1976	C
7	**Earthly Possessions** (novel)	Knopf 1977	C
		Chatto & Windus 1977	C
8	**Morgan's Passing** (novel)	Knopf 1980	C
		Chatto & Windus 1980	C
9	**Dinner at the Homesick Restaurant** (novel)	Knopf 1982	C
		Chatto & Windus 1982	C
10	**The Accidental Tourist** (novel)	Knopf 1985	C
		Chatto & Windus 1985	C
11	**Breathing Lessons** (novel)	Knopf 1988	C
		Chatto & Windus 1989	C
12	**Saint Maybe** (novel)	Knopf 1991	C
		Chatto & Windus 1991	C

Unsworth, Barry   Born in Durham, 1930.

A self-effacing and very fine writer who has been quietly publishing for longer than anyone imagines. *Pascali's Island* threatened to put him on the map following the success of the film version, as did the critical reception of *Stone Virgin*. But with *Sacred Hunger*, Unsworth would appear to have cracked it: a man to be gathered *now*.

Updike

1 **The Partnership** (novel)	Hutchinson New Authors 1966	F
2 **The Greeks Have a Word For It** (novel)	Hutchinson 1967	E
3 **The Hide** (novel)	Gollancz 1970	D
4 **Mooncranker's Gift** (novel)	Lane 1973	D
5 **The Big Day** (novel)	Joseph 1976	C
	Mason/Charter 1976	B
6 **Pascali's Island** (novel)	Joseph 1980	C
7 **The Idol Hunter** (same as 6)	Simon & Schuster US 1980	C
8 **The Rage of the Vulture** (novel)	Granada 1982	C
	Houghton Mifflin 1982	C
9 **Stone Virgin** (novel)	Hamish Hamilton 1985	C
	Houghton Mifflin 1986	C
10 **Sugar and Rum** (novel)	Hamish Hamilton 1988	C
11 **Sacred Hunger** (novel)	Hamish Hamilton 1992	C
	Doubleday 1992	C

Updike, John   Born in Pennsylvannia, 1932.

One of the most prolific writers on either side of the Atlantic (Paul Theroux doesn't do badly, either) and popular in this country mainly for the novels, his poetry barely causing a ripple. Less of a noise than latterly, though, this due to the general drift from American writers in their sixties to British writers in their thirties and forties. I do not know what American writers in their sixties make of this state of affairs.

1 **The Carpentered Hen and Other Tame Creatures** (verse)	Harper 1958	I
2 **Hoping for a Hoopoe** English edition of 1.	Gollancz 1959	G
3 **The Poorhouse Fair** (novel)	Knopf 1959	J
	Gollancz 1959	G
4 **The Same Door** (stories)	Knopf 1959	I
	Deutsch 1962	F
5 **Rabbit, Run** (novel)	Knopf 1960	G
	Deutsch 1961	E
6 **Pigeon Feathers** (stories)	Knopf 1962	F
	Deutsch 1962	D
7 **The Magic Flute** (juvenile)	Knopf 1962	E
8 **Telephone Poles** (verse)	Knopf 1963	F
	Deutsch 1963	D
9 **The Centaur** (novel)	Knopf 1963	D
	Deutsch 1963	C
10 **The Ring** (miscellany)	Knopf 1964	C

11 **Of the Farm** (novel)	Knopf 1965	D
	Deutsch 1973	C
12 **Assorted Prose**	Knopf 1965	C
	Deutsch 1965	C
13 **The Music School** (stories)	Knopf 1966	D
	Deutsch 1973	C
14 **A Child's Calendar** (prose)	Knopf 1966	C
15 **Couples** (novel)	Knopf 1968	D
	Deutsch 1968	C
16 **Bath After Sailing** (verse)	Pendulum Press 1968	E
17 **Bottom's Dream: Adapted from William Shakespeare's 'A Midsummer Night's Dream'**	Knopf 1969	C
18 **Midpoint** and **Other Poems**	Knopf 1969	C
	Deutsch 1969	C
19 **Bech: A Book** (stories)	Knopf 1970	C
	Deutsch 1970	C
20 **Rabbit Redux** (novel)	Knopf 1971	C
	Deutsch 1972	C
21 **Seventy Poems**	Penguin 1972	C
22 **Museums and Women** and **Other Stories**	Knopf 1972	C
	Deutsch 1973	C
23 **Warm Wine: An Idyll** (story)	Albodocani Press 1973	G
24 **Six Poems**	Aloe Editions 1973	G
25 **Cunts** (verse)	Hallman 1974	I
26 **Buchanan Dying** (play)	Knopf 1974	D
	Deutsch 1974	C
27 **A Month of Sundays** (novel)	Knopf 1975	C
	Deutsch 1975	C
28 **Picked-Up Pieces** (essays)	Knopf 1975	C
	Deutsch 1976	C
29 **Marry Me** (novel)	Knopf 1976	C
	Deutsch 1977	C
30 **Tossing and Turning** (verse)	Knopf 1977	C
	Deutsch 1977	C
31 **The Coup** (novel)	Knopf 1978	C
	Deutsch 1979	C
32 **From the Journal of a Leper** (verse)	Lord John Press 1978	H
33 **16 Sonnets**	Ferguson 1979	G
34 **Three Illuminations in the Life of an American Author** (prose)	Targ Editions 1979	E
35 **Problems** and **Other Stories**	Knopf 1979	C
	Deutsch 1980	C
36 **Too Far to Go: The Maples Stories**	Fawcett 1979	C
37 **Rabbit is Rich** (novel)	Knopf 1981	C
	Deutsch 1982	C

Upward

38 **Bech is Back** (novel)	Knopf 1982	**C**
	Deutsch 1983	**C**
39 **The Beloved** (verse)	Lord John Press 1983	**H**
A signed edition.		
40 **Hugging the Shore** (essays, reviews)	Knopf 1983	**C**
	Deutsch 1984	**C**
41 **The Witches of Eastwick** (novel)	Knopf 1984	**D**
	Deutsch 1984	**C**
42 **Facing Nature** (verse)	Knopf 1985	**C**
	Deutsch 1986	**C**
43 **Roger's Version** (novel)	Knopf 1986	**C**
	Deutsch 1986	**C**
44 **A Pear Like a Potato** (verse)	Santa Susanna Press US 1986	**F**
45 **Trust Me** (stories)	Knopf 1987	**C**
	Deutsch 1987	**C**
46 **The Afterlife** (story)	Sixth Chamber Press UK 1987	**G**
47 **Two Sonnets** (verse)	Wind River Press US 1987	**F**
48 **5** (novel)	Knopf 1988	**C**
	Deutsch 1988	**C**
49 **Self-Consciousness: Memoirs**	Knopf 1989	**C**
	Deutsch 1989	**C**
50 **Just Looking: Essays on Art**	Knopf 1989	**C**
	Deutsch 1989	**C**
51 **Rabbit at Rest** (novel)	Knopf 1990	**C**
	Deutsch 1991	**C**
52 **Odd Jobs: Essays and Criticism**	Knopf 1991	**C**
	Deutsch 1991	**C**

Upward, Edward   Born in Essex, 1903.

A singular literary career, and a very small output. Upward should not be underrated, however, for his little-known trilogy is very fine indeed, and quite on a par with Henry Green or Christopher Isherwood. Isherwood, indeed, was a friend of Upward's in the thirties, and glowed throughout a review of Upward's second published novel, and first of the trilogy, entitled – appropriately enough – *In the Thirties*. 'I believe,' said Isherwood, 'we are being introduced to a masterpiece.' The completed trilogy was published fifteen years later in 1977, and I should not be at all surprised to learn that it is now out of print. It is, as I say, severely underrated.

A curious bit of publishing, the handling of the trilogy. The first volume was published in 1962 and the second in 1969, quite in the normal way. Then in 1977 came the complete trilogy under the blanket title *The Spiral Ascent*, containing the first two novels as well as the newly-published third and final volume. If you come across first editions of volumes one and two, therefore, you are forced to juxtapose them with the complete trilogy in order to complete the trilogy, if you follow me.

Prices can – and should – only go, well – upward.

1	**Buddha** (verse)	Cambridge 1924	**J**
2	**Journey to the Border** (novel)	Hogarth Press 1938	**I**
3	**In the Thirties** (novel)	Heinemann 1962	**F**
4	**The Rotten Elements** (novel)	Heinemann 1969	**E**
5	**The Railway Accident** and **Other Stories**	Heinemann 1969	**D**
6	**The Spiral Ascent** Contains 3 and 4 as well as *No Home But the Struggle*, published for the first time, which completes the trilogy.	Heinemann 1977	**D**
7	**The Night and Other Stories**	Heinemann 1987	**C**

Vidal, Gore Born in New York, 1925.

Still very popular and very much read, Vidal is not as eagerly collected in this country as one might expect, and values – even for the early and scarce titles – are holding.

1	**Williwaw** (novel)	Dutton 1946	**K**
		Heinemann 1970	**C**
2	**In a Yellow Wood** (novel)	Dutton 1947	**I**
3	**The City and the Pillar** (novel) A revised edition was published by Dutton in 1965 (**C**), and by Heinemann in 1966 (**C**).	Dutton 1948 Lehmann 1949	**H** **F**
4	**The Season of Comfort** (novel)	Dutton 1949	**F**
5	**A Search for the King** (novel)	Dutton 1950	**F**
6	**Dark Green, Bright Red** (novel)	Dutton 1950 Lehmann 1950	**F** **E**
7	**The Judgement of Paris** (novel)	Dutton 1952 Heinemann 1953	**F** **D**
8	**Death in the Fifth Position** (novel) (pseud. Edgar Box)	Dutton 1952 Heinemann 1954	**I** **G**
9	**Death Before Bedtime** (novel) (pseud. Edgar Box)	Dutton 1953 Heinemann 1954	**H** **G**
10	**Death Likes It Hot** (novel) (pseud. Edgar Box)	Dutton 1954 Heinemann 1955	**H** **G**
11	**Messiah** (novel)	Dutton 1954 Heinemann 1955	**E** **D**
12	**A Thirsty Evil: 7 Short Stories**	Zero Press (NY) 1956 Heinemann 1958	**F** **D**

13	**Visit to a Small Planet and Other Television Plays** Incl. *Barn Burning, Dark Possession, The Death of Billy the Kid, A Sense of Justice, Smoke, Summer Pavilion* and *The Turn of the Screw.*	Little, Brown 1957	C
14	**The Best Man** (play)	Little, Brown 1960	C
15	**Three Plays** Cont. *Visit to a Small Planet, The Best Man, On the Marsh to the Sea.*	Heinemann 1962	C
16	**Romulus: A New Comedy**	Dramatists Play Service 1962	C
17	**Three: Williwaw, A Thirsty Evil, Julian the Apostate** (novels)	NAL 1962	C
18	**Rocking the Boat** (essays)	Little, Brown 1962	C
		Heinemann 1963	C
19	**Julian** (novel)	Little, Brown 1964	D
		Heinemann 1964	C
20	**Washington DC** (novel)	Little, Brown 1967	C
		Heinemann 1967	C
21	**Myra Breckinridge** (novel)	Little, Brown 1968	C
		Blond 1968	C
22	**Weekend** (play)	Dramatists Play Service 1968	C
23	**Reflections Upon a Sinking Ship** (essays)	Little, Brown 1969	C
		Heineman 1969	C
24	**Two Sisters** (novel)	Little, Brown 1970	C
		Heinemann 1970	C
25	**An Evening with Richard Nixon** (play)	Random House 1972	C
26	**Homage to Daniel Shays: Collected Essays 1952–1972** **Collected Essays 1952–1972**	Random House 1972 Heinemann 1974	C C
27	**Burr** (novel)	Heinemann 1973	C
		Random House 1973	C
		Heinemann 1974	C
28	**Myron** (novel)	Random House 1974	C
		Heinemann 1975	C
29	**1876** (novel)	Random House 1976	C
		Heinemann 1976	C
30	**Matters of Fact and Fiction: Essays 1973–1976**	Random House 1977	C
		Heinemann 1977	C
31	**Great American Families and Others** (non-fiction)	Norton 1977	C
		Times 1977	C
32	**Kalki** (novel)	Random House 1978	C
		Heinemann 1978	C
33	**In a Yellow Wood** (novel)	Random House 1979	C
		Heinemann 1979	C

34 **Creation** (novel)	Random House 1981	C
	Heinemann 1981	C
35 **Duluth** (novel)	Random House 1983	C
	Heinemann 1983	C
36 **Lincoln** (novel)	Random House 1984	C
	Heinemann 1984	C
37 **Vidal in Venice** (travel)	Weidenfeld 1984	C
	Summit 1985	C
38 **Armageddon? Essays 1983–1987**	Deutsch 1987	C
39 **Empire** (novel)	Random House 1987	C
	Deutsch 1987	C
40 **At Home** (same as 38)	Random House 1988	C
41 **Hollywood** (novel)	Random House 1990	C
	Deutsch 1990	C
42 **View from the Diner's Club** (novel)	Random House 1991	C
	Deutsch 1991	C
43 **Live from Golgotha** (novel)	Random House 1992	C
	Deutsch 1992	C
44 **Screening History** (non-fiction)	Deutsch 1992	C

Bibliography:
Robert J. Stanton **Gore Vidal: A Primary and Secondary Bibliography** Hall 1978

Vonnegut, Kurt   Born in Indianpolis, 1922.

Vonnegut appealed very strongly to the young in the sixties, and, while retaining that following, he seems to be appealing to the next generation in quite the same way – and, it must be said, with quite the same books, for *Slaughterhouse-Five* remains the highlight, and is the sort of thing people *mean* when they talk about Vonnegut; they do *not* mean *Slapstick* and *Deadeye Dick*, jolly though these are, in their way. Prices for English editions remain quite low, but he is very much collected in America.

1 **Player Piano** (novel)	Scribner 1952	K
	Macmillan 1953	I
2 **The Sirens of Titan** (novel)	Fawcett 1959	H
	Gollancz 1962	G
3 **Canary in a Cathouse** (stories)	Fawcett 1961	H
4 **Mother Night** (novel)	Fawcett 1961	G
	Cape 1968	E
5 **Cat's Cradle** (novel)	Holt Rinehart 1963	F
	Gollancz 1963	D
6 **God Bless You, Mr Rosewater** (novel)	Holt Rinehart 1965	F
	Cape 1965	D
7 **Welcome to the Monkey House** (pieces)	Delacorte 1968	E

8 **Slaughterhouse-Five** (novel)	Delacorte 1969	H
	Cape 1970	F
9 **Happy Birthday, Wanda June** (play)	Delacorte 1971	C
	Cape 1973	C
10 **Between Time and Timbuctoo** (play)	Delacorte 1972	C
11 **Breakfast of Champions** (novel)	Delacorte 1973	D
	Cape 1973	C
12 **Wampeters, Foma, and Granfalloons: Opinions**	Delacorte 1974	C
	Cape 1975	C
13 **Slapstick** (novel)	Delacorte 1976	C
	Cape 1976	C
14 **The Eden Express** (novel)	Delacorte 1976	C
	Cape 1976	C
15 **Jailbird** (novel)	Delacorte 1979	C
	Cape 1979	C
16 **Palm Sunday** (autobiographical fragments)	Delacorte 1981	C
	Cape 1981	C
17 **Deadeye Dick** (novel)	Delacorte 1982	C
	Cape 1983	C
18 **Galapagos** (novel)	Delacorte 1985	C
	Cape 1985	C
19 **Bluebeard** (novel)	Delacorte 1987	C
	Cape 1988	C
20 **Hocus Pocus; Or, What's the Hurry, Son** (novel)	Putnam 1990	C
	Cape 1990	C
21 **Fates Worse Than Death: An Autobiographical Collage of the 1980's**	Putnam 1991	C
	Cape 1991	C

Bibliography:
Asa B. Pieratt Jnr and Jerome Klinkowitz **Kurt Vonnegut Jnr: A Descriptive Bibliography and Annotated Secondary Checklist** Shoe String Press 1974.

Wallace, Edgar   Born at Greenwich, 1875. Died 1932.

Apart from stories and plays, Wallace wrote an estimated 150 novels in twenty-seven years. Mercifully, there is a bibliography, which ought to be acquired if one is considering collecting the entire *œuvre* of this phenomenon. It is confined to British editions only, however. Of all his well-known books, I shall confine myself to recording just one – the most desirable, although not the most rare, for those wanting merely a representation of his work.

The Four Just Men	Tallis Press 1905	**I**

The true 1st has the £500 reward advert printed on the front of its yellow cover, and not the later coloured illustration. A fold-out frontis. should be present, as well as the all-important competition slip – situated at the back of the book. It is a perforated form intended to be removed, filled in, and sent up by the hopeful owner of the volume. Collectors, therefore, seek copies from the libraries of singularly uncompetitive people.

Waterhouse, Keith Born in Yorkshire, 1929.

Although Waterhouse has long been recognized as the journalist's journalist – indeed, the columnist supreme – he has never quite received the praise he deserves for his novels and screenplays. Quite why this should be so I cannot say – he continues to be innovative in his exquisite use of language (*Bimbo* is a tour de force) which critics tend not to like – maybe there is an unspoken suspicion that Waterhouse is maybe just too much of a clever dick, who is to say? Anyway, I think he is superb – eminently readable and collectable.

1	**The Café Royal:** **90 Years of Bohemia** (non-fiction) With Guy Deghy.	Hutchinson 1955	**C**
2	**How to Avoid Matrimony** (humour) (pseud. Herald Froy)	Muller 1957 Day 1959	**C** **C**
3	**There is a Happy Land** (novel)	Joseph 1957	**G**
4	**Britain's Voice Abroad** (essay)	Daily Mirror 1957	**C**
5	**The Future of Television** (essay)	Daily Mirror 1958	**C**
6	**How to Survive Matrimony** (humour) (pseud. Herald Froy)	Muller 1958	**C**
7	**The Joneses: How to Keep Up With Them** (humour) (pseud. Lee Gibb)	Muller 1959	**C**
8	**Billy Liar** (novel)	Joseph 1959 Norton 1960	**K** **F**
9	**Billy Liar** (play) With Willis Hall.	Joseph 1960 Norton 1960	**D** **C**
10	**Can This be Love?** (humour) (pseud. Herald Froy)	Muller 1960	**C**
11	**The Higher Jones** (humour) (pseud. Lee Gibb)	Muller 1961	**C**

Waterhouse

12	**Maybe You're Just Inferior** (humour) (pseud. Herald Froy)	Muller 1961	C
13	**Celebration** (play) With Willis Hall.	Joseph 1961	C
14	**Jubb** (novel)	Joseph 1963 Putnam 1964	D C
15	**All Things Bright and Beautiful** (play) With Willis Hall.	Joseph 1963	C
16	**The Sponge Room and Squat Betty** (plays) With Willis Hall.	Evans 1963	C
17	**England, Our England** (play) With Willis Hall.	Evans 1964	C
18	**Come Laughing Home** (play) With Willis Hall.	Evans 1965	C
19	**Help Stamp Out Marriage** (play) With Willis Hall.	French (US) 1966	C
	Say Who You Are	Evans 1967	C
20	**The Bucket Shop** (novel)	Joseph 1968	D
	Everything Must Go	Putnam 1969	C
21	**The Passing of the Third-Floor Buck** (*Punch* pieces)	Joseph 1974	C
22	**Saturday, Sunday, Monday** (play) Adaptation, with Willis Hall, from the play by Eduardo de Filippo.	Heinemann 1974	C
23	**Who's Who** (play) With Willis Hall.	French 1974	C
24	**Children's Day** (play) With Willis Hall.	French 1975	C
25	**Billy Liar on the Moon** (novel)	Joseph 1975 Putnam 1976	D C
26	**Mondays, Thursdays** (*Daily Mirror* pieces)	Joseph 1976	C
27	**Office Life** (novel)	Joseph 1978	C
28	**Whoops-A-Daisy** (play) With Willis Hall.	Evans 1978	C
29	**Filumena** (play) With Willis Hall.	French 1978	C
30	**The Television Adventures of Worzel Gummidge** With Willis Hall.	Puffin 1979	B
31	**Rhubarb, Rhubarb and Other Noises** (journalism)	Joseph 1979	C
32	**More Television Adventures of Worzel Gummidge** With Willis Hall.	Puffin 1980	B

33	**Worzel Gummidge at the Fair** With Willis Hall.	Puffin 1980	**B**
34	**Worzel Gummidge Goes to the Seaside** With Willis Hall.	Puffin 1980	**B**
35	**The Trials of Worzel Gummidge** With Willis Hall.	Puffin 1981	**B**
36	**Maggie Muggins: Or Spring in Earl's Court** (novel)	Joseph 1981	**C**
37	**Daily Mirror Style** (essay)	Daily Mirror 1981	**C**
38	**Worzel's Birthday** With Willis Hall.	Puffin 1981	**B**
39	**Worzel Gummidge and Aunt Sally** With Willis Hall.	Severn House 1982	**B**
40	**Fanny Peculiar** (*Punch* pieces)	Joseph 1983	**C**
41	**In the Mood** (novel)	Joseph 1983	**C**
42	**Mrs Pooter's Diary** (fiction)	Joseph 1983	**C**
43	**Thinks** (novel)	Joseph 1984	**C**
44	**Waterhouse at Large** (journalism)	Joseph 1985	**C**
45	**The Collected Letters of a Nobody** (a follow-on from 42)	Joseph 1986	**C**
46	**The Theory and Practice of Lunch** (humour)	Joseph 1986	**C**
47	**Worzel Gummidge Down Under** (juvenile, with Willis Hall)	Collins 1987	**B**
48	**Our Song** (novel)	Hodder & Stoughton 1988	**C**
49	**The Theory and Practice of Travel**	Hodder & Stoughton 1989	**C**
50	**Waterhouse on Newspaper Style** (expanded edition of 37)	Viking 1989	**C**
51	**Bimbo** (novel)	Hodder & Stoughton 1990	**C**
52	**English Our English (And How To Sing It** (prose)	Viking 1991	**C**
53	**Jeffrey Bernard is Unwell** (play)	French 1991	**C**
54	**Unsweet Charity** (novel)	Hodder & Stoughton 1992	**C**
55	**Jeffrey Bernard is Unwell** and **Other Plays** (also contains **Mr and Mrs Nobody** and **Bookends**)	Penguin 1992	**B**
56	**Sharon and Tracey and the Rest** (columns)	Hodder & Stoughton 1992	**B**

Waugh, Evelyn   Born in London, 1903. Died 1966.

Still one of the most respected and collected authors of all. This state I see to be permanent. Every time you read Waugh, he seems to get better and better – there is *always* more to be got from the book than the last time you read it. Similarly, a Waugh first edition seems always to be more expensive than the last time one saw a copy in a shop. There is no possibility that this trend will reverse.

Many of the following were preceded by limited, signed editions.

1	**The World to Come: A Poem in Three Cantos**	privately printed 1916	W
2	**PRB: An Essay on the Pre-Raphaelite Brotherhood**	privately printed 1926	T
3	**Decline and Fall** (novel)	Chapman & Hall 1928	Q
		Farrar 1929	L
4	**Rossetti** (biog.)	Duckworth 1928	N
		Dodd 1928	K
5	**Labels** (travel)	Duckworth 1930	M
	A Bachelor Abroad	Farrar 1932	K
6	**Vile Bodies** (novel)	Chapman & Hall 1930	O
		Farrar 1930	K
7	**Remote People** (travel)	Duckworth 1931	M
	They Were Still Dancing	Farrar 1932	K
8	**Black Mischief** (novel)	Chapman & Hall 1932	O
		Farrar 1932	K
9	**A Handful of Dust** (novel)	Chapman & Hall 1934	P
		Farrar 1934	K
10	**Ninety-Two Days** (travel)	Duckworth 1934	K
		Farrar 1934	H
11	**Edmund Campion** (biog.)	Longman 1935	J
		Sheed 1935	G
12	**Mr Loveday's Little Outing** (stories)	Chapman & Hall 1936	P
		Little, Brown 1936	L
13	**Waugh in Abyssinia** (travel)	Longman 1936	M
		Farrar 1936	I
14	**Scoop** (novel)	Chapman & Hall 1938	M
		Little, Brown 1938	J
15	**Robbery Under Law** (travel)	Chapman & Hall 1939	O
	Mexico: An Object Lesson	Little, Brown 1939	L
16	**Put Out More Flags** (novel)	Chapman & Hall 1942	M
		Little, Brown 1942	I
17	**Work Suspended** (unfinished novel)	Chapman & Hall 1942	M
18	**Brideshead Revisited** (novel)	Chapman & Hall 1945	N
		Little, Brown 1945	K
19	**When the Going Was Good** (travel) Selection from 5, 7, 10 and 13.	Duckworth 1946	H
		Little, Brown 1947	F

20 **Wine in Peace and War**	Saccone & Speed	**K**
	n.d. (1947)	
21 **Scott-King's Modern Europe**	Chapman & Hall 1947	**D**
(novel)	Little, Brown 1949	**C**
22 **The Loved One** (novel)	Chapman & Hall 1948	**E**
Preceded by publication in *Horizon*.	Little, Brown 1948	**C**
23 **Helena** (novel)	Chapman & Hall 1950	**D**
	Little, Brown 1950	**C**
24 **Men at Arms** (novel)	Chapman & Hall 1952	**H**
	Little, Brown 1952	**E**
25 **The Holy Places** (essays)	Queen Anne Press	**L**
This was published in an ordinary	1952	
edition at fifteen shillings, and in a		
limited, signed edition at three guineas		
(**R**).		
26 **Love Among the Ruins** (novel)	Chapman & Hall 1953	**D**
27 **Officers and Gentlemen** (novel)	Chapman & Hall 1955	**G**
	Little, Brown 1955	**D**
28 **The Ordeal of Gilbert Pinfold**	Chapman & Hall 1957	**D**
(novel)	Little, Brown 1957	**C**
29 **Ronald Knox** (biog.)	Chapman & Hall 1959	**D**
	Little, Brown 1960	**C**
30 **A Tourist in Africa** (travel)	Chapman & Hall 1960	**D**
	Little, Brown 1960	**C**
31 **Unconditional Surrender** (novel)	Chapman & Hall 1961	**F**
The End of the Battle	Little, Brown 1961	**D**
Together with 24 and 27 it forms		
the *Sword of Honour* trilogy.		
32 **Basil Seal Rides Again** (novel)	Chapman & Hall 1963	**L**
	Little, Brown 1963	**I**
33 **A Little Learning** (autobiog.)	Chapman & Hall 1964	**D**
	Little, Brown 1964	**C**
34 **Diaries**	Weidenfeld 1976	**D**
Large parts of this first appeared in the	Little, Brown 1976	**D**
Observer Colour Magazine for 25 March		
1973, and for the succeeding seven		
issues. *The Sunday Times* published		
two more extracts immediately prior to		
book publication.		
35 **A Little Order** (journalism)	Methuen 1977	**D**
	Little, Brown 1981	**C**
36 **The Letters of Evelyn Waugh**	Weidenfeld 1980	**D**
	Ticknor & Fields 1980	**D**
37 **Charles Ryder's Schooldays**	Little, Brown 1982	**D**
and **Other Stories**		
This recently discovered story, relating		
to the narrator in **Brideshead**		
Revisited, was originally published in		

the *Times Literary Supplement*, but was
not published in book form in the UK.

38	**The Essays, Articles and**	Methuen 1983	**D**
	Reviews of Evelyn Waugh	Little, Brown 1984	**D**

Wesker, Arnold Born in London, 1932.

Still notable for a clutch of modern classics, listed below – although Wesker
has continued to produce. These, however, are the collectable ones:

1	**Chicken Soup with Barley** (play)	Penguin 1959	**C**
	This was contained in **New English Dramatists.**		
2	**Roots** (play)	Penguin 1959	**C**
3	**I'm Talking about Jerusalem** (play)	Penguin 1960	**C**
	1, 2 and 3 form the Wesker trilogy.		
4	**The Wesker Trilogy** (plays)	Cape 1960	**D**
	Contains 1, 2 and 3, for the first time in hardback.	Random House 1961	**C**
5	**The Kitchen** (play)	Penguin 1960	**B**
	This was contained in **New English Dramatists 2.** An expanded edition was published in 1962 by Cape, and by Random House.		
6	**Chips with Everything** (play)	Cape 1962	**D**
		Random House 1963	**C**

Wesley, Mary Born in Berkshire, 1912.

Quite suddenly one of the most popular authors in the country, and newly
collectable. Wesley published her first novel when she was nearly sixty (there
is hope for us all) and the humour, wisdom and sometimes rather wicked wit
found a ready audience. An author to gather up *now*.

1	**The Sixth Seal** (novel)	Macdonald 1969	**F**
		Stein & Day 1971	**C**
2	**Jumping the Queue** (novel)	Macmillan 1983	**D**
		Penguin US 1988	**C**
3	**Haphazard House** (novel)	Dent 1983	**D**
4	**The Camomile Lawn** (novel)	Macmillan 1984	**D**
		Summit 1985	**C**
5	**Harnessing Peacocks** (novel)	Macmillan 1985	**D**
		Scribner 1986	**C**
6	**The Vacillations of Poppy Carew** (novel)	Macmillan 1986	**C**
		Penguin US 1988	**B**

7 **Not That Sort of Girl** (novel)	Macmillan 1987	C
	Viking 1988	C
8 **Second Fiddle** (novel)	Macmillan 1988	C
	Viking 1989	C
9 **A Sensible Life** (novel)	Bantam UK 1990	C
	Viking 1990	C
10 **A Dubious Legacy** (novel)	Bantam UK 1992	C
	Viking 1992	C
11 **The Mary Wesley Omnibus**	Macmillan 1992	C
(contains nos. 2, 4 & 5)		

Wheatley, Dennis   Born in 1897. Died 1977.

Wheatley did not publish a book until 1933, and although today his Black Magic novels are of interest – particularly the earlier ones – prime interest is reserved for the Dossiers. In collaboration with J.G. Links, Wheatley published four of these, beginning with *Murder off Miami* in 1936. They were, quite simply, a totally new and appealing way of presenting a crime story – as a police dossier, complete with typescript pages, facsimile telegrams, notes, postcards, and clues – such as strands of hair, fingerprints, and spent matches; all this was bound in wrapps, and tied with red ribbon. A sealed compartment at the rear could be slit open to reveal the solution to the crime – and, not unnaturally, very few survive with the seal intact! They were published, unbelievably, at 3/6d – or $17\frac{1}{2}$p. Today fine copies are Grade **H**, and hard to find. Wheatley himself foresaw this, for the rear cover of *Murder off Miami* reads: '*Keep this carefully*. It is a First Edition of the first Crime Story ever presented in this way. Should others follow, it is possible that an undamaged copy of "Murder off Miami" may be of considerable interest one day.' They are undated, but later impressions announce '*N*th Thousand' on the cover.

The Dossiers:		
1 **Murder off Miami**	Hutchinson 1936	H
File on Bolitho Lane	Morrow 1936	H
2 **Who Killed Robert Prentice?**	Hutchinson 1937	H
File on Robert Prentice	Greenberg 1937	H
3 **The Mallinsay Massacre**	Hutchinson 1938	F
4 **Herewith the Clues**	Hutchinson 1939	F
Below is a short selection of Wheatley's Black Magic novels.		
5 **The Devil Rides Out**	Hutchinson 1934	D
6 **To the Devil – a Daughter**	Hutchinson 1953	D
7 **The Satanist**	Hutchinson 1960	D

White, Patrick   Born in London 1912. Australian. Died 1990.

Although White is read and collected in his own right as a very considerable author, there is no doubt that there is great nationalistic feeling, in that many Australians collect him simply because he is *their* Nobel prize-winner. Nothing wrong with that – except that very often they appear to be interested in no one else at all.

1	**The Ploughman and Other Poems**	Beacon Press (Australia) 1935	O
2	**Happy Valley** (novel)	Harrap 1939	M
		Viking 1940	J
3	**The Living and the Dead** (novel)	Routledge 1941	J
		Viking 1941	J
4	**The Aunt's Story** (novel)	Routledge 1948	I
		Viking 1948	I
5	**The Tree of Man** (novel)	Viking 1955	G
		Eyre & Spottiswoode 1956	F
6	**Voss** (novel)	Viking 1957	E
		Eyre & Spottiswoode 1957	D
7	**Riders in the Chariot** (novel)	Viking 1961	D
		Eyre & Spottiswoode 1961	C
8	**The Burnt Ones** (stories)	Viking 1964	D
		Eyre & Spottiswoode 1964	C
9	**Four Plays** Cont. **The Ham Funeral, The Season at Sarsparilla, A Cheery Soul** and **Night on Bald Mountain.**	Eyre & Spottiswoode 1965 Viking 1966	C C
10	**The Solid Mandala** (novel)	Viking 1966	D
		Eyre & Spottiswoode 1966	C
11	**The Vivisector** (novel)	Viking 1970	D
		Cape 1970	C
12	**The Eye of the Storm** (novel)	Cape 1973	C
		Viking 1974	C
13	**The Cockatoos:** **Short Novels and Stories**	Cape 1974 Viking 1975	C C
14	**A Fringe of Leaves** (novel)	Cape 1976	C
		Viking 1976	C
15	**Big Toys** (play)	Currency Press (Australia) 1978	D

16 **The Twyborn Affair** (novel)	Cape 1979	C
	Viking 1980	C
17 **The Night of the Prowler** (play)	Penguin (Australia) 1979	C
18 **Flaws in the Glass: A Self-Portrait**	Cape 1981	C
	Viking 1982	C
19 **Memoirs of Many in One** (novel)	Cape 1986	C
	Viking 1986	C
20 **Three Uneasy Pieces** (novel)	Cape 1988	C
21 **Patrick White Speaks** (non-fiction)	Cape 1990	C

Bibliography: Patrick White by Alan Lawson (OUP Australia 1974)

White, T.H.   Born in India, 1906. Died 1964.

Still a very popular author with a surprisingly large cross-section of collectors. Not easy to collect, though – in fact, not often *seen*, except for the same old few, this relative scarcity and ubiquity being reflected in the prices below.

1 **Loved Helen and Other Poems**	Chatto & Windus 1929	N
	Viking 1929	L
2 **The Green Bay Tree** (verse)	Heffer 1929	M
3 **Dead Mr Nixon** (novel) With R. McNair Scott.	Cassell 1931	N
4 **Darkness at Pemberley** (novel)	Gollancz 1932	L
	Century (US) 1933	I
5 **They Winter Abroad** (novel) Under the pseudonym James Aston.	Chatto & Windus 1932	M
	Viking 1932	K
6 **First Lesson** (novel) Under the pseudonym James Aston.	Chatto & Windus 1932	L
	Knopf 1933	I
7 **Farewell Victoria** (novel)	Collins 1933	J
	Smith & Haas 1934	G
8 **Earth Stopped: Or Mr Marx's Sporting Tour** (novel)	Collins 1934	J
	Putnam 1935	G
9 **Gone to Ground** (novel)	Collins 1935	H
	Putnam 1935	F
10 **England Have My Bones** (non-fiction)	Collins 1936	H
	Macmillan 1936	F
11 **Burke's Steerage: Or, the Amateur Gentleman's Introduction to Noble Sports and Pastimes**	Collins 1938	G
	Putnam 1939	E
12 **The Sword in the Stone** (juvenile)	Collins 1938	O
	Putnam 1939	L
13 **The Witch in the Wood** (juvenile)	Putnam 1939	M
	Collins 1940	K

14	**The Ill-Made Knight** (juvenile) 12, 13 and 14 are illustrated by the author.	Putnam 1940 Collins 1941	K J
15	**Mistress Masham's Repose** (juvenile)	Putnam 1946 Cape 1947	G F
16	**The Elephant and the Kangaroo** (novel)	Putnam 1947 Cape 1948	F E
17	**The Age of Scandal** (non-fiction)	Cape 1950 Putnam 1950	E D
18	**The Goshawk** (non-fiction)	Cape 1951 Putnam 1952	E D
19	**The Scandalmonger** (non-fiction)	Cape 1952 Putnam 1952	E D
20	**The Book of Beasts** Edited and translated by T.H.W.	Cape 1954 Putnam 1955	E D
21	**The Master: An Adventure Story** (juvenile)	Cape 1957 Putnam 1957	E D
22	**The Once and Future King** This, the complete Arthurian epic, comprises 12 with two new chapters, 13 rewritten and bearing the title **The Queen of Air and Darkness**, 14, largely unaltered, and **The Candle in the Wind**, published for the first time.	Collins 1958 Putnam 1958	E D
23	**The Godstone and the Blackymor** (non-fiction)	Cape 1959 Putnam 1959	D C
24	**America at Last: The American Journal of T.H. White**	Putnam 1965	C
25	**The White/Garnett Letters** Correspondence edited by David Garnett.	Cape 1968 Viking 1968	C C
26	**The Book of Merlyn** (novel) This concludes 22.	University of Texas Press 1977	D
27	**The Maharajah** and **Other Stories**	Putnam 1981	C
28	**Letters to a Friend:** **The Correspondence Between T.H. White and L.J. Potts**	Putnam 1982	C

Biography:
Sylvia Townsend Warner **T.H. White: A Biography** Cape/Chatto 1967. This includes a bibliography of unpublished writings.

Williams, Nigel Born in Cheshire, 1948.

An amusing and highly accomplished writer who is also a television producer – there can't be many. Becoming much better known as his output grows more regular, but still not too hard to gather. Williams may go down in history as the man who single-handedly rescued Wimbledon from the Wombles.

1 **My Life Closed Twice** (novel)	Secker & Warburg 1978	**E**
2 **Jack Be Nimble** (novel)	Secker & Warburg 1980	**D**
3 **Star Turn** (novel)	Faber 1985	**D**
4 **Witchcraft** (novel)	Faber 1987	**C**
5 **Black Magic** (story)	Hutchinson 1988	**B**
6 **The Wimbledon Poisoner** (novel)	Faber 1990	**C**
	Faber Inc US 1990	**C**
7 **They Came From SW19** (novel)	Faber 1992	**C**

Williams, Tennessee Born in Columbus, Mississippi, 1911. Died 1983. Pseudonym for Thomas Williams.

Author of over seventy books, ninety per cent of them plays, the highlights of which are listed below. A unique writer who brought us a new form of language – the inarticulacy of the misfit, this catching the feel of the fifties very well, and often memorably played by Brando in the moody black-and-white films.

1 **The Glass Menagerie** (play)	Random House 1945	**G**
	Lehmann 1948	**E**
2 **A Streetcar Named Desire** (play)	New Directions 1947	**G**
	Lehmann 1949	**E**
3 **The Roman Spring of Mrs Stone** (novel)	New Directions 1950	**E**
	Lehmann 1950	**E**
4 **Cat on a Hot Tin Roof** (play)	New Directions 1955	**F**
	Secker 1956	**D**
5 **Sweet Bird of Youth** (play)	New Directions 1959	**E**
	Secker 1961	**D**
6 **The Milk Train Doesn't Stop Here Anymore** (play)	New Directions 1964	**D**
	Secker 1964	**C**

Wilson, A.N. Born in Staffordshire, 1950.

Incredibly prolific and diverse (fifteen new titles since the last edition of this book) but still something of a puzzle to readers, critics and collectors alike. Certainly the early novels are sought after and elusive, but you will see no queues forming for *Hazel the Guinea-Pig* at one extreme, nor *The Life of John Milton* at the other. I think that with A.N. Wilson selectivity is the key.

Wilson, A.N.

1 **The Sweets of Pimlico** (novel)	Secker & Warburg 1977	**H**
2 **Unguarded Hours** (novel)	Secker & Warburg 1978	**G**
3 **Kindly Light** (novel)	Secker & Warburg 1979	**E**
4 **The Healing Art** (novel)	Secker & Warburg 1980	**D**
5 **The Laird of Abbottsford: A View of Walter Scott** (biography)	OUP 1980	**C**
6 **Who Was Oswald Fish?** (novel)	Secker & Warburg 1981	**C**
7 **Wise Virgin** (novel)	Secker & Warburg 1982	**C**
	Viking 1983	**B**
8 **The Life of John Milton** (biography)	OUP 1983	**C**
9 **Scandal** (novel)	Hamish Hamilton 1983	**C**
	Viking 1984	**C**
10 **Hilaire Belloc** (biography)	Hamish Hamilton 1984	**C**
	Atheneum 1984	**C**
11 **Lilibet: An Account in Verse of the Early Years of the Queen Until the Time of Her Accession**	Blond & Briggs 1984	**B**
12 **How Can We Know? An Essay on the Christian Religion**	Hamish Hamilton 1985	**B**
	Atheneum 1985	**B**
13 **Gentlemen in England** (novel)	Hamish Hamilton 1985	**C**
	Viking 1986	**B**
14 **Love Unknown** (novel)	Hamish Hamilton 1986	**C**
	Viking 1987	**B**
15 **The Church in Crisis** (essay) With Charles Moore and Gavin Stamp.	Hodder & Stoughton 1986	**B**
16 **Stray** (juvenile)	Walker Books 1987	**B**
	Orchard 1989	**B**
17 **Landscape in France** (travel)	Elm Tree 1987	**C**
	St Martin's Press 1988	**C**
18 **Penfriends from Porlock: Essay and Reviews 1977–1986**	Hamish Hamilton 1988	**C**
	Norton 1989	**C**
19 **Incline Our Hearts** (novel)	Hamish Hamilton 1988	**C**
	Viking 1989	**B**
20 **Tolstoy: A Biography**	Hamish Hamilton 1988	**C**
	Norton 1988	**C**
21 **The Tabitha Stories** (juvenile)	Walker Books 1988	**B**
22 **Tabitha** (same as 21)	Orchard US 1989	**B**
23 **Hazel the Guinea-pig** (juvenile)	Walker Books 1989	**B**
24 **A Bottle in the Smoke** (novel)	Sinclair-Stevenson 1989	**C**
	Viking 1990	**B**
25 **Eminent Victorians** (non-fiction)	BBC 1989	**C**
	Norton 1990	**C**
26 **C.S. Lewis: A Biography**	Collins 1990	**C**
	Norton 1990	**C**
27 **Against Religion** (essay)	Chatto & Windus 1990	**B**

28 **Daughters of Albion** (novel)	Sinclair-Stevenson 1991	**B**
	Viking 1991	**B**
29 **Jesus** (biography)	Sinclair-Stevenson 1992	**C**
30 **The Faber Book of Church and Clergy** (edited by)	Faber 1992	**C**

Wilson, Angus   Born in Sussex, 1913. Died 1991.

The great reflector of every nuance of the English and their curious personal habits died at a point when his fine body of work was being rediscovered and re-evaluated. Last year's excellent TV adaptation of **Anglo-Saxon Attitudes** gave a great boost to Wilson's reputation and sales, and now he is more collectable than ever.

1 **The Wrong Set and Other Stories**	Secker & Warburg 1949	**J**
	Morrow 1950	**F**
2 **Such Darling Dodos and Other Stories**	Secker & Warburg 1950	**I**
	Morrow 1951	**F**
3 **Emile Zola** (non-fiction)	Secker & Warburg 1952	**E**
	Morrow 1952	**C**
4 **Hemlock and After** (novel)	Secker & Warburg 1952	**D**
	Viking 1952	**C**
5 **For Whom the Cloche Tolls** (essay) With Philippe Jullian.	Methuen 1953	**D**
6 **The Mulberry Bush** (play)	Secker & Warburg 1956	**C**
7 **Anglo-Saxon Attitudes** (novel)	Secker & Warburg 1956	**D**
	Viking 1956	**C**
8 **A Bit Off the Map and Other Stories**	Secker & Warburg 1957	**D**
	Viking 1957	**C**
9 **The Middle Age of Mrs Eliot** (novel)	Secker & Warburg 1958	**D**
	Viking 1959	**C**
10 **The Old Men at the Zoo** (novel)	Secker & Warburg 1961	**D**
	Viking 1961	**C**
11 **The Wild Garden: or, Speaking of Writing** (non-fiction)	University of California Press 1963	**C**
	Secker & Warburg 1963	**C**
12 **Tempo: The Impact of Television on the Arts** (non-fiction)	Studio Vista 1964	**D**
	Dufour 1966	**C**
13 **Late Call** (novel)	Secker & Warburg 1964	**D**
	Viking 1965	**C**
14 **No Laughing Matter** (novel)	Secker & Warburg 1967	**C**
	Viking 1967	**C**
15 **Death Dance: 25 Stories**	Viking 1969	**C**
16 **The World of Charles Dickens** (non-fiction)	Secker & Warburg 1970	**C**
	Viking 1970	**C**

Wilson, Colin

17	**As If by Magic** (novel)	Secker & Warburg 1973	C
		Viking 1973	C
18	**The Strange Ride of Rudyard Kipling** (biography)	Secker & Warburg 1977	C
		Viking 1978	C
19	**Setting the World on Fire** (novel)	Secker & Warburg 1980	C
		Viking 1980	C
20	**Diversity and Depth in Fiction: Selected Critical Writings**	Secker & Warburg 1983	C
		Viking 1983	C
21	**Reflections in a Writer's Eye**	Secker & Warburg 1986	C
		Viking 1986	C
22	**Collected Stories**	Secker & Warburg 1987	C
		Viking 1987	C

Wilson, Colin   Born in Leicester, 1931.

It is a brave woman or man who sets about forming a complete Colin Wilson – by the time it was catalogued he would have published more. At least twenty new titles have appeared since the last edition of this book, so at least the *scope* is there; the classic, of course, is still his very first – *The Outsider*.

1	**The Outsider** (philosophy)	Gollancz 1956	G
		Houghton Mifflin 1956	E
2	**Religion and the Rebel** (non-fiction)	Gollancz 1957	D
		Houghton Mifflin 1957	C
3	**The Age of Defeat** (non-fiction)	Gollancz 1959	C
	The Stature of Man	Houghton Mifflin 1959	C
4	**Ritual in the Dark** (novel)	Gollancz 1960	C
		Houghton Mifflin 1960	C
5	**Adrift in Soho** (novel)	Gollancz 1961	F
		Houghton Mifflin 1961	D
6	**Encyclopedia of Murder** (non-fiction) With Patricia Pitman.	Barker 1961	G
		Putnam 1962	E
7	**The Strength to Dream: Literature and the Imagination** (non-fiction)	Gollancz 1962	D
		Houghton Mifflin 1962	C
8	**Origins of the Sexual Impulse** (non-fiction)	Barker 1963	C
		Putnam 1963	C
9	**The World of Violence** (novel)	Gollancz 1963	E
	The Violent World of Hugh Green	Houghton Mifflin 1963	D
10	**Man Without a Shadow** (novel)	Barker 1963	E
	The Sex Diary of Gerard Sorme	Dial Press 1963	D
11	**Necessary Doubt** (novel)	Barker 1964	E
		Simon & Schuster 1964	D
12	**Rasputin and the Fall of the Romanovs** (non-fiction)	Barker 1964	E
		Farrar Straus 1964	D

13	**Brandy of the Damned: Discoveries of a Musical Eclectic Chords and Discords: Purely Personal Opinions on Music** A supplemented edition, entitled **Colin Wilson on Music**, was published by Pan in 1967 (**B**).	Baker 1964 Atheneum 1966	D C
14	**Beyond the Outsider: the Philosophy of the Future**	Barker 1965 Houghton Mifflin 1965	D C
15	**Eagle and Earwig** (essay)	Barker 1965	C
16	**The Glass Cage** (novel)	Barker 1966 Random House 1967	C C
17	**Introduction to the New Existentialism**	Hutchinson 1966 Houghton Mifflin 1967	C C
18	**Sex and the Intelligent Teenager** (non-fiction)	Arrow 1966	C
19	**Voyage to a Beginning** (autobiog.)	Woolf 1966 Crown 1969	C C
20	**The Mind Parasites** (novel)	Barker 1967 Arkham House 1967	D C
21	**The Philosopher's Stone** (novel)	Barker 1969 Crown 1971	C C
22	**Bernard Shaw: A Reassessment** (non-fiction)	Hutchinson 1969 Atheneum 1969	C C
23	**A Casebook of Murder** (non-fiction)	Frewin 1969 Cowles 1970	C C
24	**The Killer** (novel) **Lingard**	NEL 1970 Crown 1970	C C
25	**The God of the Labyrinth** (novel) **The Hedonists**	Hart-Davis 1970 NAL 1971	C C
26	**Strindberg** (play)	Calder 1970 Random House 1971	C C
27	**Poetry and Mysticism** (non-fiction)	Hutchinson 1970 City Lights 1970	C C
28	**The Strange Genius of David Lindsay** (non-fiction) With E.H. Visiak and J.B. Pick.	Barker 1970	C
29	**The Black Room** (novel)	Weidenfeld 1971	C
30	**The Occult: A History**	Hodder & Stoughton 1971 Random House 1971	C C
31	**New Pathways in Psychology**	Gollancz 1972 Taplinger 1972	C C
32	**Order of Assassins: The Psychology of Murder** (non-fiction)	Hart-Davis 1972	C
33	**L'Amour: The Way of Love** (non-fiction)	Crown (NY) 1972	C

Wilson, Colin

34	**Strange Powers** (non-fiction)	Latimer 1973	C
		Random House 1975	C
35	**Tree by Tolkien** (essay)	Covent Garden Press 1973	E
		Capra Press 1974	C
36	**Hermann Hesse** (essay)	Village Press (UK) 1974	C
		Leaves of Grass Press 1974	C
37	**William Reich** (essay)	Village Press 1974	C
		Leaves of Grass Press 1974	C
38	**Jorge Luis Borges** (essay)	Village Press 1974	C
		Leaves of Grass Press 1974	C
39	**The Schoolgirl Murder Case** (novel)	Granada 1974	D
		Crown 1974	C
40	**A Book of Booze** (non-fiction)	Gollancz 1974	C
41	**Mysterious Powers** (non-fiction) This was republished in America by Doubleday in the same year as **They Had Strange Powers** (**B**).	Aldus 1975	C
		Danbury Press 1975	C
42	**The Craft of the Novel** (non-fiction)	Gollancz 1975	D
43	**The Space Vampires** (novel)	Granada 1976	C
		Random House 1976	C
44	**Enigmas and Mysteries** (non-fiction)	Aldus 1976	C
		Doubleday 1976	C
45	**The Geller Phenomenon** (non-fiction)	Aldus 1976	C
46	**Mysteries: An Investigation into the Occult, the Paranormal and the Supernatural**	Hodder & Stoughton 1978	C
		Putnam 1978	C
47	**Science Fiction as Existentialism** (essay)	Bran's Head Press 1978	C
48	**The Search for the Real Arthur** (essay)	Bossiney 1979	C
49	**Starseekers** (non-fiction)	Hodder & Stoughton 1980	C
		Doubleday 1981	C
50	**Anti-Sartre, With an Essay on Camus**	Borgo Press (US) 1980	D
51	**The War against Sleep: The Philosophy of Gurdjieff**	Aquarian Press 1980	C
52	**Frankenstein's Castle** (story)	Ashgrove Press 1980	C
53	**The Quest for Wilhelm Reich** (non-fiction)	Granada 1981	C
		Doubleday 1981	C
54	**Poltergeist** (novel)	NEL 1981	C
		Putman 1982	C

55 **Witches** (non-fiction) Illustrated by Una Woodruff.	Dragon's World 1982	C
56 **Access to Inner Worlds** (non-fiction)	Rider 1983	C
57 **Encyclopaedia of Modern Murder 1962–1982** With Donald Seaman.	Barker 1983 Putnam 1984	C C
58 **Psychic Detectives** (non-fiction)	Pan 1984 Mercury House 1985	C C
59 **A Criminal History of Mankind** (non-fiction)	Granada 1984 Putnam 1984	C C
60 **Lord of the Underworld: Jung and The Twentieth Century** (non-fiction)	Aquarian Press 1984	C
61 **The Janus Murder case** (novel)	Granada 1984	C
62 **The Essential Colin Wilson**	Harrap 1985 Celestial Arts 1987	C C
63 **The Personality Surgeon** (novel)	NEL 1985 Mercury House 1986	C C
64 **The Bicameral Critic** (non-fiction)	Ashgrove Press 1985 Salem House 1985	C C
65 **Rudolf Steiner: The Man and His Vision** (non-fiction)	Aquarian Press 1985	C
66 **West Country Mysteries** (non-fiction)	Bossiney 1985	C
67 **Afterlife: An Investigation of the Evidence for Life After Death** (non-fiction)	Harrap 1985 Doubleday 1987	C C
68 **Scandal! An Encyclopaedia** With Donald Seaman.	Weidenfeld & Nicolson 1986 Stein & Day 1986	C C
69 **Poetry and Mysticism** (non-fiction)	City Lights US 1986	C
70 **An Essay on the 'New' Existentialism**	Pauper's Press 1986 Borgo Press 1988	C C
71 **The Laurel and Hardy Theory of Consciousness** (non-fiction)	Briggs US 1986	C
72 **The Tower** (novel)	Grafton 1987	C
73 **The Delta** (novel)	Grafton 1987 Ace 1990	C C
74 **The Encyclopaedia of Unsolved Mysteries** With Damon Wilson.	Harrap 1987 Contemporary Books 1987	C C
75 **Jack the Ripper: Summing Up and Verdict** (non-fiction) With Robin Odell.	Bantam 1987	C
76 **Aleister Crowley: The Nature of the Beast** (non-fiction)	Aquarian Press 1987 Borgo Press 1989	C C
77 **The Musician as 'Outsider'** (non-fiction)	Pauper's Press 1987 Borgo Press 1989	C C
78 **The Desert** (same as 72)	Ace US 1988	C
79 **The Magician from Siberia** (novel)	Hale 1988	C

80 **The Misfits: A Study of Sexual Outsiders** (non-fiction)	Grafton 1988	C
	Carroll & Graf 1989	C
81 **Beyond the Occult** (non-fiction)	Bantam 1988	C
	Carroll & Graf 1989	C
82 **Autobiographical Reflections**	Pauper's Press 1988	C
83 **Lord Halifax's Ghost Book** (non-fiction)	Bellew 1989	C
84 **Written in Blood: A History of Forensic Detection**	Equation 1989	C
	Warner 1991	C
85 **Existentially Speaking: Essays on the Philosophy of Literature**	Borgo Press 1989	C
86 **The Untethered Mind** (essays)	Ashgrove Press 1989	C
87 **The Decline and Fall of Leftism**	Pauper's Press 1989	C
88 **Serial Killers** (non-fiction) With Donald Seaman.	W.H. Allen 1990	C
89 **Murder in the 1930's** (non-fiction)	Robinson 1992	C

Bibliography
The Work of Colin Wilson: An Annotated Bibliography and Guide
by Colin Stanley, Borgo Press US 1989

Winterson, Jeanette   Born in Lancashire, 1959.

A woman to watch: quite possibly the Muriel Spark *de nos jours*. Preceding her drily comical *Oranges Are Not the Only Fruit* (yes, titles *are* getting weird, these days) Winterson published one of these mandatory 'How-To-Be-A-Woman-And-Live-To-The-Full-And-Kick-Men-God-Help-Us-All' sorts of books, which we shall ignore. Below is the fiction.

1 **Oranges Are Not the Only Fruit** (novel)	Pandora Press 1985	F
	Atlantic Monthly Press 1987	C
2 **Boating for Beginners** (novel)	Methuen 1985	D
3 **The Passion** (novel)	Bloomsbury 1987	C
	Atlantic Monthly Press 1988	C
4 **Sexing the Cherry** (novel)	Bloomsbury 1989	C
5 **Written on the Body** (novel)	Cape 1992	C

Wodehouse, P.G.   Born in Guildford, 1881. Died 1975.

That Plum is (along with Graham Greene) the most collected author in Britain amply demonstrates that we have not yet lost our sense of proportion, let alone humour. It's the sheer what'd'you-m'call-it of the feller that makes him so utterly, well – you know what I mean, don't you now?

Mind you, Wodehouse collectors are fussy coves. It is true to say that there is almost no such thing as a common first edition *fine in dust wrapper*, but an awful lot of titles come up in fair-to-middling (i.e. nasty) condition that fail to find buyers because everyone has the *book*, but in similarly horrid condition. This rule applies particularly to the books of the late forties and early fifties: *Cocktail Time, Full Moon, Spring Fever*, etc. But the early stuff – and these days, that means pre-war – continues to be sought-after even *without* the much-vaunted dust wrappers, but the values double-to-quintuple *with* them. Whether you think this is sane or not, is up to yourself; if it is *not* sane, then I am privileged to know an awful lot of loonies. The *prehistoric* stuff, however (pre-1918) is worth fortunes. Each one is the equivalent of roughly one-and-a-half gold bricks, but is infinitely more fun. Collect him: you only live once. And just think – if the whole boom collapses overnight, and all books are declared *worthless* – you'll be one of the few who still has something to laugh about.

Finally, a word or two about pronunciation: *Psmith*, Plum informs us in characteristic style, is pronounced with a silent 'p', as in 'pshrimp', *Ukridge* is pronounced with the 'U' as in 'U' and 'non-U', and Wodehouse is pronounced 'Wood house' (as in log cabin) and *not*, as one still hears, 'Woe-dowse'. Learn.

1	**The Pothunters** (novel)	Black 1902	**R**
	This first book is bound in blue, with silver ornament, and not the later pictorial cover. No adverts. Very, very scarce.	Macmillan (US) 1924	**M**
2	**A Prefect's Uncle** (novel)	Black 1903	**Q**
		Macmillan 1924	**K**
3	**Tales of St Austin's** (stories)	Black 1903	**P**
		Macmillan 1923	**J**
4	**The Gold Bat** (novel)	Black 1904	**Q**
		Macmillan 1923	**K**
5	**William Tell Told Again**	Black 1904	**N**
	This retelling of the classic tale is scarce in any edition, but the 1st may be recognized by the date on the t/p, and the absence of the publisher's address.		
6	**The Head of Kay's** (novel)	Black 1905	**P**
		Macmillan 1922	**K**
7	**Love Among the Chickens** (novel)	Newnes 1906	**R**
	A 'Popular Edition' revised and entirely rewritten by the author was reissued by Jenkins in 1921 (**E**).	Circle Publishing Co. 1909	**P**
8	**The White Feather** (novel)	Black 1907	**Q**
		Macmillan 1922	**J**
9	**Not George Washington** (novel) With Herbert Westbrook.	Cassell 1907	**R**

10 **The Globe By the Way Book**   Globe 1908   **V**
Again written with Herbert
Westbrook, this paperback was a
compilation of the 'By the Way'
columns from the *Globe* paper.

11 **The Swoop** (novel)   Alston Rivers 1909   **S**
A pictorially wrappered paperback.

12 **Mike** (novel)   Black 1909   **Q**
The second part of this novel was   Macmillan 1924   **M**
reissued as **Enter Psmith** Black 1935
(**H**); the whole novel was then revised
and reissued in two volumes – **Mike
At Wrykn (H)** and **Mike and
Psmith (H)** Jenkins 1953.

13 **The Intrusion of Jimmy** (novel)   Watt (US) 1910   **O**
   A Gentleman of Leisure   Alston Rivers 1910   **O**
Not to be confused with the Newnes
reissue of 1911.

14 **Psmith in the City** (novel)   Black 1910   **O**
15 **The Prince and Betty** (novel)   Watt 1912   **M**
16 **The Prince and Betty** (novel)   Mills & Boon 1912   **O**
An almost entirely different book to 15.

17 **The Little Nugget** (novel)   Methuen 1913   **O**
      Watt 1914   **M**
18 **The Man Upstairs** (stories)   Methuen 1914   **O**
19 **Something New** (novel)   Appleton (US) 1915   **M**
   Something Fresh   Methuen 1915   **M**
20 **Psmith Journalist** (novel)   Black 1915   **O**
Another version of 15.

21 **Uneasy Money** (novel)   Appleton 1916   **N**
      Methuen 1917   **L**
22 **Piccadilly Jim** (novel)   Dodd Mead 1917   **L**
Wodehouse's first book with Jenkins.   Jenkins 1918   **K**
23 **The Man with Two Left Feet**   Methuen 1917   **M**
   (stories)   Burt 1933   **F**
24 **My Man Jeeves** (stories)   Newnes 1919   **P**
The first Jeeves title. This small red
volume was issued in Newnes 1/9d
Novel Series.

25 **Their Mutual Child** (novel)   Boni & Liveright 1919   **K**
   The Coming of Bill   Jenkins 1920   **I**
26 **A Damsel in Distress** (novel)   Doran 1919   **J**
      Jenkins 1919   **J**
27 **The Little Warrior** (novel)   Doran 1920   **J**
   Jill the Reckless   Jenkins 1921   **J**
28 **Indiscretions of Archie** (stories)   Jenkins 1921   **K**
      Doran 1921   **K**

29 **The Clicking of Cuthbert** (stories)	Jenkins 1922	J
The 1st lists only eight titles on the verso of the half-title.		
Golf Without Tears	Doran 1924	I
30 **Three Men and a Maid** (novel)	Doran 1922	K
The Girl on the Boat	Jenkins 1922	I
English edition revised from original American.		
31 **The Adventures of Sally** (novel)	Jenkins 1922	L
Dated 1923.		
Mostly Sally	Doran 1923	J
32 **The Inimitable Jeeves** (stories)	Jenkins 1923	J
This must list ten titles on the verso of the half-title.		
Jeeves	Doran 1923	I
33 **Leave it to Psmith** (novel)	Jenkins 1923	I
	Doran 1924	H
34 **Ukridge** (stories)	Jenkins 1924	K
Thirteen titles must appear on the verso of the half-title.		
He Rather Enjoyed It	Doran 1926	H
35 **Bill the Conqueror** (novel)	Methuen 1924	I
	Doran 1925	H
36 **Carry On, Jeeves** (stories)	Jenkins 1925	K
	Doran 1927	H
37 **Sam the Sudden** (novel)	Methuen 1925	J
Sam in the Suburbs	Doran 1925	J
38 **The Heart of a Goof** (stories)	Jenkins 1926	J
Divots	Doran 1927	J
39 **Hearts and Diamonds** (play adapt.)	Prowse 1926	G
With Laurie Wylie.		
40 **The Play's the Thing** (play adapt.)	Brentano's (US) 1927	G
41 **The Small Bachelor** (novel)	Methuen 1927	I
	Doran 1927	H
42 **Meet Mr Mulliner** (stories)	Jenkins 1927	L
	Doran 1928	I
43 **Good Morning, Bill** (play)	Methuen 1928	I
44 **Money for Nothing** (novel)	Jenkins 1928	J
	Doran 1928	G
45 **Mr. Mulliner Speaking** (stories)	Jenkins 1929	I
	Doubleday 1930	G
46 **Fish Preferred** (novel)	Doubleday 1929	I
Summer Lightning	Jenkins 1929	I
47 **A Damsel in Distress** (play)	French 1930	E
With Ian Hay.		
48 **Baa, Baa, Black Sheep** (play)	French 1930	E
With Ian Hay.		

Wodehouse

49 **Very Good, Jeeves** (stories)	Doubleday 1930	J
	Jenkins 1930	J
50 **Big Money** (novel)	Doubleday 1931	I
	Jenkins 1931	I
51 **If I Were You** (novel)	Doubleday 1931	K
	Jenkins 1931	L
52 **Jeeves Omnibus** (anthol.)	Jenkins 1931	G
53 **Leave It to Psmith** (play)	French 1932	E
With Ian Hay.		
54 **Louder and Funnier** (essays)	Faber 1932	O

Wodehouse's only book of humorous
essays, and his only book from Faber.
Only those copies in yellow cloth,
with the Rex Whistler d/w, are the
first issue. Sheets were later bound in
green for the Faber Library series.
(H)

55 **Doctor Sally** (novel)	Methuen 1932	J
56 **Hot Water** (novel)	Jenkins 1932	J
	Doubleday 1932	G
57 **Nothing but Wodehouse** (anthol.)	Doubleday 1932	E
58 **Mulliner Nights** (stories)	Jenkins 1933	J
	Doubleday 1933	G
59 **Heavy Weather** (novel)	Little, Brown 1933	J
	Jenkins 1933	J
60 **Candlelight** (play adapt.)	French 1934	D
61 **A Century of Humour** (ed. P.G.W.)	Hutchinson 1934	D
62 **Library of Humour:**	Methuen 1934	E
P.G. Wodehouse (anthol.)		
63 **Right Ho, Jeeves** (novel)	Jenkins 1934	J
Brinkley Manor	Little, Brown 1934	G
64 **Thank You, Jeeves** (novel)	Jenkins 1934	J
	Little, Brown 1934	G
65 **Enter Psmith** (novel)	Black 1935 (see 12)	H
66 **Mulliner Omnibus** (anthol.)	Jenkins 1935	E
67 **Blandings Castle** (stories)	Jenkins 1935	J
	Doubleday 1935	G
68 **The Luck of the Bodkins** (novel)	Jenkins 1935	I
	Little, Brown 1936	F
69 **Anything Goes** (play)	French 1936	E
70 **Young Men in Spats** (stories)	Jenkins 1936	J
	Doubleday 1936	G
71 **Laughing Gas** (novel)	Jenkins 1936	I
	Doubleday 1936	F
72 **The Three Musketeers** (play)	Chappell 1937	D
With Gifford Grey and George	Harms 1937	D
Grossmith.		

73	**Lord Emsworth and Others** (stories)	Jenkins 1937	J
	Crime Wave at Blandings	Doubleday 1937	G
74	**Summer Moonshine** (novel)	Doubleday 1937	I
		Jenkins 1938	I
75	**The Code of the Woosters** (novel)	Doubleday 1938	L
		Jenkins 1938	L
76	**Weekend Wodehouse** (anthol.)	Jenkins 1939	E
		Doubleday 1939	D
77	**Uncle Fred in the Springtime** (novel)	Doubleday 1939	H
		Jenkins 1939	H
78	**Wodehouse on Golf** (anthol.)	Doubleday 1940	E
79	**Eggs, Beans and Crumpets** (stories)	Jenkins 1940	J
		Doubleday 1940	G
80	**Quick Service** (novel)	Jenkins 1940	H
		Doubleday 1940	F
81	**Money in the Bank** (novel)	Doubleday 1942	G
		Jenkins 1946	G
82	**Joy in the Morning** (novel)	Doubleday 1946	G
		Jenkins 1947	G
83	**Full Moon** (novel)	Doubleday 1947	F
		Jenkins 1947	E
84	**Spring Fever** (novel)	Doubleday 1948	E
		Jenkins 1948	E
85	**Uncle Dynamite** (novel)	Jenkins 1948	E
		Didier 1948	E
86	**The Best of Wodehouse** (anthol.)	Pocket Books (US) 1949	D
87	**The Mating Season** (novel)	Jenkins 1949	D
		Didier 1949	D
88	**Nothing Serious** (stories)	Jenkins 1950	F
		Doubleday 1951	D
89	**The Old Reliable** (novel)	Jenkins 1951	F
		Doubleday 1951	D
90	**Best of Modern Humor** (ed. P.G.W.)	McBride (US) 1952	D
91	**The Week-End Book of Humo(u)r** (ed. P.G.W.)	Washburn (US) 1952	D
		Jenkins 1954	D
92	**Barmy in Wonderland** (novel)	Jenkins 1952	F
	Angel Cake	Doubleday 1952	D
93	**Pigs Have Wings** (novel)	Doubleday 1952	D
		Jenkins 1952	D
94	**Mike at Wrykyn** (novel)	Jenkins 1953	H
95	**Mike and Psmith** (novel)	Jenkins 1953	H
	For 94 and 95, see 12.		
96	**Ring for Jeeves** (novel)	Jenkins 1953	G
	The Return of Jeeves	Simon & Schuster 1954	E
97	**Bring on the Girls** (autobiog.)	Simon & Schuster 1953	G
	Written with Guy Bolton.	Jenkins 1954	G

The English edition was rewritten
from the original American, and
has a different selection of
photographs.

98	**Performing Flea** (letters)	Jenkins 1953	G
	An extensively revised edition,	Simon & Schuster 1962	G
	entitled **Author! Author!**, was		
	published in America		
99	**Jeeves and the Feudal Spirit**	Jenkins 1954	F
	(novel)		
	Bertie Wooster Sees It Through	Simon & Schuster 1955	F
100	**Carry on, Jeeves** (play)	Evans 1956	D
	With Guy Bolton.		
101	**French Leave** (novel)	Jenkins 1956	F
		Simon & Schuster 1959	D
102	**America, I Like You** (autobiog.)	Simon & Schuster 1956	G
103	**Over Seventy** (autobiog.)	Jenkins 1957	F
	A revised edition of 102.		
104	**Something Fishy** (novel)	Jenkins 1957	E
	The Butler Did It	Simon & Schuster 1957	E
105	**Selected Stories by P.G.**	Modern Library 1958	D
	Wodehouse		
106	**Cocktail Time** (novel)	Jenkins 1958	D
		Simon & Schuster 1958	D
107	**A Few Quick Ones** (stories)	Simon & Schuster 1959	D
		Jenkins 1959	D
108	**The Most of P.G. Wodehouse**	Simon & Schuster 1960	D
	(anthol.)		
109	**How Right You are, Jeeves** (novel)	Simon & Schuster 1960	E
	Jeeves in the Offing	Jenkins 1960	E
110	**The Ice in the Bedroom** (novel)	Simon & Schuster 1961	D
	The English edition lacks the word	Jenkins 1961	D
	'The' in the title.		
111	**Service with a Smile** (novel)	Simon & Schuster 1961	D
		Jenkins 1962	D
112	**Stiff Upper Lip, Jeeves** (novel)	Simon & Schuster 1963	E
		Jenkins 1963	E
113	**Biffen's Millions** (novel)	Simon & Schuster 1964	D
	Frozen Assets	Jenkins 1964	D
114	**The Brinkmanship of Galahad**	Simon & Schuster 1965	D
	Threepwood (novel)		
	Galahad at Blandings	Jenkins 1965	D
		Simon & Schuster 1967	D
115	**Plum Pie** (stories)	Jenkins 1966	D
		Simon & Schuster 1967	D
116	**A Carnival of Modern**	Delacorte 1967	D
	Humo(u)r (ed. P.G.W.)	Jenkins 1968	D

This, along with 90 and 91, was edited in association with Scott Meredith.

117	**The World of Jeeves** (anthol.)	Jenkins 1967	**D**
118	**The Purloined Paperweight** (novel)	Simon & Schuster 1967	**D**
	Company for Henry	Jenkins 1967	**D**
119	**Do Butlers Burgle Banks?** (novel)	Simon & Schuster 1968	**C**
		Jenkins 1968	**C**
120	**A Pelican at Blandings** (novel)	Jenkins 1969	**D**
	No Nudes is Good Nudes	Simon & Schuster 1970	**C**
121	**The Girl in Blue** (novel)	Barrie & Jenkins 1970	**D**
		Simon & Schuster 1971	**D**
122	**Much Obliged, Jeeves** (novel)	Barrie & Jenkins 1971	**D**
	Jeeves and the Tie That Binds	Simon & Schuster 1971	**D**

This novel was published to coincide with P.G.W.'s ninetieth birthday.

123	**The World of Mr Mulliner** (anthol.)	Barrie & Jenkins 1972	**D**
		Taplinger 1974	**C**
124	**Pearls, Girls, and Monty Bodkin** (novel)	Barrie & Jenkins 1972	**C**
	The Plot That Thickened	Simon & Schuster 1973	**C**
125	**The Golf Omnibus** (anthol.)	Barrie & Jenkins 1973	**C**
		Simon & Schuster 1974	**C**
126	**Bachelors Anonymous** (novel)	Barrie & Jenkins 1973	**C**
		Simon & Schuster 1974	**C**
127	**The World of Psmith** (anthol.)	Barrie & Jenkins 1974	**C**
128	**Aunts Aren't Gentlemen** (novel)	Barrie & Jenkins 1974	**C**
	The Cat-Nappers	Simon & Schuster 1974	**C**
129	**The World of Ukridge** (anthol.)	Barrie & Jenkins 1975	**C**
130	**The World of Blandings** (anthol.)	Barrie & Jenkins 1976	**C**
131	**The Uncollected Wodehouse** (stories and articles)	Seabury Press (US) 1976	**E**

Edited by David Jasen, introduced by Malcolm Muggeridge

132	**Vintage Wodehouse** (anthology)	Barrie & Jenkins 1977	**C**

Edited by Richard Usborne.

133	**Sunset at Blandings** (novel)	Chatto & Windus 1977	**D**
		Simon & Schuster 1977	**C**

Unfinished, posthumous novel, edited by Richard Usborne.

134	**Wodehouse on Wodehouse**	Hutchinson 1980	**C**

Contains his three autobiographical works: **Bring on the Girls, Performing Flea**, and **Over Seventy**.

135	**Tales from the Drones Club** (anthology)	Hutchinson 1982	**C**
136	**Wodehouse Nuggets** (anthology)	Hutchinson 1983	**C**

Chosen by Richard Usborne.

137	**The World of Uncle Fred** (anthology)	Hutchinson 1983	C
138	**Four Plays** Contains **The Play's the Thing, Good Morning Bill, Leave it to Psmith** and **Come on Jeeves.**	Methuen 1983	C
139	**Sir Agravaine** (story) This is a landscape-format illustrated version of a story which first appeared in **The Man Upstairs** (1914).	Blandford 1984	D
140	**The World of Wodehouse Clergy** (anthology)	Hutchinson 1984	C
141	**The Globe by the Way Book** I put this in because you haven't a hope in blue blazes of coming across (or affording) the true 1st, and this is a beautiful facsimile of the original one shilling paperback, in an optional (expensive) slipcase. Actually, only 500 were printed, so you might have already missed your chance.	Heinemann/Sceptre 1985	G
142	**The Hollywood Omnibus** (anthology)	Hutchinson 1985	C
143	**Wodehouse on Cricket** (anthology)	Hutchinson 1987	C
144	**The Parrot and Other Poems**	Hutchinson 1988	C
145	**The Aunts Omnibus** (anthology)	Hutchinson 1989	C
146	**Yours, Plum** (letters)	Hutchinson 1990	C
		Heineman 1990	C
147	**A Man of Means** (story) With C.H. Bovill. Limited to 200 numbered copies.	Porpoise Books 1991	G

There are now over thirty books about Plum and all his works, but from the collector's point of view the essential work is:

Bibliography
P.G. Wodehouse: A Comprehensive Bibliography and Checklist by Eileen McIlvaine, Louise S. Sherby and James H. Heineman (Heineman 1991)

Wolfe, Tom   Born in Virginia, US, 1930. American.

Still the greatest hep-cat, groovy journalist, and now author of what will be seen (is *already* seen, actually) as a key post-war novel. Not an easy man to collect, but he's *so* Kandy-Kolored Kool it's just *got* to be worth the effort.

1	**The Kandy-Kolored Tangerine Flake Streamline Baby** (essays)	Farrar Straus 1965	H
		Cape 1966	G
2	**The Electric Kool-Aid Acid Test** (essays)	Farrar Straus 1968	G
		Weidenfeld & Nicolson 1968	E
3	**The Pump House Gang** (essays)	Farrar Straus 1968	E
4	**The Mid-Atlantic Man and Other New Breeds in England and America** (same as 3)	Weidenfeld & Nicolson 1969	E
5	**Radical Chic and Mau-Mauing the Flak Catchers** (journalism)	Farrar Straus 1970	D
		Joseph 1971	D
6	**The Painted Word** (journalism)	Farrar Straus 1975	D
7	**Mauve Gloves and Madmen, Clutter and Vine and Other Stories** (essays)	Farrar Straus 1976	D
8	**The Right Stuff** (journalism)	Farrar Straus 1979	D
		Cape 1979	C
9	**In Our Time** (essays)	Farrar Straus 1980	C
10	**From Bauhaus to Our House** (non-fiction)	Farrar Straus 1981	C
		Cape 1982	C
11	**The Bonfire of the Vanities** (novel)	Farrar Straus 1987	G
		Cape 1988	E

Woolf, Leonard   Born in London, 1880. Died 1969.

Not just the Brian Epstein of the Bloomsbury Group, but himself the author of a large number of books – many of a political nature – the highlights of which are listed below. As founder of The Hogarth Press, he would no doubt be gratified by the fact that there are many collectors around eager for anything in first edition that was issued by the Press, and not just the undisputed highlights from Virginia. This is a very rare distinction for a publisher, for despite the name, The Hogarth Press was not a press in the sense of Golden Cockerel or Nonesuch; the Press was a trade and commercial publisher, by far the greatest part of its ouput being ordinary productions at ordinary prices. Hogarth Press books, then, are not collected for their intrinsic beauty, but because of their importance in the history of publishing. The only other house that I can think of that shares this distinction is Penguin: I have yet to hear of a Cape collector, or a Faber collector – or indeed any other trade publisher.

Stories about the primitive workings of the Press abound, the most droll centring around Leonard's thriftiness. If it is true, though, that he hung Hogarth Press galley and page proofs in the lavatory in place of something more customary, today's collector thinks not 'how mean!' but only of Leonard's consummate extravagance!

Woolf, Virginia

1 **The Village in the Jungle** (novel)	Arnold 1913	**K**
	Harcourt Brace 1926	**E**
2 **The Hotel** (play)	Hogarth Press 1939	**G**
	Dial Press 1963	**D**
3 **Sowing** (autobiog.)	Hogarth Press 1960	**E**
	Harcourt Brace 1960	**D**
4 **Growing** (autobiog.)	Hogarth Press 1961	**D**
	Harcourt Brace 1962	**D**
5 **Beginning Again** (autobiog.)	Hogarth Press 1964	**D**
	Harcourt Brace 1964	**D**
6 **Downhill All the Way** (autobiog.)	Hogarth Press 1967	**D**
	Harcourt Brace 1967	**D**
7 **The Journey Not the Arrival Matters** (autobiog.)	Hogarth Press 1969	**D**
	Harcourt Brace 1970	**D**

Woolf, Virginia   Born in London, 1882. Died 1941.

Who was or is the greatest female English novelist? Many people would come up with Jane Austen, or a Brontë. Many more, I think, would go for Virginia Woolf. Her reputation is mighty, and the vast amount of posthumously published material has – far from having had a diminishing effect – enhanced it still further, for with her letters, and most particularly with her diary, we have master works of the first order; the five-volume diary really could come to be ranked amongst her finest works. The young seem to approach the lady with trepidation, and are very often surprised to find how very much at one with her they are. Within a traditional framework, she comes across as intensely modern and unforgettable; it is difficult to read *The Waves* and remain indifferent.

To many, Virginia Woolf *is* the Bloomsbury Group. She is certainly the greatest talent to have emerged from this singular circle. The Bloomsbury gravy train steams on for ever, though, for the public (and the review pages) seem never to tire of the latest discoveries about Lytton and Duncan and Vanessa and Carrington and Vita and Ottoline and all.

1 **The Voyage Out** (novel)	Duckworth 1915	**Q**
	Doran 1920	**M**
2 **Two Stories** Cont. **The Mark on the Wall** by Virginia, and **The Three Jews** by Leonard. It is notable for being the very first Hogarth Press publication, printed in an edition of 150 wrappered copies.	Hogarth Press 1917	**R**
3 **Kew Gardens** (story) 150 copies printed, in wrpps.	Hogarth Press 1919	**O**
4 **Night and Day** (novel)	Duckworth 1919	**O**
	Doran 1920	**L**

5 **Monday or Tuesday** (stories)   Hogarth Press 1921   **N**
Woodcuts and cover design by Vanessa   Harcourt Brace 1921   **K**
Bell.

6 **Jacob's Room** (novel)   Hogarth Press 1922   **M**
   Harcourt Brace 1923   **K**

7 **Mr Bennett and Mrs Brown** (essay)   Hogarth Press 1924   **K**
No. 1 in the Hogarth Essays series.

8 **The Common Reader** (essays)   Hogarth Press 1925   **M**
   Harcourt Brace 1925   **K**

9 **Mrs Dalloway** (novel)   Hogarth Press 1925   **N**
   Harcourt Brace 1925   **K**

10 **To the Lighthouse** (novel)   Hogarth Press 1927   **O**
   Harcourt Brace 1927   **L**

11 **Orlando: A Biography** (novel)   Crosby Gaige (NY)   **P**
The Gaige edition was limited to 861   1928
copies, 800 numbered and signed for   Hogarth Press 1928   **K**
sale at $15.   Harcourt Brace 1929   **I**

12 **A Room of One's Own** (essay)   Fountain Press/
The 1st joint American-English edition   Hogarth Press 1929   **Q**
was limited to 492 copies, 450 for   Hogarth Press 1929   **K**
sale, and each signed.   Harcourt Brace 1929   **H**

13 **Street Haunting** (essay)   Westgate Press (San
Limited to 500 signed copies.   Francisco) 1930   **N**

14 **On Being Ill** (essay)   Hogarth Press 1930   **O**
Limited to 250 signed copies

15 **Beau Brummell** (essay)   Rimington & Hooper   **N**
Limited to 550 signed copies.   (NY) 1930

16 **The Waves** (novel)   Hogarth Press 1931   **P**
   Harcourt Brace 1931   **M**

17 **A Letter to A Young Poet** (essay)   Hogarth Press 1932   **E**
No. 8 in the Hogarth Letters series.

18 **The Common Reader:**   Hogarth Press 1932   **J**
Second Series (essays)   Harcourt Brace 1932   **G**

19 **Flush: A Biography**   Hogarth Press 1933   **F**
   Harcourt Brace 1933   **D**

20 **Walter Sickert: A Conversation**   Hogarth Press 1934   **H**
(essay)

21 **The Roger Fry Memorial**   Bristol 1935   **M**
Exhibition (address)
Only 125 copies printed, and none for
sale.

22 **The Years** (novel)   Hogarth Press 1937   **L**
   Harcourt Brace 1937   **I**

23 **Three Guineas** (essay)   Hogarth Press 1938   **H**
   Harcourt Brace 1938   **E**

24 **Reviewing** (essay)   Hogarth Press 1939   **E**
No. 4 in the Hogarth Sixpenny
Pamphlets series.

Woolf, Virginia

25	**Roger Fry: A Biography**	Hogarth Press 1940	**H**
		Harcourt Brace 1940	**E**
26	**Between the Acts** (novel)	Hogarth Press 1941	**H**
		Harcourt Brace 1941	**E**
27	**The Death of the Moth** (essays)	Hogarth Press 1942	**G**
		Harcourt Brace 1942	**D**
28	**A Haunted House** (stories)	Hogarth Press 1943	**F**
		Harcourt Brace 1944	**D**
29	**The Moment and Other Essays**	Hogarth Press 1947	**E**
		Harcourt Brace 1948	**C**
30	**The Captain's Death Bed** (essays)	Hogarth Press 1950	**F**
	The American edition actually preceded by one week.	Harcourt Brace 1950	**D**
31	**A Writer's Diary**	Hogarth Press 1953	**F**
		Harcourt Brace 1954	**D**
32	**Virginia Woolf & Lytton Strachey: Letters**	Hogarth Press 1956	**F**
		Harcourt Brace 1956	**D**
33	**Granite and Rainbow** (essays)	Hogarth Press 1958	**F**
		Harcourt Brace 1958	**D**
34	**Contemporary Writers** (essays)	Hogarth Press 1965	**E**
		Harcourt Brace 1966	**C**
35	**Nurse Lugton's Golden Thimble** (story)	Hogarth Press 1966	**H**
	With pictures by Duncan Grant.		
36	**Mrs Dalloway's Party** (story)	Hogarth Press 1973	**C**
37	**The Flight of the Mind:**	Hogarth Press 1975	**D**
	The Letters of Virginia Woolf 1888–1912	Harcourt Brace 1975	**C**
38	**Moments of Being** (autobiog.)	Sussex University Press 1976	**C**
39	**The Question of Things Happening: The Letters of Virginia Woolf 1912–1922**	Hogarth Press 1976	**C**
		Harcourt Brace 1976	**C**
40	**Freshwater** (comedy)	Hogarth Press 1976	**C**
41	**The Diary of Virginia Woolf Volume I: 1915–1919**	Hogarth Press 1977	**C**
		Harcourt Brace 1977	**C**
42	**Books and Portraits** (essays)	Hogarth Press 1977	**C**
		Harcourt Brace 1977	**C**
43	**A Change of Perspective: The Letters of Virginia Woolf 1923–1928**	Hogarth Press 1977	**C**
		Harcourt Brace 1977	**C**
44	**The Pargiters** (fiction)	Hogarth Press 1977	**C**
		Harcourt Brace 1977	**C**
45	**The Diary of Virginia Woolf Volume II: 1920–1924**	Hogarth Press 1978	**C**
		Harcourt Brace 1978	**C**
46	**A Reflection of the Other Person: The Letters of Virginia Woolf 1929–1931**	Hogarth Press 1978	**C**
		Harcourt Brace 1978	**C**

47 **The Sickle Side of the Moon:**	Hogarth Press 1979	C
The Letters of Virginia	Harcourt Brace 1979	C
Woolf 1932–1935		
48 **The Diary of Virginia Woolf**	Hogarth Press 1980	C
Volume III: 1925–1930	Harcourt Brace 1980	C
49 **Leave the Letters Till We're**	Hogarth Press 1980	C
Dead: The Letters of Virginia	Harcourt Brace 1980	C
Woolf 1936–1941		
50 **The Diary of Virginia Woolf**	Hogarth Press 1982	C
Volume IV: 1931–1935	Harcourt Brace 1982	C
51 **The London Scene** (essay)	Hogarth Press 1982	C
	Random House 1982	C
52 **The Diary of Virginia Woolf**	Chatto & Windus 1984	C
Volume V: 1936–1941	Harcourt Brace 1984	C
53 **The Essays of Virginia Woolf:**	Chatto & Windus 1986	C
Volume I		
54 **The Essays of Virginia Woolf:**	Chatto & Windus 1987	C
Volume II		
55 **The Essays of Virginia Woolf:**	Chatto & Windus 1988	C
Volume III		
56 **Paper Darts: The Illustrated**	Collins & Brown 1992	C
Letters (ed. Frances Spalding)		

Biography:
Quentin Bell **Virginia Woolf** (2 vols) Hogarth Press 1972; Harcourt Brace 1972.

Bibliography:
B.J. Kirkpatrick **A Bibliography of Virginia Woolf** Hart-Davis 1957.

Wyndham, John   Born in Birmingham, England, 1903.
Died 1969.
Pseudonym of John Beynon Harris.

The early books are scarce, and quite avidly collected. Wyndham will always be known for his *Day of the Triffids*, though – a cautionary tale for gardeners everywhere.

1 **Foul Play Suspected** (novel)	Newnes 1935	J
(pseud. John Beynon)		
2 **The Secret People** (novel)	Newnes 1935	I
(pseud. John Beynon)		
3 **Planet Plane** (novel)	Newnes 1935	I
(pseud. John Beynon)		
Reissued by Michael Joseph in 1972 as		
Stowaway to Mars (**B**).		
4 **The Day of the Triffids** (novel)	Joseph 1951	J
	Doubleday 1951	G

5	**The Kraken Wakes** (novel)	Joseph 1953	**G**
	Out of the Deeps	Ballantine 1953	**D**
6	**Jizzle** (stories)	Dobson 1954	**D**
7	**The Chrysalids** (novel)	Joseph 1955	**E**
8	**Re-Birth** (stories)	Ballantine (NY) 1955	**C**
9	**The Seeds of Time** (stories)	Joseph 1956	**E**
10	**The Midwich Cuckoos** (novel)	Joseph 1957	**E**
		Ballantine 1957	**C**
11	**The Outward Urge** (stories)	Joseph 1959	**C**

11 'With L. Parkes'.
Lucas Parkes is another of Wyndham's
pseudonyms, apparently used because
the author considered the stories to be
unlike his usual style.

12	**Trouble with Lichen** (novel)	Joseph 1960	**D**
13	**Consider Her Ways** and **Others**	Joseph 1961	**C**

13 (stories)
The title story first appeared in
Sometime, Never Eyre &
Spottiswoode 1956; Ballantine 1956.

14	**The John Wyndham omnibus**	Joseph 1964	**C**
	Cont.4, 5 and 7, the last two appearing	Simon & Schuster	**C**
	in America for the first time.	1966	
15	**Chocky** (novel)	Joseph 1968	**C**
16	**The Man from Beyond** (stories)	Joseph 1975	**C**

ACKNOWLEDGEMENTS

I should like to thank Julian Rota of Sotheby's and Giles Gordon of Sheil Land Associates for their help with various bits and bobs connected with this book. Gratitude is also due to the following literary agents, who gave of their time when they really didn't have to: Curtis Brown & John Farquarson, A.M. Heath & Co. Ltd, The Peters Fraser & Dunlop Group Ltd, Murray Pollinger, and A.P. Watt Ltd.

Thanks are also due to Mr Charles Connolly who from day one kept asking whether the book was finished yet, thus adding a certain vibrancy to the entire caper.

Gratitude too to the following publishers, whose dustwrapper artwork is reproduced in this book, with apologies for any omissions:

Jonathan Cape Ltd, Faber & Faber Ltd, John Murray (Publishers) Ltd, Victor Gollancz Ltd, HarperCollins Publishers, William Heinemann, Michael Joseph Ltd, Chatto & Windus, Secker & Warburg, Weidenfeld & Nicolson Ltd, Longman Group Ltd, Macmillan London Ltd, Cassell plc.

Scales of Values

A	up to £5	J	up to £125	S	up to £1500
B	up to £10	K	up to £150	T	up to £2000
C	up to £20	L	up to £200	U	up to £3000
D	up to £30	M	up to £250	V	up to £4000
E	up to £40	N	up to £300	W	up to £5000
F	up to £50	O	up to £400	X	up to £6000
G	up to £60	P	up to £500	Y	up to £8000+
H	up to £80	Q	up to £750	Z	up to £12000+
I	up to £100	R	up to £1000		